THE COLOR OF FAMILY

# THE
# COLOR
## OF
# FAMILY

HISTORY, RACE,
AND THE POLITICS
OF ANCESTRY

# Michael O'Malley

The University of Chicago Press    *Chicago and London*

The University of Chicago Press, Chicago 60637
The University of Chicago Press, Ltd., London
© 2024 by The University of Chicago
Published 2024
Printed in the United States of America

33 32 31 30 29 28 27 26 25 24      1 2 3 4 5

ISBN-13: 978-0-226-83590-7 (cloth)
ISBN-13: 978-0-226-83591-4 (e-book)
DOI: https://doi.org/10.7208/chicago/9780226835914.001.0001

Library of Congress Cataloging-in-Publication Data

Names: O'Malley, Michael, author.
Title: The color of family : history, race, and the politics of ancestry / Michael
    O'Malley.
Description: Chicago : The University of Chicago Press, 2024. | Includes
    bibliographical references and index.
Identifiers: LCCN 2024011380 | ISBN 9780226835907 (cloth) |
    ISBN 9780226835914 (ebook)
Subjects: LCSH: Families—United States—History. | Irish American
    families—United States—History. | Racially mixed families—United
    States—History. | Race awareness—United States. | Racially mixed
    people—Race identity—United States. | Irish Americans—United States—
    Genealogy. | Genealogy—Political aspects—United States. | Identity
    politics—United States. | United States—Genealogy.
Classification: LCC CS69 .043 2024 | DDC 929.20973—dc23/eng/20240402
LC record available at https://lccn.loc.gov/2024011380

♾ This paper meets the requirements of ANSI/NISO Z39.48-1992
(Permanence of Paper).

*To my father, Jeff O'Malley,*
*and my daughter, Frances O'Malley*

# CONTENTS

# NOTE ON THE TERMINOLOGY OF RACE

Nineteenth-century Virginians mostly used the word "colored" as we tend to use the word "black." When they wanted to indicate a person with European and African ancestry, they would also sometimes use the word "mulatto." "Mulatto" did not confer any special legal status, although it might hint at an elevated social status. People described as "mulatto" in one census might appear as "black" or "colored" or even as "white" in another. Someone called "mulatto" was a colored person, and in law, a colored person was a black person. The law understood people with Native American ancestry differently. They could not be legally enslaved, for example. Walter Plecker spent his time in Richmond insisting that there were no "Indians" in Virginia, only "colored" people, by which he meant "Negro" or what we would think of as "black." If you feel none of this quite makes sense, you're right: it revolves around treating an imaginary construct, "race," as if it were real.

# NOTE ON SOURCES

Much of the research for this book was done using the online resources at Ancestry.com and Familysearch.org, which present a problem of citation. A citation to Ancestry.com, for example, is useless unless the reader has a subscription. FamilySearch.org is free, as of this writing, but does not always have the same resources as Ancestry.com. Although both include page images of the census returns, they don't organize them the way an archive would. On its website the National Archives, where the original census returns reside, encourages users to search online. It says, "Federal Census records have been digitized by several of NARA's [National Archives and Record Administration's] partners, and will eventually be available as well through the National Archives Catalog." If users click on the link to search, they find links to Ancestry.com and FamilySearch.org. Citations establish the authority of your claims. Citing a document located in the National Archives conveys a different kind of authority than citing the same document in the database of a commercial firm, and this is central to what the book explores. In general, and unless an endnote says otherwise, if the text describes a record from a US decennial census, or a state record, the reference can be assumed to point to the records scanned and transcribed at FamilySearch.org.

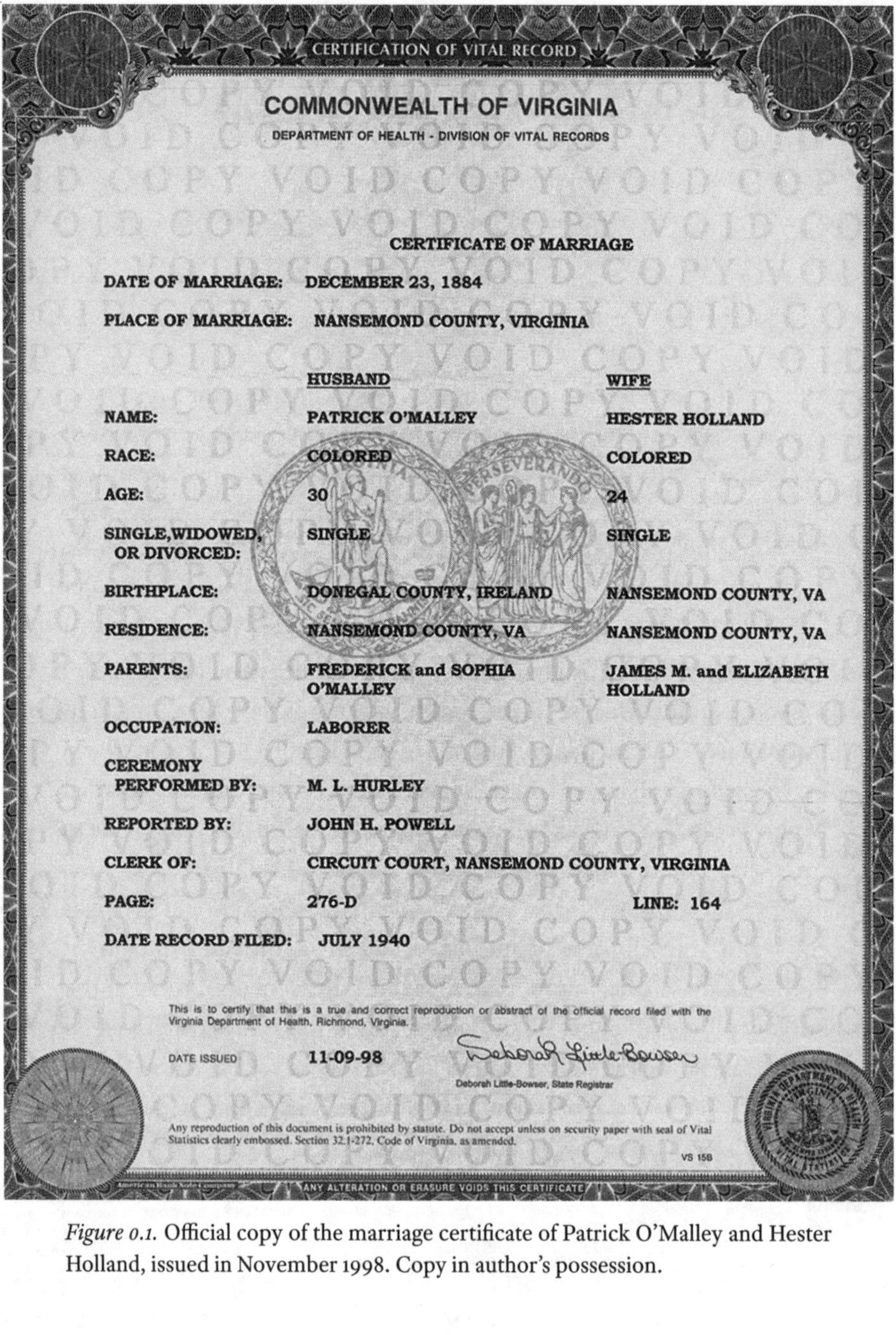

CERTIFICATION OF VITAL RECORD

COMMONWEALTH OF VIRGINIA

DEPARTMENT OF HEALTH - DIVISION OF VITAL RECORDS

CERTIFICATE OF MARRIAGE

| | | |
|---|---|---|
| DATE OF MARRIAGE: | DECEMBER 23, 1884 | |
| PLACE OF MARRIAGE: | NANSEMOND COUNTY, VIRGINIA | |
| | HUSBAND | WIFE |
| NAME: | PATRICK O'MALLEY | HESTER HOLLAND |
| RACE: | COLORED | COLORED |
| AGE: | 30 | 24 |
| SINGLE, WIDOWED, OR DIVORCED: | SINGLE | SINGLE |
| BIRTHPLACE: | DONEGAL COUNTY, IRELAND | NANSEMOND COUNTY, VA |
| RESIDENCE: | NANSEMOND COUNTY, VA | NANSEMOND COUNTY, VA |
| PARENTS: | FREDERICK and SOPHIA O'MALLEY | JAMES M. and ELIZABETH HOLLAND |
| OCCUPATION: | LABORER | |
| CEREMONY PERFORMED BY: | M. L. HURLEY | |
| REPORTED BY: | JOHN H. POWELL | |
| CLERK OF: | CIRCUIT COURT, NANSEMOND COUNTY, VIRGINIA | |
| PAGE: | 276-D | LINE: 164 |
| DATE RECORD FILED: | JULY 1940 | |

This is to certify that this is a true and correct reproduction or abstract of the official record filed with the Virginia Department of Health, Richmond, Virginia.

DATE ISSUED 11-09-98

Deborah Little-Bowser

Deborah Little-Bowser, State Registrar

Any reproduction of this document is prohibited by statute. Do not accept unless on security paper with seal of Vital Statistics clearly embossed. Section 32.1-272, Code of Virginia, as amended.

VS 15B

ANY ALTERATION OR ERASURE VOIDS THIS CERTIFICATE

*Figure 0.1.* Official copy of the marriage certificate of Patrick O'Malley and Hester Holland, issued in November 1998. Copy in author's possession.

# ARLINGTON

Like millions of Americans, my father started doing family history when he retired. He got mildly obsessed with it, making trips to distant churches, writing to obscure semi-relatives, collecting documents. You may have a relative like this, or you may be that relative yourself. In 1998, at a family Christmas party, he announced startling news. He called everyone into the living room, where stood an easel, covered. He pulled the cover off, and we beheld the marriage certificate of his great-grandparents, enlarged. Gradually it dawned on the people in the room that both of them were listed as "colored." Amazement and laughter ensued, with some dismay from some of the oldest people in the room, who could remember a time when the American Irish were a bit more marginalized and the family's status more precarious.

Our family strongly identified with Philadelphia and had consisted almost entirely of Irish Americans marrying other Irish Americans as far back as anyone had ever looked. Family gatherings are full of Pats, Mikes, Kevins, Eileens, Kathleens, Maureens, and Maggies, people who turn red as boiled lobster on the slightest exposure to a bright sun. So it was something of a shock to find out my family had a Virginia branch, implicated in the state's racial politics, and that by Virginia law I might be considered a black person, or might actually *be* a black person according to America's confused racial reckonings.

I was fascinated by the document. He was born in Ireland, but they called him "colored"? She was colored? We had a picture of the couple

on or near their wedding day: a photo of two people who seem unambiguously white. Looking at their picture (figure 0.2), scrutinizing
their faces and bodies for evidence of African ancestry, reenacts the
racial surveillance demanded of everyone at the time the photo was
taken in 1884. By the early twentieth century, Virginia law insisted "every person in whom there is ascertainable any Negro blood shall be
deemed a colored person." "Ascertainable" could refer to what people
looked like, or it could refer to documents, records, like the marriage
certificate Virginia sent to my father.[1]

The marriage certificate had some odd details. It was a modern
transcription, dated 1998, of some original document. But although
they married in 1884, the certificate said, "date record filed: July 1940."
Why was a record from 1884 "filed" in 1940?

For decades I tried to figure out how to write about this. During
that time a growing historical literature looked at how immigrants,
often at each other's throats in Europe, became simply "white" in the
US. Several books considered the Irish, and how they "became white,"
and multiple books looked at the career of Walter Plecker, the man
responsible for the 1940 filing.[2]

Like a lot of historians, I was critical of genealogy, which seemed
to have only one argument that it made over and over and over: "this
person is a relative, and this person and this person," until eventually
someone famous was produced, Charlemagne or Genghis Khan perhaps. But people doing family history are trying to figure out, like any
historian, what the past means, and in particular what family and ancestry mean to the present. What does *anyone's* past mean? Patrick, it
would turn out, was quite a rogue and not at all what he often seemed.[3]

Genealogy draws its material mostly from records generated by
governments—census and tax information, birth and death certificates, marriage licenses, draft records, and military service records
all stem from local and national government's desire to know who
their citizens are and what they're up to. To do this, governments had
to "individualize" their citizens and create a stable record of identity
that persisted over time. The desire to track people has a disquieting

*Figure 0.2.* Patrick O'Malley and Hester Holland, on or about their wedding day in late December 1884. Copy of family photo in author's possession.

and sinister aspect of surveillance and control, but it also guarantees people the benefits of citizenship, protects them from evildoers, and secures property.

This book puts ancestry as a form of identity in tension with the rise of "individualism" as a way of thinking about people. Before the nineteenth century, people mostly understood themselves as members of communities, castes, social classes, or families. In a rural community, you were known by neighbors and kin. In the city, an ordinary stranger had no easy way to prove who they were. Their clothes might testify to their social status, or someone socially prominent might speak for them or write a letter on their behalf, but before roughly 1800 documents of identity of the sort we carry in wallets or on phones didn't exist. Gradually the force of kin and community gives way to an idea of individuals as "discrete," separate from family and community, stable over time and place. This identity, this "administrative individualism," was created by the administrative records family history relies on.

Administrative individualism was a radically new way of seeing people that cut them loose from traditional sources of identity. An "individual" in this modern sense has an identity derived only from themselves, not from their family; always the same no matter where they go, the same person on a desert island as they are in a crowded city; the same person at death as they were at birth. Birth certificates, driver's licenses, fingerprints, retinal scans: these things construct a unique identity. Of course people had "personhood" before: they had a legal identity if they had property, and in theology they had a soul distinct to them. But most of the people genealogists trace only exist to us as individuals because of the records documenting their existence. In this sense genealogical records create individuals, and genealogical records produced by governments mark the rise of "individualism." Individualism is an idea about what people are and how they relate to each other: documents of identity are the tools and machinery that make the idea function.

Over the nineteenth century, county and state governments began building paper records of identity and claiming authority over who was who: in the process state agencies gained ever more precise and granular information in ever larger files. Genealogy puts these records of individuals into the service of family, but throughout US history these same records of individualism served to track people and assign them a race. The improbable blackness of Patrick O'Malley and Hester Holland shows how a record of stable individual identity also served to create a stable racial identity, stable across space and time. Much of Virginia's record keeping aimed to police bloodlines and prevent subversion. That impulse required birth and death certificates, marriage licenses, and multiple other documents aimed at fixing people in their "real" place. An increase in the number and extent of records of citizens — birth certificates, marriage licenses, death certificates — is an increase in individualism. This book explores how the problem of race is also, always, a problem of individualism.

We often see "individualism" described as the alternative to racism, but the stories told here show individualism and modern, scientific racism strolling hand in hand through county courts, state capitals, and federal record offices. Individualism as the foundation of a system of government arose at exactly the same time as the modern idea of race, and this isn't a coincidence: it's a major reason why the most prominent speakers for individual freedom were slaveholders. Fixing people as individuals was the first step toward fixing them as members of a race. Imaging individualism as the solution to the problem of racism is like imaging clocks as the solution to the problem of punctuality. Clocks produced the idea of being "on time" in the first place. They created the possibility of punctuality and then made it possible to be late or early by a precise measure: they can't eliminate a problem they created.

Understanding people as individuals, rather than as peasants or nobles or members of a kin group, also always sets up a separation between what people appear to be and what they "really are." At all times people in individualist societies likely misrepresent themselves in some way — pretending to have skills they don't have so they get the job, or pretending to be younger or older than they are, or promising something they know they may not be able to deliver—always trying to put "their best face" on a situation rather than their not so great regular face. Individualism called up a detective impulse, a desire to peer through what people seemed to be and find the real person. Formal records could tell you if this person was who they claimed to be, and they could also tell you if an ambiguous-seeming person was really white or really black or really Indian. This book explores how racial identities, like the identities of Patrick and Hester, were created by, and policed by, the same records that created stable individual identities.

In the twenty-first century, authority over identity has started to shift from records generated and held by governments to records held by commercial genealogy services linked to DNA databases. Individualized records of my DNA, combined with the state and federal records now available via Ancestry.com, promise to reveal whether I'm "really black" or not: here again, individualism and racism stroll hand in hand.

I'm writing from Arlington, Virginia, named after Robert E. Lee's plantation home. Like communities all over the US, Arlington is rethinking the past. Lee Highway is now Langston Boulevard, named for John M. Langston, Virginia's first congressman with known African ancestry. The county logo used to include a drawing of Arlington House, but that image is gone, after much Sturm und Drang about "the erasure of history." But attempts to "erase" Lee are not new. The Union confiscated Lee's home during the war, and Union general Montgomery Meigs turned it into Arlington Cemetery, so the Lees could never live there again.

Visitors to Arlington Cemetery often see the Tomb of the Unknown Soldier, holding the unidentified remains of soldiers from WWI, WWII, Korea, and Vietnam. This profound and moving memorial, guarded continually in all weather, stands for the idea of the nation. The unknown soldier could be, theoretically, anyone—any "race," any background, any color. The unknown soldier is not individualized: that's the point. That's what gives the monument its power. But in 2012 Arlington National Cemetery announced they were removing the remains of the soldier from Vietnam. They had identified his DNA: they knew his name, and his date of birth, and *now he had a race*. Individualism and race, once again, are not opposed ideas: they arrive at the same moment. Plans were underway to identify the remains from other wars, but the cemetery seems to have dropped the idea. The memorial dramatizes a notion of relatedness built on the social rather than the biological, on what people do rather than what they are, and individualizing the remains destroys the memorial's symbolic meaning.[4]

The need to detect what people "really are" comes from a false premise built into individualism itself. It's easy to argue people aren't *really* anything. We are born with a genetic blueprint, but we have will, creativity, and ambition, and we modify or exploit that blueprint. What kind of friend are you, what kind of neighbor, what kind of parent, what did you do with your life, what did you create: this is what matters about people, not the circumstances of their birth. How we deal with the bodies we're born with changes over time, as the bodies change and as politics change. Genetics, and ancestry, does not wholly define anyone, and why would we want it to?

At the same time, people doing genealogy want to know what the past of their family means, and why would any historian ignore how people in the past understood themselves? Family histories reveal individual people's desire to define themselves but also the powerful social constraints ideas of race imposed. People with dark skins typically had no choice in the matter of how society defined them, and it would be preposterous to ignore hundreds of years of that lived experience. This book focuses mostly on people on the margins—people whose skin color or features or social status made their identity ambiguous. There were of course millions of people whose appearance defied renegotiation, whose identities could never be negotiated away. I focus on "mixed" people, or people on the margins, because as the walls of a house reveal its fundamental structure, the structures that form the idea of "race" are laid bare at its boundaries and edges.

The first two chapters tell the remarkable story of Dempsey Hare, "the richest negro in southern Virginia," a man with a largely invisible racial essence who could easily have passed for white. It's a story of actual murder and betrayal: Hare disinherited his daughter because she married a dark-skinned man, and was buried face down to keep his uncanny spirit from rising. Hare's wife shared a surname, and possibly "blood," with Hester Holland, Patrick's wife, who lived three miles away. The next three chapters tell Patrick and Hester's story, from his origins in Ireland to their home near Dempsey Hare's farm. Patrick was a slippery character, who "passed" in order to assimilate. He confronted forms of racecraft that, on the one hand, sought to make the Irish a different, lesser race, but, on the other, offered a path into assimilated whiteness.

Patrick and Hester's 1884 marriage license was "filed" in 1940 because of Walter Plecker, a man who weaponized genealogy by deliberately and systematically merging racism with state records. Many historians have written about Plecker, focusing on his vendetta against people with Native ancestors. My focus here is on his centralized administrative authority as "state genealogist" and how he mobilized the new technologies of individual identity to solidify ideas of race. Chapter 6 tells how, from his office in Richmond, Plecker drew on eugenics to sort out who was "really" white and who merely passed for white, carrying in them the dangerous secret of magically tainted blood. Had Patrick and Hester stayed in Virginia, Plecker would have found the "trace" that made them both colored, and their children could not have married people regarded as white.[5]

Family history is also more and more practiced through DNA research, and commercial genetic testing, which foregrounds biology above all. Commercial DNA tests will report you are, say, X percent Hungarian and X percent Gambian, and a historian will right away want to point out that Hungarian and Gambian are modern ideas and nobody regarded themselves as either in 1700. Ancestry.com, the subject of the last chapter, has digitized an amazing range of the records generated by the government, and combined them, for a hefty subscription fee, with DNA testing. Genetic records offer a new set of tools for managing and marketing records of identity: they often serve as the racial "blood test" Walter Plecker dreamed of. Chapter 7 looks at ancestry as property: property of families, or governments, or regions, ancestry as personal and now commercial property.

Historian Barbara J. Fields, and her sister, sociologist Karen E Fields, coined the term "racecraft" to describe the practices and spells that make "race" seem real. I've used their work throughout this book: it offers a powerful way to rethink the relation of ancestry to "race." Barbara Fields argues that we should stop saying "so-and-so is black" or "is white" and instead say, "she has ancestors from Africa and the Americas" or "ancestors from Europe and the Middle East." Thinking of people as "having ancestors from Asia" rather than *being* Asian would allow us to connect more with the history of human movement and interchange, instead of an imaginary static idea of race. It allows for particularity: Where in Asia? Where in Africa? It would turn genealogy away from strictly biology and toward history and culture. Family history can offer us a way to escape the spells of "racecraft" by focusing on historical experience, and historical experience in turn makes it clear how racecraft, practiced through individualized records, has operated to produce inequality.

It might seem at first that the stories told here are unusual, but I would insist that they are not. Stories of choosing to pass or not to pass are deeply rooted in the experience of Americans with African ancestors, and very few African Americans will be surprised at Dempsey Hare's tale. The book shows multiple other examples of people with European ancestors, like Patrick and Hester, named as "black." But beyond that, every family's history contains evidence of courage and weakness, honesty and mendacity, and heroic perseverance and fecklessness. Every family's history is equal parts epic, mundane, and fantastic, if you know how to look.

# ONE

# NANSEMOND

On a dreary winter day in 1901, they lowered Dempsey Hare into the ground. "There was no preacher," wrote the *Virginian Pilot*, just a layman who spoke a few words. The late January weather didn't stop "a large crowd of persons including many white people," from gathering near the home of "the richest negro in southern Virginia," on Holy Neck Road in Nansemond County. Hare owned up to three thousand acres of land; the safe up at his house, visible across his level fields, held an unknown amount of cash. "Though colored himself," the deceased "was so familiar with several prominent business and professional men in Suffolk that it was his wont to address them by their first names." Hare "had believed in white people," the reporter added, and now he counted on them to extend his will beyond the grave.[1]

Hare was a canny and opportunistic farmer and businessman, the child of a father descended from Europe and a mother with ancestors in Europe and Africa. Newspapers called him "eccentric and shrewd," also "fractious." They repeated rumors that Hare had once asked a surgeon to "change his blood" from black to white. In 1897, about seventy-four years old, Hare had traveled the forty miles to Norfolk and ordered a marble vault and eight-foot-high carved marble marker. Nansemond County was table-flat, much of its sandy soil reclaimed from swamp, and local burials required a stone or brick vault below ground level. Hare laid out paths and a garden around the gravesite. From his front porch, he'd watched travelers pass his future resting place. Now the law was executing his final scheme.[2]

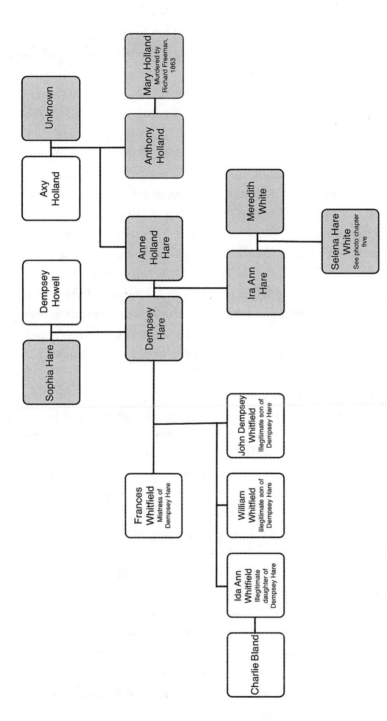

*Figure 1.1.* Partial family tree of Dempsey Hare. People not discussed in the book are omitted. Shaded boxes indicate people identified in public records as having ancestors from Africa. The African ancestry of Frances Whitfield's children was concealed.

Crowds gathered because Hare's will left his daughter, Ira Ann White, only ten dollars. Ignoring his demands, she had fallen in love with and married a dark-skinned man. In spite and bitterness, Hare bequeathed all his land and nearly all his money to two prominent local white men who shared his late wife's surname, Edward Everett Holland and Dr. Job Holland. The story made newspapers as far away as Texas, Nebraska, Boston, and Connecticut. "Being a bright mulatto himself, he would not associate with dark negroes," wrote the *Baltimore Sun*. "He had one daughter, whom he had stated he was rearing to be the wife of a white man. When she married a negro the father would have nothing more to do with her." The story flattered people who understood themselves as white: of course this crazy rich man wanted to be white, didn't everybody? A Pennsylvania newspaper mocked him as "a vain colored man." What madness made him think his daughter could change her race? The story repeated things people already liked to believe, and so newspapers reprinted it widely. Hare was light but could not be white: his wealth would go to white people, not his daughter.[3]

A day later, some of those newspapers printed a sensational new development. "It was learned today that Dempsey Hare, Nansemond's richest negro, was yesterday buried with his face down and his feet toward the west." Before the burial someone had opened his coffin and rearranged his body, so that he would lie face down in the grave, looking not toward the heavens but toward the center of the earth.[4]

In both Africa and in Europe, "prone burial" indicated the dead person was evil or dangerous. "Burial face down is a practice used for 'Nyongo' witchcraft practitioners in coastal Cameroon," wrote one scholar of West Africa. Among the Ibibio people, of coastal Nigeria, "undesirables whose return is not wished are placed in the grave face downward." Whoever placed Hare face down might have drawn on African traditions. But face down burial also appeared in Europe, particularly in the burial of suspected witches or criminals. Hare had turned his face from part of his community and in a brutal judgment, someone in the community turned the act back on him. His white friends summoned the undertaker, Solomon Holland, to exhume the corpse, turn it face up, and reposition it so the feet faced the rising sun.[5]

## *Racecraft*

Historian Barbara Fields uses the term "racecraft" to describe how race and racism work. "Witchcraft," Fields points out, is a body of ideas, knowledge, and practices people in Europe, Africa, and North America all found useful for navigating the world. "Witchcraft" might explain why someone got sick or died or why people had visions. The practices of witchcraft—incantations, herbs, cryptic symbols, potions—always reinforced the idea that witches existed: "witchcraft" has the witch as its object; it tries to "produce" the witch. It looks at events in the world and points to the witch at work.

But witches themselves rarely appeared, and were hard to spot, because in ordinary life the essence of "witchiness" was invisible: one had to "see behind appearance" to discover the witch. Halloween caricature aside, what made a witch was internal, unseen, not on the skin. Despite this invisibility, in societies committed to witchcraft, it's absolutely common sense that a witch caused someone's illness or sickened their cow or blighted a crop. Daily life in, say, Puritan New England was full of gestures, practices, and superstitions designed to ward off or uncover witches. Most famously in Salem, the common sense of witchcraft led to the execution of twenty ordinary looking people as witches.

Fields argues "racism" is to "race" as witches are to witchcraft: racism is a set of practices that aims to bring about and make real the thing it imagines, "race." Racecraft is the tools racism uses to produce race. It blames race for things produced by the practice of racecraft, just as witchcraft blames someone called a witch for various social ills. In Virginia racism showed up most obviously in slavery: people were enslaved *because* of their race, as if race caused it. But *racism* caused it and blamed it on this thing called "race." Racism also imposed unequal taxation, lack of voting rights, and a range of restrictive laws on free people with African ancestors like Dempsey Hare. As intended, these social and political acts worked to keep brown-skinned people in poverty: the poverty was then understood as a product of race, a product of some inward, invisible essence every bit as imaginary, and as dangerous, as the witch's power. Witch hunters looked for signs and practices that might reveal a hidden essence, and then called it out: "your crops failed because this woman is a witch!" Racecraft similarly tries to produce a thing that isn't visible: "those people are poor because of their race!"

But race isn't invisible, you might say, surely there really are black people: it's common sense! People don't look alike though, even people of the same "race." Skin color varies widely, and *people* vary widely. Racecraft works to make the idea of race into common sense: everyone *must* have a race and their race is the same regardless of what they actually look like. "Having African ancestors" is understood as "being" black: racism generates race from the complications of ancestry. But the various things claimed to stigmatize African-descended people were all inward and invisible traits of this thing called race. They weren't really "sensible" in that you couldn't see or hear or taste them. Laziness is not written on the body; crime is not written on the body: both dark and light children are routinely born poor. Racecraft attributes poverty or crime to race.[6]

Consider Dempsey Hare, a child of Europe to all appearances, but supposedly having in himself, like the secret of witchery, the internal traits of "race," invisible and never provable at the time by any concrete means. He tried to "change his blood," newspapers reported. Racecraft located race in blood, but as Hare discovered you could not see "black blood" any more than you could see witch blood: all blood looks the same to the naked eye. In common usage "blood" referred to the red fluid flowing in the veins, but also to an internal essence or character. Blood could contain courage or cowardice, virtue or vice, even though the blood of the hero and the coward, spilled on the ground, looked the same. These ideas about secret essences in blood converged in genealogy, in family histories revealed in local knowledge, in local people's memories, and increasingly over the course of Hare's life, in administrative records on paper.

The newspaper articles about Hare's prone burial amount to racecraft. By describing him as black, they help make it so: they tell you how to understand him. So does the way I've retold the story, quoting newspapers that insisted on dividing people into white / black even though neither dark skin nor the alleged traits of race were present. Hare looked like a European. He was smart, energetic, rich, and left a lot of property, but disposal of his property after death turned emphatically on the question of blood, not on visible signs in skin or hair, and blood was tracked through genealogy.

As they lowered him into the ground, lawyers prepared their cases. Hare's daughter was contesting the will. Was Hare insane on the question of race? What would that even mean? The state would have to intervene: money and property were at stake. And so here in his prone burial, aimed at keeping his spirit from rising, we see witchcraft and racecraft and statecraft merging.[7]

That Hare's beneficiaries dug him up and reburied him vindicated his belief in the local Euro-Americans, but Hare's will also specified a bequest of $500 in trust, "the interest on which is to be used in keeping the cemetery in my home place in good condition." It insisted that upon the deaths of E. E. and Job Holland "other trustees are to be appointed by the County Court of Nansemond County," so as to keep his grave in good repair. Hare "believed in white people," and had faith in the law and faith his monument would endure.[8]

### Hare's Grave

That faith was naive. Searching the fields, woods, and swamps along Holy Neck Road reveals no trace of Dempsey Hare's eight-foot marble cenotaph. I spent a lot of time driving up and down local roads trying to find it, and searching satellite photos of the area. Property deeds from that period do not include a map or plat or street addresses: they simply describe the property and say "adjacent to the property of X," naming the owners of the lots surrounding the land in question. So it's impossible to get a precise sense of where a plot is located. The road itself changed course at some point. Testimony in the case of *Hare v. Darden*, described in chapter 2, says Dempsey Hare lived on the north side of Holy Neck Road near South Quay Road, and that he had gates opening onto Holy Neck Road. Newspaper accounts say Hare was buried on his own land near the road. Hare at one point allowed members of the African American community to worship in a brush arbor church on his land, but after some sort of dispute the parish moved nearby and eventually built the stately, attractive, and lovingly tended Mount Sinai Baptist Church. Descendants of Hare's disinherited child worship there today. Near that general location, roughly two hundred yards west of the Mount Sinai Church and east of what's now called Old South Quay Road, stands a nineteenth-century farmhouse, much modified and cut up for apartments, that would have suited a prosperous farmer in 1900. It seemed likely this was the place.[9]

I was very conscious of being a stranger while driving up and down on Holy Neck Road, with my vestigial Philadelphia accent and my odd interest in this terrible story, and also aware that I was looking into the racially charged history of living people who might not like what I'd find. So I decided to confine myself as far as possible to using only public records. But, on the other hand, my ancestors had lived just a few miles away: my great-great-grandmother Hester Holland was born and raised in Nansemond County; she and my great-great-grandfather started a family here. I had "deep roots" in this soil, according to records. So armed with this sense of vague entitlement, and overcoming the historian's general preference for working with dead people, I knocked on the farmhouse door and stumbled through an explanation of what I was looking for, the grave of Dempsey Hare. The woman who answered listened patiently and said, "well, there's graves right over there," pointing over my shoulder. I'd driven right by them a dozen times and never noticed.

Where she pointed were six graves, just off the road, none with headstones, each oriented strictly east to west. Four of the graves were concrete, and two had lettering identifying the deceased: one had cursive letters incised into a thin scrim of smooth cement, now indecipherable. Two clearly dated to the mid-twentieth century. Three were just weathered brick, with no identifiers, one set apart from the others. All these clues suggest the one set apart is Hare's grave, that his beneficiaries sold the land and let it fall into disrepair, and that the marble was plundered and later owners of the land buried their own family members, Benjamin Howell and Washington Brown among unknown others, near Hare's grave in an act of reclamation, erasing his name.

Hare's life seems like something out of Faulkner, or Toni Morrison, a story of driving ambition and the moral madness that turned ancestry into race. The son of "Sophia, of Hare," a free woman of European and African descent, and Dempsey Howell, presumed Euro-American, he married a woman of mixed ancestry named Anne

*Figure 1.2.* Author photo of what I believe to be Dempsey Hare's house. The graves are near the road, out of frame to the left.

Holland in 1848. During the Civil War, he saw his sister-in-law, Mary Holland, murdered by a man angry at her barking dog. He invested himself in the politics of Reconstruction, on behalf of the freed people, but then when Reconstruction failed, turned his mind to farming and prospered. He took a mistress, a Euro-American woman, and had at least two children with her. Disinheriting his legal daughter and giving two prominent men named "Holland" his estate merged racecraft and statecraft. It bought his illegitimate children passage into legal whiteness despite their "black blood." When able, Hare used statecraft, the formal state and local administrative records, the apparatus of state and local government, to work his will. But he remained snared in the "common sense" demand that individuals must have a race.

At Hare's birth in about 1824, Virginia had no formal birth certificate requirements, and reporting on marriages and deaths was casual and sporadic. Census takers and county clerks mostly guessed at age. By the time he died, records had become much more precise, specific, and regular; much more effective at preventing renegotiation and eliminating ambiguity; and much more effective at making an individual's race into a durable, lasting, and inheritable proposition. This chapter examines the evolution of racecraft and the state in antebellum Virginia, looking at how administrative standards coexisted with, and eventually supplanted, community norms. It highlights a tension between blood as some sort of static essence recorded in law and blood as genealogy and lived history. We still grapple today with those evolving standards of making sense of people, and of people's relationship to the past, and we still practice racecraft with both the best and the worst of intentions. The social history of ordinary families shows how racecraft worked, while still acknowledging the history of racism and the way it operated in daily life.

Nansemond County, where Hare lived and died, no longer exists. Suffolk Town was Nansemond's county seat, but in 1974 the county became the city of Suffolk, the largest city, geographically, in Virginia. It's in the far southeast corner of the state, bordered by North Carolina to the south and to the east by "the Great Dismal Swamp," still dismal and still great but less great than in George Washington's day, when its boggy woodlands covered as much as a million acres. At one time ship captains prized the swamp's tannic, tea-colored water, "commonly called juniper water." Stored in casks, it stayed fresh longer. The waters of Lake Drummond, in the center of the swamp, were "so highly esteemed that people whose health is impaired frequently go there to drink."[10]

The swamp also served as refuge for people on the margins of society: Native Americans, escaped slaves, and free people, collectively termed "Maroons," eked out a living or found refuge in its spongy depths. When Nat Turner's attack on slavery in neighboring Southampton County failed, Nansemond residents expected Turner would head to the Dismal Swamp to hide out. Harriet Beecher Stowe even wrote a novel about escaped "Maroons" in 1856: *Dred: A Tale of the Great Dismal Swamp*. The swamp was a microcosm of the county as a whole, which had a mixed population of Native peoples, European settlers of English and Ulster Irish descent, and persons with roots in Africa, both enslaved and free.[11]

## Forms of Unfreedom

To understand these communities we have to understand the various forms of "unfreedom" in US history and their relation to changing ideas of selfhood. In the broadest sense, into the nineteenth century there were three categories of unfree people: slaves, indentured servants, and apprentices. *Apprentices* were nearly always young people bound to a craftsman, who owned them legally until adulthood. They contributed their labor and in return learned the master's trade. *Indentured servants* had a limited term of unfreedom: perhaps three to seven years but possibly longer. They might agree to an indenture contract to fund a voyage or because they were down on their luck; or they might suffer indenture as punishment for a crime, but in all cases indenture was limited. During the term of indenture, they were property. Their master might treat them as he or she pleased or sell them. Europeans, Native Americans, Africans, or mixed people could all wind up as indentured servants, but their children were born free. *Slaves* were unfree for life, and their unfreedom was inherited via the mother: the child of a female slave was a slave. Before about 1700, Native people were often enslaved, but in Virginia after 1705, slavery only applied to people with African ancestors.

Colonial Americans frequently blurred these categories of unfreedom, for example, using the term "servant" to describe both slaves and indentured servants and sometimes making it hard for historians to tell them apart. The first people of African descent arrived in Virginia as indentured servants, and indentured servitude of Africans predominated for the first thirty years or so, but once they discovered tobacco and cotton as cash crops, and mortality rates in the new colony declined, the English settlers quickly adopted enslavement along with indenture.[12]

The multiple forms of unfreedom confuse people. Consider this advertisement from the *Connecticut Gazette* in 1764: "just imported from Dublin, in the brig Darby, a parcel of Irish servants, both men and women, to be sold cheap." Some people, mostly Irish Americans, see something like this and conclude "the Irish were slaves too." They were not: rather, forms of legal unfreedom were ubiquitous, and brutish "inhuman" treatment both common and casual. Ben Franklin estimated that at the time of the American Revolution roughly one-half of Pennsylvania's labor force was legally unfree, mostly indentured servants; Young Franklin himself was indentured to his older brother and dodged local sheriffs when he ran away from Boston to Philadelphia. Later, as publisher of the *Pennsylvania Gazette*, he felt no qualms about owning enslaved people himself or about running an advertisement for "a parcel of English and Irish servants, men and women," just arrived in Philadelphia and "to be disposed of" by sale on the Market Street wharf. Owners often cared less about strict definitional categories between servant and slave than they did about getting unfree labor in the most convenient form possible.[13]

Over time, distinctions between servants and slaves grew more formal. By 1800, indentured servitude and apprenticeship were vanishing, replaced by a system of heritable, permanent racial slavery. Slavery by then was a legal category restricted to persons with African ancestors. Not just a system of labor exploitation, slavery depended on racecraft, on an idea of white supremacy, black inferiority, and a belief in profound, nonnegotiable differences between Native Americans, Africans, and Europeans. But that belief took a lot of effort to sustain, because it was founded in nonsense and like witches vanishing in the dark, race was always winking in and out of sight.

Just as ideas about freedom and unfreedom evolved, definitions of "race" have continually evolved. The word "Caucasian" as a generic term for a supposed "white race," for example, didn't appear until the 1780s. People of course could see visible differences, but as always, the question was how to make sense of those visible differences: What did they *mean*? And what did it mean when those differences blurred and merged, as with someone like Dempsey Hare?

## *The Co-Dependence of Individualism and Racism*

We can get a vivid look at how Americans understood freedom, individualism, and race in the past by looking at advertisements for indentured servants and enslaved persons who ran away. The examples below come from the *Pennsylvania Gazette*, Ben Franklin's newspaper, the most widely read newspaper in North America. The *Gazette* includes more than seven hundred examples of runaway advertisements between 1728 and 1800, and these advertisements reflect a very different understanding of personhood.[14]

Modern readers will notice right away, from just a few examples, how poorly the ads identify their subjects. This typical example comes from April 5, 1729:

Run away the Second Day of the Fair, from Mary Stockdale, of Evesham, in the County of Burlington, a Servant Man named John Finley, a Farmer, aged about 20. He had an old Beaver Hat, a striped yellow and blue Cotton Cap, a blue grey Worsted and Woollen Coat, a yellow homespun Jacket, Ozenbrigs Breeches, a new pair of grey Woollen Stockings, a new pair of Neat's Leather Shoes. He has a brown swarthy Complexion, and thick Legs, his Hair newly cut off. Whoever secures the said Runaway, so as his Mistress may have him again, and gives Notice to John Breintnal in Chesnut street, shall have 40s. Reward, and reasonable Charges paid by me, Mary Stockdale.

The ad does not give Finley's "race," and only gives a very general one-sentence description of his appearance. Despite his Irish name, he has "a brown swarthy complexion." Does he have African ancestors? Why does the ad not give his race? We might say "racecraft" is not being practiced well here, or not very energetically. This ad does not even bother to tell us the color or texture of Finley's "hair newly cut," though it takes great care to describe his yellow and blue striped cap and other clothes: they mark his personhood, rather than his individual physical attributes. He isn't effectively individualized *or* effectively racialized: the tools are not precise enough yet. Neither the sense of race nor the sense of individualism conform to modern ideas.[15]

Today we would expect a photograph, or footage from surveillance cameras, or a composite drawing. On their website in 2022, for example, the Chicago police department explained "how to describe a suspect." It told people to look for "sex, Race or national origin," also for "Age (estimated): Height—use comparisons with your own height, a door, or some other standard measure; Weight (estimated): Build—fat, husky, slim, muscular, etc." It also suggests people note hair texture, hairline, hair style, also possible dyes or wigs. "Note forehead height," it continues, "and whether the skin is smooth, creased or wrinkled." It asks witnesses to consider "eyes—note the color, shape (round, slanted), whether clear or bloodshot, and the heaviness of eyelashes and eyebrows." Consider each part of the face, it continues—nose, ears, skin color and porosity, cheekbone prominence: a long list of facial details that several hundred years of forensics have measured, considered, recorded in databases, and made part of the package of features that individualize a suspect and make him distinctive, to the point where we now have facial recognition software that can theoretically pinpoint identity remotely. The Chicago police website reflects a far more developed sense of individualism and a settled sense of race.[16]

Modern policing mixes racecraft—the need to give suspects a race—with statecraft, the state's archive of records and databases. It *individualizes* the subject, regarding that person independently of community and family. An earlier era read John Finley's clothing, his "Ozenbrigs breeches" and striped cap, for signs of social status and caste. The modern era produces individualized records of nearly every person born, and a baby's footprints on a card make a record of distinct personhood independent of breeches or caps. "Individualism" is a political idea: documents that track people make the idea real. Fingerprints, genetic codes, facial recognitions, retinal scans all individualize us. We often understand individualism as freedom or the exercise of consumer choice. Modern commerce, mapping your purchases and anticipating preferences, doesn't really care about your family. But it individualizes people to an even greater extent than the government. Individualism and race, freedom and surveillance, have a much closer relationship than commonly understood.

The Chicago police website devotes only a few lines to the subject of clothing, while the bulk of the call for John Finley concerns what he wears. In that sense runaway ads invert the modern sense of individualism, locating it not in the individual body but in body covering. Clothing cost more then. It marked status much more clearly. Specific fabrics and colors told a tale of class background. Very likely the owner of the servant also owned the clothing on the servant's back, possibly worth more than Mr. Finley himself.

But it's also likely Finley's owner did not quite see him as human, or at least not human to the same degree, and despite living in the same household never bothered to pay attention to Finley, the person. He was a possession, not a person, a member of a lesser caste and class.

Individualizing him, knowing him, was hardly worth the bother. From the *Gazette*, October 2, 1729:

> Run away on the 10th of September past, from William Dewees . . . a Servant Man named Melchizedeck Arnold, of a middle Stature, and reddish curled Hair: he had on when he went away, a good Felt Hat, a dark Cinnamon colour'd Coat, black Drugget Jacket, mouse colour'd drugget Breeches, grey Stockings, and new Shoes. Whoever secures the said Runaway . . .

Melchizedek's curled red hair must have helped mark him, but "middle stature" does little, and here again the bulk of the text concerns clothing. William Dewees of Germantown seems to know nothing at all about Melchizedeck Arnold. Did he have freckles or scars? Fair skin or dark? Blue eyes or brown? Was he religious? Irreverent? Quick witted? Shy? Clumsy? Did he love to dance? Did he stammer when lying? All these things might help identify him, yet he barely exists in the ads, possibly because he barely existed to William Dewees except as an inventory of clothing and a source of labor. We would probably have regarded him as a white man, but again the ad does not bother to say. He was not yet racialized in the modern sense of the word.[17]

It was very common to find Irish runaways identified as "black" or "brown" or "dark." For example, an ad in 1768 described "John Meshefrey, born in the North of Ireland, a thick well set Fellow, about 5 Feet 7 Inches high, of a black Complexion, and talks broad." It gave an estimate of his height but as usual spent far more time on the "blue Coat, whitish Jacket, Buckskin Breeches, grey Stockings, a Pair of Brass Buckles, and an old Felt Hat, tarred on the Top of the Crown" that he wore. Did Meshefrey's black complexion indicate he had African ancestors, despite being born in Ulster? We might also wonder about "James Downing, an Irish Man," who ran off in 1738: "short of Stature, black Complexion, broad Shoulders, bandy Legs, hooper arsed, walks as if he was Hip shot." A 1775 ad described "a certain Thomas Mallen," as of "low stature, black hair and visage." "Irish servant man"

John McCarter was also "of a very dark complexion" when he ran off in 1772, and four years later so was "Manus O'Cannon, aged about 30 years, 5 feet 5 inches high, much marked with the smallpox, of a very dark complexion." Each of those latter ads spent more time on clothes than on personhood, but pointedly identified Irish people as dark, suggesting racial difference.[18]

What do we make of the 1785 advertisement for "BILL, a miller, about 5 feet 8 inches high, of a swarthy complexion and down look, with short black hair and thick lips." Bill was "a good fidler, fond of musick, company and spirituous liquors . . . when afraid, or his passions in any manner agitated, his face becomes remarkably dark coloured." "He called himself Mullon," his owner added. Was Bill a person with African ancestors, or the child of an Irishman named Mullon, or both? The unusually long ad continued with a description of "GEORGE," of light complexion, "addicted to swearing, fond of spirituous liquors" and also "fond of the fiddle." Bill and George, it turns out, were twins, "descended, by their mother, from an Indian female slave their grandmother, and by bastardy not to be distinguished from white persons." Remarkably, the ad continued, both, "as they talk on the Scotch-Irish dialect, may pass for Irishmen." It's fascinating to imagine what sort of music the swarthy twin descendants of a Native American woman and an Irishmen, both either speaking Irish or with heavy Irish accents, might have played on their fiddles. It's also fascinating that they can't be racially placed with precision or clearly identified as either slaves or indentured servants or Irishmen. It's not that Irish people were seen as a different race, at least not exactly: it's that "race" itself was not as clearly defined, and neither was individualism. Readers of the *Gazette* did not demand the sort of answers we see as routine.[19]

A decade before the American Revolution, with its sweeping rhetoric about individualism and individual freedom, we see a markedly different understanding of both. From the *Gazette*, June 5, 1766:

> Carlisle Goal, in Cumberland County . . . NOW in said Goal, the four
> following described Fellows, all committed on Suspicion of being

Runaways, viz. Daniel Holburn, about 21 Years of Age, 5 Feet 9 Inches
high, pale faced, slender built, with yellow Hair, a long Nose, very ragged Cloathing, and says he is an Englishman. James Steven, an Englishman, 5 Feet 8 Inches high, well set, about 30 Years of Age, of a dark
Complexion, short black Hair, and very ragged. John Logan, a well
set chunkey Irishman, and declares himself to be a Servant to James
Alexander Gardiner near Philadelphia. John Henderson, alias George
Smith, a short well set Fellow, about 35 Years of Age, of a dark Complexion, down Look, short black Hair, tries to pass for a Fool; he had
with him, and is now at Hay, in said Town, a large black Mare, 16 Hands
high, 7 Years old, shod all round, a natural Pacer, a little white on her
Forehead, and near each Nostril, her near hind Foot white, and lame
in one of her Footlock Joints. The Masters of said Fellows (if any) are
hereby notified to come and take them away, otherwise they will be
sold six Weeks after the Date hereof, for Cost and Fees, by HENRY
CUNNINGHAM, Goaler.

The word "Goal" here means "jail": Noah Webster would not publish
his first dictionary of American English till 1806, fifty years in the future, and spelling was not yet standardized.

In these descriptions we see more about the physical features, and
less about the clothes, as in "goaler" Henry Cunningham's opinion that
"John Henderson, alias George Smith," has a "dark complexion," a
"down look," and "tries to pass for a fool." "Dark complexion" shows us
again relative indifference to racecraft: is he white or not, and why are
they not telling us? Is his darkness a mark of what we would call race, or
a mark of being lower class, a sign that he works outside in the hot sun?
Or just that he was understandably dismayed and frowning at finding
himself in jailer Cunningham's minimal care? James Steven is also "of a
dark complexion" despite being named explicitly as "an Englishman."
Was he a person with African ancestors? We can't tell. But notice that
*the horse* gets a more fulsome and precise description than any of
the four men. Jailer Cunningham has a much more detailed vocabulary for individualizing horses than he does for describing persons.[20]

The ad gives estimates of height, but like spelling, weights and measures were not standardized in 1766. Age is a guess: there were no legal requirements for birth certificates. Sometimes a village clerk or a church might write a birth record, and literate families might make a note in a family Bible, but the idea of standard legal birth certificates was more than one hundred years away. So the jailer guesses John Holburn at "about 21 years of age": Holburn himself likely had no real idea. In the present, twenty-one often marks a significant age, old enough to drink alcohol, and a bartender can demand precise legal proof of age that any thirsty patron must produce on demand. No such documents of individual identity existed in 1766.[21]

And notice finally that these men sit in jail as suspected runaways: they have no way to prove their free status unless someone comes to the jail and either vouches for them as free or claims to own them. Otherwise jailer Henry Cunningham will sell them. The *Gazette* includes hundreds of advertisements like this, wherein the jailer has arrested some stranger, clapped the person in a cell, and then advertised for the owner to come and get them, "otherwise they will be sold six weeks after the date hereof, for cost and fees." It was nearly impossible to fix the identity of a stranger with precision, so the security of individual personhood and individual freedom was precarious. Standards for identification were nonexistent, and public officials had no qualms about selling people into legal unfreedom. Modern individualism, produced and secured by administrative records, is not in place.

This is a world regarding personhood, and the rights of persons, very differently. They lacked the administrative technology to track people precisely, at least partly because they had no need for it. Imprecision served almost everyone's interest. The runaways could benefit from the fact that their owner offered no precise description: it made them harder to find. The jailer could certainly benefit by rounding up sources of income from the streets, wharves, and taverns. Any person looking for laborers for the coming harvest could just buy one or more of these men if no one arrived to claim them. In this world one's individual status depended much more on the appearance of wealth and social rank and on community. People who knew you and could speak for you shielded you from arrest or from enslavement, not identity cards or fingerprints. That would change.

## Free People of Color

Virginia had a particular problem, because it had an unusually large community of free people with Native or African ancestors, working as laborers, farmers, and artisans. By 1860, Virginia had about 550,000 people in slavery, roughly one-third of the state's population, and roughly sixty thousand free people with African ancestry. Half of those free people lived in the tidewater region, the coastal plains of the southeast, including Nansemond County. Many of them, later called "free issues," were born free: the children of formerly indentured servants. Others bought their way out of slavery, or had relatives who bought them, or were emancipated by their owners. In Nansemond County, by 1860, "there were 2470 free negroes" and only 581 slaves. Tobacco did not thrive in Nansemond County's soil, and neither did cotton. You will see cotton growing today in farms around Holy Neck Road, and in December tufts of cotton that escaped the harvester blow away and collect in small drifts, but at the time cotton production mostly took place elsewhere. "The chief industries of the county before the Civil War were the manufacture of tar, turpentine and staves." Dempsey Hare grew up on land with a "tar kiln" for rendering resin from pine logs. His father built houses for "his negroes," meaning both his children with Sophia Hare and as many as seven people held as slaves. Most Nansemond County slaveholding households held less than ten people in slavery, so while slavery was common in Nansemond County, free people with African or Native ancestors were much *more* common.[22]

"I was born in Nansemond County, Virginia on my father's place near the center of the County," recalled Reverend Frank Boone in 1937: "I was born free." The Works Progress Administration interviewed Boone, born about 1858, about life before the Civil War: the interview can tell us some details about the world Dempsey Hare lived in. Boone grew up in Nansemond in "what is known as Free Colonies. They were Negroes that had always been free. The first landing of the Negroes in America, they claimed, formed a colony. The Negro men who came over, it is said, could buy their freedom and a number of them did," Boone remembered. "My ancestors were a white man and an Indian woman. He was my great-grandfather." Boone remembered their home as a two-room log cabin, chinked with mud, with the exterior covered in weatherboards so "you couldn't tell it was a log house." It had a separate kitchen. Typical of the region's farmers, "they raised corn, peas, wheat, potatoes, and all things for the table. . . . I never saw a pound of meat or a peck of flour or a bucket of lard or anything like that bought. We rendered our own lard, pickled our own fish, smoked our own meat and cured it, ground our own sausage, ground our own flour and meal from our own wheat and corn we raised." "My grandmother on my father's side owned slaves," he told the interviewer, thinking back to when he was five or six years old. "The law was that colored people could own slaves but they were not allowed to buy them. I don't know how many slaves my grandmother owned. I didn't know they were slaves until the War was over."[23]

As Boone's recollections suggest, free people "of color" complicated everything. They were neighbors, and possibly relatives of people regarded as "white," but they threatened the regime of slavery in multiple ways. They took surnames, lived independently, earned money, raised children, went to church, and lived perfectly well without an owner. Some were understood as Indian, exempt from slavery after 1705. Some had obvious African ancestors, some had ambiguous ancestry. The bodies of "mixed" people demanded the practice of racecraft to make them sensible.

Local people in Nansemond County had a good idea of who their neighbors were and how they'd gotten to be who they were. They knew Dempsey Hare's mother was not his father's legal wife. But strangers or people who moved from place to place posed a different set of problems. How could you know with any certainty if a person claiming free status was actually a runaway slave or servant? Runaway ads specific to Nansemond County have a lot to say about how free people of African descent interacted with their neighbors.

## Free People and the Enslaved

The *Virginia Gazette*, published from Williamsburg, had a much smaller and more local circulation than Franklin's *Pennsylvania Gazette*. On November 15, 1775, it announced, "BROKE jail on Monday the 13th . . . a very remarkable light mulatto slave, named DICK." It gave his age and height and added that he had a "down look" and a scar on his upper lip, with short dark hair. He had a "red lappeled sailor's waistcoat, narrow osnabrug trousers and shirt, a cocked hat, and shoes and stockings." The rest of the ad tells an interesting history of movement between freedom, servitude, and slavery. Dick "has been run away for 18 months past, and went by water as a freeman, till last summer, when he enlisted as a soldier, in Princess Anne county." Princess Anne County, now Virginia Beach, was on the Atlantic coast. In the British Army, he went "by the name of Will Thompson, and came to this city, where he was taken up, and committed to jail." John Lamb, owner, added "I imagine he will again try to pass for a freeman, and endeavour to get on board some vessel, or return to Nansemond, where I hear he left a crop of corn."[24]

While the advertisement foregrounds Dick's mixed ancestry, it clearly shows the state's inability to track its people. Dick can escape and pass as a free man because there is no solid way to tell who he is aside from a "down look" and some sort of scar on his lip. For unclear reasons he took a new name, enlisted in the army, and wound up in jail in Williamsburg, where he escaped and will again pass for a free man, perhaps going back to sea. Somewhere between working on the water and serving as a soldier, Dick managed to plant a crop of corn in Nansemond County, on someone's land. This is a state that lacks effective police power, because it can't track identity: it's also a state having trouble making its racial categories stick. Individualism and racism aren't fully developed yet. Racecraft and statecraft haven't yet merged.

In April of 1787, the *Virginia Gazette* announced a reward for "FRANK, a mulatto man." Frank was of middling height, about twenty-five, "stout and strong made." The notice listed his clothing in detail and added, "I have been informed that he has a free pass, with four or five different person's names to it, and passes as a free man. He formerly belonged to a person who calls himself a Quaker, and of whom I purchased him last summer. I imagine he will endeavour to get among the negroes that have been emancipated by the Quakers in Nansemond or Isle of Wight, where he has been seen." Frank's putative owner added that he had "remarkable large legs" and "a scar near one of his temples, but do not recollect which." Neither of these descriptors would offer much certainty.[25]

Frank's "free pass" is interesting and will be discussed below. But as the ad shows, Nansemond County had a community of free "colored" people, and they helped each other and the enslaved. Nansemond had also had a community of Quakers, Euro-Americans increasingly opposed to slavery. Frank Boone affirmed, "there was one set of white people in Virginia called Quakers. Their rule was to free all slaves at the age of twenty-one. . . . My mother who was a Negro woman was freed under this rule." Warren Milteer writes that in the late eighteenth and early nineteenth centuries, "the combination of social and political changes led slaveholders across the South to reconsider the enslavement of their bondspeople. Manumissions driven by antislavery thinking were common in the Upper South." He adds slaveholders cited ideas of "natural rights" and expressed moral qualms about slavery when they finally decided to manumit.[26]

In 1787, many people regarded slavery as evil or at least as problematic: their ranks included men like George Washington and Thomas Jefferson, whose awareness of slavery's evils failed to stop them from fattening on its proceeds till the day they died, but also principled men and women who formed the beginnings of the abolitionist movement. We should not mistake them for proponents of racial equality, but they were willing to aid a person seeking freedom. O'Kelly Road runs north from Holy Neck Road in Nansemond County. The name comes from Reverend James O'Kelly, an Irish-born Methodist who later helped found the Disciples of Christ. O'Kelly preached against slavery and when in charge of his church on Holy Neck Road, "had a shed added to it, for accommodation of the colored people." O'Kelly spoke against slavery, yes, but kept people with known African ancestors in a separate building.[27]

### Individualism and Racism Emerge Together

To resolve this "problem" of free people with African ancestry, Virginia in 1793 passed a remarkable statewide law requiring that "free negroes or mulattoes shall be registered in a book to be kept by the town clerk, which shall specify age, name, color, status, and by whom and in what court emancipated." The act also specified that "annually the negro shall be delivered a copy of the certification for twenty five cents" and that "every free negro shall once in three years obtain a new certificate." The free person would report to the local clerk. The clerk would eyeball them, ask questions, and then produce a written record naming and describing them. The record would often include height, weight or "build," skin color, teeth, and scars from smallpox, accidents, or ill treatment. Free persons would then pay twenty-five cents to get a certificate, popularly nicknamed "free papers," attesting to their status. The law demanded they reappear every three years to renew the certificate.

The law mandating free papers was an unprecedented instrument for producing individualism and race at the same time. The federal government kept records of soldiers, for example, but they consisted of little more than the person's name and place of induction. As Milteer writes, "the state mandate for registration effectively became a government identification service for free people of color." The law represented a new way of tracking African-descended people, but also the beginnings of a new way of thinking about individuals and the state.

The state came up with records of individuals for the purposes of racial surveillance: individualism and racial surveillance are the same thing here. The document that asserts individual identity does so to assert racial identity.[28]

Other states quickly adopted the idea of "free negro registers," and the law requiring free papers joined a larger set of changing ideas about how to secure identity. A few years later, the federal government passed a law for the protection of sailors, then routinely subject to "impressment" by British naval vessels. The captain of a British ship, short of manpower, could simply "press" sailors into his crew, since sailors had no proof of citizenship. Under this new act, the government would issue "seaman's protection papers," which "listed the sailor's name, identifying characteristics—height, complexion, tattoos, scars, and the like—and the location of his birth."[29]

In 1782 the Continental Congress charged the Department of Foreign Affairs with the responsibility for issuing formal passports, which were becoming increasingly common as documents of international identity. By 1811, passports, although not yet fully standardized, included space for a standard physical "description of his person, embracing the following particulars: Age, years; stature, feet; inches; forehead; eyes; nose; mouth; chin; hair; complexion; face." Distinct administrative individualism is beginning to emerge.[30]

The acts that created "free papers," "protection papers," and passports sought to create a stable record of individual personhood linked to state and federal government, along with a bureaucracy to record, track, and certify identity. They also tried to draw a line of legal identity around "negroes": that is, they tried to instate an idea of race in law and compel people to police each other in accordance. They show us racecraft and statecraft working together to produce a racial identity that could transcend time, space, and community. Dempsey Hare had to troop down to the county courthouse, submit to visual inspection, and register himself. The certificate fixed him as "colored" and, beyond that, established a racial identity that his ancestors would inherit, no matter what they looked like or who they married.[31]

Passports, protection papers, and free papers all grew from a shift in thinking about the nature of individualism, a desire to see people distinct from family, class, and community. These tools were part of what James Scott called "seeing like a state." In the nineteenth century, industrializing nations developed an intense desire to map and track their populations, to make them more "legible" to administration. Scott drew on French philosopher Michel Foucault, who described how during the era of the Enlightenment, European nations began to weigh and measure and assess people once dismissed as mere peasants, aiming to make them more productive and less troublesome. In this line of thinking, we have become more and more subject to state-directed authority and less free over the last 250 years. These arguments will be familiar to anyone who finds websites serving them advertisements for things they were just reading about, and countless movies imagine a sinister surveillance state. There is plenty of ground for that kind of thinking, but people quickly learned to subvert the bureaucratic aspiration for control.[32]

## The Uses of Administrative Individualism

Frederick Douglass used the similarity between free papers and sailors' protection papers to escape from slavery. Douglass had a friend "who owned a sailor's protection, which answered somewhat the purpose of free papers." The sailor's protection "described his [friend's] person" and certified that he was a free American. On board a train headed north, the conductor asked Douglass if he had his free papers. Douglass, dressed as a sailor, replied that he never took his free papers to sea, but he had his sailor's protection. Douglass had worked as a ship caulker in Baltimore's harbor and knew the ways of sailors. Persuaded by Douglass's clothes and manner, the conductor took only a cursory look at the paper, missing the fact that the sailor's protection described "a man much darker than myself." His confident nautical bearing carried more authority than the formal document.

In the same passage, Douglass described "free papers" "giving the

name, age, color, height and form of the free man . . . together with
any scars or other marks upon his person." But many people could
fit the often vague descriptions, and European-descended people often let their enthusiasm for stereotyping replace careful examination.
"Hence many slaves could escape by personating the owner of one set
of papers." An enslaved person would find a free person of color who
looked roughly similar and borrow their free papers, planning to mail
them back once he or she reached freedom. These instruments used
individualism to create race: the two ideas are intimately linked. But
they also opened paths to escape enslavement.[33]

Runaway ads show this clearly, people being individualized and
racialized at the same time, in the same document. An advertisement
in the *Richmond Enquirer*, June 17, 1833, called for the apprehension of
"a negro man, named James." The subscriber noted that "I understand
he calls himself JAMES POLLARD," so as "to suit some free papers he
has procured." The ad gave an estimate of his height but noted "some
persons think he has a scar about his face, others think on his upper
lip: I cannot say, though I have owned him for many years." James had
secured an administrative instrument that gave a precise account of
what "James Pollard" looked like, but the weak link is James's owner,
who lacks precise information that would distinguish James, enslaved
person, from James Pollard, free man of color, a paper identity that
the runaway assumed.[34]

An 1829 ad from the same newspaper tried to use precise knowledge of the runaway's appearance to prevent the escape of "my man
Ben," a "bright mulatto" who "has been taken for a white man." The ad
described Ben as five feet and nine or ten inches, about fifty-five, having "a white spot on the front of his head," and added that he "has lost
a piece of his left ear—has very large feet." Ben could read and write,
the listing continued, and "I have no doubt he has procured free papers, and will endeavor to make his escape to a Northern State." Ben
might have tried to escape by passing for white; he had done so in the
past, but here chose not to. White men did not have to carry certificates of freedom. But forged or borrowed papers gave Ben's imposture

the color of law, despite his former owner's precise description. He might have passed for white, but it was more useful to be individualized on paper as "black" but free. The paper identity mattered more than what he actually looked like. Authority is shifting to administrative records, and the paper document determines his race, independent of what he looks like or who bore him.[35]

## Imposture and the Pursuit of the Real

These ways of tracking people, as the ads suggest, center on racecraft and the security of human property, but they also stem from the problem, inherent in individualist societies, of imposture. A society committed to the idea that anyone can be what they want, that people can transform themselves from poor to rich, has to face the fact that at any given moment, no one is quite what they seem. The escaped slave passing for a free person is only a few degrees away from an ambitious person passing for the thing they hope to become. The difference between an ambitious man and a fraud, trickster, or con man might be only a few degrees further. The most famous example is probably another Ben, young Ben Franklin, hoping to establish himself as a printer, making a big show of pushing a wheelbarrow full of paper through Philadelphia's streets. "To show that I was not above my business," Franklin remembered, "I sometimes brought home the paper I purchas'd at the stores thro' the streets on a wheelbarrow. Thus being esteem'd an industrious, thriving young man." Franklin prospered while his rivals failed. Franklin realized that making a show of being busy could lead to actually being busy. The difference between a busy man and a man busy seeming busy was hard to parse. He was a man ahead of his time.[36]

Franklin had been a runway apprentice himself and had worried about being caught, and he later published hundreds of ads for runaways in which owners tried to figure out effective ways to identify their elusive property to strangers. In these tracking documents, with their descriptions of bodies, we also see a broad cultural interest in the problem of detection, in seeing through surface appearance, figuring out who people "really are," and fixing that identity in their descendants. One of the foundational categories for who people "really are" would be race.

"Free papers," on the one hand, demonstrate gross injustice: once indentured servitude ended as a practice, Euro-Americans never had to prove entitlement to freedom. Aimed at tracking and controlling free people of color, "free papers" also gave them both protection from enslavement and a tactic for escape. They also created a record, a trace, for history and genealogy. People doing genealogical research now use free papers and sailors' protections as sources and will often find a free person of African descent in 1850 described with precision and privacy-violating detail that's lacking in records of even affluent Euro-Americans people from the same era. The present knows them better because of the injustices perpetrated in the past.

The Free Negro Registry of Albemarle County, for example, tells the descendants of Johnson and Rachel Smith that Johnson Smith was fifty-one in 1814, about five foot four and a half inches tall, that he was "very dark" and had a "small blemish on the right eye next the nose, a scar on the left side of the left leg just below the knee." Descendants would probably not have photographs of Johnson or Rachel, who was forty-two in 1814, but they learn that she was also "very dark," barely five feet tall, with "large eyes, a large scar on the left breast near the shoulder, a small scar of about one inch in length on the right thumb, the middle finger of the right hand hath been split."[37]

Genealogical records are often the records of pain, the pain and anxiety inflicted by law on the weak, the pain of slavery or indenture or imprisonment, the pain of emigration or displacement. Rachel Smith's scars and "split" finger attest to a hard life. Genealogical records might also be records of joy, the joy at the birth of a child or a marriage, but even then they represent a moment when an ordinary person, clutching money scraped up to pay a fee, traveled to an intimidating office to confront the majesty of the law. Sheriffs, judges, clerks, immigration inspectors, or police could grant legitimacy, or the right to marry, or right of entry into a new country, but each encounter amounted to a test the subject might fail.

Because the Nansemond County Courthouse burned down in 1866, only eight "free negro certificates" from that county survive. Figure 1.3 shows the certificates of John Eloy Ash, sixteen, of dark complexion, five foot five inches with scars on his right wrist, on the right corner of his mouth, and over his right eye; and "Caty of Copeland," a woman of "yellow" complexion precisely "the height of five feet, two and one fourth of an inches," twenty-eight years old with four scars, one on the right cheek, one of the left wrist, "one just above the wrist and one on her finger next the little one on her left hand." Both county clerks showed a strong interest in precision, especially with Caty, whose lighter skin made her identity more ambiguous. Ash was registered by Peter B. Prentis, one of the central figures in chapter 5 and the man who declared Hester and Patrick to be colored. Earlier we saw people who were Irish but had a black complexion or whose dark complexion was noted but was race was not specified. These certificates insist that both John Ash, with dark complexion, and Caty of Copeland, of "yellow" complexion, were "negro." The certificates established both individual free status and individual racial identity: they make individuals as they make race.

In historical research individual personhood mostly emerges like this, from interactions with the state. Famous people may leave permanent records of their actions in newspapers and books, or video, but outside of the arts, we tend to remember mostly criminals, politicians, military leaders, or explorers, all roles formed in some relation to state authority. We know ordinary people almost entirely from state records. Family stories and lore matter but may be unreliable and rarely survive the family: when they do it's often through local and state historical societies and archives. The record of Dempsey Hare's life exists in census and marriage and tax records and through legal disputes about property and inheritance: all interactions with the state. Like Johnson and Rachel Smith, or Caty of Copeland, he exists to history only because of the state's interest in tracking individuals so they can assign race and make it stick.[38]

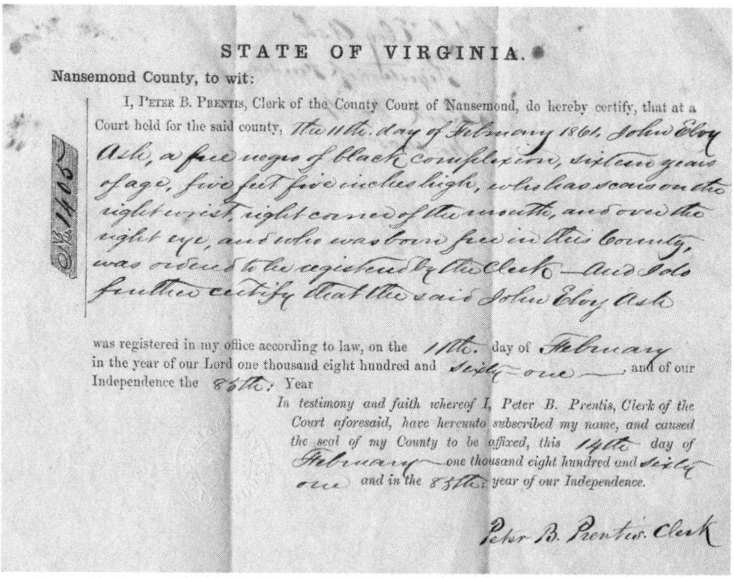

STATE OF VIRGINIA.

Nansemond County, to wit:

I, PETER B. PRENTIS, Clerk of the County Court of Nansemond, do hereby certify, that at a Court held for the said county, *the 11th day of February 1861, John Eley Ask, a free negro of black complexion, sixteen years of age, five feet five inches high, who has scars on the right wrist, right corner of the mouth, and over the right eye, and who was born free in this county, was ordered to be registered by the Clerk — And I do further certify that the said John Eley Ask*

was registered in my office according to law, on the *11th* day of *February* in the year of our Lord one thousand eight hundred and *sixty-one*, and of our Independence the *85th* Year.

*In testimony and faith whereof I, Peter B. Prentis, Clerk of the Court aforesaid, have hereunto subscribed my name, and caused the seal of my County to be affixed, this 14th day of February one thousand eight hundred and sixty one and in the 85th year of our Independence.*

*Peter B. Prentis, Clerk*

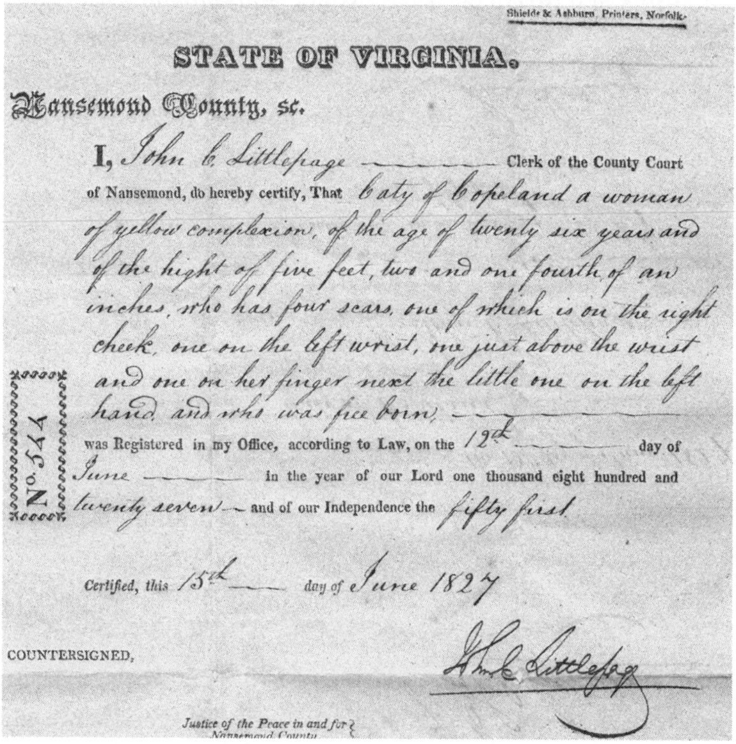

Shields & Ashburn, Printers, Norfolk.

STATE OF VIRGINIA.

Nansemond County, sc.

I, *John C. Littlepage* ———— Clerk of the County Court of Nansemond, do hereby certify, That *Caty of Copeland a woman of yellow complexion, of the age of twenty six years and of the hight of five feet, two and one fourth of an inches, who has four scars, one of which is on the right cheek, one on the left wrist, one just above the wrist and one on her finger next the little one on the left hand and who was free born.* ———

was Registered in my Office, according to Law, on the *19th* ———— day of *June* ———— in the year of our Lord one thousand eight hundred and *twenty seven* — and of our Independence the *fifty first*

Certified, this *15th* —— day of *June 1827*

COUNTERSIGNED,

*John C. Littlepage*

Justice of the Peace in and for
Nansemond County

*Figure 1.3.* "Free Negro Certificates" from Nansemond County dated 1827 and 1861. Part of "Virginia Untold: The African American Narrative," online at https://lva -virginia.libguides.com/virginia-untold.

## The Lingering Power of Community in Law

The aspiration toward a more modern and precise administrative record of personhood might work against the enslaver, or it might help
catch the runaway, but it was in tension with the lingering power
of community norms. Free people with African or Native ancestors
formed a vital part of Nansemond County and the South as a whole,
writes Milteer, who found "a common willingness among white people
to celebrate the positive attributes of the free people of color among
them, even as they allowed their elected representatives to spew in-
flammatory rhetoric that depicted free people of color as corrupt and
threatening."[39]

The logic of slavery and racecraft encouraged the Virginia legislature to think in terms of black and white, but politicians also felt ob-
ligated to legally recognize persons of mixed European and American ancestry, precisely because the line between them might blur. In
1705, Virginia created a legal category of people termed "mulatto,"
defined as anyone with at least one African parent, grandparent, or
great-grandparent. But you couldn't always see the evidence of such
African ancestry. In 1785, the legislature changed the definition of "mulatto" to anyone with one African grandparent, rather than one great-
grandparent, that is, from one-eighth to one-fourth. The state could
never settle on what the term meant.[40]

And the law had no way to actually define any of these categories
in ordinary life: without legal requirements for documents of identity,
there was no way to measure "percentages of blood" except through
a visual test or local memory of the ancestor in question. By 1853, the
legislature debated a proposal to declare that all persons "who may
be known or proven to have negro blood in them" as Negroes. The
measure failed, but they also debated, and rejected, a similar proposal to extend the definition of "negro" to anyone with an African
great-great-great-grandparent. The flailing inability to define what
these terms meant, while at the same time insisting on their solemn
legal force, gives another perfect example of the overlap between

racecraft and statecraft. In ordinary life a person with one-eighth African ancestry, sometimes informally called an "octoroon," might look white. But "one-eighth" does not account for an already-mixed great-grandparent. Imagine a person with one "black" grandparent, that grandparent herself only one-eighth African. The law would term the granddaughter one-eighth, a "mulatto," but she would be closer to one thirty-second African genetically. We might as well say "a left-handed person is anyone one-eighth left-handed." The confusion and ambiguity here is what "racecraft" tries to resolve, imposing a fixed idea of race on the ambiguity of real life.

Adding to the confusion, no legal advantages attached to "mulatto" status in Virginia. "Mulattoes" as we have seen were regularly enslaved. "Mulatto" free people also labored under a set of laws designed to check and restrict "free negroes." In addition to having to register themselves, for example, the law insisted free people of color had to leave the state within a year of gaining their freedom. This law was not strictly enforced in Virginia, but the register of state enactments is full of declarations that such and such a free person of color has been granted the right to remain in Virginia. Even if they remained, "by 1832, Virginia 'free negroes' had lost the right to carry guns, preach, sell liquor, and purchase slaves other than their enslaved relatives." Three years later, "the laws of every state in the South excluded free people of color from the franchise."[41]

Still, Milteer points out that "racial hierarchy was not the only form of hierarchy helping to uphold the social order." "Hierarchies based on wealth, gender, occupation, reputation, and religion coexisted with ideas promoting white supremacy." So if, on the one hand, laws sought to register free people with African "blood" and fix them in place, custom proved more flexible. "Individuals shifted in and out of the category, just as people in more recent times have moved back and forth between racial categories," and "someone considered 'of color' in one community might pass for white in another." Well into the early nineteenth century, if evidence of African heritage receded far enough, a family might pass wholly into whiteness, depending on how much property they owned, their religiosity, respectability, and deportment, or their "precise footing in the community." "Whiteness did not always require the mythical 'purity' it would later entail."[42]

### Defining Identity through Ancestry, Not Records

When racial status came before the courts, lacking formal documents judges often had to establish a genealogy based on nothing more than local memory. In the 1792 case of *Jenkins v. Tom*, Virginia's Court of Appeals had to decide whether a group of people held in slavery were Indian or African in origin. They could not tell by looking, but if termed "Indian," with no African ancestry, they could not be enslaved. So "the plaintiffs had offered in evidence sundry depositions of ancient people to prove that certain women named Mary and Bess, when they came first into this country, were called Indians; and had a tawny complexion, with long straight black hair." The plaintiffs produced a witness claiming "he heard a certain other person now dead, say in the year 1701, that when he was a lad about 12 years old, these women were brought to this colony in a ship, and were called Indians." Lacking a means of clear identification, an administrative record, the court accepted ninety-year-old hearsay testimony from a dead person. The court used what they could not see—ancestry—to make the individual person belong to a "race"—"Indian"—not actually visible on their bodies.[43]

In *Pegram v. Isabell*, 1808, Isabell, "styling herself an Indian and a pauper," insisted, "she was descended in the maternal line from an Indian who had been imported into this country . . . on which ground, her mother Nanny had recovered her freedom." The court accepted the word of George K. Taylor, who relied on "a witness, whose name the said Taylor did not particularly recollect, but whom he believes to have been one Francis Coleman, a very old man." Taylor added that he "believes, but does not positively know," that Coleman was "since dead." Coleman had said, "Nanny was descended according to general reputation, in the maternal line, from an Indian ancestor." Taylor had tried and failed to find a living witness to prove the same point. Isabell's freedom thus depended on the secondhand testimony of a man who might be dead.

George Taylor had been a federal judge and was the brother-in-law of US Supreme Court justice John Marshall, and his reputation as a jurist no doubt helped Isabell's case. But as above, in *Jenkins v. Tom,* the court's inability to certify identity and assign race was part of the problem "free negro registers" aimed to solve. These cases took place before the certifying documents of individualism existed, so Isabell appears to the court as other people's recollection of her ancestors. Had the "free negro registers" existed at Isabell's birth there would have been no need for a trial: the register would have assigned her an individual identity that also established her legal race. Administrative individualism was crucial to controlling race.[44]

That same year the Supreme Court of Appeals of Virginia heard the remarkable case of *Hudgins v. Wright*, appealed from the Richmond District Chancery Court. Jackey Wright and her children had been enslaved based on a belief that they had African ancestry. No African "blood" was visible in Jackey, who was "perfectly white, with blue eyes." George Taylor, arguing on Wright's behalf, dramatized the point: "this is not a common case of mere blacks suing for their freedom; but of persons perfectly white." The court admitted they could not tell "whether they are white or not."

Jackey Wright did not try to claim she was white: rather she claimed to be "in the maternal line descended from Butterwood Nan, an old Indian woman," who "was 60 years old, or upwards, in the year 1755." A witness described Nan "as an old Indian"; still other witnesses recalled "that [Nan's] daughter Hannah had long black hair, was of a copper complexion, and generally called an Indian among the neighbors." Neither Jackey nor witnesses knew for sure if Nan was Jackey's great-grandmother or her great-great-grandmother. As the court admitted after hearing multiple witnesses, "their genealogy was very imperfectly stated." With only imperfectly stated genealogy based on witness memory to go by, the judges concluded that since Wright's ancestors had looked Indian, not African, she should be freed, and added that henceforth, the enslaver must demonstrate conclusive evidence of African ancestry if it was not visible. This again is racecraft and statecraft in an embryonic stage. In the absence of documents of identity, her "race," invisible, has to be divined by other means: in this case some local people's memory of her genealogy.[45]

The respectability of her attorney, again George Taylor, must have helped the Wrights. But if Taylor had not taken her case Jackey Wright would have gone South and deeper into slavery. An invisible Indian racial essence, existing only in the sketchy recollections of local people, saved the family from "being black" while looking "perfectly white" but "actually" Indian. These are the kinds of problems administrative individualism aimed to solve.

Multiple scholars have described how before the Civil War, before the tools of individualism were well established, status for mixed people often depended on intangibles, on "respectability." When trying to determine race, Ariela Gross concluded, judges and juries "had to read not only bodies but also actions, demeanor, character," all the ways in which the person in question performed their identity. In addition to looking white, or "white enough," did they go to church? Had they ever voted, or served on juries? Were they respectable? Gross called this the "common sense" of race in antebellum America: "juries used common sense to make visual inspections and hear testimony about reputation." As late as 1833, the Virginia legislature could declare, to give but one example, that "certain parties named Wharton," residing in Stafford County "who heretofore were held in slavery and acquired their freedom since 1806 are not negroes or mulattoes but white persons, although remotely descended from a colored person." One hundred years later, a declaration like this would have been impossible: Virginia in 1930 declared "every person in who there is ascertainable any Negro blood shall be deemed a colored person." By 1930, Virginia had one hundred years of carefully collated birth, death, and marriage records to draw on: these would provide the trace for bureaucrats to ascertain. But in 1833 things were less rigid. That "common sense" also "depended on local knowledge and public memory" or, as in the legal cases described here, on "genealogy" established by the faltering memories of local people living and dead.[46]

## The Record on Dempsey Hare and His Family

We don't have Dempsey Hare's record in the free Negro register, because the Nansemond County Courthouse burned down in 1866, taking the records with it. Hare's father, Dempsey Howell, had a long-term relationship with a free woman of color known as Sofia Hare, or, in some census records, as "Sophia of Hare." The census calls Howell "white," but census records starting in 1830 showed Sophia as a free woman of color, who also would have made the trek to the clerk's office for inspection, description, and certification, so freedom would fall automatically on young Dempsey and his siblings. Census records tell us that Sophia kept her own house and that she couldn't read or write. They show children with her last name living in her house, and we know they are Dempsey Howell's children because Howell willed land to his children by Sophia, and because in 1887 his son Dempsey Hare filed a lawsuit against a local man and witness testimony described, carefully and delicately, the relationship between Howell and Sophia Hare.[47]

The free Negro registers were the first step in a general demand for more information: the 1850 census gives more information about Sophia Hare than the census gave a decade earlier. It tells us she was a "mulatto," and that she was born in 1805, and that she lived in a household with eight free people of color, some likely her grandchildren, all equally described as "mulatto." The census gathered more and more precise information, and that impulse appeared in state law as well. In 1853, the state passed a new law requiring that "every commissioner of the revenue shall make annual registration of the births and deaths in his district" and instructed said commissioner to record the name, place and date of birth, the sex, and the "color" of the child. The 1853 law established something like a legal birth certificate for the first time. The records are individualism in the service of race, individualism as an idea written into documents to make race out of ancestry.[48]

The year 1850 marks Dempsey Hare's first appearance in the census, which describes him as "Dempsey Hare of S," a way of naming Sophia as his mother. It called him twenty-four years old, "mulatto," a farmer with real estate valued at $800. The census recorded his wife, Anna Hare, and a child, Ira M. Hare, age two, both also listed as "M" for "mulatto." Hare had married Ann, Anne, or Anna Holland in 1848, in Gates, North Carolina, just south of the state line. The marriage record suggests that he could not sign his name: it says "Dempsey Hare, his mark" with a cross added. But none of the other census records suggest illiteracy.[49]

Dempsey and Anne lived on Holy Neck Road, on land gifted to them by his father. Howell's other children with Sophia lived nearby. By 1860, Dempsey's property in land had increased to $830, and he had acquired personal property worth $300. He and Ann lived with their daughter, Orra, age eleven. "Orra" was surely Ira, whom the census taker mistakenly called a boy in 1850.

Ann's brother Anthony Holland, a free laborer, lived nearby as well. All available records call their mother Axy, Asa, or Axa Holland, a white woman, but call Anthony and Dempsey Hare's wife, Ann, "mulatto." The 1860 census termed Anthony's wife, Mary, "black": they had three daughters under fifteen, one described as "black" and two as mulatto. In July of 1860, the Civil War was less than a year away, and the war would change everything for them.

"The facts of the case are as follows," wrote Captain John W. Barnes. "On the 22nd. day of December 1863, Mary Holland (Colored) wife of Anthony Holland, was sitting in her husband's house with her two children, Sophia Ann Holland (now Faulk), and Nancy." As Mary "engaged in her usual household duties," along came a white man, Richard Freeman, on horseback. "Freeman came riding by," Barnes continued, "on the premises of the said Anthony Holland, when the dog of Anthony barked at Freeman." He then "told of Mary Holland, that, if she did not take the dog away that he would kill her." "When she replied, 'the dog is at home,' Freeman then replied 'God d——n you, if you repeat those words again I will come there and kill you,' which she Mary did." In a rage Freeman dismounted, went into the house, picked up a butcher knife, "and then stabbed and cut Mary Holland until she died; this was done in the presence of the two children above named, who were then of age to be competent witnesses."

The children ran toward the house of their neighbor, Dempsey Hare. Anthony Holland's sister, Dempsey's wife Ann, "saw Freeman leave the house, as she was going there on a visit, and the children came running and crying and saying Freeman had killed their Mother, and when she got in the house Mary was dead."[50]

TWO

# HOLY NECK ROAD

Richard Freeman, murderer, must have lived nearby, because while Mary lay dying, another neighbor, William Byrd, "went in search of a magistrate" and found one, Dawson C. Parker, who happened to be at Freeman's place killing hogs. Byrd wanted Freeman arrested, but Parker the magistrate "would take no notice of the request." While Byrd argued with Parker, Freeman returned to his home, "and asked Byrd if the D——n B——h was dead, and said if she was not that he would go back and kill the whole d——n family."[1]

We can just imagine the horrific scene: the smell of the blood of slaughtered hogs; Byrd urgently telling the story of murder, pleading for action; Parker refusing. And then Freeman arrives, covered in Mary Holland's blood, viciously boasting about the crime and threatening more killing. Why did Parker, the magistrate, do nothing? What prompted Freeman's rage, and why did he believe he could murder with impunity? Why is the letter, describing a murder committed in 1863, dated September 1867?

Parker, the magistrate, did nothing because Richard Freeman was his stepson. Census and marriage records show Freeman's mother had married Dawson C. Parker, farmer and corrupt magistrate, after her first husband died. Freeman had the greatest confidence in his father-in-law's discretion, which confidence in 1863, during the Civil War, turned out wholly justified.[2]

## The Civil War in Nansemond

In early 1863, six months before Freeman killed Mary Holland, the Union Army under General John Peck occupied the town of Suffolk, Nansemond's County seat. Peck fortified the town and sent out foraging parties to feed his troops. Newspapers claimed that "Yankee vandals" were "roaming the counties of Nansemond . . . stealing negroes, bacon, and horses, and arresting every citizen whose loyalty to the Confederate States is known." From James Dillard, of Nansemond, "the Yankees stole some eight or ten thousand pounds of bacon and lard." They sent Dillard to jail, "because he refused to take the oath of allegiance to the Lincoln government." Nansemond County was partially occupied, and by 1863 Suffolk Town was garrisoned as a Union stronghold.[3]

In response Confederates under General James Longstreet laid siege to the town. A few relatively small engagements failed to dislodge the Yankees, and Longstreet concluded he could serve the Confederacy best by seizing food for Lee's army further north: he named it as his "principal object." The rebel soldiers took "enough meat to feed Longstreet's army of 20,000 men for nearly a month," one historian claimed. A Confederate told his family that "we have already gotten about 1,000,000 pounds" of bacon from Nansemond and northern North Carolina. A Texan exulted, "all the time we have an immense wagon train hauling out bacon, corn, wheat, flour, and great droves of beeves." Both armies plundered the countryside.[4]

In summer 1863, Longstreet moved his army north, to join Lee at the Battle of Gettysburg, and the Union evacuated Suffolk. But Union and Confederate raiding parties continued to plunder the area, and for the duration of the war, the region experienced "acute shortages and constant raiding." The Freemans and the Hollands would all have likely experienced the tender regards of foraging parties, or at least have hidden livestock and harvested crops from hungry soldiers in blue or gray. Free people of color could end up having to work for either side:

Exum White, whose brother Meredith would marry Dempsey Hare's daughter a decade later, was forced to work on the rebel works and on the railroad near Manassas for sixty days, along with one hundred other men. On his return to Nansemond in 1862, he "worked on Union fortifications around Suffolk for two or three months." In October of 1862, members of the Eleventh Pennsylvania Cavalry came to his home and confiscated "10 hogs and hundreds of fencing rails." White eventually filed a claim for compensation and was awarded $390. Confederate pay records show Richard Freeman receiving sixty-nine dollars for "forage" and renting a team of four horses to the Confederate Army for $4.50 a day, but pay in nearly worthless Confederate dollars probably offered him little comfort.[5]

During the occupation enslaved people crossed Union lines "in large numbers, large enough that General Peck had to set up a contraband camp on the banks of the Nansemond river." As early as 1862, the *Richmond Daily Dispatch* had complained that "the Yankees have employed for some time past a lot of free negroes, who scour the country, tamper with slaves, and use every means to entice them from their owners." When the Union entrenched itself at Suffolk, more and more enslaved people left. Frank Boone, interviewed about his childhood in Nansemond County in 1938, remembered, "when the War broke out, the free colored people became fearful. There was a great deal of stuff taken away from them by the Confederate soldiers. They moved into the Yankee lines for protection. My family moved also."[6]

Northern generals at first had no idea what to do with people who crossed Union lines. Before the Emancipation Proclamation in 1863, slavery remained legal, and enslaved people who came into Union camps remained the property of their owners every bit as much as horses or cattle. But returning them to their owners not only violated the abolitionist spirit that animated some Northerners; it also gave aid and comfort to the enemy. General Benjamin Butler, operating on the James River in Virginia, settled on calling them "contraband of war," confiscated property. Newspapers in the North and South reported on very large numbers of "contrabands" entering Union camps. The

*Philadelphia Inquirer* claimed, "In Suffolk contrabands arrive daily, and report themselves to the Provost Marshal. If they keep on coming in, there will be no hands left on any of the plantations south of this point." The *Chicago Tribune* wrote that "loyal Africans are coming in numbers into Suffolk" and that "petitions from three hundred and three slaveholders, for 1,078 slaves, have already been filed with the District Commissioners." Southern newspapers admitted the large numbers, but insisted the "contrabands" wanted to return home. "Hundreds of the contrabands here have had already quite enough of liberty and abolition philanthropy," declared the *Raleigh Daily Progress*: "They would gladly return to their masters and mistresses, but they have no power to do so." Enslavers constructed all sorts of pleasing fictions, but thousands of African Americans demonstrated their feelings about slavery, and the people who enslaved them, by leaving.[7]

"Contrabands" also offered valuable intelligence to Union commanders: they knew the land and the people. Butler began putting the "contrabands" to more and more soldierly duties, eventually arming them. The service of contrabands helped convince Lincoln, by 1863, to allow African Americans to enlist in the Union Army. Not long after, Nansemond citizens saw men with visible African ancestry dressed in Union blue and fighting for their people's liberation. Frank Boone recalled, "my father volunteered and went to the army in 1862. He served with the Yankees." He added, "you know Negroes didn't fight in the Confederate armies. They was in the armies, but they were servants"[8]

The Civil War cost Richard Freeman dearly: not just confiscated crops, but the loss of human property. The 1850 census listed Freeman as a "farmer," married with two children, owning real estate valued at $8,000 and "real property"—slaves—valued at $8,500. Owning nine people put Freeman above the average for slaveholding Virginians but far, far below the small number of elite families enslaving more than one hundred people.[9]

The census of slaves does not mention the names of the enslaved, only their ages. That he owned three women of childbearing age draws the eye. The census calls Freeman "farmer," but by 1860 Virginia's

leading export was human beings, raised in Virginia and sold to the
deeper South, and Richmond had the second largest slave market in
the country. Freeman's household had four adult women in it, his wife,
Mary, and three women held in slavery. The enslaved had no legal
rights; an enslaved woman had no right to refuse her owner's carnal demands. Freeman might have been a trader in slaves or engaged in some
"trading" of children and other people. But the war brought an end to
that trade and probably to his aspirations. By December 1863, when he
killed Mary Holland, the South's loss at Gettysburg made the Confederacy's defeat seem more likely by the day. If his former slaves had fled,
they took both his labor force and his accumulated wealth. Did reversal
of fortunes draw him, in a murderous rage, to the Holland home?[10]

## The Administrative State in Reconstruction

The Confederacy's defeat left the South in disarray. In 1867, John
Barnes, our letter writer, worked for the Freedmen's Bureau, a federal agency established in 1865, after the Union victory. The war had
freed four million people. With much of the South still "unrecon-
structed," under military rule, the Freedmen's Bureau tried to adju-
dicate disputes, review contracts, and in general assist freed people
in the transition to freedom.

The bureau, active till 1872, "was responsible for the supervision
and management of all matters relating to refugees and freedmen, and
of lands abandoned or seized during the Civil War." It "issued rations
and clothing, operated hospitals and refugee camps, and supervised
labor contracts." It managed labor disputes, "assisted benevolent societies in the establishment of schools, helped freedmen in legalizing
marriages entered into during slavery, and provided transportation
to refugees and freedmen who were attempting to reunite with their
family." Each of these activities left a paper trail; the trail led from
farm cabins to local officials to local district offices to regional offices
to a central office for each of the five military districts the bureau administered. No other federal agency had ever attempted such a huge

task. Free Negro registers, described in the previous chapter, were an innovation in record keeping by state and local governments, but the Freedmen's Bureau, and Reconstruction, involved administrative record keeping, and administrative individualism, on a vastly bigger scale, a national scale.[11]

The war demanded new forms of statecraft. It dramatically increased federal authority and the size of the federal bureaucracy. Roughly two million men fought for the North. The government owed them a pension—initially only for wounded veterans but by Reconstruction the number eligible had expanded dramatically. Each pension case demanded individual consideration of paper records of the man's rank, length of service, nature of wounds received. Widows and heirs could claim benefits, and someone had to review those claims. Was this person claiming a pension actually his widow or his child? In a society where birth and marriage certificates were uncommon, how would you know? African Americans made up 10 percent of the Union Army by the end of the war. Could the widow of a formerly enslaved veteran claim his pension, if the law forbid enslaved people to marry? This latter question involved the Freedmen's Bureau: the agencies had to coordinate. It amounted to a massive job of information management at a time before typewriters, paper clips, rubber bands, staples, ring binders, or vertical file cabinets. Chapter 1 describes the persistence of community standards for identity. Now ordinary people found themselves in new relationships with political authority, where community mattered less than identity on paper.[12]

You can see the revolution in statecraft and individualism if you visit the National Building Museum in Washington, which was built to house the Pension Bureau following the Civil War. General Montgomery C. Meigs had been quartermaster general of the Union Army, an immense administrative task that involved, among many other things, securing supplies for the army, directing shipping and transport, paying contractors, filing receipts, and making sure the taxpayers weren't cheated. Meigs was tasked to design a building that would memorialize the veteran's service, offer efficient storage and access to records, and also provide a grand ceremonial space for inaugural balls and similar events. The eccentric and spectacular building included tracks that ran around the walls of each floor. Office workers, when they finished their part of the work on someone's case, would place the files in a hanging basket on rollers, and push it down the track to the next office. Meigs also designed a row of sculptural niches along the very top of the building's central court. He asked the Smithsonian "to make casts of some of the Ethnological heads Savage & Civilized" so he could place them in the niches. Since the 1870s, the Smithsonian had been collecting skulls, taking photographs, and making busts of representative "types" of humanity, mostly from people who had no choice in the matter. The building combined the racecraft of ethnology, which we will see in more detail in subsequent chapters, with statecraft as information management and as symbolic representation of an ideal of nation.[13]

In 1867, the army and the Freedmen's Bureau administered Virginia as the "First Military District." An 1866 report to Congress by Major J. K. Stone of the Freedmen's Bureau described the climate of Nansemond County at that time and the implacable hostility freed people faced. "It is one of the unpardonable sins for a 'nigger' to complain to the Yankees," Stone wrote, "and terrible threats are muttered against him." He judged that "the purpose of a majority of the whites is to keep the freedmen intimidated, and they succeed." If he suggested a freed person should bring a legal action, Stone testified, "the customary reply" is, "He shoot me, sartain sure."

The intimidation extended well outside the law. Stone wrote, of the local freed people, "I cannot induce them to make the least effort in the matter of schools, although anxious to send their children, provided they are not required to contribute a cent. I had great difficulty in finding one of them unselfish enough to board, at any price, a colored teacher recently arrived. They do not want the trouble." Stone attributed this to character flaws in the freed people, but a modern reader will clearly see the dual problems of poverty and intimidation. For example, in March of 1866, four white men, L. H. Norfleet,

E. F. Norfleet, J. A. Haslett, and W. S. Hunter, burned down a Quaker school intended for "colored" children in Nansemond County. They went unpunished after Barnes, acting for the Freedmen's Bureau, referred the case to civil authorities.

Stone did note that "in the matter of schools in Nansemond county," "on the Holy-Neck Chapel road, about twelve miles from Suffolk, the Society of Friends have a colored school, of from 50 to 108 scholars, with two teachers." The Holland and Hare families lived on Holy Neck Chapel Road, and that school stood on Dempsey Hare's land. Hare enjoyed the rents the Freedmen's Bureau paid him for the land's use while braving the risks. Under Freedmen's Bureau protection, Hare's in-laws felt able to bring an action against the man who murdered Mary Holland, wife and mother, in front of her children, over a barking dog.[14]

## Reconstruction Empowers the Freed People

Mary's survivors saw Reconstruction, and the federal administration it was built on, as an opportunity for justice. Mary herself exists to history almost entirely because of administrative records generated by the Freedman's Bureau. In 1867, Captain Barnes heard the complaints of the Holland family—that Mary's murderer lived among them unpunished—and he wrote to Lieutenant Edward Murphy, commissioner for Nansemond County in the Virginia Military District, requesting that Freeman "may be arrested and tried by a Military Commission, as a trial by Civil Authority at this late day would be a farce, and he would be acquitted." In 1863, Freeman had gotten away with murder because his stepfather refused to act: Barnes, like Major Stone, had little reason to believe things had changed.

Lieutenant Murphy examined Freeman, and the available evidence, and directed the local jailer to arrest Freeman "and confine in jail until the orders of the Commanding General in his case are Known." Murphy forwarded the record of the arrest to General Orlando Brown, in charge of the military district of Virginia for the Nansemond region.

But after twenty days, on October 25, Freeman escaped the jail. Murphy wrote, "he probably picked the lock, which was a poor one with a nail or some such instrument. The Jail itself is not secure it being much damaged during the war."

Freeman, apparently not well, returned to his home near Holy Neck Road. Murphy wrote his commanding officer enclosing "certificates from the Physicians attending him who state that in all probability it would Cause his death to remove and again confine him in jail." Murphy told the county sheriff to secure Freeman in his home and made the sheriff responsible for his safekeeping "until the question of his being bailed is decided by the Comdg. General." Two days later Freeman died at home, thwarting the Holland family's desire for justice.[15]

The *Alexandria Gazette* reported on what it termed the "melancholy death," calling Freeman "a prominent and esteemed citizen of Nansemond county." He was charged, the *Gazette* continued, "with killing a negro woman during the war, with whom he had a fight. He protested that it was done in self defense, and the statement was so generally accepted, that no arrest was made." The *Gazette* felt it an injustice that "long after the war was over," "he was arrested and thrown into prison, where confinement caused his health to rapidly give way." Indeed, added the *Gazette*, "with a premonition that he was soon to die, he managed to escape from the jail, and went directly home, about fifteen miles distant, where he was prostrated and died on Monday last." Did he die of melancholy and despair? Did he die of whatever mental imbalance caused him to fly into a rage at the barking of a dog? Was he helped along to death by members of the Holland family who did not trust local justice? The official record of his death on November 8, 1867, says only "disease of the lungs."[16]

Mary Holland's murder has all the elements of the epic of Reconstruction, "America's unfinished revolution," as Eric Foner termed it. Reconstruction lasted from the end of the Civil War through 1877, although some states, like Virginia, were declared "reconstructed" earlier. If you believe the Hollands, downtrodden African Americans aspired to civil equality and justice under the protection of temporarily idealistic Northerners. Or, if you believe Freeman, vengeful African Americans and misguided Yankees lashed out at their betters.

Starting in the 1890s, Euro-American historians tended to explain Reconstruction as a story of zealous, angry elites, the Radical Republicans, seeking to punish the South by imposing racial equality. In this view of Reconstruction, often known as the "Dunning school" after historian William Archibald Dunning, the former slaves were not ready for the task of self-government, and unscrupulous Northern "carpetbaggers" exploited them, using the votes of corrupt African Americans to lard the Southern states with debt. The South's natural leadership, termed "redeemers," reasserted itself in the 1870s and restored white rule. This view, endorsed by Woodrow Wilson among many others, entered the American mainstream in multiple ways, including D. W. Griffith's notorious and widely popular film *Birth of a Nation*, which depicted the masked and robed Ku Klux Klan as the heroes of Reconstruction. The idea that poor suffering Richard Freemen expired of sorrow while in jail for killing an aggressive black woman in self-defense fits this version of Reconstruction.

African American scholars, notably W. E. B. DuBois, argued conversely that Reconstruction represented a moment when America tried to live up to its best ideals, and to reform Southern society on a basis of civic equality. Reconstruction governments were no more corrupt than Northern state governments during the Gilded Age, DuBois noted, and African American participation in politics led to positive goods like increased land ownership, the formation of public schools, and the beginnings of an African American middle class. DuBois documented how African American elected officials worked pragmatically with white politicians to build a foundation of future prosperity. In his view Reconstruction failed because the North lacked the stomach to see the struggle to the finish. Eric Foner's magisterial account of Reconstruction brought DuBois's interpretation into the mainstream of historical thinking. Most historians today see Reconstruction not as "revenge" but as a failed effort to bring about something like civil equality. We can see evidence for DuBois's view in the Holland family's determination to use the Freedman's Bureau to seek justice for Mary's death.[17]

The claim that Richard Freeman murdered Mary Holland in self-defense strains belief, and the *Alexandria Gazette* demonstrated the extent of habitual, systemic racecrafting when it called him an "esteemed citizen" but never bothered to even give the name of the woman he killed: she simply did not matter and neither did her family's grief. But the version her children told to Barnes, that she just meekly let him walk into her house, pick up a butcher knife, and kill her, seems equally unlikely. Mary Holland was a free woman, on her own property: Barnes wrote that Freeman rode "on the premises" of Anthony Holland, Mary's husband. Would she simply let this arrogant man do as he wished? "The dog is at home," she told him, and when he dared her she repeated it. That's what her children, the only witnesses, told the man from the Freedmen's Bureau, four years later, four years in which they retold each other the story of their mother's murder, polishing and honing the memory as people do. The Holland family asserted the integrity of home, they implied, and they told Richard Freeman the dog had rights he didn't have. The innovative statecraft of Reconstruction expanded rights for people like the Hollands. They had the law ostensibly on their side, and by 1867 they could vote or run for office themselves: they could make appeals for justice to the federal government.

### Reconstruction and Prosperity for Dempsey Hare

Dempsey Hare took his own advantage of Reconstruction. His name appeared on the poll list of Nansemond County in 1867, the first year African Americans could vote. He must have seen promise in politics, because in 1871 Hare attended the nominating convention for the Republican Party in Suffolk. He managed his land well—in 1860 he had raised thirty-one hogs and four hundred bushels of corn, along with three hundred bushels of sweet potatoes, making him probably "the leading farmer among the free people of color in the region." As a substantial landowner, he occupied a socially prominent position: shortly after the war's end in 1866 or 1867, a group of African Americans built a brush arbor church "on Dempsey Hare's farm." But some sort of dispute arose and the congregants moved, eventually building Mount Sinai Baptist Church on Holy Neck Road. Something of a leader in the community, he also put himself at odds with his neighbors.[18]

The school for freed people mentioned above by Major Stone also stood on Dempsey Hare's land: a single room, fourteen by eighteen feet, heated by a fireplace and termed the Mount Moriah school. The school enrolled fifty-two students in its first year. Hare took a chance by having the school on his property, because as Stone indicated, the freed people greatly desired education but rightly feared the risks involved. In response to the question, "what is public sentiment as to the education of Freedmen and Poor Whites," the inspector of schools in October of 1868 answered, "the feeling towards colored schools is not good." He noted that there were no schools for white children, which conveys the degree to which, as W. E. B. DuBois had observed, the idea of *public schooling*, not just racial equality, was a key innovation of Reconstruction.[19]

The end of Reconstruction in Virginia reversed some of the political gains African Americans had made. In 1874, former Confederate general James Kemper entered the Governor's Mansion in Richmond, declaring "let it be understood of all, that the political equality of the races is settled, and the social equality of the races is a settled impossibility." He added, "let it be understood of all, that any organized attempt on the part of the weaker and relatively diminishing race to dominate the domestic governments, is the wildest chimera of political insanity," and counseled Virginians of African descent to know their place. "Let each race settle down in final resignation to the lot to which the logic of events has inexorably consigned it." Hare appears to have dropped politics and focused on economic advancement.[20]

African Americans entered into "truck farming," which involved marketing a produce not locally but to cities accessible by boat and

rail: Baltimore, Washington, Philadelphia. By the 1870s, Dempsey
Hare, not alone, prospered from the rise of truck farming. Stephen
Hahn's study of African American politics in the South quotes a British traveler marveling at the "large black proprietary" in the Tidewa-
ter region, owning "small patches of land and their own cottages."
By the early twentieth century, Virginia had the highest number and
percentage of African American landowners in any state of the former Confederacy.[21]

Hare bought out the land of two of his siblings in the 1880s, and
continued buying land into the 1890s, so much so that he had accumulated at least two thousand acres by 1900, and possibly as much as
three thousand, when newspapers described him as "the richest negro in eastern Virginia."[22]

### A Lawsuit Reveals and Conceals

In 1887, Hare sued a neighbor, Elisha Darden, in a dispute over land.
Hare claimed to have inherited the parcel, on the south side of Holy
Neck Road, from his father. He aimed to stop Darden from cutting
timber on that land. Darden, Hare claimed, had cut down "line trees"
that marked the boundary between their two properties. When the
Nansemond County Courthouse burned in 1866, it took the deeds
with it. The more than one hundred pages of testimony in *Hare v.
Darden*, intended to establish ownership, show Hare using the law
aggressively in his interests, while illuminating the way Nansemond
County residents thought about race and family.[23]

Individual depositions show that everyone knew and agreed Dempsey Howell was Hare's father, and multiple witnesses agreed that Howell, the father, had given land on the south side of Holy Neck Road to
people witnesses referred to variously as "his black folks," "his black
people," or "his negroes." This might mean people held in slavery, or it
might mean his free mixed ancestry children, or both. Dempsey Hare
was born about 1824. The census of 1820 shows his father, eighteen
years old, living in a household with four enslaved people. By 1830,

*Figure 2.1.* Nansemond County Courthouse, in the town of Suffolk, author photo. A fire in 1866 destroyed the records, but not the structure, which is still standing in Suffolk and now houses the Suffolk Visitor's Center. Many of the events described in the book took place here: Dempsey Hare's lawsuit against Elisha Darden, and Ira Ann Hare's two suits against her father and his will. Patrick O'Malley got his marriage license here, later received the deeds to his land, and took the oath of citizenship. The ledger declaring he and his wife "colored" was compiled and stored here.

Howell's household included twelve people, seven in slavery and the rest free, including two free mixed ancestry girls under ten, and one free mixed woman between twenty-four and thirty-five. Howell built houses, a "cooper shop" and a "tar kiln" for rendering pine resin from logs, witnesses said, while he lived on the other side of the road. At some point those structures were removed: Washington Copeland, a man with African ancestors and then eighty-nine years old, remembered the houses were moved to the north side because "there were patrollers, and they pestered his negroes so." Virginia communities used "patrols," semi-legal groups of men on horseback, to ride country roads and maintain curfews, keeping African Americans from communicating, visiting, or escaping slavery.[24]

An example of the anxiety that led to patrollers had occurred on Holy Neck Road in 1858, when the *Richmond Daily Dispatch* reported, "this morning about 1 o'clock, information reached this town that an insurrection of the blacks had broken out between South Quay and Holy Neck, in Nansemond county, and that some white families had been massacred." The rumor was not true, but "the town instantly rose in arms and sent out a scouting party on horseback to near the scene of the reported outrages." It turned out that "a deranged negro man, belonging to Mr. Benton, of Gates county, N.C., had attacked a white man, named Whitmel Jones, on the road near South Quay, and murdered him, splitting his skull open. The negro then went to the house of Mrs. Harrison Howell, a widow woman, whom he murdered likewise." Harrison Howell had lived on the land, across the road from Dempsey Hare, which Darden claimed in 1887. The Hares would have heard the news and worried about an angry mob. Newspaper accounts did not give the man's name, or a motive, saying only that he had been "hired out to work on a railroad." In one account he first murdered Mrs. Howell, then killed Whitmel Jones, but the newspapers were content to simply describe the nameless man as "deranged." The posse eventually shot the murderer after he tried to hide in a swamp. There was no inquest or legal investigation. The dehumanization apparent in the indifference to his name and motive, and the panic at an imaginary insurrection, shows how insecure slave owners were. Dempsey Howell for good reason had cared enough about the safety of "his people" to move them away from the patrollers.[25]

The witnesses in *Hare v. Darden* all talked around the nature of Howell's marital relations, acknowledging Dempsey Hare's father but never naming Sophia Hare. Washington Copeland, asked about Howell, remembered visiting the house of "Dempsey Howell, who went for Dempsey Hare's father." The phrase "went for" showed some hesitation in naming Hare's parentage. Copeland knew Howell "when [Howell] was a young man, before he got married and soon after he got the land from his father." Copeland also referred to "his woman who he had for his first wife." He used the phrase twice: "the woman he had for his first wife moved back there with her children and she hired me to cut wood." But Copeland also said he came often to Howell's place because "a good many of his negroes were kin to me." Thomas Holland, also African American and in his eighties, remembered, "Mr. Howell had a woman belonging to him who was said to be my sister."

The pathos of Thomas Holland's statement remains vivid nearly 150 years later: he does not really know his siblings with any certainty, because slavery made family impossible to maintain. Or possibly he knows, but they won't let him say. Enslaved people could not legally marry, and nothing at all prevented an enslaver from selling couples apart from each other or selling children away from parents. A slave owner might not acknowledge his own mixed race children. Thomas Holland and Washington Copeland had to tiptoe around the knowledge of their own families. Copeland knew many of the people at Howell's house were relatives, but in court he could not say exactly how: Thomas Holland, over eighty years old, near death, was still imagining and trying to realize the family slavery and white supremacy denied him.[26]

Beyond lack of freedom, physical abuse, and theft of labor, this last marked slavery's most egregious injustice. It made families impossible to maintain. Two people might fall in love and have children, but at any point the master might sell any of them away. By 1830, the

profits of slavery in Virginia came mostly from selling the enslaved to
the Deep South: selling families apart was the foundation of slavery's
profit. Once the Civil War ended, freed people thronged the roads
trying to reunite their severed families. Slavery shattered the sense of
family, and the racecraft on which white supremacy depended meant
Dempsey Hare could not speak openly about his mother.[27]

Racecraft deliberately set out to destroy the families of enslaved
people, to prevent them from forming emotional bonds slavers would
have to respect. Today, people of African descent use DNA evidence
to reconstruct family ties. While free people of color were highly individualized, statecraft before the war gave enslaved people only the
most minimal identities, often nothing beyond a gender and an age
range. DNA testing can reveal relatives crushed out of knowing by
slavery's brutality. It can reveal ancestors of African descent but also
of Native descent, or from Europe. Genealogist Andre Kearns, from
whom I first learned about Dempsey Hare, has written about discovering his German ancestry, and his living German relatives, via the
man who enslaved one of his ancestors. As Alondra Nelson argues,
"genetic ancestry testing provides a lexicon with which to continue
to speak about the unfinished business of slavery and its lasting shad-
ows: racial discrimination and economic inequality. DNA-based tech-
niques allow us to try—or try again—to contemplate, respond to, and
resolve enduring social wounds." But this genetic individualism is at
odds with ideas of community. Kim TallBear points out, "gene dis-
courses and scientific practices are entangled in ongoing colonialisms.
What 'they' think and do have always determined how much trouble
'we' have." DNA testing requires Native people to adopt racial terms
not part of their historical culture. DNA testing raises fundamental
questions about self-understanding and who gets to control it. Hare's
legal identity, even in this dispute about land boundaries, depended
on his ancestry and what that ancestry meant, but that understanding
was and to a large extent still is, controlled by people who made unmixed European heritage the foundation of their claim to authority.[28]

In his testimony, Hare remembered, "when I was a small boy living with my father," but referred only to "my father's wife," avoiding the inconvenient fact of his biological mother altogether. Along with his long-term relationship with Sophia, Howell also married a woman named Elizabeth Langston. Her brother T. E. Langston testified that he never saw them married, but they were living there as man or wife "and she would not have been living there if they had not been married." North Carolina records show an Elizabeth Langston marrying Dempsey Howell in 1832. They had no children. She died, Langston said, in 1843, shortly after Howell, and the land "was turned over to the guardianship of Dempsey Hare," then about twenty years old. In the courtroom, apparently, much remained unspoken. No one wanted to overtly mention Howell's relationship with a woman of color, even as everyone knew about it and a child of that relationship sat before them, plaintiff in a court of law.[29]

We can't know what Dempsey Howell, the legally white man, felt for Sophia. She was a free woman, not enslaved by Howell, so while it might overstate the case to simply call it a consensual relationship it does not fit the model of rape in slavery. His eldest son took his first name, suggesting Howell acknowledged his offspring, but not his last name, demonstrating the limits of acceptance. He gave his children with Sophia land on his death and built them houses and apparently moved those houses to protect them from aggressive patrollers. Sophia Hare, illiterate, later lived as a free woman in a house of her own, not with Howell. The census names most of the Nansemond people mentioned here, including Howell, as illiterate. But Dempsey Hare could read. Someone—Sophia, Howell, Dempsey himself—made the effort to get him an education.

Dempsey's mother, Sophia Hare, a free woman, might have loved Howell, or she might have used him strategically to try to improve the lives of her children. Or both: racecraft tainted and complicated all motives. The complex story is again made far more complex by the simultaneous insistence on "race" as a real thing, and by the evident and even ubiquitous violation of racial rules we see in the Holland and Hare families.

Modern Americans might tend to celebrate this evidence of crossing the color line and cherish the fact that people were attracted to
each other despite the forces of law and prejudice. That tendency runs
against the fact that most instances of "race mixing" came under slavery and involved situations where the women could not consent. But
historians have also uncovered many instances of European-descended
women choosing African American men as partners. Dempsey Hare's
mother-in-law, Axy Holland, was regarded as a white woman in legal
documents: her children were not. Celebrating these ubiquitous instances of "intermarriage" risks downplaying the brutality that often
lay behind them. Though the Holland and Hare families stemmed from
relationships among free people, none of the history of racial mixing
protected Mary Holland from Richard Freeman's rage.[30]

Dempsey Hare's testimony in *Hare v. Darden* shows him well prepared, self-possessed, and aggressively asserting his claims. In 1887,
despite the failure of Reconstruction, people of color in Virginia had
more legal room to maneuver than they would have after the 1890s,
when regimes founded on radical racism came to power across the
South. Hare exercised a keen form of stewardship: he knew the land
closely, especially the species and the value of trees on the property
in question: "lightwood" (pine and fir), sweet gum, black gum, "Bow-
Tree" (Osage orange), "Blackjack Oak." Each tree had specific properties and uses. He had helped survey the property, carrying the sur-
veyor's chains as a young man, and claimed to know its boundaries
exactly. He might have been left-handed: he tried to establish that
Darden's men had cut down "line trees" by pointing out they were
right-handed and a right-handed man had done the chopping.[31]

Darden's lawyer brought in witnesses of his own, who testified
to ambiguity about ownership. They pointed out that the road had
been relocated, that a new road had been cut, and that the boundary
markers may have decayed over time or that Hare himself might have
cut some down. Testimony showed little apparent acrimony, except
in one instance. Hare's lawyer cross-examined D. B. Jones, asking if
anything has "caused you to feel unfriendly" toward Dempsey Hare.

Jones replied, "Yes sir, Hare cursed me on the occasion of the controversy between himself and Whitfield."[32]

## *Ira Ann Hare White and Her Half Sister, Twinned*

This controversy is central to Hare's story, but obscured in the record. In 1887, Dempsey and Annie's only child, their daughter, Ira Ann, lived with her husband, Meredith White, "a good man, an educated man, a landowner, a farmer and a teacher at a colored school in Nansemond during the reconstruction era." The couple had married in 1870. Ira Ann probably saw him coming to teach at the school then located on her father Dempsey Hare's land, when the federal government was still engaged in its unprecedented effort to administer a new society. She must have admired the handsome young man, committed to the education and improvement of the freed people: a man surely possessing more than the ordinary measure of courage, ambition, and will. It marked a moment of possibility, the possibility of using federal power to renegotiate what African ancestry meant. But the North's support for Reconstruction waned, and Dempsey Hare made very different choices.[33]

The 1870 census showed Ira Ann had moved out, to be with her husband, Meredith White, but Dempsey and Anne Hare's household now included a Frances Whitfield, aged thirty-five, and her two children, William and John D., ages ten and three. The census taker marked Dempsey and Anne "M" for "mulatto," while listing all three Whitfields as "W." He named Dempsey as a farmer and Anne as "keeping house," but wrote "works on farm" after the Whitfields' names. Ten years later the 1880 census shows Frances Whitfield still living with Dempsey and Anne, along with the aforementioned William and John, but now with an eight-year-old daughter, Ida Ann Whitfield, born in 1872.

The similarity in names is remarkable. *Ira* Ann Hare was born to Dempsey and Anne about 1850. She is variously listed as "Orra," "Laura," or "Isa," but by 1900 official accounts had settled on "Ira Ann," a sign of the greater precision of state and local records. *Ida* Ann Whitfield was born in 1872 while her mother and brothers lived in Hare's household. All the Whitfields appear in the controversy over Hare's will at his death in 1901. "The trouble with Whitfield" that D. B. Jones remembered drawing a curse from Hare probably had to do with the fact that Whitfield's children, as we will soon see, were likely also Hare's. The presence of the Whitfields might help explain why the census taker listed Dempsey and Anne as white in 1880.

Edward Everett Holland defended Elisha Darden in the case of *Hare v. Darden*, and he also appeared in Hare's 1901 will, as a primary beneficiary. Judge Wilbur Kilby ruled in *Hare v. Darden* that Hare should pay $150 to Elisha Darden, getting in return clear and unambiguous title to land he claimed he already owned. Darden was enjoined from cutting wood on that land. Darden got the money, Hare got the land, and the law settled the question of title.[34]

In 1893, Ira Ann White sued her father for "trespass in assumpsit," meaning failure to uphold terms of an agreement in common law. It might have been over property he promised but failed to deliver. The Circuit Court records show little detail, but the case of *White v. Hare* went to a jury of twelve men, who found Hare guilty and assessed damages of $400. As an example of the purchasing power of $400, three years later Dempsey bought seven acres of land in "Holy Neck District" for just seventy dollars. The court required Hare to pay his daughter the $400 on October 12, 1893.[35]

As he approached the end of his life, Hare was known as "the richest and most eccentric colored man in this section." By 1900, Anne Holland Hare had died, and Dempsey lived alone, on a farm free of mortgage. Sometime around 1900, he tried to woo a much younger woman named Mary B. Scott, described as "an intelligent mulatto school teacher" or "a nearly white school teacher." Scott said Hare offered her "$1000 to cook for him one week," newspapers related, and "he promised her all his property if she would become his wife. They had a protracted correspondence." She refused to marry Hare because of what newspapers called "her peculiar religious and social views and because of his unsound mind." "She said Hare claimed to be white, and he said she was white, and declared that if any man said otherwise he would spend every dollar he owned in prosecuting him."[36]

"Ordinary people" often turn out to be not so ordinary. Mary B. Scott was "star witness" for the defense, said the *Virginian Pilot*. Newspapers run by people understood as white rarely used the adjective "intelligent" when it came to persons they regarded as black, unless that person was doing something pleasing to white people. Mary Scott emphatically rejected Hare's advances, but also his attempts to redraw the color line. "The teacher told Hare he was not white but could not convince him," wrote the *Pilot* in approval. But what was in their "protracted correspondence"? What were "her peculiar religious and social views"? She must have made them clear to the court. Scott was likely part of the emerging political networks of educated women of color who, through organizations like the National Association of Colored Women's Clubs, set the foundation for women's suffrage and the campaign against Jim Crow. Light enough to pass, like Ira Ann White, she embraced an identity as African American. Did her protracted correspondence aim to persuade Dempsey to put his wealth to better uses? Mary B. Scott was not famous—I searched briefly, but could find little on her. Someone's family history probably includes Mary B. Scott: hers seems like a story worth telling.[37]

About that same time, the 1900 census taker, Lester Daughtry, came by Hare's house and recorded his details. Hare corrected him, demanding that he cross out the original birth dates Daughtry had written and cram new dates into the form's small boxes. Daughtry had listed Hare as "B" for "black," then presumably at Hare's insistence scribbled over the "B" leaving racecraft unresolved.[38] Hare died

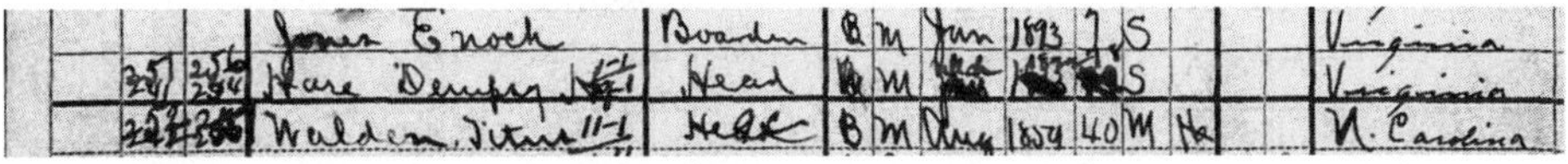

*Figure 2.2.* Entry for Hare in 1900 census. Column 6, for race, has been scribbled over, leaving his race ambiguous while the two men around him are listed as "black."

on January 29, 1901, at age seventy-seven, and then the news broke that he had left almost his entire estate to Edward Everett Holland and Dr. Job Holland.[39]

The *Sun* described Hare's funeral: "The remains of Dempsey Hare, Nansemond's richest negro, were this afternoon borne to the grave by white pallbearers." "A white layman read the burial service" rather than a minister. "It is understood," the *Sun* continued, "that Hare's valuable real estate goes to State's Attorney Edward E. Holland, of Suffolk, and Dr. Job G. Holland, of Nansemond county. Laura [*sic*] Ann White, Hare's only daughter, whom he had reared for a white man's wife and who incurred his displeasure by marrying a negro, is 'cut off' with $10." An auction of his chattels and personal effects followed: reportedly his safe contained $1,000 in cash.[40]

The next day newspapers reported "that Dempsey Hare, Nansemond's richest negro, was yesterday buried with his face down and his feet toward the west." The *Sun* told readers that "interested persons had the body exhumed and put it away in proper shape. Undertaker Sol W. Holland did it." Solomon Holland was a white man, although there was also an African American Solomon Holland with a connection to the Hare will. In the same article, the *Sun* noted that Hare's daughter, Ira Ann White, had resolved to challenge the will.[41]

### Was Hare Sane?

Why did he leave his estate to Edward Everrett Holland, a banker then serving as state's attorney, and Dr. Job Holland, then practicing in the nearby town of Holland, Virginia? Were the two men related in some way to Hare's late wife, Anne Holland? It seems possible—the surname "Holland" is *extremely* common in Nansemond County: the author's great-great-grandmother was Hester Holland, declared to be colored. According to the 1910 census, Job Holland's household included his wife and children as well as his brother, Solomon Holland, listed in the census as "black." Under "occupation" it listed "butler." Incredibly, Dr. Job Holland appeared to have his half brother of mixed ancestry working in his house as a butler. Perhaps Dempsey imagined a relation between his late wife and Job Holland. E. E. Holland had been Darden's attorney in the case of *Hare v. Darden*. Dempsey must have been impressed with his work. But none of these seem like adequate explanations.

Understandably, Ira White challenged Dempsey Hare's mental competence. "Ira Ann White (colored) is seeking to break the last testament of her father, Dempsey Hare," wrote the *Baltimore Sun*, "who was seven-eighths white, who hated negroes, who was the largest landholder in Eastern Virginia, and who cut off his only daughter with $10 because she did not marry a white man." Her lawyer, the report continued, argued that "Hare's prejudice against negroes amounted to a delusion; that the testator's mind was weak and unsound, and that he was unduly influenced to write the will three weeks before death."[42]

At the trial in late 1901, Ira White told her story. She testified that "my papa permitted my husband [Meredith White] to visit me two years before our [1870] marriage, but was always saying he and I were white and I should not marry a negro man. He told me the name of the white man he had picked out, but I didn't love him. I loved the man I ran away to marry, despite papa's wishes." She had chosen the young teacher at the colored school, in the optimism of Reconstruction, when her cousins tried to use the legal system to get justice for her aunt Mary Holland's murder. But she continued, "besides, I knew I had negro blood, and the Virginia laws wouldn't let me marry a white man."[43]

Virginia laws as we might expect were incoherent and ever changing on the subject. In 1866, the legislature had declared that "every person having one-fourth or more Negro blood shall be deemed a colored person," but as always "negro blood" was a vague term. Sophia Hare's "percentage of blood" can't be determined, neither can we tell anything about the "blood" of Ira White's mother, Anne Holland Hare, except that Ira had mixed European and African ancestry. But the law acted as if "percentage of blood" had an objective reality. That same year, 1866, the law required ministers to "make a record of all marriages and state in the record whether the persons are white or colored" and return a copy to the county clerk. Absent birth records, as had nearly always been the case before 1853, this declaration by the minister would then become the controlling document, regardless of what the law said about percentages of blood, since the law had no objective way to measure such a thing and would still have to rely on what the minster reported and what local people assumed.[44]

Laws prohibiting intermarriage date back at least as far as 1681, when the legislature had punished any English or other white man or woman who married a negro, mulatto, or Indian with banishment from the colony. In 1705, the colony imposed a fine of ten pounds and six months in jail for any "white man or woman who shall intermarry with a negro," and added a fine of ten thousand pounds of tobacco on the minister who performed the service. In 1792, it reiterated the jail term of six months for intermarriage and upped the fee to thirty dollars, while fining the celebrant $250. In 1878, eight years after Ira Ann and Meredith White married, Virginia passed a law stating, "any white person who shall intermarry with a Negro, or any Negro who shall intermarry with a white person, shall be confined in the penitentiary from two to five years." So Ira Ann was right that marriage to a man regarded as white would be illegal, even though the law could not objectively measure the thing it regulated.[45]

"When he heard of my marriage Papa got very mad and never afterward recognized me as a daughter," Ira Ann testified. At the hearing, witnesses called Hare "a man of unsound mind" and claimed that "he always maintained that he was a white man, and could not be reasoned with on that subject, notwithstanding the fact that his mother was a negress." Witnesses added that "he repeatedly said that no d——d negro should ever have his money." Dempsey Hare seems like an awful person, but his "sanity" here has to be evaluated in terms of an insane set of laws, laws that required that people pretend that what they saw—that Dempsey Hare could be declared "white" on the 1880 census—was not real and that what they could not see, his African ancestry, was the sum of his identity. Ira Ann, who must have looked like a European herself, had accepted the role racecraft created for her and married a man whose racial identity was easier to believe in.[46]

Along with disinheriting Ira Ann, Hare's will had several interesting and strange provisions. He left $100 in cash and a sewing machine to Frances Whitfield, "provided she outlives me," but if not, he willed the cash to a Charlie Bland Jr. and the sewing machine to *Ida* Ann Bland. Frances Whitfield, recall, lived in Hare's house in 1870 and 1880. Around 1872, she had her daughter, named Ida Ann Whitfield — nearly the same first names as Hare's legal daughter, Ira Ann Hare White. In 1889, Ida Ann Whitfield married Charles Bland Jr., described in census and marriage records as a white man. Their marriage certificate from 1889 lists Frances Whitfield, white, as Ida's mother and her father as unknown. Was Ida Whitfield Bland, regarded as white, married to a man also regarded as white, the daughter of Dempsey Hare and Frances Whitfield? When D. B. Jones remembered, "Hare cursed me on the occasion of the controversy between himself and Whitfield," Jones seemed to believe he referred to something everyone in court knew about.[47]

At the trial Ira Ann White produced an earlier undated will, witnessed by three men also named Holland, in which Dempsey Hare declared, "it is my will and desire that after my death, Willie Whitfield son of Frances Whitfield, shall have one hundred acres of the choice of my land near Hain Oke Ferry, to him and his heirs forever." The will added, "it is also my will and desire, that after my death John Dempsey Whitfield, son of Frances Whitfield, shall have my home plantations and all the balance of my estate real and personal, including the balance of my land near Hain Oke Ferry, to him and his heirs forever." While it's not clear where "Hain Oke Ferry" was, it seems very clear there was a personal connection between Hare and Frances Whitfield's children. They gave the second child "Dempsey" as a middle name, in addition to willing him Hare's house and most of his estate.[48]

Ida Ann Whitfield, born about 1872, is not mentioned in the first will, so it seems reasonable to assume this will was drafted between 1870, when *Ira* Ann Hare married Meredith White, and *Ida* Ann

Whitfield's birth in 1872. It also seems as if Hare was trying to replace Ira Ann with Ida Ann. The Whitfields were likely his children, and Hare was trying again to engineer his descendants into whiteness. The case record is partially typed. When the court declared its intention to consider the validity of the two wills, it listed as plaintiff Ira Ann Whitfield. Someone then crossed out "Whitfield" and handwrote "White." Even the court was confused about the two women, likely half sisters. In this case their racial ambiguity made their individual identities ambiguous as well.[49]

Why did Ira Ann Hare White, Dempsey's legal daughter, introduce the will, which also pointedly left her nothing? Hare had used knowledge of genealogy, in the form of land given by his father, to advance himself, but now in death his reputation ran up against the inexorable practice of racecraft. Sophia Hare was of mixed African and European ancestry, Dempsey Howell was understood as white, and Anne Holland was a mixed ancestry person herself: their daughter must have appeared very light, and Hare tried to force her into whiteness. She rebelled against his particular version of racecraft, and he died trying to escape the meaning society placed on his genealogy.

The record of the case of *White v. Holland* does not include witness testimony, but does include judge Robert Riddick Prentis's statement to the jury. "The Court instructs the jury that if they believe from the evidence that Dempsey Hare, at the time of executing the will in question, was laboring under a delusion that he was a white man, or that his mother, was not his mother, or that his daughter was not his daughter, or that he was of—different race or blood from them or either of them, and that such delusions were insane delusions and . . . then the will is invalid and they must find it so." But, he added, if they believe "that his remarks on the subject were only a species of boasting, and if they believe that he well knew his daughter was his daughter, and that he well knew he had negro blood in his veins . . . then the will was properly executed."[50]

In other words, if Hare believed that he and his daughter were white, he was insane; if he merely boasted about his mixed background, and hers, then he was not. He was sane if he ignored the evidence of the senses, objective reality, and insisted on an invisible racial identity. He was sane if he believed in something he could not see. But if he insisted on seeing his father when he looked in a mirror, then he was insane. If he dwelled on his mother Sophia's European ancestry, rather than her African ancestry, he was insane. The issue of sanity or insanity then turns on a question that, again, the law could not effectively measure. Imagine, to borrow an analogy from Walter Benn Michaels, that Dempsey Hare was five feet tall, but one of his mother Sophia Hare's ancestors was six foot four. Would we insist that Dempsey Hare was "really tall" or "of mixed height?" When he stood in a low doorway, should he have forced himself to duck because of his tall heritage? In this absurd situation, "sanity" insists on severing seeing from believing. An idea of "race" is being summoned in law, but the specter thus summoned has no substance: it lives in stories about ancestry. It's racecraft at work, the idea of race as a real thing called into being by the court's action.[51]

Ira Ann White, on the other hand, is clearly sane because she accepts that she "really is" something she does not look like or only looks a little bit like, and that invisible blood conditions her identity. In chapter 5 you will see a picture of Ira Ann White's daughter, Selena White Holland, and a link to a photo of Josephine Hare, Dempsey's niece. Ira Ann White married a darker man by choice, knowing the social connotations and costs that attached to the act. She well knew how people understood and used the idea of race, and she embraced that identity. Most people today, myself included, will probably view hers as the honorable or the admirable choice and will see Hare as craven or lacking in self-respect. We might also applaud her for not wanting to erase her African forebears, or even, if we accept the logic of racism, applaud her for being true to "what she really was." The judge mostly wanted to highlight that she "brought this on herself" by marrying Meredith White, so he could support the will's legitimacy.

Judge Prentis added that if the jury believed from the evidence that Dempsey Hare "was insane upon the subject of the races, that by reason of such diseased mind he hated the negro and loved the white man, and that he cut off his only daughter in his will, because of this

mania, because she is a negro, then the jury must find against the will."
But here again the written statement reflected intense confusion about
what was actually under discussion. The judge, or whoever transcribed
Judge Prentis's remarks, had originally written "because she *loved* a
negro," and then crossed the word "loved" out and penciled in "*is* a
negro." That is, the judge himself was confused about her racial status. Was she white and disinherited for loving a darker man? Or was
she black and disinherited for not being white? He changed the fault
in question from *being* a black woman to *choosing* to love a dark man.
The judge told the jury to condemn her choice, which went against
her father's wishes. But he also told them that if she was disinherited
merely because she was black, the will should not stand.[52]

The judge added the remarkable fact that the defendant, Edward E.
Holland, was Hare's attorney and had drawn up the will, and "that the
defendant Job G. Holland was his physician and tended him in that capacity at the time when the will was made." Ira Ann White quite rea-
sonably suggested that the two men had conspired to take advantage
of the unsound mind of an elderly man, but the judge reminded the
jurors that evidence of an unsound mind could not rest simply upon
one party's dislike of the will's terms. The two Hollands not surprisingly testified that Hare had been just fine, mentally.[53]

Frances Whitfield herself appeared and testified as to the legitimacy of the *second* will, the one that left her with $100 and a sew-
ing machine, rather than the earlier will that left her two sons all of
Hare's estate. At the time she lived as a white person in Norfolk with
her daughter Ida and son-in-law Charles Bland, both termed white.
Had the first will stood, her sons would have been substantial landowners, but they also would have been identified as having African
ancestry. So she testified to the validity of the second will. Whiteness
was worth more than land.

### Dealing in Race

It seems likely that Everett and Job Holland struck a deal with Dempsey
Hare: we get your estate, and we insure that your illegitimate children

get to be white. There's no evidence of such a deal, and no one would have written, "we agree that your illegitimate children will be allowed to live as white people if you give us your estate." But it seems very clear that Ida Bland was Hare's daughter, and that the jury knew this. The court records even reflected confusion about the two women: again their racial ambiguity mirrored the ambiguity in their individual identities. We saw in chapter 1 how people could sometimes pass into whiteness if the community approved of them. Why else would Hare have given his entire estate to two younger men who bore him no relation, unless as a compensation for some service? Of course it's possible both E. E. Holland and Job Holland *were* relatives of Hare's, in some unspoken and willfully undocumented way. In that case they collaborated to disinherit their own relative, Ira Ann. We might see Hare as a sad person, deluded and obsessed, or might see him as a bitter, warped trickster, playing a joke on Virginia's race laws by whitewashing Frances Whitfield's children.

According to newspapers, Ira Ann White's lawyer presented their case "in elegant language and oratorical beauty such as is seldom heard in courthouses of the present day," and it seemed at his conclusion as though she might win. But then the judge "went over the evidence in part and made what he called his plain talk to the jury, closing with a flight of oratory which carried one from the little rivulet to the mighty waves which swept across the ocean's bosom to the shore of other lands." At the end of the judge's speech, "it was hard to conjecture what the verdict would be."

The jury reached a verdict very quickly, in only a few minutes, upholding the validity of the will and leaving Ira White disinherited. When they announced the verdict, someone in the room cried, "I told you so." And indeed, what sane person would believe a jury regarding itself as white would allow thousands of acres of land, and thousands of dollars, to slip from the grasp of the state's attorney and a prominent doctor and into the hands of a couple who the law had wrapped in the spells of racecraft? Ira Ann White filed an appeal, based partly on the judge's windy instructions to the jury, but the court again upheld the legitimacy of Hare's will.[54]

Less than a year later, "Constable Whitfield [a relative of Frances] today at Holland Va conducted what he believes to be one of the largest land sales . . . ever held in Nansemond county He was selling off some farms left by the late Dempsey Hare." A year later the two Hollands were still disposing of Hare's estate.[55]

The two men appear to have ignored Hare's wishes and left the grave untended: what is most likely the grave is unmarked, surrounded by other graves added later. Edward Everett Holland, banker in the towns of Suffolk and Holland, Virginia, eventually became a Virginia state representative, spent ten years in Washington as a congressman, and ended his career as a Virginia state senator. A lifelong Southern Democrat, he was thus one of the people upholding the regime of white supremacy. Doctor Job Holland's house and office, still standing in the tiny town of Holland, Virginia, were added to the national register of historic places in 1983.[56]

Hare rejected community and tried to construct his memory out of economic transactions and law, out of the merger of racecraft with statecraft. He was successful in the sense that he managed to secure Ida Bland in whiteness—unless her descendants take a DNA test.

The real insanity here lies perhaps not with Hare, or with his daughter, but with a system of laws that continually tried to magic "race" into solid existence. Many readers of this story probably long ago thought something like "why can't people just be who they are?" Why couldn't Dempsey Hare just be . . . a person? And the answer of course is because Virginia insisted on the primacy of the black/white divide and built its social and economic order around racial division and the "racecraft" required to maintain it. And the further answer is that individualizing was inextricable from racializing. By 1900, contrary to reason and the evidence of the senses, no percentage of "white blood" would make Dempsey or his daughter white. She accepted this, indeed embraced it; he refused to accept it.

But further, asking "why can't people just be people" misses the power of history and family. Some of the "mixture" in Hare's background probably came as a result of rape in slavery and so represents a fundamental injustice, a gross imbalance of power. African Americans have a history and experience forged under the pressure of systemic inequality: they have a heritage of thriving and combating, making meaningful lives in a world where law limited opportunities and where the powerful conspired against them. Why would anyone want to ignore or discard that powerful history of resource, faith, and creativity under pressure?

We could use ancestry here as an alternative to "race" and simply say "Dempsey Hare had ancestors from Africa and from Europe." But treating him this way obscures or minimizes the force of racecraft in history. He knew what he was doing: he knew the law would never accept him as white, and he turned his back on his mother's African ancestors. Genealogy shows us complicated ancestry: racecraft simplifies ancestry into race. History would regard all the people in the courtroom as related and focus on the structure of injustice and inequality that led him to punish his daughter for marrying the man she loved.

In the 1880s, into this Faulknerian landscape of murder, sin, and half-acknowledged family, came an exotic creature indeed: Patrick Melley, not long off the boat from Donegal, Ireland, with a thick brogue and traveling under a new name, Patrick O'Malley. He joined a branch of the Holland clan and lived about three miles from Dempsey Hare. Patrick ended up, unknowingly, crossing the color line himself.

# THREE

# GLENTIES

In 1890, Patrick O'Malley made the fifteen-mile trip to the Nansemond County Courthouse in Suffolk. He might have traveled the railroad he'd helped to build. He told Wilbur Kilby, the judge who had decided the case of *Hare v. Darden,* that he came from County Donegal, in Ireland, and when they asked for a more specific place he told them "Glenties." Glenties was both a town and the name of a large administrative district: it's an answer that would have made sense to British officials in Ireland, but says little about where he actually came from. He didn't tell them his birth name was not "O'Malley" but "Melley," or that he was once married to a woman in Summit Hill, Pennsylvania, named Mary Murphy, and had never divorced her. He did not say that the witness to their marriage was probably executed as a "Molly Maguire" in 1877. There was a lot he didn't say.

Patrick told family members and American officials his parents' names, but he anglicized them to Frederick and Sophia. My father remembered his grandfather telling him the real name was "Feargal" or "Farrigle," Irish names in the Irish language that both the British and the Catholic Church would have frowned on in 1854, when Patrick was born. The church taught in English and wanted children to have the names of Catholic saints, and so Patrick's older siblings— the ones who went to America first and thereby left a record of their existence—were named Bridget, Cornelius, Anne, and Mary. No records at all document their mother, Sophia, possibly born with the Irish name Siobhán, but there is a death record for a "Farrigle Melley," a married farmer who died in 1865 at the age seventy in the townland of Derrydruell, in the district of Glenties.[1]

## Administering Donegal

Ireland has more than sixty thousand individual "townlands": the term predates English conquest and, contrary to what the English word suggests, does not name a village or cluster of houses. Townlands in Ireland usually have origins lost in history and no local government. No signage tells the tourist in Donegal they now enjoy the view from Farragans, Ranny, Meenacarn, or Toome, all within a few miles of Derrydruel. People know the distinctions locally. Family stories suggest Patrick was from the townland of "Madavagh," just north of the Gweebarra River.

It seems plausible. In 1824, the British began the Ordnance Survey map of Ireland, a twenty-year project to draw the island in precise detail. A year later they appointed Richard Griffith to survey and record tenants in Ireland and the values of their leases. The two projects together represent a massive bureaucratic intervention in the life of Ireland, an effort "at making the human and physical landscape, most especially property in land, intelligible to administrators." And like the bureaucratic innovation of "free negro registers," they created a record of existence historians can track.[2]

By the time of Patrick's birth, which he told Americans was February 15, 1854, the British had finished surveying Madavagh. Griffith recorded multiple Melleys/ Mallys living there, close to each other, and the cemetery in Lettermacaward, just down the road, holds the remains of eighty-three Melleys from Madavagh, spelled as "Maigh Dabhcha" in Irish, and the neighboring townlands known in English as Toome, Farragans, Ranny, Meenacarn, Boyoughter, and Dooey and in modern Irish as Tuaim, Na Fargáin, Raithnigh, Mín an Chairn, Bá Uachtair, and An Dumhaigh. Irish townland names often referred to local geography. "Maigh Dabhcha" might mean "field of flax pools," for retting flax to make linen; Bá Uachtair means "Upper Bay"; Raithnigh means "ferns." The English word "Derry" likely comes from "doire," which means "grove" and probably refers to oak trees, once abundant in Ireland. English names replaced local history and knowledge with nonsense sounds.[3]

The name "Melley" is an anglicization of a name in the Irish language, Ó Meallaigh. English-speaking administrators might record it as Malley, Mally, Mellay, Melly, or possibly Malloy or Mealey or Meelly or many other variants. The multiple variants mark the ill fit between colonizers and the colonized—Englishmen trying to sort out what these people called themselves and render it into English—and mark the relative disinterest in individualizing. Of course in England as well—as in most nations of Europe—naming practices were still mostly local, casual, and customary, and administrative individualism not yet fully in place. Donegal schoolmaster Hugh Dorian recalled the ways the Catholic residents of Donegal understood each other. Especially after the famine, the church typically insisted on baptizing children with the names of Catholic saints. There were "no Abels, no Adams, no Noahs, no Samuels, no Isaacs, but of Johns, Pats there was no end, also James and Michaels, often with the same last name." In Donegal people would refer to "John the son of James (John Hemus); John the son of Pat (John Paddy); John the son of young Pat, John John Ogue; John Bawn (blond); John Roe (red)." He added, "Often the mother's name was introduced as Hugh Kitty Thomas, that is Hugh the son of Kitty, the daughter of Thomas." You might refer to someone by their family's occupation: "Mícheál the pub" might refer to Michael, the son of the pub owner. These names situated people in a local community and context. Modern systems of understanding and tracking individual identity had not yet triumphed.[4]

The British did their best to install them. The Ordnance Survey produced a six-inches-to-the-mile map of the entire island. That map can be correlated to Griffith's valuation, a similarly arduous and long project of surveying primary tenants and their holdings, and then it becomes a social map historians can read. Brian Freil's play *Translations* brilliantly describes Donegal in the midst of the mapping process, local traditions and aspirations in conflict with administrative demands for order and legibility. The survey map and the valuation together show abundant Melleys living near Lettermacaward but no Frederick or Sophia, or Feargal or Siobhán. A "Patrick Mally" lived in a small cluster of houses in Madavagh, with four other households named "Mally." But Frederick and Sophia may have been subtenants, leasing from other, more fortunate Melleys, and so not recorded by Griffith. Subtenants were of no account.[5]

## Family History and Absence

Sooner or later nearly anyone examining family history runs into a place where they fall off the edge of the map and there's nothing. The edge of the map comes up pretty quickly in Donegal. There's no way to know if the Farrigle Melley who died in Derrydruel was Patrick's father. Records from Donegal are notoriously poor: there are no records of Frederick and Sophia's births, marriage, or deaths, and no records of their children's baptisms, aside from what they told American officials. They might have appeared in census records, but in an egregious act of ineptitude and indifference, the records of the census the British conducted every ten years between 1821 and 1851 were destroyed in the Irish Civil War in 1921. The census returns from 1861 to 1891 were destroyed by the British after they had summarized the results. These spectacular erasures make it extremely difficult to track ordinary people in Ireland.

Who gets recorded for history, and why? The wealthy document their bloodlines, so they can assure the transfer of property and title. In monarchies, genealogy legitimates political power. Ordinary people only appear when state or religious authorities take an interest in them, usually to mark a sacrament, secure an obligation to support the local church, or to keep a record of taxes owed and paid. No one was interested in Farrigle and Siobhán, neither church nor state. They only existed in the minimal recollections of their children. In the US, the census determined how many representatives a state would get in Congress. Virginians also tracked free people with African ancestors to determine who they could enslave, and to know who married who and how to class them as in the case of Dempsey Hare's children. That led to more energetic and attentive methods of tracking identity than we see in Ireland.[6]

Donegal church records improve later in the century, and they show a different Patrick Melley, also born in 1854, also to parents named Frederick and Sophia. But that Patrick never left Ireland. The British ran workhouses to manage the Irish poor, grim and notorious institutions. Workhouse records from Glenties show a Patrick Melley, age thirteen, admitted for a "sore foot" in 1866. He is listed as a schoolboy, a Roman Catholic, and as "destitute." He stayed a bit more than a month. The age is right, but it may be the other Pat Melley, because the workhouse listed his home place as "Glenties, Glenties," probably meaning the town of Glenties as well as the larger administrative district.[7]

Donegal sits at the far north and west of Ireland. It rains a great deal there, and rarely gets much above seventy degrees. In Ireland, Donegal has a distinctive regional accent and somewhat of a reputation for rustic backwardness. Summer vacationers today come to enjoy the rugged scenery, but in prosperous modern Ireland people from Donegal, take vacations in places like Spain or Florida, where they can warm themselves under a more forthcoming sun. Madavagh is north of Glenties village and a few miles from the sea on the Gweebarra River. It's a "Gaeltacht," meaning a region where the Irish language persisted longest and is still commonly spoken. Most of the Gaeltacht are in the far west of Ireland, where English colonial authority was weakest.

A few years ago, I went to Madavagh, part of a research trip for this book. I climbed a local hill, also called Toome, foolishly choosing the boggy side. Alternatively hopping on rocks and sinking halfway up to my knees in wet sphagnum, I reached the windswept top and could see the entire region of Patrick's nativity. After struggling back down, I repaired to Elliott's Traditional Irish Bar, a wonderful local pub, and started sending photos back to my family. This was their ancestral home.

*Figure 3.1.* Looking north toward the Rosses, from Toome. Author photo with shadow of author included.

What does that mean exactly? It's only the ancestral home of my father's paternal line. I've got "ancestral homes" near Malin head in Donegal and in Fermoy in County Cork, and in Dublin and multiple other places in Ireland, depending on what branch I'd choose to follow on my father's or mother's side. I'd invested a lot of time in Patrick by this point and related this to Daniel, the bartender, as he poured a pint of Guinness at the appropriately slow pace. Irish people are somewhat long-suffering about Americans with Irish ancestors who come over searching for a sense of belonging, which they won't find, but the dollars are welcome. Daniel patiently heard my story—yet another Yank, seeking roots—and said, yes, there were many people named Melley in the area, but no records. Frederick and Sophia and Patrick and his siblings all came from there, but there's no clear trace of them, except perhaps in DNA, which Irish people are somewhat uneasy about since the DNA record conjures people, like Patrick and his parents, whose memory emigration erased.

The bar was cozy and friendly, a late October fire burning in the fireplace, and music was starting. A whole family, grandparents, parents, and grandchildren, had come in, all with instruments: fiddles, flutes, tin whistles, and concertinas. In the course of research for an earlier book, I'd gotten interested in Irish traditional music and had taught myself the rudiments of the "Irish flute." So I pulled the flute from my backpack. Not long after, in walked Michael Rooney, harpist, and June McCormack, flute player, two very well known and extremely accomplished Irish musicians, joining the rest of their family. They were all vacationing nearby, it turned out. They graciously welcomed me to huff and struggle through a few tunes. These were wordless tunes Patrick surely would have heard in his childhood, and there I was, with a pint of Guinness and wet feet, encountering and enacting "my roots."

In this moment the genetic ancestral connection to Ireland had the least meaning. No one knew anything about poor people who had left 150 years before, or cared, and why should they: emigration has been a constant theme in Irish history, and the pain of every departure was balanced by the relief at one less mouth to feed. People left continually, millions of people, and Ireland mostly forgot whatever they'd known about them, but Irish Americans concocted a sentimental attachment to the old sod. As the Pogues put it, "Where e'er we go, we celebrate / The land that makes us refugees." That celebration calls attention to history and a sense of belonging or entitlement rooted in "blood," but also in my case a desire to bring some useful information back from the trip. The Rooney and McCormack family welcomed me not because I had Irish ancestors, but because I had obviously put in the time to learn a few tunes, engaging in the *practice* of a form of Irish culture. The music I played in Elliott's pub is available to anyone who likes the music and wants to work at it. If genetics played a role in it, I'd be a far better player than I am.[8]

### Irish Poverty

The chapter that follows documents how Ireland was described in the years before Patrick left. It's a hard subject to write about, partly because it's personal. Historians are generally trained to avoid the personal, for good reason. An objective account of fact is a worthy goal, even if it's impossible to fully accomplish. The personal, in this book, is political: the historical record of Irish oppression and poverty is startling. Frederick Douglass traveled in Ireland on the eve of the great famine and was shocked by what he found. "I had heard much of the misery and wretchedness of the Irish people, previous to leaving the United States. . . . But I must confess, my experience has convinced me that the half has not been told." There was "much to remind me of my former condition," he wrote. Irish poverty was made all the more shocking by the fact that they were white people. Or were they?[9]

Irish Americans have coupled legends of ancestral misery with shamrock hoodoo about Ireland in order to dismiss other people's suffering. You still see memes claiming "the Irish were slaves too," so African Americans should just shut up. Research librarian Liam Hogan has extensively debunked these claims of Irish slavery. People who make this claim are confused about the difference between indentured servitude, described in chapter 1, and slavery. But the myth persists and makes talking about Irish poverty, and the Irish as racially "other," a tricky proposition. Ancestry is made meaningful by knowledge of history and by the practice of cultural traditions, not biology, and while suffering is general in history, each experience of misery is unique.[10]

England's invasion and colonization of Ireland took hundreds of years to accomplish. Put simply, starting in the east, English rule gradually extended throughout the island, especially after Henry VIII and the conversion of England to Protestantism. English and British landlords seized tens of thousands of acres by force till by 1800, 95 percent of the land in Ireland was owned and controlled by British nobility and their underlings, many of whom never visited their Irish estates, simply leaving them to managers who forwarded the rents so lord and lady might live splendidly in London. By 1800, the Marquess Conyngham, Farrigle Melley's landlord in Derrydruel, controlled 123,300 acres in Donegal, 27,613 acres in County Clare, and 7,060 acres in County Meath: "landlord king of about 40,000 people." Thomas Campbell Foster, a lawyer and journalist for the *Times of London*, described

Conynghim's Donegal lands from 1846, eight years before Patrick
Melley's birth.[11]

"I proceeded to Glenties, a village which is the property of the
Marquis of Conynghim," Foster wrote. "Almost the whole barony of
Boylagh belongs to this nobleman, together with the island of [Arran-
more] on the west coast." Foster noted that "once in the course of his
life, two years ago, the Marquis of Conynghim visited this estate for
a few days." Otherwise, Conyngham's lawyer, a London man named
John Benbow, "usually comes once a year, and the sub-agents visit the
tenants every half-year to collect their rents." Every few years Benbow himself visited individual farms "to see what increased rent they
will bear, and this is the extent of the acquaintance of the Marquis of
Conyngham with his tenants."[12]

The National Library of Ireland holds the Conyngham Papers, an
extensive and uneven collection of mostly letters from his Irish estate agents, reporting how much money he got from his tenants in
Ireland. The agents sent Conyngham lists, pages long, of townlands
and the sums extracted from them. Sometimes there would be names
with amounts listed: "C. Boyle, 1£ 1 s.," "Pat Sweeney 2£ 3s." More often the rents extracted from a given townland would be totaled up to
several hundred pounds and presented for his lordship's satisfaction.
The small sums added up: in 1840 Conyngham drew the equivalent
of more than a million dollars just from his estate in Mountcharles
alone.[13]

Tenants who could not pay were often "ejected." In 1821, Conyngham's agent in Ireland wrote to tell him of "proceedings for recovery of
rent in the Rosses. 39 people ejected and turned out." "It is my honor
to inform your Lordship that I have ejected & turned out all the tenants of the lands of Brockagh the arrears on which is lost they being
totally unable to pay it." He added, "I was obliged to go & pull down
the houses and on the first farm I had ejected finding the tenants had
returned after being turned out." "This I understand has had the desired effect of obliging them to give up any idea of occupancy," he assured Conyngham. We can imagine the range and variety of sorrows

*Figure 3.2.* Francis, 2nd Marquess Conyngham, holder of various titles acquired by bleeding rent from people whose lands his family had confiscated. Courtesy of National Portrait Gallery, London.

those terse sentences concealed: the ejected had no other place to go; they knew no other home, so the local police, in Conyngham's employ, destroyed their home and they fell off the map, went to some place history cannot follow or just conveniently died. That same year, his agent wrote that "it grieves me to be obliged to state to your Lordship the prospect of starvation and distress in this district is becoming every hour more manifest. I fear many will starve." He acknowledged, "such a picture cannot be pleasant to your lordship but the truth on such an occasion ought to be supported." And then he got to the question Conyngham cared about: "how the rents are to be had until the crops come round is to me a great source of anxiety & necessitates that there will be many defaults."[14]

Twenty-five years after that famine, on the eve of an exponentially worse famine, Foster wrote that Conyngham "bears the character of a kind hearted, generous man, fond of yachting and amusement, and having an excessive distaste for every kind of business or trouble." But "from one end of his large estate here to the other, nothing is to be found but poverty, misery, wretched cultivation, and infinite subdivision of land."[15]

"Infinite subdivision of land": there's the core of the grim tale. The British, settler colonialists, controlled most of the land in Ireland. Irish natives had to pay rent to live on land they once owned. The lord reserved the best land for himself, for cash crops or for lovely estate gardens and parks of the sort beloved by the BBC and Hollywood Anglophiles. Tenants could acquire very long term rights to land, leases extending to several "lives," but they could never purchase the land. Salable crops belonged to the landlord or went to pay his rents and taxes. "Such is poor Ireland," wrote Donegal schoolmaster Hugh Dorian, "England's pantry." A farmer worked in fear of eviction, and "never to be banished from the mind, never to be forgotten, always oppressing the brain, from the month of May till November and from November till May: the rent—the rent." A tenant fortunate enough to hold more than thirty acres would probably sublease it, and that subtenant, if he could, might sublet it further. A tenant who had children might subdivide the family's small holdings further still: infinite subdivision of land, with families existing on plots as small as an acre, leading to a degree of poverty that appalled the Euro-American world.[16]

Thomas Campbell Foster, quoted above, wrote that "there are no gentry, no middle class," in Ireland: "all are poor, wretchedly poor. Every shilling the tenants can raise from their half cultivated land is paid in rent, whilst the people subsist for the most part on potatoes and water." The British discouraged industrialization in Ireland, and "so they are driven to the land for support, till they infinitely subdivide it." "Every rude effort that they make to increase the amount of the produce is followed immediately by raising their rents in proportion—as it were, to punish them for improving."

Foster spoke with one Donegal farmer who told him "that for the half of this year, whilst his cows gave no milk, he had to subsist on pepper and water and potatoes. He could not afford to eat butter." Potatoes became nearly the only source of food for millions of people: other crops went to pay the rent. The farmer told him, "Not a bit of bread have I eaten since I was born," for "we must sell the corn and the butter to give to the landlord." "I have the largest farm in the district," he added.[17]

The potato, introduced from the New World, proved both a blessing and a curse. The Irish lived on potatoes because they grew well in poor soil—the only soil available for subsistence—and the varietal mostly commonly grown in Ireland, nicknamed the "lumper," was highly nutritious, capable of feeding an entire family on as little as an acre. Thanks to potatoes, population grew dramatically in Ireland in the early nineteenth century, which meant more and more subdivision of land and more and more boggy, rocky, marginal plots converted to potato fields. In Donegal's Fánaid peninsula, for example, population "was probably no more than 4,000 in 1766; by the turn of the century it was in the region of 6,000; twenty years later it was 8,846, and in 1831 it was 9,596 and still rising." As a result "two generations saw snug farms frittered into beggarly patches: in one instance a holding of 37 acres—one third of them bog—that had supported a single family in 1781 was divided among the occupier's six children; by 1823 these six holdings had become thirteen, and they were supporting 91 persons." "In consequence of the immense increase of population, and the minute subdivisions of land in many places," wrote Thomas Price in 1829, "the people now subsist upon potatoes and water."[18]

Potato monoculture would have disastrous results a year after Foster's visit, when the infamous potato blight wiped out the island's entire crop. But the potato's enthusiasm for poor soil also enabled the growth of what economists liked to call "surplus" or "redundant" population. Ireland's population in 1845 was estimated at about 8.5 million people, roughly the same as today. These people were only "surplus" because the political economy of land management insured that Ireland exported food while its population starved. "The Irishman," Alexis de Tocqueville wrote, "raises beautiful crops, carries his harvest to the nearest port, puts it on board an English vessel, and returns home to subsist on potatoes. He rears cattle, sends them to London, and never eats meat."[19]

Travelers visiting Ireland were astonished by the extent of poverty. Gustave de Beaumont toured Ireland with his friend Alexis de Tocqueville, the French aristocrat most famous for *Democracy in America*, his account of the US in the 1830s. De Beaumont told his readers that "misery, naked and famishing, that misery which is vagrant, idle, and mendicant, covers the entire country; it shows itself everywhere, and at every hour of the day; it is the first thing you see when you land on the Irish coast, and from that moment it ceases not to be present to your view." "It follows you everywhere," he lamented, "and besieges you incessantly; you hear its groans and cries in the distance." De Tocqueville told his father, "you cannot imagine what a complexity of miseries five centuries of oppression, civil disorders, and religious hostility have piled up on this poor people." "I defy you," he told his cousin, the Countess of Grancey, "whatever efforts of the imagination you may make, to picture the misery of the population of this country."[20]

Travelers in Ireland focused on the infamous dwellings of mud or stone the British called "fourth class cabins." Frederick Douglass wrote to a friend in the US that "of all places to witness human misery, ignorance, degradation, fifth and wretchedness, an Irish hut is pre-eminent." He described "four mud walls about six feet high, occupying a space of ground about ten feet square, covered or thatched with straw a mud chimney at one end, reaching about a foot above the roof—without apartments or divisions of any kind—without floor, without windows, and sometimes without a chimney." Furniture consisted of "a piece of pine board laid on the top of a box or an old chest—a pile of straw covered with dirty garments." "A few broken dishes stuck up in a corner—an iron pot, or the half of an iron pot, in one corner of the chimney," served for eating, with "a little peat in the fireplace, aggravating one occasionally with a glimpse of fire, but sending out very little heat." In this cabin you might find "a man and his wife and five children, and a pig." Pigs were vital: kept not for food, but to pay the rent. "Here you have an Irish hut or cabin such as millions of the people of Ireland live in. And some live in worse than these."[21]

De Beaumont published his widely read account of Ireland in 1839. He too described "four walls of dried mud, which the rain, as it falls, easily restores to its primitive condition; having for its roof a little straw or some sods, for its chimney a hole cut in the roof, or very frequently the door, through which alone the smoke finds an issue." He also reported, "the single apartment contains the father, mother, children, and sometimes a grandfather or grandmother; there is no furniture in this wretched hovel; a single bed of hay or straw serves for the entire family. Five or six half-naked children may be seen crouched near a miserable fire, the ashes of which cover a few potatoes, the sole nourishment of the family. In the midst of all lies a dirty pig." De Beaumont insisted, "this dwelling is very miserable, still it is not that of the pauper, properly so called; I have just described the dwelling of the Irish farmer and agricultural laborer."[22]

In Donegal, Foster visited the cottages of John and Charles M'Cabe, who lived on Conyngham's land in slightly better cabins made of stone. "The mud floor was uneven, damp, and filthy," he wrote. The family shared the house with a pig, and "two chairs, a bedstead of the rudest description, a cradle, a spinning wheel, and an iron pot constituted the whole furniture." This house had two rooms. In the second room, "six children slept on loose hay, with one dirty blanket to cover them. The father, mother, and an infant slept in the first room, also on loose hay, and with but one blanket on the bed." The barefoot, nearly naked children wore the castoff rags from their parents. "I give you these as examples, without any kind of selection, of the universal condition of the tenantry around on this estate."[23]

These examples of Irish poverty likely describe how Patrick Melley's family lived. Patrick's parents were not substantial enough to show up in Griffith's valuation, or notable enough to appear in any records, and so we have to consider them as living among the anonymous Irish poor described here, and all the evidence suggests they shared a mud hut with a pig, if they were lucky. This is not an especially pleasing notion, although pretty much every human being's ancestors shared their home with livestock if you go back far enough. But looking at the dusty packets of letters in the Conyngham Papers at Ireland's National Archives was extremely unsettling. Year after year, decade after decade, people living in rags sent rents to Conyngham while he sported in London. And what value did he return? He kept "order," meaning he enforced a set of laws designed entirely to protect his property and the orderly collection of his rents. I certainly never suffered personally from these historically distant things, but these estate records, and others like them, are a starting point for any explanation of why there are so many Irish in America and possibly for how Patrick Melley could be regarded as a black man. What did Conyngham care about people who left, or about the deaths of people he never saw? The archive answers, "not at all, except to the degree that it hindered the collection of rent." The poverty he created made his tenants "other": weird and primitive, savage, alien, like a strange race.

### The Irish as a Savage Race

The homes of the Irish poor reminded de Tocqueville of his time in America: "I should have believed myself returned to the huts of my friends, the Iroquois," de Tocqueville wrote, "if I saw a hole made to allow the smoke to escape. Here the smoke goes out by the door, which gives, according to my weak lights, a decided advantage to the architecture of the Iroquois." Douglass thought the Irish lived "in much the same degradation as the American slaves." Recalling a meeting of more than five thousand people he had attended, he insisted "that these people lacked only a black skin and wooly hair, to complete their likeness to the plantation negro."[24]

De Beaumont argued that "like the Indian, the Irishman is poor and naked . . . he is destitute of the physical comforts which human industry and the commerce of nations procure." But "in the midst of his greatest distress, the Indian preserves a certain independence," he thought, "which has its dignity and its charms. Though indigent and famished, he is still free," whereas "the Irishman undergoes the same destitution without possessing the same liberty; he is subject to rules and restrictions of every sort: he is dying of hunger, and restrained by law." De Beaumont did not think Irish, Indians, and African American slaves were *the same*, but like Douglass he thought they were comparable: the Irish person "has neither the liberty of the savage nor the bread of servitude." *The Illustrated London News* described the Irish cabin as "on the same scale of comfort as the hut of the Esquimaux, or the wigwam of the North American Indian." These accounts reduce the Irish poor to a state of nature: nearly naked, barefoot, in marginal huts barely distinguishable from the earth and plants from which they are made. Pigs share the house. And so the Irish seem like a different "race."[25]

The accounts of poverty are similar enough, and numerous enough, that they must be true to some extent, but of course they don't show the whole picture. Ireland had towns, stores, and merchants. There was an Anglo-Irish aristocracy and its less wealthy familiars. It had political leaders engaged in struggle for independence or for more autonomy. It had relatively prosperous "strong farmer" tenants who managed to gain lease of more than fifty acres of land. The Library of Ireland has photos of fair day in Glenties dating from sometime between 1880 and 1910. You see a prosperous-seeming street and people not in rags engaged in commerce. If these photos date from 1900, then they reflect more than fifty years of the continual emigration of people like Patrick.

Ireland had shocking mass poverty, but even the poorest and most "primitive" people have "culture": they tell stories, sing songs, hold rituals celebrating births and mourning deaths. They have religious beliefs. They have complicated kin relations; they gossip and maneuver for advantage. They resist political coercion where they can. What we see here is both accurate and a product of the social distance settler colonialism establishes and depends on: what we see is the tools of racecraft. The people who caused this poverty had to find some means to explain it besides their own actions. Comparing the Irish to the Iroquois, "Esquimaux," and African Americans gets to questions racecraft poses: were the Irish poor because they were a different, inferior race?[26]

## Irish Indians

England first sent its armies to Ireland at the same time it was colonizing North America, and "as numerous historians and geographers have pointed out, there are countless parallels between the English plantations in North America" and the plantations in Ulster, Ireland's northernmost province, between 1585 and 1640. Many of the military men who settled Virginia also settled Ulster, and they often compared the Irish to Indians. The Irish were pastoralists: they practiced "transhumance," meaning they moved with cattle to mountains in the summer, living in a rustic "booley house," and then back down to the lower country in the winter. "The English took the Irish practice of transhumance as proof that the Irish were nomads, hence Barbarian," and "at the opposite pole of civilization from themselves."[27]

No less than Virginia explorer John Smith described Powhatan wearing "a fair robe of skins as large as an Irish mantle." Martin Pring, exploring Cape Cod in 1603, similarly reported an Indian wearing "a bear's skin like an Irish mantle over one shoulder." Another New England settler called attention to the leggings Virginia Indians wore, "a kind of leather breeches and stockings . . . which they tie and wrap about the loins after the fashion of the Turks or Irish [trousers]." George Percy, walking in the woods near Jamestown in 1607, remarked how "by chance we espied a pathway like to an Irish place." "The wild Irish and the Indian doe not much differ," one English observer who was familiar with both had written in 1646, "and therefore [they] should be handled alike." Nicholas Canny noted how English writers implied that American Indians and the Irish the "were descended from the same primitive ancestors or that they were at the same retarded state of cultural development." English observers often compared them to the "savages" of North America and sometimes to the "Hottentots" of South Africa. These comparisons made colonial subjugation easier to justify.[28]

## Confusing Celts

Nineteenth-century observers often understood the Irish to be "Celts," a term still bandied about widely, from historical conferences to Renaissance Fairs, with little concern for what it actually might mean. The literature of the "Irish race" in the nineteenth century is a shaky concoction of Latinate nouns seasoned with fantasy and wish fulfillment, "racecraft" at its finest. Some observers, reading accounts of barbarian Celts written by the Romans, concluded the ancient Celts "had yellow hair" and "that they were tall and fair," while other insisted that "the Celts of Wales, Ireland, and Scotland, at this day, have black curled hair, and brown faces." Were they the same people? "Dark-fair racial divisions were fundamental for both British and Irish race scientists," writes Richard McMahon in his admirable survey of racial literature, and many nineteenth-century race theorists imagined a contrast between tall, blond, "true Celts" and a lesser race of "Celts" said to have arrived in Ireland from, variously, Iberia, the Berber regions of North Africa, "Turania," or even the lost continent of Atlantis: these latter made up the "small, dark, inferior 'black Irish,' a type pro-British writers had remarked for centuries." By the time Patrick

Melley arrived in America, European race theorists increasingly relied on physical anthropology to back up their claims. At the eve of World War II, Euro-American social scientists went to Ireland to measure heads and excavate tombs, hoping in vain to find traces of the blond "Aryan Celt."[29]

In the heyday of the Roman Empire, "Celtic" was a geographically widespread language group, with some common decorative motifs and styles found from central Europe to the Emerald Isle. But turning this linguistic group into a "race" makes little sense. A language group does not translate into a "race": millions of people around the world speak English as a majority language, for example, and consume American media, but Jamaicans, Australians, Asian Indians, and Barbadians don't fit anyone's idea of a "race." In the US, demands that everyone speak English will not turn people from China, Japan, India, Vietnam, Ireland, Italy, El Salvador, or any of the many other countries from which Americans claim ancestry into a single "race." So we could regard efforts to turn "Celtic" into a race as equally misbegotten. In his thorough survey of the origins of the Irish people, using evidence from archaeology, mythology, linguistics, and DNA, J. P. Mallory offered "a word of warning for those who seek some form of Irish genetic purity: it doesn't exist."[30]

The idea of an Irish race had strategic advantages and disadvantages. It served both detractors and those who made claims for independence from England, asserting "we the Irish, are a distinct race entitled to independence because of our racial distinctiveness." It worked particularly well for upper-class Anglo-Irish men who imagined the true Celtic race as pale, blond, and plagued by annoying dark Celtic peasants requiring leadership. But racecraft could more often work to support oppression, as when Benjamin Disraeli in 1836 claimed the Irish race, "hate our free and fertile isle. They hate our order, our civilisation, our enterprising industry, our sustained courage, our decorous liberty, our pure religion. This wild, reckless, indolent, uncertain and superstitious race have no sympathy with the English character. . . . Their history describes an unbroken circle of bigotry and blood."[31]

## Savage Catholics

English administrators often used the term "savage" or "wild" to describe the Irish. De Beaumont observed that "in Ireland, the justices of the peace, the judges, and the jury, treat the accused as a kind of idolatrous savage, whose violence must be subdued, as an enemy that must be destroyed." De Beaumont agreed: "the Irishman displays the most ferocious cruelty in his acts of vengeance. . . . The punishments which he vents in his savage fury cannot be contemplated without horror." De Tocqueville reported, "all the rich Protestants that I saw in Dublin speak of the Catholic population only with an extraordinary hatred and contempt. They are, to all intents, savages incapable of recognizing a kindness, fanatics led into every disorder by their priests."[32]

The colonizers of Ireland after the 1530s were Protestants: the Irish remained stubbornly Catholic. But until the late nineteenth century, they practiced forms of Catholicism that particularly offended Protestants. "Popular Irish religion was tribal, traditional, and permeated with magic," wrote one historian of religion, involving sacred objects and holy wells, still found in Ireland today. Wakes and weddings typically involved remarkably earthy rituals invoking fertility and resurrection. Wakes combined wailing, keening grief with dancing, manly contests of strength, and openly sexual games involving sowing and planting as metaphors for sexual acts. Breandán Mac Suibhne, in his superlative account of nineteenth-century Donegal, writes that in the mid-1850s, "the people vibrated between two cosmologies, one ancestral or fairy and the other Christian. Central to the non-Christian system were ritualized gatherings around fires or wells, often on dates determined by solar or lunar cycles." In Glenties "on the night of 23 June, every house had a bonfire, and in some townlands there was one large fire, around which people from all houses gathered, and when the fire had burned out, they would take the cinders and scatter them through the fields of growing crops and they would rub the ashes on their cattle." They called that night "*Oíche Fhéile Eoin*, St John's Eve," Mac Suibhne continued, but its connection to John the Baptist was superficial at best: instead it marked the summer solstice, and if Patrick's family joined in the celebration, they would have looked like savage pagans to the English. "We came to this country as conquerors, we English Protestants," historian John Patrick Prendergast told de Tocqueville, and Protestant conquerors detested that kind of pre-Christian practice. "The aristocracy of this country has always regarded the Catholic population as a bunch of savages; they have treated them as such," he continued, and now "the Catholic population has really become savage." Colonizers want regularity, predictability, and docility from the colonized: they turn these things into "virtues" and imagine their absence as evidence of savagery.[33]

If we see descriptions of Irish poverty as a species of racecraft, many American and British observers of Ireland saw "priestcraft" as the root of Ireland's difficulties. Priestcraft merged with the superstitious belief in banshees, *púca*, and the panoply of magical beings encompassed by fairy lore. Scottish politician John Campbell Colquhoun called the Irish people "who believe in hobgoblins, and witches, and fairies—who tremble at an evil eye, and trust in a charm." The same people who fear the banshee "visit holy wells, and submit to cruel penances at the command of their Church." Colquhoun linked crime in Ireland to the power of priests, claiming priests controlled elections through magic. "One priest threatened that the very moment a freeman who voted for me returned home, he would clap a pair of horns on his head." Another claimed, "he would, on the spot, turn his rebellious parishioners into [marsh plants]." "A third gravely told them that the food should melt in their hands; whilst a fourth swore that if they went against him, he would turn them into four-footed beasts, and put them on their bellies for the rest of their lives!" Indeed, wrote another source, "that hell-forged armour of superstition and priestcraft" kept the Irish in savagery. "Those, who like the writer and his companions, have been on the spot, and thoroughly tested the spirit of Irish priestcraft" know well "that the priests in Ireland should be capable of exciting thousands of their depraved and wretched votaries to deeds of violence and blood in the name of the Christian religion."

When he arrived in Pennsylvania in 1871 Patrick Melley found these same ideas about savage Catholics prevailed.[34]

## Resistance to the Colonizer

Again even the poorest people have culture: these religious practices, the fairy lore merged with "priestcraft," were, like all religious practices, an effort to moralize the world and make sense of birth and death, life's joys and cruelties. Fairy lore looked like witchcraft: it *was* witchcraft, in that it found coherent explanations for events in the supposed actions of typically invisible beings. Irish people did not worship the *Aos Sí*, the fairies, but they did fear them, tell entertaining and cautionary stories about them, and take care to placate them. Witchcraft and superstition persisted in many Christian countries, including Puritan New England, but to Protestants administering Ireland these practices looked like savagery.

Rural Irish culture expressed itself not just in customs blending the pagan and the Christian, but in overt acts of "savage" resistance to British rule. Historians sometimes use the term "prepolitical" to describe acts of protest or violence by people who have no effective access to the political process, or who confront a political process, as in Ireland, rigged to protect, serve, and enforce the desires of landlords. In Ireland, rural protest took the form of attacks on the persons and property of landlords and their agents, on rent collectors, or on people suspected of collaborating with the authorities.[35]

The organizations that engaged in these protests had many names. "All who remember the year 1821," wrote Colquhoun, "have heard of Captain Rock and his followers." "Those who know more particularly the history of Ireland, have read of the Carders and Righters, the Shanavats and Caravats, the White boys and the Peep-o'-day-boys, the Thrashers and Riskavallas, the Black hens and Ribbonmen, the Lady-Clares and Terry-Alts." Participants typically dressed up in some sort of outlandish costume and left notes in which they gave themselves fanciful titles and described the source of their anger. "These factions," he insisted correctly, "have existed all over Ireland." Indeed, he declared, "the lower classes of Ireland are entire savages in all their feelings with regard to law. The power of force they recognise, (as all savages do), but law they utterly despise."[36]

In southwestern Ireland, an agrarian secret society called the "Whiteboys" conducted attacks on local landlords and elites, sometimes marching in large bands of several hundred men. The "Whiteboys" blackened their faces with charcoal and often wore long smocks in emulation of women: they dressed symbolically as black women. This "blackface" or gender transgression had less to do with people from Africa than with a sense of the ordinary order inverted: white becomes black, men become women, chaos, boundaries in collapse, disorder loosed. Agrarian protesters would often describe themselves as women, or in Donegal, as "the children of Molly Maguire." The actual causes of the violence lay squarely in the dispossession of the native Irish and the system of extracting rents from subdivided plots. But the prepolitical vigilante violence, supported allegedly by "priest-craft," superstition, and masquerade, reinforced the idea of the Irish as a savage race.

One Crown prosecutor admitted, "the peasantry have always had objects connected with the land. I have traced the origin of almost every case I prosecuted, and I find that they generally arise from the attachment to, the dispossession of, or the change in the possession of land." Obtuse British politicians like Colquhoun tended to see political violence directed toward the possession of land as evidence of savagery. In Galway in 1831, for example, Colquhoun wrote of "a number of the peasantry putting up wigwams, like savages, and establishing themselves upon the proprietor's land, and saying, 'Now we will cut and parcel out this land'; and they have been found disputing and dividing the land amongst themselves." He noted, "they will do anything rather than be turned out of their holdings." Their willingness to do *anything* to avoid homelessness and starvation—an entirely understandable desire—here passes as evidence of an alien, savage racial character.[37]

Colquhoun looked at starving Irish tenants putting up temporary shelters on the lord's land and saw wigwams: racecraft shaped what people saw, and statecraft turned this visualization into policy. Racecraft taught people how to see "race" as witchcraft taught people how to see the witch.

Americans adopted this language. In 1851, *Harper's Monthly* published "A Scene of Irish Life," a short story in which tenants angry at eviction murder the local landlord. The author described the two assassins as types of "fellows who are as plentiful on Irish soil as potatoes." "Had they been travelers over a plain of India, an Australian waste, or the Pampas of South America," the author added, "they could not have been grimmer of aspect, or more thoroughly children of the wild. They were Irish from head to foot." He further insisted, "the Celtic physiognomy was distinctly marked—the small and somewhat upturned nose; the black tint of skin; the eye now looking gray, now black; the freckled cheek, and sandy hair." The entire remarkable passage is racecraft at work: the Irish are like Asian Indians, or indigenous South American Indians, or Aboriginal Australians: a racially distinctive people. Confusingly, they have "black tinted skin" and freckles, eyes that shift color, and sandy hair. Racecraft is a way of seeing: it teaches how to see the signs of "race," in order to explain the tenant's rage at the local lord as a phenomenon of racial savagery, not politics. The article told Americans to *see* the Irish as Australian Aborigines, South American Natives, or as Asian Indians then also grappling with English colonialism. It insisted on a physical difference: "black" tinted skin and an upturned nose. In 1858, in a fierce late night debate over whether to admit Kansas as a slave state or a free state, frustrated congressmen had gotten into a fistfight on the House floor. The *New York Tribune* mocked the spectacle of "some fifty middle-aged and elderly gentlemen pitching into each other like so many Tipperary savages." The Irish as Indians, or as racially exotic, was as with American Indians, both a negative stereotype and a source of romantic attraction, a relief from middle-class restraints.[38]

*Figure 3.3.* Drawing by Arthur Young, who traveled in Ireland from 1776 to 1779 and published *A Tour of Ireland* in 1780. This drawing depicts the era *before* the population increase that led to the astonished descriptions of poverty described in the text. The drawing shows potato fields laid out with an exact regularity unlikely in the real world, and abundant livestock, scattered randomly with barefoot, idle adults, naked children, and an overgrown, dilapidated hut barely distinguishable from nature. Part of a similar hut appears on the left. Rather than guessing whether or not it's an accurate depiction of Irish life, we could look at it as a compound of colonial fantasies about orderly production of resources mixed with understandings of the Irish as indolent "savages." Courtesy of National Library of Ireland, Dublin.

The three photos comprising figure 3.4 come from a series of seven stereopticon images taken in Killarney, County Kerry, some time between 1860 and 1883. Stereopticon cards contained two images taken from a slightly different position. Placed in a simple binocular viewer, they gave a convincing and fascinating 3-D effect. Most Americans will probably think these are images of Native American women, maybe vaguely recalling the photos Edwin S. Curtis took of Native people in the Southwest. Some of my students see central Europe in those faces. The photographer, according[s to the National Library of Ireland, was either James Simonton or Frederick Holland Mares, both of whom worked as commercial photographers in Ireland and England, producing images of Ireland for general sale to a public interested in real and virtual tourism.[39]

"The Irish Colleen," rustic, demure, erotically appealing, was a stock image in popular culture by the time these images were taken. Did the photographer choose these women to represent the *colleen* because they looked maybe like Indians, or because they looked "racially other?" Or did he make them look more exotic? Did they habitually go barefoot, or were they asked to take their shoes off for effect?

*Figure 3.4.* "Full-length portrait[s] taken at the Gap of Dunloe, Killarney, Co. Kerry," between 1860 and 1883. *Left to right*, Bridget Sweeney, Mary Sullivan, Norah O'Connell. Courtesy of National Library of Ireland, Dublin.

Did they normally pull their hair back in a severe center part, or did the photographer style their hair? Two of them wear a broad loop of cloth around their skirts—why? The photographer scratched their names on the original printing plate, authenticating them as Irish. The images, on the one hand, seem to offer us an example of what Irish people "actually looked like" in the nineteenth century, and they suggest that at least some Irish people looked different from the idealized Caucasian. But the photographers may have set out to make them "look like" some preexisting idea of the Irish. For example, one of the women photographed for the series, not shown here but viewable online, wears the same shawl as the woman on the right, Norah O'Donnell. All of the women in the series carry one or two of what look like the same bottles and an identical glass. These details show the photos were staged.

And in fact it turns out these photos reflect the tourist trade. Well before Patrick was born, "as soon as it became fashionable to admire romantic scenery," the rugged beauty of the Killarney region made it a tourist destination, as it still is today. By 1853, tourists could reach Killarney by rail from Dublin. Visitors described local people flocking to sell them things. "About a score of them were in attendance as we reached a group of wretched hovels at the foot of the mountain; and the crowd grew like a snow-ball as it moved onwards," one wrote. A blind fiddler played for coins, women offered hand-knit stockings, and "girls with bare feet carrying goat's milk tormented us to buy of them. Very beringed handsome girls with smart shawls over their heads." The girls vended goat's milk and also *poitín*, homemade Irish whiskey. Thus comely maidens with bare feet became a designated tourist attraction, and local people, in a region with marginal land for agriculture, quickly found ways to meet expectations and commodify themselves as exotic spectacle. If they had shoes, they knew to take them off when tourists approached or for the photographer. It was so much a trade that by 1888 travelers were complaining about the local girls "who sell deplorable photographs of themselves and the huts in which they live," and suggesting "this pass of Dunloe would be very lovely if we could only be alone with Nature." The landscape of Ireland would be lovely, he suggested, without the Irish.[40]

In this way staging, props, and tourism reframe the problem of Ireland's poverty and violence: it's not the fact that someone like the Marquess of Conyngham controlled over two hundred square miles of Donegal, or that he only ever visited the land once, or that he casually demanded rents tenants could not pay and then had the law evict them. It's not that dispossessed people have to hustle an exoticized image of their own poverty. The problem lies instead in the racial character of the Irish, who are like Indians, Indians who were similarly dispossessed and similarly resented it and saw their entirely justifiable resentment cast as "savagery." The Celts are "natural savages, and regarded as such by all writers of all ages," insisted Thomas Price, "for they are savages—have been savages since the world began; and will be forever savages, while a separate people; that is, while themselves, and of unmixed blood."[41]

## The Famine and the Evictions

Most of the primary accounts quoted so far come from before 1847 and the calamity that Ireland suffered that year when virtually the entire potato crop succumbed to a blighting virus. The potato blight struck with supernatural, unnerving speed. A man might leave his fields in the morning and return in late afternoon to notice a sickly sweet smell, the sign of the blight, and find his entire crop turned black and rotting. It very quickly spread all over the island, and all those people described above, teetering on the edge of starvation, fell into its maw. In desperation people ate the pig or the cow whose butter paid the rent and were evicted. Witnesses recall seeing evicted tenants dead on the side of the road, their mouths full of the grass they tried to eat. They packed into workhouses, marked by shocking mortality rates and very quickly, mass graves to hold the accumulating dead. At least a million people died of starvation, others of disease or exposure. In the hardest hit areas, population dropped by half in two years.[42]

Even before the famine, British politicians had tried to address the extensive poverty by encouraging poor people to leave. By the 1840s, landlords, even those as thickly insulated from the reality of Irish life as Conyngham, had realized that they could make more money by ejecting the lesser peasants wholesale from their miserable cabins and subdivided plots and converting the land to cattle pasture. In 1838, economist and publisher Robert Torrens had asserted, "there is in Ireland a redundant population, which must continue to occasion the most frightful misery, unless maintained in workhouses, or assisted either to migrate to Great Britain, or to emigrate to the colonies" or to the United States. "A regulated and extensive system of emigration is the appropriate remedy for Ireland's social disease," he insisted. British administrators, Irish landlords, and Catholic tenants who held substantial land all seized on the opportunity to clear off the "surplus population" and rationalize production. Marginally productive potato plots that barely paid rent could make profit if you removed the people and set grazing cattle loose. "Every good tenant soon found out that a broken tenant being put out might mean a substantial gain to himself," wrote one landlord in self justification. Tenants holding more than thirty acres benefited from the famine as a result. The famine and the reorganization of landholding invigorated a stream of emigration that would continue for more than one hundred years.[43]

## White Chimpanzees

Oxford history professor Charles Kingsley toured County Mayo in 1860, when Patrick Melley was six years old, and saw how the famine and emigration had emptied the land. "The country which I came through yesterday moves me even to tears. It is a land of ruins and of the dead. You cannot conceive to English eyes the first shock of ruined cottages; and when it goes on to whole hamlets, the effect is most depressing." Kingsley described a land depopulated by famine and emigration, through "English eyes." He rationalized the empty landscape as a necessity. "I suppose it had to be done," he wrote, "with the people dying of starvation" even before the famine, "but what an amount of human misery each of those unroofed hamlets stands for!" "Still," he repeated, "it had to be done."[44]

Kingsley's empathy for the sorrowing land had decided limits. He described his journey north through Sligo to his wife. "I am haunted by the human chimpanzees I saw along that hundred miles of horrible country," he wrote. "I don't believe they are our fault," he told her, and added, "they are happier, better, more comfortably fed and lodged under our rule than they ever were" before the famine. "But to see white chimpanzees is dreadful." "If they were black, one would not feel it so much, but their skins, except where tanned by exposure, are as white as ours." This was the crux of his problem: they were enough like himself to evoke something like compassion. They had skins "as white as ours," but through "English eyes" they remained racially disturbing, "white chimpanzees," not quite human but not quite different enough to fully silence the pull of sympathy. Kingsley was an Oxford- and Cambridge-educated member of the establishment, a well-regarded novelist and private tutor to the Prince of Wales. He knew perfectly well that British settler colonialism had caused the bleak, empty landscape that brought him to tears, but he distanced himself from the reality by imagining the Irish as white chimpanzees, a different race. He later observed that "the differences of race are so great, that certain races, e.g., the Irish Celts, seem quite unfit for self-government." He tried to convince himself that "we did not do it," but rather something called "necessity" did it, in the passive voice: "It had to be done."[45]

As we saw in Virginia, racecraft doesn't really need skin color or even distinguishing physical features to work its sinister magic: it can roll on relentlessly in the complete absence of physical evidence for its claims. That Dempsey Hare looked white did not matter. Racecraft taught "English eyes" to see the Irish differently; merged with an idea of "necessity," it dried Kingsley's tears. Obvious physical differences make racecraft easier to work, but poverty and class can make do. The London satirical magazine *Punch* constantly racialized the Irish who had settled in London in 1862, referring, for example, to "two colonies of savages who have settled in [Gray's Inn Lane]: the Kerry Indians and the Tipperary Indians," and then blaming priestcraft: "Like the other natives of the Hibernian wilds, both these tribes of savages have their spiritual medicine-men, whom they call Fathers, and beneath whom they all alike grovel in the most abject prostration."

"A creature manifestly between the Gorilla and the Negro is to be met with in some of the lowest districts of London and Liverpool by adventurous explorers," wrote the English *Punch* that same year. "It comes from Ireland, whence it has contrived to migrate; it belongs in fact to a tribe of Irish savages: the lowest species of the Irish Yahoo. When conversing with its kind it talks a sort of gibberish. It is, moreover, a climbing animal, and may sometimes be seen ascending a ladder laden with a hod of bricks." Here the labor of Irish emigrants, displaced by the famine the British helped to create, serves to mark the laborer racially: he carries a hod of bricks because of his race, but it has nothing to do with what he looks like, unless you have been trained by racecraft.[46]

Patrick Melley would probably have looked like a gorilla or a "white chimpanzee" to the readers of *Punch*, or to the learned Professor Kingsley, although Patrick could read and write English, no small accomplishment and relatively rare. In Glenties and nearby Ardara, only 11.4 percent of males over five years old could write; "the figure for females over 5 was 6.7 per cent." Indeed, while Patrick could read and write, his sister Anne could not, and his other sisters, Bridget and Mary, were probably the same. The British were embarrassed by the lurid accounts of Irish poverty and ignorance, and Patrick likely went to the Lettermacaward National School, part of a system of what Americans would call public schools set up to teach the English language, the sciences, and English history. The National Schools, begun in 1831 and gradually spread across the island, taught lessons in English that ignored Irish history and culture altogether. Speaking Irish was prohibited and might bring punishment, and so while Patrick undoubtedly grew up hearing Irish, and speaking it at home, the language was being steadily erased. One school inspector, in 1850, noted that through the National Schools "we are quietly but certainly destroying the national legend, national music, and national language of the country." In 1850, four years before Patrick's birth, "around 1,500,000 westerners and south-westerners were to some degree bilingual and around 300,000 spoke only Irish." By the late nineteenth century, only about seventy-five thousand children still spoke Irish at home. "The English language came in greatly in my own time," Donegal weaver Charles McGlinchy recalled, "in the one generation Irish went away like the snow off the ditches."[47]

## *The Reorganization of Land*

In Donegal, as in other parts of Ireland, tenants before the famine often lived under a practice of land management loosely termed "Rundale." Under the "Rundale" system, groups of people, usually related to each other, clustered as tenants on a parcel of land that they divided into "infields," the good farming land, and "outfields," the land for grazing animals. Each year, a leader, sometimes termed the "king," would assign different families sections of the tenancy to farm. The rotating assignments assured that no one family got all the best land and perpetuated a sense of land held in common, not divided into individual plots. But as families had children, the plots under consideration grew smaller and more complicated. Tourists in west Donegal saw lots of "clachans," clusters of small huts and cabins in which all the inhabitants worked the same areas of land in turn. The cluster of Mallys that Griffith's valuation found in Madavagh, which may have included Patrick's family, probably reflects the practice of Rundale.[48]

In the famine's aftermath, English landlords accelerated the process of rationalizing and reorganizing landholdings. They resurveyed their lands and broke up the Rundale fields. "Squaring" or "striping" the fields involved plotting precise boundaries and assigning individual plots to individual people, for the length of the lease. Griffith's valuation shows Thomas Conolly as the landlord of many of the Melleys in the Madavagh area. An 1881 account of land reform in Ireland by the journalist Finlay Dun described the history of Conolly's Irish estates. "The Conolly estates were once the finest in the north-west of Ireland," it claimed. The management was "of the old fashioned, free and-easy, feudal type," the article continued, and "rents were low" and "irregularly paid." But "subdivision and subletting, and the introduction of squatters unchecked ran to a ruinous extent." Around the time of Patrick's birth, "Conolly vainly endeavored to reduce this overcrowding and double up his small holdings." "On many townlands the farms were squared or striped."[49]

Striping and squaring broke up communal ties, and if one family got exclusive access to good land, the less fortunate family might fall to eviction or see a lucky neighbor acquire a lease on the evicted man's land. Thanks to Griffith's valuation and the reorganization of land, "the ideal of individuals paying rates on property—rather than headmen representing groups of land—and householders—could now be realized." The breakup of Rundale imposed new kinds of boundaries on the landscape, a new way of understanding individuals and communities. "After the late divisions [of the land] the tenants were in spite of themselves within limits; a straight line and in nearly all cases a fence formed the boundary between man and man, and between them and the landlord's part, 'the reserves,' and everyone must now keep inside of his lines." Land occupancy went from communal to individualized, with each farmer assigned a specific plot.[50]

## The Molly Maguires

When English landlords broke up Rundale holdings and imposed new boundaries on land in Donegal, men calling themselves "Molly Maguires" or "the children of Molly Maguire" issued threatening notices and conducted violent attacks on local elites and their agents. Various legends describe an actual Molly Maguire as a woman wronged by landlords: Breandán Mac Suibhne points out that whatever the origin of the name, in predominantly Irish-speaking west Donegal it made a double entendre that amplified menace. "*Clann Mhailí*, Molly's Children, sounds like *clann mhallaithe*, cursed, infernal clan."[51]

"Molly Maguires," wrote Steuart Trench, "were generally stout, active young men dressed up in women's clothes, with faces blackened, or otherwise disguised; sometimes they wore crape over their countenances, sometimes smeared themselves in the most fantastic manner with burnt cork about their eyes, mouths and cheeks." In one 1847 instance in Donegal, "upwards of 100 people headed by a man attired in women's clothes had attacked the house of Patrick Doherty, a schoolmaster cum land agent." Like the Whiteboys or the traditions of mummers, the Molly Maguires had a carnivalesque quality: Molly Maguire attacks often took place at the time of traditional holidays. Elites tended to depict the Molly Maguires as a well-organized secret terrorist army and used the excuse of this possibly imaginary army to bring in more police, more officials, more administration, and to tighten their hold on the countryside. "In 1851, there had been 317 Constabulary officers" in County Donegal; "by 1861 there were 627." Patrick lived during this crackdown.[52]

The disruption of communal life in Madavagh came along with improvidence and foolishness on the part of landlord Thomas Conolly, living proof that intelligence and sagacity are not inherited. From his family's mansion, Castletown House, in County Kildare, to his home in London, Conolly was known for his lavish spending of his tenants' rents, and soon "horse-racing and gambling brought serious difficulties on the generous-hearted but improvident country family." Conolly, like others of his class, sympathized with the Confederacy in the US Civil War: he admired the fact that "they have their darkies as the lower & and the whites as completely an aristocratic class as ever the Helots and Athenians of old represented." He cooked up a scheme to make a fortune by running the Union blockade. The scheme failed, but Conolly toured the South in the last days of the Confederacy. His diary of the trip shows him flirting with ladies, fawning over Robert E. Lee, and blithely predicting Confederate victory even as Richmond fell around his ears. He enjoyed that degree of indifference to reality only vast piles of money can confer, but "running the American blockade is said to have sacrificed a quarter of a million sterling," and so by 1881 "large portions of the Conolly property ha[d] been sold in the Encumbered Estates Court."[53]

"Thank God a sale of a portion of the property will set you right," Conolly's brother wrote him in 1866. "I hope and trust" that from henceforth the "infernal word 'sale' . . . shall be banished from our family's vocabulary." But a year later, Conolly "resolved some of his Lettermacaward estate, occupying 5,500 acres in the barony of Boylagh, on Gweebarra Bay," by selling it to an English physician, Charles Deazeley. Those acres held families named Melley among "239 tenants." Most of those tenants paid two pounds a year or less in rent: only six paid more than ten pounds. "The estate was striped, which is the first stage of evolution from the ruder state of Rundale." "Several lots of about 100 acres of sandhills, rough pasture, bent grass, and rabbit warrens were held as common among ten to twenty adjacent tenants," the article continued: after "striping," the rents went up to twenty-five pounds or more an acre, an increase of well over twelve times.[54]

These were the lands I could see, windswept and sodden, from the top of Toome, the hill overlooking Lettermacaward and Madavagh to the south and the general region of the Rosses to the north. Patrick's landlord was either Conolly or Conyngham: from the top of the hill, I could see both men's Donegal property. These few sentences, describing the "striping" of poor lands held by tenants in common, the wreck of older patterns of community, or the increase in rents occasioned by Conolly's foolishness, could very well be the only specific reason I'll ever find for Patrick's departure. But the cause was general: when Patrick left for America in 1871, he followed one brother and three sisters, who had departed starting a decade earlier.[55]

He joined an exodus of men and women from west Donegal who went overwhelmingly to one place: the anthracite fields of Pennsylvania. "From the end of the American Civil War in 1865, the leave-takings had intensified," as one by one people "left for the mine patches." For those who stayed behind, the anthracite towns "Hazleton and Wilkes

Barre, Mauch Chunk and Summit Hill became more vividly imagined at their own firesides than towns in neighboring counties." In Summit Hill, Patrick would find thousands of Donegal people, and talk of the Molly Maguires, and as in Ireland, a ruling class convinced that the Irish were primitive, savage, and unfit for self-government.[56]

Were the Irish truly considered a different, nonwhite race? They were routinely compared to Africans and to Native Americans: they were regarded as innately savage and incapable of self-government; they were described as chimpanzees and gorillas and their poverty was displayed as an exotic natural fact for the reader's shuddering interest. At the same time, there is no equivalent to the "mulatto" in discourse about the Irish, and not much talk about "mixed blood" or miscegenation. The United Kingdom never passed laws saying "a person 1/8 Irish is Irish," while Virginia lawmakers kept revisiting the issue of what mixture made someone "black." The Irish were held in debt peonage but not enslaved. Religion and social class play a major role in anti-Irish sentiment, racecraft exaggerated or imagined physical difference and taught people to see it.

Thomas Conolly's ancestor William was born a Catholic in Donegal in 1662, the son of a mill owner. He converted to Protestant, went into law, and married a member of the Conyngham family. Those connections and skills made him the wealthiest man in Ireland, mostly from buying and selling the lands confiscated from Catholic Irish during the Williamite war, when Catholic James II lost his battle for the throne of England to William of Orange. British aristocrats sometimes mocked Conolly's low birth and profession as a lawyer: "this gentleman was lately an attorney, his father keeping an ale house in the north of Ireland, this being too notorious to be stifled," one British lord wrote. But conversion to Protestantism could make "race" irrelevant. Sir Richard Cox, historian and a contemporary of William Conolly, claimed: "we know no difference of nation but what is expressed by Papist and Protestant. If the most ancient natural Irishman be a Protestant, no man takes him for other than an English man." Cox imagined an "ancient natural Irishman" but also insisted it made no difference as long as the man forswore the pope: the natural Irishman would become an Englishman. Being the richest man in Ireland no doubt helped considerably. Slave owners, on the other hand, had no problem at all enslaving baptized Protestants, if they had African ancestry.[57]

But Protestants from Ireland remain a problem in American thinking about ancestry: Were they Irish or not? And if Irish, were they white? Well before the American Revolution, Anglican missionary Charles Woodmason complained bitterly about the "ignorant, mean, worthless, beggarly Irish Presbyterians," who he saw as invading the Carolinas. He called them "the Scum . . . and Refuse of Mankind" and "the worst Vermin on Earth," "the most lowest vilest Crew breathing," people who "delight[ed] in their . . . low, lazy, sluttish, heathenish, hellish Life." They were "run[ning] wild . . . like Indians," "as rude in their Manners as the Common Savages, and hardly a degree removed from them . . . differing in Nothing save Complexion."[58]

After Catholic famine immigrants started to arrive in large numbers, Americans embraced a term, "Scotch Irish," or "Scots Irish." The term aimed to make religious difference into a difference of "blood" or race. "Scotch Irish" refers more or less to "Protestants from Scotland who lived in the North of Ireland for a while and then moved to the US." In 1889, four years after Patrick married Hester Holland in Virginia, a group of Americans founded the Scotch-Irish Society to differentiate themselves from the "Irish Irish," insisting, "We are not a band of aliens, living here perforce and loving the other land across the sea. We belong to this land, and only recall the old that we may better serve the new, which is our own." In 1905, Thomas Dixon, published his best-selling novel *The Clansman*, celebrating the connection between the Scotch Irish clans and the Ku Klux Klan: he called the rise of the KKK "one of the most dramatic chapters in the history of the Aryan race." His Scotch Irish were Aryan, not Celtic. In an example of the enduring power of "blood" and race to substitute for history, no less a personage than Admiral James Webb, formerly secretary of defense and once a candidate for president, referred to the "Scots Irish" as a "race" in his 2004 book *Born Fighting*, and imagined "Scottish blood" flowing in his veins. He hoped to undo the tendency to "lump the Scots-Irish in with the Irish themselves," while admitting that "a considerable number of Scots-Irish immigrant families did carry Irish as well as Scottish blood, just as many of them also carried English blood." In a version of the Dempsey Hare story, he insisted on magical "blood" while acknowledging the reality that history hadn't respected those same boundaries.[59]

As de Beaumont noted, the Catholic Irish in Ireland were not free but not property, and so Frederick and Sophia, likely subtenants on someone else's lease, were literally of no account. The only record of their existence is their children's memories, tersely related to American officials. When Patrick Melley arrived in America, he had to navigate these competing ideas of what Irish meant, first in Pennsylvania, where "Scotch Irish" dominated the mining industry, then, improbably, in the farmland of Virginia, where he made an effort to "account for himself" by changing his name, marrying a Protestant woman descended from Ulster, and converting to Protestant, hoping to escape his ancestry.

# FOUR

# SUMMIT HILL

The colored Patrick Melley first enters history on the manifest of the steamship *Helvetia*, docking in New York City on June 7, 1871. Built in England and owned by the "National Steamship Line," the ship had sails and a steam-driven propeller. It was one of many making regular runs to New York from Liverpool or Queenstown (now Cobh) in County Cork. The National Line alone owned eleven ships that year, with one more under construction: their boats left Liverpool for New York twice weekly. *Helvetia*, under Captain George Griggs, sailed on May 20, so Patrick spent over two weeks at sea. He may have left from Derry, on the eastern border of Donegal, a point of departure common enough to have inspired songs. But he might have taken a smaller ship to Liverpool, or perhaps *Helvetia* made a stop in Derry. Advertisements for the National Line in American newspapers offered "prepaid steerage tickets from Liverpool, Queenstown, Londonderry [Derry] and Glasgow, $32 currency."[1]

### The Bustling Business of Emigration

Emigration from Ireland and England was a nonstop business. *Helvetia* carried 722 passengers; that same day *Java*, sailing under the Cunard line, also unloaded more than seven hundred passengers. A narrow majority of *Helvetia*'s passengers came from Ireland, along with migrants from England, Sweden, Norway, France, Holland, Poland,

Germany, and Americans returning home. According to the *Annual Report of the Commissioners of Emigration of the State of New York*, the year 1869 saw over 257,000 arrivals. It was a typical day in New York Harbor when Patrick stepped off the boat.[2]

*Harper's Weekly* explained immigration to a national audience in 1874. "They come from every part of Europe," the article asserted, "flying from hopeless poverty and repression, to seek in the New World the freedom, prosperity, and happiness denied them in the Old." After this tone of welcoming clichés, the author described the steerage class, saying conditions had improved over the last decade, if "judged by the popular standard of what is due the poor and ignorant classes in return for value given by them." He added, "a great amount of discomfort among the emigrants arises from their own ignorance and life-long habits. Many of these poor people have lived in hovels in comparison with which the steerage cabin of a steam-ship is a palace." This probably described young Patrick. By 1871, the transatlantic passage was much safer than it had been, and conditions on ship were more closely regulated, but steerage passengers were still relegated to cramped shelf-like bunks in a windowless hold. It must have been an extraordinary voyage for a seventeen-year-old, alone, alternatively exhilarated, anxious, and bored for long stretches in the crowded steerage.[3]

In New York on that Friday in June of 1871, *Helvetia's* passenger manifest listed "Pat Millay," a solitary nineteen-year-old laborer from Ireland. But two months earlier, a twenty-two-year-old "Ptk Malley" had arrived on *City of Brussels*: in early May, *City of Washington* had brought a nineteen-year-old Pat Malley into port from Ireland. On June 27, another Irish Pat Malley, seventeen, steamed into New York on *Nevada*. A month later, on July 3 of 1871, Patrick Melly, also a laborer from Ireland, also nineteen, disembarked from *Oceanic*. All these ships steamed from Liverpool, with human cargoes including five ambiguous Melleys. As late as 1871, individualization was still incomplete.[4]

In 1887, as part of the process of becoming a citizen, my great-great-grandfather Patrick traveled to the Nansemond County Court and swore that he had arrived in New York City on the seventh day of June 1871. On that same legal declaration, he gave his birthday as February 15, 1854, which would have made him seventeen when he arrived, not nineteen, and he gave his name in Virginia as "Patrick O'Malley." He had entered into a new world of record keeping. Can we assume the "Pat Millay" of June 7 is the same man?

An 1890 cartoon from *Harper's Weekly* (figure 4.1) shows the increased demand for documents of identity, and the Irish immigrant's lack of records and even comprehension of the demand. An Irish immigrant is trying to cash a check at the bank. He has stepped up to the teller's window and has announced himself as "Malone." The teller says, "I can't help it if your name is Malone: you can't get the money on that check unless you are identified." Malone says he will go get a friend, Jim Maginnis, and Maginnis will make an introduction. Malone has confused "identity," the legal record of discrete existence, with "introduction," an artifact of the social realm. The artist used stereotypes of Irish buffoonery to convey that by 1890, twenty years after Patrick arrived, more precise records of identity were routinely required.

In genealogy, the entire point is knowing which specific Pat is my ancestor, but it's very difficult to know that because they aren't effectively individualized in records. From a historian's perspective, the answer might be "who cares?" It's likely these various Melleys were all from Donegal, and *all* related at some level, if you go back far enough. The important thing to history is less the individual person than the social and political forces, the settler colonialism and land "reforms," that in this case pushed five young single Irish laborers with more or less the same name to arrive in New York within a few months of each other.

## *Tracking Immigrants*

By the time he started for citizenship in Virginia, in 1887, Patrick had grasped the demand for increased precision in records, and he furnished the Nansemond Court with exact dates that may or may not

FERTILE IN EXPEDIENTS.

PAYING TELLER. "I tell you I can't help it if your name is Malone: you can't get the money on that check unless you are identified."
MALONE. "Hould a bit, wid ye! Oi'll bring Jim Maginnis in an' inthroduce ye to him, an' begorra he kin oidentifoy us both. Phat name, sir?"

*Figure 4.1. Harper's Weekly*, February 1, 1890, 92, courtesy of HathiTrust.

have been accurate: it's impossible to tell, because Ireland kept no records of his birth. While it might seem unlikely he would remember the exact date seventeen years later, it's even more unlikely that he would have randomly hit on a date that happened to include "Pat Milay" arriving. But why would he expect anyone to check? Did he imagine the local clerks in Virginia mailing to New York to check passenger manifests? Was he in some degree intimidated by the judge and the clerk when it came to citizenship? The date might have stuck in his mind as a moment of transition, the beginning of a new life in a new country. But if he remembered the arrival date correctly, he either made up the date of his birth, or told officials at Castle Garden he was two years older than he was, or he shaved two years off his age in Virginia. Researchers in family history want a degree of precision that officials in 1871 showed no interest in, but all these Melleys entered a world of increased record keeping—not so much precise records of individuals, at least not at first, but aggregated records of huddled masses, ostensibly yearning to breath free.

The State of New York in 1871 produced detailed statistics about immigrants arriving at Castle Garden, the immigration processing center at the foot of Manhattan. It tracked what countries immigrants came from and noted that "the alien emigration of the past year, as contrasted with that of 1869, shows a falling off of 45,369." Within that number, they thought it important to record that "the number of German emigrants arrived last year was 72,350, being less by 27,255 than that of the year 1869," while the number of Irish emigrants arriving in 1870 was 65,168," 1,036 less than the year before.[5]

They told the legislature that "the number of persons who have received relief from the commission in the year 1870 was 71,579, being about 1,700 less than the number so relieved in 1869." It checked them for illness or insanity and if necessary referred them to a nearby hospital on Ward's Island. The hospital, in 1869, cared for 13,911 people and recorded 447 births and 497 deaths. All these numbers show the state's increased interest in aggregating and tracking data about who was coming. They needed this information partly for budgeting, so they would know how much money might be required for the next year, but also we have already seen, because of a general interest in the racial makeup of the population. Were the people coming over in such large numbers capable of life in an industrial republic?[6]

## The Irish as Racial Other in America

Americans echoed English claims about the alleged racial character of the Irish. Joseph Simms, in *Nature's Revelations of Character*, 1873, argued, "we find quite as much variation among different nations as between so-called different races, why not call every nationality a distinct race?" The Europeans, he said, may be divided thus:

| | |
|---|---|
| English | Cockney or Devonshire |
| Scotch | Highland or Celtic and Teutonic |
| Russians | or Slavs |
| Germans | or Teutonic |
| Hollanders | or Dutch |
| French | or Celts |
| Irish | " |
| Welsh | " |
| Danes | or Scandinavians |
| Spaniards | or Iberian and Celts |

Like the theorists mentioned in chapter 3, he made the "celts" into distinct subraces.[7]

In 1871, *New Physiognomy, or Signs of Character, as Manifested through Temperament and External Forms* stressed a fundamental difference of racial character between the Irish and Anglo-Americans, comparing Florence Nightingale, a real person, to someone it made up out of stereotypes, "Bridget McBruiser." It similarly compared the profile of an upper-class Protestant English woman to a "bog trotter" and "Princess Alexandra" to someone it imagined named "Sally Muggins."[8] The Irish are depicted as "prognathous": their mouths and jaws

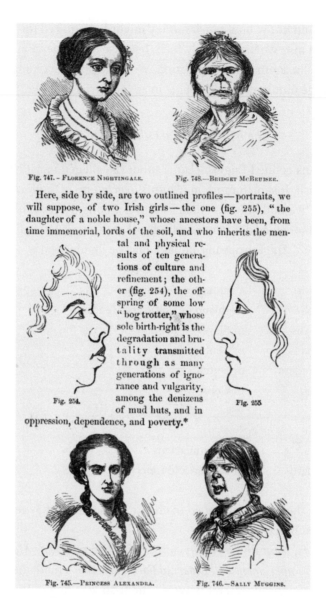

Fig. 747. – FLORENCE NIGHTINGALE.    Fig. 748.—BRIDGET MCBRUISER.

Here, side by side, are two outlined profiles — portraits, we will suppose, of two Irish girls — the one (fig. 255), "the daughter of a noble house," whose ancestors have been, from time immemorial, lords of the soil, and who inherits the mental and physical results of ten generations of culture and refinement; the other (fig. 254), the offspring of some low "bog trotter," whose sole birth-right is the degradation and brutality transmitted through as many generations of ignorance and vulgarity, among the denizens of mud huts, and in oppression, dependence, and poverty.*

Fig. 254.    Fig. 255.

Fig. 745.—PRINCESS ALEXANDRA.    Fig. 746.—SALLY MUGGINS.

*Figure* 4.2. Images from Samuel Roberts Wells, *New Physiognomy, or Signs of Character, as Manifested through Temperament and External Forms and Especially in the Human Face Divine* (S. R. Wells, 1871), 188, 537, 536. Internet Archive.

thrust forward. Prognathism would identify the Irish in stereotype for next one hundred years.

Arriving in 1871, Patrick might have seen copies of *Miss Columbia's Public School* in the bookstores. The anti-Catholic fable, published that year, had illustrations by Thomas Nast, the foremost political cartoonist of his day and no fan of the Irish. The plot involved "Miss Columbia" teaching students about the virtues of the Republic, which manage to include both "no established church" and the Protestant Bible as its foundations. The Irish pupils, perhaps understandably confused, ignore the lessons, fight, and try to take the Bible out of school, literally. Nast drew his Irish pupil, struggling with a comically oversized Bible, as both ape-like and vaguely "African," with "nappy" hair and a

" Put that Bible back !"

*Figure 4.3.* Charles Henry Pullen and Thomas Nast, *Miss Columbia's Public School, or, Will It Blow Over?* (New York: Francis B. Felt & Co., 1871), 36, courtesy of HathiTrust.

broad nose. He has the "prognathous" features regarded as both Irish and a sign of racial inferiority.

Nast consistently drew Irish characters as prognathous and racially ambiguous, as in figure 4.4, showing an Irish politician. The harp on his desk and the Catholic texts leaning against it indicate his nationality, but his features mark him as racially "other" to the white men in the room.[9]

As we saw in the brief mention of Irish runway servants in chapter 1, Americans had often singled out the Irish as particularly low and unworthy and used color to express their bad character. The Irish were low in status, and the ads expressed their low status by seeing them as black, brown, or dark. In a gesture to racecraft, their class difference was "seen" as physical difference. Ralph Waldo Emerson saw that in Concord, "in Irish districts men deteriorated in size and shape, the nose sunk, the gums were exposed, with diminished brain and brutal form." With the condescension characteristic of libertarians whose mothers do their laundry, Henry David Thoreau imagined one of his Irish neighbors as a sort of dull monster, having "wading webbed bog-trotting feet," "born to be poor," doomed to poverty, "not to rise in this world, he nor his posterity."[10]

Thomas Henry Huxley in 1870 imagined a difference between what he called the "Xanthochroi, or fair whites" who, "on the south and west" of Europe, come into contact and mix "with the 'Melanochroi,' or 'dark whites.'" Huxley saw this "dark type" in "many Irishmen, Welshmen, and Bretons, by Spaniards, South Italians, Greeks, Armenians, Arabs, and high-caste Brahmins." Irish people were perhaps a different kind of white person, more closely related to the Mediterranean or India than to England.[11]

In 1864, David Croly published *Miscegenation: The Theory of the Blending of the Races, Applied to the American White Man and Negro*. Croly hoped to peel Irish voters away from Lincoln and the Republican Party by claiming Lincoln promoted racial intermarriage, an accusation Lincoln had been dodging since he first entered politics. The Irish "are a more brutal race and lower in civilization than the Negro,"

THE CHAIRMAN OF THE HANGING COMMITTEE.

*Figure 4.4.* Charles Henry Pullen and Thomas Nast, *Miss Columbia's Public School, or, Will It Blow Over?* (New York: Francis B. Felt & Co., 1871), 18, courtesy of HathiTrust.

Croly wrote. "The Irish are coarse-grained, revengeful, unintellec-
tual, with very few of the finer instincts of humanity." "Take an equal
number of negroes and Irish from among the lowest communities of
the city of New York, and the former will be found far superior to the
latter in cleanliness, education, moral feelings, beauty of form and
feature, and natural sense." "Miscegenation" would thus improve the
Irish, who are "thin-legged, pot-bellied, with mouth projected, head
sloped, nostril distended; in short they exhibit all the characteristics
by which we have marked the lowest type of the negro. The blending
of the Irish in this country with the negro will be a positive gain to the
former." This is racecraft in process, trying to imagine physical difference into "race." It's clear Irish people were seen as different, but what
did that difference mean? We can't simply say "the Irish were considered nonwhite" because it's also clear the Irish rarely if ever appeared
as racially "other" in law.[12]

In New York, and across the US, Irish immigrants and African
Americans often held the same jobs and lived in the same neighborhoods. A substantial literature describes the close relations, antago-
nisms, competitions, partnerships, and brawls between Irish and African American working-class people. In cities and waterfronts, what
Christopher Smith calls a "creole synthesis" emerged in US culture,
blending language, dance, and musical styles. Much of American ur-
ban culture at mid-nineteenth century came from and involved Irish
and African Americans and stereotypes of both.[13]

But as in England, the idea of the Irish as savage Indians persisted.
In 1871, Mark Twain published a short story, "A Visit to Niagara" in
which the naive protagonist goes to Niagara Falls, hoping to see ste-
reotypical Indians he's read about in fiction. But each group he meets
responds in an increasingly agitated Irish brogue—"An' it is mesilf,
Dennis Hooligan, that ye'd be takin' for a dirty Injin!"—and finally
they throw him off the falls. Dying, he tells the doctor, "it is an awful
savage tribe of Indians that do the bead work and moccasins for Niagara Falls, doctor. Where are they from?" The doctor replies, "Lim-
erick, my son."[14]

It's easy to find examples of drunken, ape-like, stupid, and violent Irish people in nineteenth-century newspapers and magazines. Nast alone published dozens of them: angry, skulking, menacing, animalistic. In theaters, the bumbling and comically bellicose "stage Irishman," with his ragged antique clothing and incomplete grasp of English, vied for popularity with minstrel show stereotype Jim Crow, the bumbling, comic and comically ragged African American field hand who similarly mangled the English language. But it's also easy to find demeaning stereotypes of the Chinese, or the Germans, or later the Italians and the Jews and every other immigrant group that took its place on the lower ranks of the economic food chain. When we see these caricatures, we see not that the Irish suffered uniquely, but rather racecraft at hard work, trying to turn differences of class and culture into "race," and ranking the Irish with the "melanochroi," white but differently white. In the nineteenth century, the spells of racecraft still had some conjuring power when it came to light-skinned immigrants in general, and again racecraft was about teaching people how to see. As Matthew Jacobson put it, "an earlier generation of Americans saw Celtic, Hebrew, Anglo-Saxon, or Mediterranean physiognomies where today we see only subtly varying shades of a mostly undifferentiated whiteness." Caricatures taught people what they were supposed to see when they looked at Irish immigrants. In figure 4.5, we see images comparing Irish people to apes almost into the twentieth century.[15]

It's easy to overstate this. In *Three Years among the Working-Classes in the United States*, published in 1865, James Burn argued that "Irishmen are not less industrious than Germans, but they lack the caution and frugality of the latter, and their easily excited feelings and impulsive nature frequently lead them into difficulties." Even so, he continued, "In New York there is scarcely a situation of honor or distinction, from the chief magistrate down to the police, that is not filled by a descendant of some Irishman who lived in savage hatred of England" back in the old country. It was possible to imagine Irish people as racially distinct but assimilated.[16]

Searching newspapers for the phrase "the Irish race" from 1874 to

RATHER SENSITIVE.
Boss. "What's the matter, Pat? You're not leavin'?"
Pat. "Oi am that."
Boss. "Why, ain't the work and the wages all right?"
Pat. "The wur-ruk is all roight, an' the wages is all roight, an' yer not so bad yersilf, but oi'll not wur-ruk on the same job wid a thing that looks as much loike a munkey as *that!*"

*Figure 4.5. Harper's Weekly, May 23, 1891, 387, courtesy of HathiTrust.*

1888 nearly always turns up not denunciations of the Irish, but Catholic clerics making hortatory speeches about the distinctive greatness of the Irish race, or Fenians calling for Irish independence. The idea of the Irish as a race could work in multiple ways. As in Ireland, it could anchor claims for independence based on an idea of racial difference. Irish people were stigmatized, and the tendency to stigmatize would persist over the next two decades, but other groups were stigmatized as well. Hostility to the Irish did not stop them from playing an out-sized role in politics, the police force, and the fire companies; and they worked everywhere as laborers.[17]

## Getting to Work

Starting in 1868, Castle Garden had established a Labor Exchange, which called attention to the entire point of allowing immigrants in the first place: cheap labor. Immigrants right off the boat could go to the Labor Exchange and find employers seeking their specific skills, or more likely grunt labor for digging or loading. "During the past year employment has been procured for 34,955 emigrants, nearly 4,000 more than the previous year," the *Annual Report* for 1869 noted. The Labor Exchange was an early example of a very modern desire, a com-prehensive national "database" — the word would not be coined till the 1950s — that connected employers with laborers. "The success of this department," concluded the *Report*, "is doubtless attributable to its connections with every part of the country, which enables it to ob-tain a complete survey of the whole labor market." If social scientists were trying to identify the physiognomy of the Irish race, they were also working to systematize and rationalize labor markets.[18]

Immigration officials had detailed aggregate records of "the masses" but no reliable way, as above, to distinguish five different Pat Mellys/Malleys arriving in the summer of 1871: no fingerprints, no birth certificates, no passports. The free Negro registers had tried to fix one body to one name, but the names on passenger manifests are nonstandard, imprecise, and possibly "wrong," not yet "sticky." His ambiguous individual status mirrors his ambiguous racial status. Pat-rick would later exploit this lack of precision to escape one life and start another.

I imagine him arriving at Castle Garden, passing inspection, and asking, in a heavy Donegal brogue, if they had a message for "Pat Millay." Castle Garden's directors reported that "during the last year

9,723 letters have been received for emigrants, containing money, railroad tickets, or information, and 5,524 telegraphic messages were sent from the office in Castle Garden, and 1,563 messages received." Certainly Patrick might have found one of those messages waiting or a letter with tickets or cash. They would have needed to ask him who it was from, to make sure he was the right man, and he most likely told him it was from one of his siblings already living in Summit Hill or Coaldale.

How else could he afford the cost of the trip across the ocean? He grew up in an area of Donegal, recall, where people struggled to pay two pounds a year in rent; he might have been the Patrick Melley who had spent five weeks in the Glenties workhouse, destitute, just four years earlier. In 1871, an unskilled laborer in the US might make $500 to $600 a year; the average for an unskilled worker in Great Britain was about half that; in Ireland, lower still. The ticket would have been from two-thirds to more than three-quarters of an American worker's monthly pay. It's also possible a landlord anxious to clear out his low-rent tenants offered Patrick a subsidy to leave. Especially in the decade of the famine, landlords and workhouses had subsidized passage to America for paupers or less desirable tenants. As late as 1860, Conyngham's Boylagh estate agent recorded sixteen pounds going to "pay the passage of the McElwes to America."[19]

But it seems far more likely that siblings who had gone to America ahead of him sent him a ticket for the sea voyage, and then either met him in New York or furnished him a ticket to Pennsylvania. Irish immigrants sent over $200 million back to Ireland between 1869 and 1900. In New York they used the Emigrant Savings Bank, which made remittance payments relatively easy. An 1880 illustration (figure 4.6) shows Irish Americans withdrawing money to send back home. The artist mostly avoided the usual stereotypes and depicted a respectable Irish middle class.

The siblings who left Donegal before him—his brother Cornelius, his three sisters Ann, Mary, and Bridget—might have met him at Castle Garden. All four now made their living in the coal fields. But alone or in company, Patrick most likely boarded the Central of New Jersey line for the roughly 125-mile trip to the town of Mauch Chunk,

NEW YORK CITY.—IRISH DEPOSITORS OF THE EMIGRANT SAVINGS BANK WITHDRAWING MONEY TO SEND TO THEIR SUFFERING RELATIVES IN THE OLD COUNTRY.—SEE PAGE 27.

*Figure 4.6.* Depictions of the Irish were by no means all negative. This March 1880 illustration shows well-dressed emigrants lining up to send money home. Library of Congress, Prints and Photographs Division.

Pennsylvania, now also known as "Jim Thorpe." The town marks the eastern end of one of three anthracite ridges that run roughly east to west across Pennsylvania: local signage describes the region as "the Panther Valley." Anthracite mining continues there today in the towns of Summit Hill, Lansford, Coaldale, and Tamaqua. Nathan Shaler, later a Harvard professor of geology, described "a naturalist's trip" through the region around Tamaqua in 1873, not long after Patrick arrived.

### The Anthracite Valley

What Shaler saw displeased him: "scanty forests robbed of every tree which could be used in shoring up the galleries of the mines": "gnarled and worthless pines spread their ragged limbs against the sky line of the hills." The brooks, he added, "are turbid with the waters pumped from the innumerable shafts," and the water meanders around "enormous piles of black waste dumped into their valleys." He described "squalid little wooden hamlets" and "files of grimy sheds. "On every hand run the coal rail ways down which pour unending trains of coal."

The miners he called "shapeless, hulking fellows, shuffling over the ground . . . their clothing sordid, their faces blear-eyed and dull. Whiskey has made its mark on nearly every face, visible even through the soot which hides almost every other expression of their sinister countenances." Shaler had been camping and sought comfort in the remaining woods. They "seemed wild enough, but they were everywhere cut by paths which are traversed by the mine people on their way to and fro. We recoiled at the prospect of camping among these unpleasant-looking neighbors." Patrick, who seems to have settled in Summit Hill, would have been one of those "mine people," the "unpleasant-looking neighbors" cutting paths through the woods.[20]

Shaler wanted to go camping, but Patrick wanted work. Stepping off the train in Mauch Chunk, he would have seen things differently: a thriving industrial river town, with barges and train cars departing constantly. He would have seen carloads of coal come racing down the Switchback Railroad, the second railroad ever built in the US and famous in its day. From Mauch Chunk, mules and later steam-driven cables pulled empty cars nine miles up to Summit Hill, a gain in elevation of over nine hundred feet. There men loaded them with coal and sent them back down, powered by gravity. Very likely Patrick would have ridden one of the empty cars to the top.

A year after he arrived, a new conventional railroad reached the town of Lansford, just below Summit Hill, and local entrepreneurs converted the Switchback Railroad to a roller coaster–like tourist attraction, rattling down the nine miles of haphazardly graded hill at fifty miles an hour. Summit Hill had a bandstand and an armory and hotels where people riding the Switchback railroad could stay. It had mines, and also a mine fire that started burning in 1859 and continued burning underground till the 1920s, when strip mining finally exposed the coal seam. Tourists came to experience the burning mine, the smoke rising through the ground, the sulfur smell, the glowing coal visible on moonless nights in deep crevices.[21]

Pennsylvania's southernmost anthracite region originally fostered small coal operators who ran individual mines, some of which started at places where surface erosion had revealed a coal seam. By the time Patrick arrived, tunnels and lifts took men hundreds of feet down. Miners, mostly Welsh or Irish Protestants, did the skilled digging at the coal face, deciding where to dig and where to place explosive charges. They earned a relatively high salary and controlled the terms and pace of their work. The actual miner might just work a few hours a day, setting off a dynamite charge that filled the tunnel with smoke, dust, and large chunks of coal and rock blasted from the face of the seam. Mine *laborers* stayed below to hack at the broken face and shovel the raw coal into rail cars. The coal came out of the ground as small boulders and large chunks, too big to easily burn. Once it left the mine, it was dumped onto conveyors that brought it to the top of the "breaker building," typically a large building up to ten stories tall. Machines crushed it into smaller pieces, and steel grids of different sizes sorted it. The sized coal then went down narrow chutes. "Breaker boys" sat across the chutes picking out shale. Grown men tended the pumps that kept ever-present water from flooding the mine or the ventilators that kept poisonous, explosive gasses at bay, or they built and maintained the rails on which mine cars and miners traveled up and down. They fed the steam engines that drove machinery. They went down into the mine and loaded big chunks of coal into cars or installed timbering to keep the mine from collapsing. It was dirty, dangerous, low-paying work, in the tunnels with the rats, work that choked the lungs with dust and meant that for six months a year you only rarely saw the sun.[22]

Patrick might have lived in Summit Hill, but he also might have lived on a "patch," one of the clusters of rudely built shacks that formed near actual mine entrances. In 1875, four years after he arrived, a mob of forty men broke into a boarding house in "Wiggans Patch" owned by

Margaret O'Donnell, from Gweedore in Donegal. They murdered her son and her pregnant daughter. Patrick had entered a violent world.

## Ireland in the Coal Fields

Small operators who worked the region before the Civil War lacked the capital to dig deep or buy the equipment needed to process the coal at a large scale, and increasingly corporate ownership controlled the Schuylkill and Carbon County mines. As large operators gained control, miners bought supplies at a company store, which deducted the costs from their pay, and increasingly rented their homes from the company. The Reading Railroad, led by Franklin Gowen, the child of a Protestant Irish immigrant himself, set out to establish a monopoly over the region, buying small mines and local real estate till his Pennsylvania Coal and Iron Company owned virtually every aspect of the regional anthracite market: the coal face, the mine towns, the stores where miners shopped, the rails and rail cars on which the coal traveled, and the wharves and docks where men in Philadelphia auctioned it off.

Mine workers resisted this monopolization in many ways. They resorted, as in Ireland, to prepolitical violence, beating or killing mine supervisors and foremen or damaging company property. In the 1860s, men attacking mine operatives sometimes called themselves "Molly Maguires" as they had in Donegal. The Wiggans Patch massacre targeted the sons of Margaret O'Donnell, suspected of being a Molly Maguire. But miners also began to form unions, hoping to gain a monopoly over labor power as Gowen had built a monopoly over production. The Workingmen's Benevolent Association managed to combine more than thirty thousand Welsh and Irish workers: in 1875, it called a strike. Gowen determined to fight this threat with every means at his disposal, and though the WBA deplored any acts of violence, Gowen and his allies in the press increasingly emphasized what he termed a sinister, secret conspiracy of thuggish murderers, imported from Catholic Ireland to destroy the American way of life, the "Molly Maguires."

For good and for ill, it would have been a familiar world for Patrick. Town names like Tamaqua and Mauch Chunk were nonsense sounds replacing names the Lenape had used before colonization, the same way English colonialism replaced "Maigh Dabhcha" with "Madavagh." Not just rumors of the Molly Maguires, which he would have heard back in Donegal, and not just his siblings nearby: names from Donegal were everywhere. He could hear the accents, the Irish language stories. "Peasant superstitions — 'hobgoblins, ghosts, witches, fairies, banshees and many signs and omens' — were also transplanted wholesale to the hills of Pennsylvania." Oral histories of the region recall Irish music in saloons and *céilí*, house dances. Starting in the 1880s, Father Daniel J. Murphy began collecting *sean-nós* (old-style) songs in the anthracite towns and in Philadelphia, songs in the Irish language. His collection of more than one thousand songs includes three people named Melley singing in Irish in Coaldale and Summit Hill. The Irish language preserved memories and kept secrets. The social world centered, for women, around church and boardinghouse and *shebeen*, private homes where one could find a congenial drink, and for men, around saloons and pubs and the Ancient Order of Hibernians.[23]

The AOH offered an Irish Catholic counterpart to the Masons, a fraternal secret society that combined what we might term "networking" with a social safety net or emigrant aid society. It began in New York City and quickly grew to influence in Schuylkill and Carbon Counties. The AOH endorsed political candidates, invariably Democrats, and it opposed abolitionism and, during the Civil War, the draft. Irish Americans rejected abolition for the most part: they worried about competition for unskilled labor jobs but also quickly grasped that in the US, the first step on the path of advancement almost invariably lay across the backs of people with African ancestors.

The AOH had a complicated relationship to the Catholic Church, which resented secret societies for claiming loyalties the church perceived as due to itself. The church in turn had to stave off the constant and intense attacks of anti-Catholic nativists, who dominated newspapers in the coal region and kept up a constant stream of invective about "Papist mummery." "You are the minority," one newspaper editor warned Catholics: "you are in the power of the Protestants, and must ever remain so, as long as you remain in this country."[24]

When Patrick Melley encountered the kind of hostility to the Catholic Irish he had known in Ireland, membership in the AOH and the church offered him some protection and a community of people very much like himself—so much like himself in fact that between 1867 and 1878, six different men named Patrick Melley or Mally married in Summit Hill, Pennsylvania. Indeed, Patrick's older sister Mary Melley in 1875 married a man named . . . Patrick Melley. Their sister Anna witnessed the marriage. The Irish of Summit Hill came disproportionately from the same region of Ireland and carried not just Irish surnames, but Irish customs, practices, and beliefs with them in the Pennsylvania mountains, including the tradition of antielite violence.[25]

### The Molly Maguires

In 1863, shortly after Halloween, men with blackened faces broke into the home of mine supervisor George Smith and shot him dead. The *New York Times* and other papers termed it "Molly Maguires on the rampage." In December 1871, not long after Patrick Melley's arrival, someone assassinated Morgan Powell, a mine company foreman, as he walked along the streets of Summit Hill; in 1875, the Wiggans Patch murders occurred, possibly in retaliation for Molly Maguire actions. But any violence might be attributed to the Molly Maguires, however tenuous the link. "Elsewhere in the coal country the outlawry is great," newspapers claimed. In Clarion County, 250 miles away and closer to Pittsburgh, allegedly ten Mollys "took possession of the Evangelical church in the township of Farmington." They refused to let parishioners leave. The next night they returned "and made an indiscriminate and murderous attack upon the worshippers with pistols, clubs, bludgeons (a favorite weapon with the Molly Maguires), stones and other death-dealing things." The only alleged connection to the

Molly Maguires in this case was the commonly used weapons. Accusations of criminal violence undermined unionization, and in July of 1875 the "long strike" called by the Workingmen's Benevolent Association failed, crushing the Union. Mine workers had been reduced to foraging in the woods for food. Gowen's victory initiated another wave of violence. In that year two men assassinated John Jones, holding the same position as Morgan Powell at the same mine.[26]

Between 1868 and 1878, at least sixteen people were killed, amid a much larger number of smaller crimes of assault, sabotage, and destruction of property. Gowen blamed these crimes on the Ancient Order of Hibernians and what he regarded as its militant wing, the Molly Maguires. He produced as evidence "coffin notices," warnings allegedly sent to mine officials by the Mollies, and he wrote endlessly about the Molly Maguire menace, with help of newspapers eager to please the man who owned virtually the entire southern anthracite field. This too must have felt familiar to Patrick—a tenant on land someone else owned, under a police force beholden to the landlord, in a political and legal system stacked against the Irish Catholic laborer.

Did the Molly Maguires ever exist as described by the mine owners and their allies in the press? There is no doubt that men using the term "Molly Maguire" carried out acts of violence against mine property and mine officials, following traditions brought from Ireland. But other examples of "Molly Maguire" violence look more like disorganized retaliations against a hated foreman, interethnic rivalry between Irish and Welsh or English miners, or sometimes just brawling. The Ancient Order of Hibernians existed as a formal organization, but "the Molly Maguires themselves left virtually no evidence of any actual existence, let alone their aims and motivation," concluded Kevin Kenny. They existed mostly in the fervid testimony of Franklin Gowen and the men he hired to destroy the burgeoning miner's union, a "moral panic" ginned up to legitimize official violence. In Pennsylvania, in the 1870s, the campaign against the Molly Maguires figured the Irish as savage, tribal, primitive, superstitious, and hostile to democracy., The Mollies "objects and aims sink to the level of the meanest animal

instinct of wreaking revenge for wrongs," capable of the "most sicken-
ing wholesale assassinations that the heart of savage ever conceived."[27]

These assumptions and rhetorical devices allowed Franklin Gowen
to establish a private army, the Coal and Iron Police, to enforce the law
as he saw it. "Like other things in Pennsylvania," wrote the reformer
Henry George of the coal fields, "the coal and iron police are sugges-
tive of Ireland." "Their functions on the coal estates are a combination of those performed for the Irish landlords by the 'rent warner,'
the 'process server' . . . and the Royal Irish Constabulary. They are the
spies, informers, collectors, writ-servers, and guards of their employers, licensed always to carry arms and make arrests."[28]

Gowen also hired the Pinkerton Detective Agency to infiltrate the
Molly Maguires. Allan Pinkerton, born in Scotland, had worked as a
spy for the Union Army during the Civil War. After the war, for a large
fee, the self-promoting Pinkerton could supply gangs of replacement
workers to any company facing a strike or operatives who could infiltrate a union. Calling them "detectives" helped link unions to crimi-
nality in the public imagination.[29]

Pinkerton hired an Irish immigrant, James McParlan, to go "under-
cover" in the anthracite region. McParlan gave much of the testimony
against men accused of being Molly Maguires, and historians have long
suspected him of provoking violent acts he then blamed on others. In
1878, Pinkerton published a highly fictionalized account of McParlan's
activities, *The Molly Maguires and the Detectives*, which Arthur Conan
Doyle would later use as the basis for the Sherlock Holmes detective
novel *The Valley of Fear*. In the anthracite valleys we see race, individualism, and detection coming together.

## Detection and Imposture

Edgar Allen Poe often gets the credit for inventing the detective story,
with his 1841 story "The Murders in the Rue Morgue" and two subsequent stories featuring his detective, Auguste Dupin. Poe's detective used keen powers of observation and deductive reasoning to see

through the surface of things and find the truth. Like the free Negro registers and the state's interest in labor statistics, detective fiction imagined a more legible world. In Donegal there was little need to standardize identity: people knew their neighbors and custom governed their interactions. A rigid class system and poverty foreclosed economic mobility. Detective stories made little sense in that world: people might lie about small matters, but for the most part no one could be other than they seemed; there was little to detect. Detective stories make sense in a world of strangers, where ambitious individuals constantly pretend to be something they are not in hope that by pretending, they might make their dream come true. What if they dream evil, criminal dreams? The detective sees through pretense, establishes individual identity, and restores order.[30]

In his book Pinkerton changed McParlan's name to McKenna. Detectives in fiction typically imitated the thing they aimed to "detect." McKenna imitates, through careful study, the customs, speech, and clothing of the Irish miners and "sings, fights, and dances his way into popularity." At times McKenna himself seemed confused about the difference between who he was and who he pretended to be: on his arrival in Pottsville, "when the young man glanced at his figure, as reflected in a mirror, he found it difficult to believe he was really himself and not some wild vagabond who had usurped his place."

In chapter 1, we saw the central role clothing played in the runaway ads. Pinkerton gave a minute description of McKenna's clothing, but as part of a carefully contrived performance aimed to deceive. He wore "a grayish coat of coarse materials, which had, from appearances, seen service in a coal bin, and, while never very fine in make or fashion, was considerably the worse about the cuffs and skirts, both being frayed out to raveled raggedness." His vest "was originally black, but the years had come and gone in such numbers since, that the dye was washed away, and with it had fled the surface of the cloth." His wool pants, "too large for him in the body," were "worn strapped tight at the waist with a leather belt, which, from its yellowish and broken condition, might have been a former bell-thong off the neck of some

farmer's cow." His gray shirt had no collar, but he had "a red yarn cra-
vat, or knitted comforter, drawn closely around the wearer's neck and
tied in a sailor's knot in front." The miners had no other way to track
or identify the stranger called McKenna: the detective's minute attention to detail allowed him to pass. These details, like the dancing and
singing, indicated authenticity, or rather *performed* authenticity, but
also excess. "McKenna was the most eccentric and savage appearing
Mollie Maguire" in the anthracite fields, Pinkerton wrote.[31]

Pinkerton salted his narrative with ersatz Irish phrases and ex-
pressions designed to convey the genuineness of the tale he told, but
the tale itself was false—Pinkerton was hired to make Gowen's claims
about the Molly Maguires seem real, and he admitted in his preface
that the story "reads much like fiction, and that it will be accepted
as romance by very many." It's easy to see why: Pinkerton describes
his meeting with Gowen, who tells Pinkerton, "The Mollies rule our
people with a rod of iron. . . . They elect or defeat whomsoever they
may please. They control, in a measure, the finances of the State. Their
chiefs direct affairs this way, and that way, without hindrance. Men
without an iota of moral principle, they dictate the principles of otherwise honorable parties." Pinkerton has Gowen saying: "wherever
anthracite is employed is also felt the vise-like grip of this midnight,
dark lantern murderous-minded fraternity."[32]

People only talk this way in fiction, or perhaps on a stage. The gassy
rhetoric conceals the fact that if anyone ruled the anthracite region
with a rod of iron, it was Franklin Gowen: Gowen, who had his own
private police force, who owned the housing and the stores, who had
engineered a virtual monopoly, and who counted on a compliant press
to advance his claims about the all-powerful Molly Maguires. In 1877
and 1878, twenty men went to the gallows as Molly Maguires. They
ranged from young unskilled laborers to middle-aged former miners turned local politicians, but all shared an Irish heritage. Franklin
Gowen himself was prosecuting attorney in several cases, and detective McParlan helped convince the judge and jury they were savage
criminals.

In Virginia, record keeping developed out of the necessity of tracking race, determining who people "really were" underneath what they appeared to be. The Irish occupied an ambiguous racial position, and they were immigrants trying to pass for Americans or, in Gowen's view, criminals passing for the law-abiding. Both racial tracking and immigrant tracking shared a detective impulse. Is this individual who they seem to be? Will they make good on this loan? Do they have the skills they claim? Are they honest? Is their scheme a good investment? It's the plot of countless movies and streaming media episodes: someone is pretending to be something they're not. Sometimes the difference between appearance and reality reads as sinister deception, sometimes as heroic ambition, sometimes as laughable comic pretentiousness.

### Family History and Detection: Was Patrick a Molly Maguire?

Genealogy is popular for much the same reason as detective stories. The genealogist finds small clues and scraps of information to reveal a larger narrative. Genealogy constantly raises, but rarely answers, questions about motive: Why did they move? Why did they marry? Genealogy, like detective stories, promises to resolve uncertainty in a world of ambitious strangers. When Patrick Melley looked in a mirror, did he recognize himself or, like McParlan, see himself in costume, a new character he devised to cope with America? Did he see a Donegal Irishman or the new American self of his imagination?

Young Patrick Melley left very few clues. If we would consider the same kind of immigrant today, we would likely find birth certificates, passports, identification numbers, fingerprints. We would have a record of credit card transactions, cell phone movements, video from security cameras. All these things are part of the general apparatus of detection, the impulse to classify, track, and recall information about individuals, both detection of consumers and detection of criminals. We use the phrase "undocumented immigrant" to describe someone who has evaded surveillance by documents. Patrick had no documents, and none were demanded when he arrived. Patrick's history presents the same problem both Franklin Gowen and the Molly Maguires faced: limited information about identity.

Patrick was exactly the sort of person, young, male, with little to lose—likely to be drawn into antielite or interethnic violence. He had come to Summit Hill in 1871, in time for the murder of Morgan Powell. He probably had a job in the mines, and he certainly would have rubbed shoulders with members of the AOH, although he does not appear on its membership rolls. He would have heard miners' angry complaints and muttered threats, and rumors of violent retribution. He would have noticed how, three thousand miles from Donegal, Irish people still remained subject to Protestant authority. He was not much different from James McParlan: a person of uncertain identity establishing himself not through formal records, but through his ability to fit in with local customs and traditions.[33]

In February of 1876, the governor of Pennsylvania heard and apparently granted a pardon to "John Downey, Patrick Maley, and James Conners, of Schuylkill County," for the crime of "assault with intent to kill." As mentioned, multiple Patrick Melleys/ Malleys/ Maleys lived in the area: a saloonkeeper, identified as "Pat Maley" and also as "Paddy Melly," appeared in some Molly Maguire trial testimony. The pardon might have gone to that man. Or it might have been our Patrick Melley, young and impetuous, drawn into some sort of brawl.[34]

Family stories, related in the 1980s by the great-grandson of Patrick's brother Cornelius in Summit Hill, recall "a scandal that involved a woman that caused Patrick to leave the area. She was subsequently known as Mrs. Black, and a Mrs. Mary Black shows up in the 1880 census living in Summit Hill." The records of Saint Joseph's Church in Summit Hill show that in 1874 a Patrick Melley married a woman named Mary Murphy, born in the US to parents from Derry. She was nineteen; Patrick either twenty or twenty-two. Witnesses to the marriage included Bridget Boner—a common surname back in Madavagh, in Donegal—and a young man named James Boyle. James worked at the number 5 colliery below Summit Hill, which suggests Patrick might have worked there as well.[35]

Three years later, James Boyle, of Summit Hill, went to the gallows for the murder of policeman Benjamin Yost, alongside six other alleged Molly Maguires executed that day at Pottsville, Pennsylvania. Newspaper accounts say he carried a single rose in his hand, which fell to the ground when the trapdoor swung. Two of Boyle's relatives later went to jail for perjury after the court rejected their efforts to provide James an alibi.[36]

Of course more than one James Boyle lived in the area in 1874, when Patrick and Mary Murphy married. Three men named James Boyle married in Saint Joseph's Church between 1870 and 1877. But only one lived in Summit Hill, and he was the right age. If Patrick had the executed James Boyle as a witness to his wedding, it seems very likely he had at least proximity to people termed Molly Maguires; if he was the Pat Maley pardoned by the governor for assault in 1876, he may have been more deeply involved in antielite violence, and so it's possible the scandal that drove him from Summit Hill might have had less to do with Mary Murphy than with Molly Maguire. But James Boyle belonged to the Ancient Order of Hibernians, while Patrick was not listed as a member.

If you visit the picturesque town center of Mauch Chunk/Jim Thorpe today, you see the long, steep slope Patrick would have ascended to reach Summit Hill, now a hiking trail. You can visit the jail where four of the Molly Maguire suspects were hung, including Alexander Campbell, who left a handprint on the wall of his cell, swearing it would never fade as proof of his innocence. And there you can see but not photograph the handprint, which, you are led to believe, has survived multiple attempts at overpainting and removal. The Mauch Chunk jail looks remarkably like a smaller version of Kilmainham, the Dublin jail where the British kept Irish rebels. Molly Maguires live in the history of the anthracite towns more as heroes and martyrs than as villains. You would expect Irish family stories to stress doomed rebels rather than love affairs gone wrong, or as in many songs, love affairs doomed because of participation in rebellion. Did Patrick leave because of involvement in the Mollie Maguires?

Speculation like this is pleasant but impossible to resolve. It puts the modern person back in the place of the ancestor. What would I have done in that situation? I would prefer to see Patrick as a bold rebel against oppression, but surely Patrick himself didn't know what to do. There were young men all around him angry at obvious injustice. It would be tempting to join them and give that foreman the beating he deserved. But, on the other hand, he had ambitions: he hadn't left green Ireland to live a *worse* life; he could have been thrown in jail in Donegal and saved himself the trouble of an ocean voyage. He might have been held back by religious scruples. Lacking more information, historians also end up doing detective work, relying on context to try to piece the story together. What sort of truth can we derive from these fragments of information?

## A New Life, a New Identity

By 1877, and the executions, the Catholic dioceses of Philadelphia and Scranton had both formally excommunicated members of the Molly Maguires—who again, possibly did not actually exist as an organization—*and* the Ancient Order of Hibernians, which Gowen claimed *was* the Molly Maguires in all but name. The Hibernians earned their way back into grace by repudiating all forms of violence and swearing renewed allegiance to the church.

But Patrick simply left: sometime after his 1874 marriage to Mary Murphy, Patrick walked away from Summit Hill and seemingly never returned. We know he was gone before 1880, because in that year Mary Murphy married John Black, with no evidence of divorce or an annulment of her marriage to Patrick. This is no trivial matter: Mary must have left the Catholic faith to marry John Black, because they remained in Summit Hill; at least two of their children were buried in a Presbyterian cemetery. This would indeed be a scandal—how could she marry John Black in a smallish town where likely everyone knew she had been married to a Catholic a few years earlier? Perhaps Patrick abandoned the marriage, or perhaps she left it. If he had some degree of Molly Maguire involvement, it might have soured their relationship or his enthusiasm for Summit Hill. His association with James Boyle could have led to blacklisting in the mines, making him unemployable. But Patrick Melley vanishes from history, until he turns up, oddly, in 1884, as "Patrick O'Malley," the newlywed husband of Hester Holland of Nansemond County, Virginia: Protestant and colored man.[37]

He must have experienced a great deal in Summit Hill. An impressive effort to unionize the mines collapsed in failure while he was there. He might have been among those foraging the hills for wild food during the strike. He witnessed the execution of the Molly Maguires. The James Boyle who went to the gallows on flimsy evidence was likely the best man at his wedding. Boyle was the victim, as in Ireland, of a thorough and repressive state apparatus that seemed bent on keeping the Catholic Irish down. The church itself, Patrick might have felt, turned its back on the men who tried to fight the mine bosses. He might have been disillusioned with the church for failing to support the executed men or feared the wrath of the church or Mary's family for abandoning his marriage.

## *The Catholic Colonization Movement*

Winding up in Virginia makes little or no sense, *historically*. Immigrants nearly always went where their people settled. Philadelphia or New York would have been the obvious and unsurprising choices for someone like Patrick: both had very large Irish Catholic communities and many jobs for unskilled labor. One explanation might be found in the "Catholic colony movement."

Patrick was married by Father James Brehony, parish priest at Saint Joseph's in Summit Hill. Brehony accompanied at least one of the executed Molly Maguires on his walk to the gallows. In 1877, apparently disgusted with prospects in the coal fields, Brehony and Charles Boyle, from Glenties in Donegal, led a group of one hundred men from Schuylkill and Carbon Counties to Texas. They formed a Catholic colony called, for a time, "Brehony," near the present-day town of Luling. The *Reading (PA) Times* reported on "a colony of about one hundred men from the vicinity of Tamaqua, Schuylkill county, and Summit Hill, Carbon county," who "passed through Reading on their way to Texas, where they intend to take up land, and prepare homes for their families." The *Times* noted, "most of the men are young, or in the prime of life, intelligent and industrious. Several of them are skilled mechanics." More than a week away by train, Luling in 1877 resembled "the wild west" of popular myth. Charles Boyle, who led the colonists in Texas, claimed "Texas is no place for twenty-one year old babies or children in pantaloons," but insisted "manly men and sensible women" would do well there. Did Patrick join that effort?[38]

The national Catholic colony movement sought to draw mostly Irish Catholic immigrants to mostly rural areas, where they could escape the crowded cities, settle as farmers, practice Catholicism freely, and enjoy the allegedly moralizing effects of hard toil in country air. The movement combined religious and speculative zeal. Promoters of a colony in Edina, Missouri, in the 1860s, for example, urged Catholics to head west before all the land is "gobbled up by persons who are opposed to us and to our Church" and to "lead the advance before the New England puritans fill up the country." Catholic colonies succeeded most notably in Minnesota under Bishop John Ireland, who in the 1870s and 1880s worked with state government and the railroads to settle more than four thousand families on land recently appropriated from the Sioux.[39]

If Patrick went to Texas with Father Brehony, he left no record, but other colonization efforts might have drawn his interest. A Catholic newspaper in New Orleans reported in 1877 that "the Colonization movement among the Irish Catholics of the North is taking practical form and already we read of the transfer of numbers of families from the coal mines of Pennsylvania and the large cities of the East, to settlements in North Carolina, Texas and Arkansas."[40]

Patrick might have joined an ambitious colony in Charlotte County, Virginia, about one hundred miles to the west of Nansemond County. In 1877, a group called the Philadelphia Colonization Society, itself

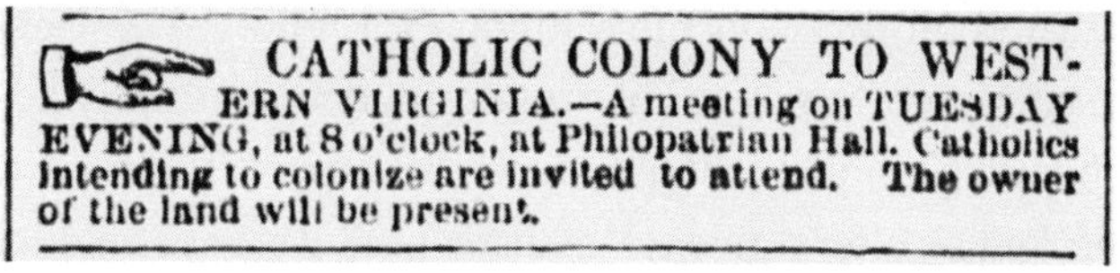
CATHOLIC COLONY TO WESTERN VIRGINIA.—A meeting on TUESDAY EVENING, at 8 o'clock, at Philopatrian Hall. Catholics intending to colonize are invited to attend. The owner of the land will be present.

*Figure 4.7.* Advertisement for the Barnseville / Keileyville colony, *Philadelphia Times*, April 15, 1878, 3.

part of the Irish Catholic Benevolent Union (ICBU), had purchased seven thousand acres north of Clarksville near the North Carolina border, hoping to start a community. The land, apparently owned by planter and former slave trader Samuel Barnes and known as Barnesville, eventually included a grist mill, a sawmill, a blacksmith shop, and forty frame houses, formerly slave quarters, in which the colonists would live. The ambitious promoters addressed meetings in Philadelphia and other cities and placed ads in newspapers describing abundant land on good terms. “Ho for Virginia!” one newspaper announced in 1878: “The Barnesville colonists getting ready to depart.” The article described but did not name the initial thirty colonists and their occupations and announced the Richmond and Danville Railroad had offered free transportation to any colonist buying more than one hundred acres.[41]

Catholic newspapers like the *Boston Pilot* thereafter gave regular updates on the colony, renamed “Keileyville” after the Irish American mayor of Richmond, who was also president of the ICBU. In 1879, the colony’s leader reported, “today there are two hundred, comfortably settled, while seven more families have purchased land here and will shortly come to take possession of it.” The letter to the *Pilot* described a grand Saint Patrick’s Day celebration in that same year: “we had a parade around the village. We turned out 75 men, with ten flags, in line. We formed the line at the post office, and marched out Reilly Street to Hardy Street and Keiley Avenue, and down to the church, where Father Burke’s lecture on St. Patrick was read,” along with a speech of Irish Nationalist hero Robert Emmett.[42]

Like the colonization movement as a whole, the Keileyville colony, with its enthusiastic Hibernianism, demonstrated the degree to which Irish Catholics still felt themselves apart. The colony movement marked an alternative to "melting pot" style assimilation: Keileyville colonists could have prosperity, land, and spiritual autonomy, something they could only dream of in the Ireland they had left. A Catholic colony would mark off a line between themselves and other Americans, a community away from the evils of city life and away from the hostility of Protestants, with boundaries they could maintain and police.

Did Patrick join them? It would have been a reasonable idea: land had a fierce hold on the imagination of people who suffered eviction at the hands of English landlords. We can imagine Patrick in Summit Hill discussing the idea of Texas or Virginia with his wife, Mary, and Mary not wanting to leave her home and family. We can imagine Patrick going ahead to scout out the place and then planning to write her to join him: perhaps she went with him, but returned home. In the absence of hard evidence, we can imagine lots of things.

The colony mostly sought to attract families, but welcomed single laborers as well. Along with a blacksmith shop, they established a foundry and began smelting iron. The glowing letters to newspapers concealed troubles, however. In 1879, the priest assigned to the colony, himself in poor health and with other flocks to tend, described "the colony's aspect for the present" as "somewhat gloomy." The ICBU, it turned out, did not have clear title to the land: Barnes still retained ownership. The revelation of this dual ownership rocked the ICBU and led to the resignation of Keileyville's chief booster under a taint of scandal.[43]

In addition, "one great drawback is that most colonists have not had any experience in farming." "The Southerners welcome emigrants with open arms," a 1878 letter to the *Philadelphia Times* complained, but "it is hard to get them to name a price for any service in advance . . . they think all Northerners are loaded down with money." The letter added, "the greatest drawback to colonizing the South is the high rates of freight and passage on the railroads. Though the Richmond and Danville Company have offered unusual inducements to us, they are very slow in fulfilling them, and their station agents appear to think that the public was made for the use of railroads and not the railroads for the public." In that same decade, in Nansemond County, Dempsey Hare thrived by selling crops out of the docks at Portsmouth: the Keileyville colony had to sell crops by rail north. The Richmond and Danville Railroad enjoyed a monopoly on rail traffic from Keileyville, making it a much more expensive proposition.

The colony suffered other reversals—in 1880 the steam-powered sawmill exploded "with noise like thunder," killing one man and scalding and wounding five others. Without a full time priest, the men lingered near death without the comfort of the last rites, in a colony founded specifically for the practice of the Catholic faith. Fire destroyed several houses and killed several children. Catholics settlers continued to live in the area, but the colony as a self-contained unit failed by the mid-1880s.[44]

The 1880 census shows no Patrick Melley or O'Malley or any similar variants in Charlotte County or nearby, but census records were never complete. If Patrick joined the Keileyville colony, the only possible evidence is a record of a "Mr. Melloy," farmer, living there in 1880. But the fact of the Keileyville colony might explain how he ended up in Nansemond County. Keileyville boosters had reported in 1879 that along with a working blacksmith shop, "our foundry is nearly ready now. Mr. Fallon expects to 'run off a heat' on the Fourth of July." Like the sawmill and gristmill, a blacksmith shop and foundry would need laborers. In the 1900 census, Patrick would give his occupation as "Iron Merchant," while the 1910 census listed two of his sons, Frederick and Patrick, both employed as "blacksmiths" in Philadelphia. Frederick in fact continued semiprofessional smithing throughout his life. My father clearly remembers the time, in the early 1950s, when he told Patrick's son Frederick that he planned to go to medical school. Grandfather Fred replied, "doctors are a dime a dozen: you should be a blacksmith," advice my father rejected. These details lend slight credence to the idea that Patrick might have worked at the Keileyville foundry and picked up some familiarity with smithing and ironwork.[45]

## Railroad Speculation

In 1882, around the time the Keileyville colony began failing in earnest, the newly incorporated Atlantic and Danville Railroad announced a plan to connect the port of Portsmouth to Danville through Suffolk, Nansemond County, and Holland, Virginia. The proposed right-of-way passed about ten miles south of Keileyville and could have been reached by water on the Roanoke River. The line would have given Keileyville residents an alternative path to market their crops, to the same ports Dempsey Hare used. Patrick would later buy land on that very railroad line. If he spent time at Keileyville, perhaps he saw opportunities in the new venture and left Keileyville to work on the rail line through Nansemond County. Family stories claim Patrick was a railroad engineer, building bridges, even taking classes in engineering, but no evidence for this exists.[46]

The map in figure 4.8 completes an admittedly flimsy argument

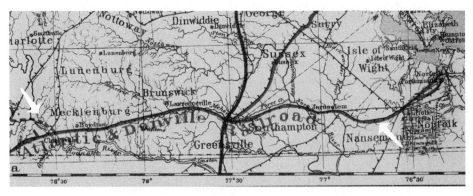

*Figure 4.8.* Map of the Atlantic and Danville Railroad, 1886. The white arrow on the left shows the approximate location of Barnesville / Keileyville. The arrow on the right shows the approximate location of Patrick's house on Elwood Road where it crossed the Atlantic and Danville. Library of Congress, Prints and Photographs Division.

for why Patrick Melley may have wound up in Nansemond County, Virginia. It's a reasonable suggestion and makes economic sense. It's also entirely possible Patrick was sick of the Irish and sick of being Irish: tired of being associated with violence or regarded as an ape-like savage, tired of a religious faith that made him stigmatized in Ireland and the US, which had excommunicated the Molly Maguires and the AOH, and which had lured people to settle in Keileyville on land they didn't own. He made a big break with the past: in December 23, 1884, Patrick married Hester Holland, a Protestant, in Suffolk. He joined the vast multihued Nansemond clan of Hollands, which included, by marriage, Dempsey Hare. What made this Irishman exile himself to Nansemond County and abandon his Catholic identity? And what led to either of these people being understood as "colored"? Did the understanding of the Irish as a savage race follow him there? Or was Hester herself of African ancestry?

# FIVE

# ELWOOD STATION

On December 15, 1884, Patrick Melley and Hester Holland walked into the county clerk's office in Suffolk, Virginia, to get a marriage license. The clerk, Peter Bowdoin Prentis, took out a large sheet of good paper, ornately bordered and lettered, with a vignette of Cupid, holding an arrow, in a cart pulled by doves. He laid it on his desk. Pen in hand, he asked them their names. He wrote "Patrick O Malley," with just a hint of an apostrophe after the "O," which is heavier, and darker, as if Prentis had added it after recharging the pen with ink. He wrote "Hester Holland," and the date, and signed it. The same piece of heavy paper served as a marriage certificate when, eight days later, they came back to the courthouse and Prentis filled in the details. He recorded that Patrick was born in Donegal, Ireland, and that he was a laborer, thirty years old. He recorded his parents' names as Frederick and Sophia, born in Ireland. He recorded Hester as twenty-four, and listed her parents, "James Holland (of James)" and "Elizabeth, his wife." Where the form asked for "color," he wrote "white." But Prentis left a smudge underneath the word, as if reservations afflicted his steady hand.

The minister, M. L Hurley, filled out his portion of the bottom of the form. Hurley belonged to the Southern Christian Convention, which later became the United Church of Christ. He helped found Elon College in North Carolina and had come to the church by the influence of James O'Kelly, who we saw in chapter 1 building a shed

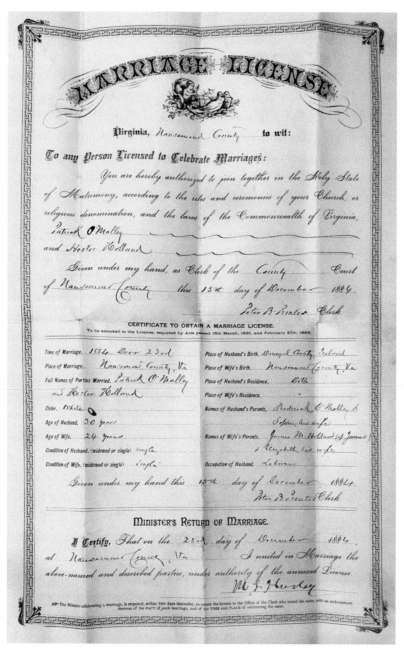

*Figure 5.1.* Original marriage license of Patrick O'Malley and Hester Holland, author photo from original in Suffolk Circuit Court, Suffolk, Virginia.

for the colored worshippers. Patrick and Hester Holland might have
taken O'Kelly Road to get to Suffolk. O'Kelley and Hurley are both
Irish names and so, for that matter, is "Holland": an English name but
also an Irish name related to "Mulholland" or "Halland." The surname
Holland is not uncommon in Ireland and most notably attaches to Irish
engineer John Phillip Holland, from County Clare, the father of the
US submarine service. Patrick might have been the only Catholic in
the county, but he wasn't the only Irishman, depending on how you
understood the word "Irish." And of course, by this act of marriage
he was both a criminal bigamist and no longer a Catholic.[1]

The young couple had their photo taken around the time of the
marriage: the photo appears in the introduction. Hester, hair up, hand
on hip, wears a light skirt and darker close-fitting jacket with a hair clip
like a tiara; she looks eager to get started on the rest of her life. Her
earrings seem to have been added later with a retoucher's brush. Patrick, pleased with himself, with an energetic and intense gaze, looks
like a laborer wearing his best clothes. He was far from family, far from
the Irish Catholic world of Summit Hill, far from Donegal, with a new
name and a new wife.

In Pennsylvania's coal fields, poor Irish Catholics took the worst
jobs, just as in Ireland, and they kicked against their betters as they
had in Ireland and were put down hard, and everyone outranked the
savage and superstitious Irish Catholic laborer. In Virginia the other
laborers would be African American, relegated by law and custom
to the lowest place, and Patrick's whiteness could confer a higher
status. The comparative advantages of whiteness were clear at every
construction site, every rail camp. He would get the better jobs, and
the boss's favor, and his hard work would find more certain reward.
Throwing off his faith would grant him a higher status still. The costs
of being Catholic were high. He was ready to stop paying them.

Peter Prentis, the clerk, went back to his office after the happy
couple left and opened the county register of marriages, the register
state law required him to keep. The record of each marriage spanned a
single line on two facing ledger pages. He entered the same information

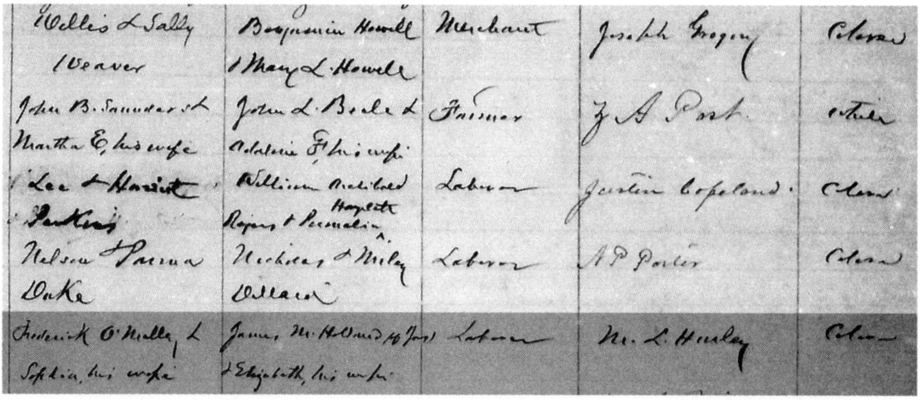

*Figure 5.2.* Excerpt of original marriage register in which Patrick and Hester were declared to be colored. Their parents are in the two left columns, bottom row. Nansemond County Marriage Register 1, 1866–99, microfilm reel 60, Library of Virginia, Richmond.

he put on the marriage certificate. The last column in the ledger was labeled "remarks," and Prentis used it to record "race," as required by law. For Patrick and Hester, he wrote the name of Hurley, the minister, and right next to it he wrote "colored." Figure 5.2 is an image of the ledger, taken from microfilm. You can see on the bottom line their parents' names, Patrick's occupation, Hurley's name, and then "colored."

What was Prentis thinking? This would not have been a mistake — he deliberately wrote this entry about a couple he had just seen and listed as white. In their sight he recorded them as white people, but in the privacy of his office he changed his mind. What form of race-craft, what suspicion or intuition or rumor, motivated him? Answering this question requires looking at Hester's family and the Hollands of Virginia.

## Hester's Family

In early July of 1846, a large group of Virginia men met to celebrate the nation's birth at Carrsville, on the western border of Nansemond County. The Isle of Wight County Riflemen invited the Nansemond

County Riflemen to feast and drink, and to congratulate and flatter each other. Formal proceedings started with toasts to

1. The Day we celebrate.
2. The Constitution of the United States.
3. The President of the United States.
4. The Ex-Presidents.
5. The Army and Navy.
6. The Militia.
7. Agriculture, Manufactures and Commerce.
8. The Heroes of the Revolution.
9. The Signers of the Declaration of Independence.
10. The Freedom of the Press, the Bulwark of Liberty
11. General Taylor, and the Heroes of the Rio Grande.
12. Woman.

Then other men took their turn, toasting various icons of patriotism and progress. James M. Holland of Nansemond County offered a barbed toast to "the health of Gen. Z. Taylor: his services in the Army of the United States . . . entitle him to the gratitude of his country, but, as his studies have been on the field, we will keep him in the field." Taylor, a Whig, was then a war hero and future president. Holland was a Democrat, like most Southerners.

A year later a larger group of men met in Amelia County, west of Richmond, to celebrate the seventy-first anniversary of the nation's birth. After a generous feast, they got to the business of drinking toasts, first the "regular toasts," tiresomely identical to the ones listed above from a year before. Americans in those days had a much greater appetite for speeches than we do now, and repetition troubled them little. The nation, the Constitution, General Washington, all past presidents, the current president, the current vice president, "the people," "US forces then fighting in Mexico," "the Ladies"—the list of toasts went on and on finally settling on "the volunteer toasts" from groups including the "Isle of Wight Riflemen and Nansemond Cavalry." First, the officers spoke, then the regular members including again James M. Holland, a young man on the rise, who offered them a toast to themselves: "The Isle of Wight Riflemen and Nansemond Cavalry: Men who know how to appreciate the liberty which they enjoy, and who will maintain it at any hazard." No doubt they all nodded and cheered.

By "maintaining liberty" Holland mostly meant "maintaining slavery." The South had a special enthusiasm for militia and military training, because white Southerners worried constantly about slave insurrections. "There were ninety six military colleges, military academies, and universities with cadet programs in the slave states in the years 1827–60," but "only 15 similar schools in the free states in the same period." Slave owners boasted about the happy loyalty of their unfree laborers, when Yankees asked about it, but they drilled and rode and patrolled the lanes at night to quash rebellion and stop slaves from communicating with each other. Frank Boone remembered as a young child in Nansemond County, "they had a class of white people known as patrollers. They would catch the slaves and whip them." Patrollers had "pestered" Dempsey Howell's people enough that he moved their homes to the other side of Holy Neck Road. James Holland might have been among them.[2]

James Holland's membership in the Militia signaled his enthusiasm for the regime of slavery and his willingness to actively defend it. Earlier in 1847 Holland had attended a meeting of the "Democratic Vigilance Committee" of Nansemond County. Similar ominously named committees appeared in both Southern and Northern states: they functioned to make sure Democratic voters made it to the polls, or possibly to make it more likely Whig voters did not. A Democratic Vigilance Committee in Virginia certainly extended its vigilance to any sign of abolitionism, an increasingly powerful influence in national political life. So James Holland had some degree of political ambition and an investment in maintaining the status quo.

In 1832, Holland, born in about 1814, had married Elizabeth Moore and started a large family: after 1850 either family life or political disappointment seems to have kept him out of newspapers. The 1850 census lists the couple having eight children, ranging in age from seventeen to ten months. He held real estate valued by the census taker at $225, which put him about in the middle of his neighbors. For comparison, that same year Dempsey Hare held real estate valued at $800. The 1850 census of slaves shows one twelve-year-old girl in the Holland's household, name unknown: she may have been hired out to the Hollands, since they show no personal property.[3]

These Hollands betrayed some consciousness of Virginia history in their naming practices. Their oldest son, Alexander Washington Holland, was nineteen; one of the daughters, age eleven, enjoyed the name "Pocahontas Holland." All the Hollands could read and write: the story of Pocahontas, John Smith, and John Rolfe was well established in Virginia lore. Claiming descent from Pocahontas would later gain people a special exemption from race law. But if these Hollands descended from Pocahontas and John Rolfe, the record shows no evidence.

Ten years later, on the eve of the Civil War, Holland is still a farmer, now living in "Lower Parish," but his real estate value has more than tripled, to $800, and he has $3,000 in personal property. That $3,000 tallies human property; the 1860 census of slaves shows five in the household: a man, forty; a woman, fifty-seven; a woman, eighteen; a "black" girl, three; and one infant, nine months old. All are listed as "B" for black rather than as M for "mulatto." James Holland has one house for enslaved people, the census says. As an example of the relative value of slaveholding, Dempsey Hare, in 1860, had real estate valued at $850 and personal property worth $500.[4]

By that time two children had moved out of the Holland home, but two more had arrived, so six children and James Butler, an illiterate white laborer, shared the house with James and Elizabeth. James himself may have recorded the census: on the line "enumerated by," the form is signed "Jas. M. Holland." But another James M. Holland of roughly the same age, also married to a woman named Elizabeth, lived relatively nearby, so either man might have written the record: most records refer to our man as "James M. Holland, of James" or "of Jas." Peter Prentis listed him that way on the marriage certificate.[5]

## The Meaning of Ancestry

The war took its toll on these Hollands. Yankee soldiers may have arrested James: the *Richmond Dispatch* for August 4, 1862, includes a report, from the Suffolk region, of a James M. Holland among "gentlemen [who] have been arrested, some of them manacled and dragged off to the Rip Raps" by the Union Army. Alexander, the son, seems to have joined Company A of Sixteenth Virginia Infantry, a volunteer unit, in which he served for the duration of the war: his record shows two desertions and a "confinement" at Fort Monroe, which would have made him a prisoner of the Union.[6]

But as with Richard Freeman, the war reduced the Holland family's circumstances dramatically, by eliminating their human property. James M. Holland's enslaved people might have "run off" when the Union occupied Suffolk. But the war drove a stake through slaveholding and through James's modest prosperity. The 1870 census shows James M. Holland now living in Chuckatuck Township, to the north of "Lower Parish," with land valued at $500 and personal property of $250. By comparison, Dempsey Hare in 1870 had $1,200 in land and personal property worth $158. James and Elizabeth have added a daughter, born very late in their childbearing years: Esther or Hester Holland, age nine in 1870. She is my great-great-grandmother.

I'd prefer to have discovered that James M. Holland, her father, was not a slave owner, but the evidence is clear: Holland invested in human property and used the labor of unfree people. He held three adults and four children in slavery, subject to sale at his whim. One of the questions genealogy raises, in the minds of people trapped in conversation about family history, is "so what? who cares?" That's largely what this book is about: What does the past mean, and what does the past of family mean? Should we care, and why? It's the question Dempsey Hare was trying to force an answer to and the question asked by the free Negro registers: What does a specific ancestry mean? History is built on the idea that the past matters: if it matters that some ancestor might have been famous and noble, it matters that some other

ancestor was a slaveholder. But how does it matter? What is the rele-
vance of one slaveholding three-times-great-grandparent among the
thirty-one other three-times-great-grandparents of the same generation, who didn't own slaves? In the case of Dempsey Hare, one person
with African ancestors, out of many, controlled his identity. I would
like to tell myself that one slaveholder, out of many, should not control mine. But Hester's family was formed in the practices of slavery
and the racecraft of white supremacy: James chose to stake his family's prosperity on slave owning.

History looks at Nansemond County and says, "*all* these people
are *related*," in that they inhabit the same political economy, the
same structure of laws. They walked the same roads, faced the same
droughts, and were wetted by the same rains. If we think about an
ecosystem, we imagine all living things in the ecosystem as related,
but occupying different roles, some as predators, some as prey. James
Holland was in the upper half of the Nansemond County ecosystem,
certainly, eager to exploit those on the bottom. We saw that already
in his enthusiasm for militia duty in support of the white suprema-
cist status quo.

This puts me in a doubled state of relationship to slavery: they are
direct ancestors, and slavery conditioned the choices he made and the
choices Hester made, though slavery was gone by the time she was
three. I have an ethical obligation to know the past and think about
what the past means, because if the person in the past is to some extent a distant version of myself then their actions are particularly rel-
evant to how I conduct myself in the present. A related person made
these choices, took these actions: will you choose the same? But of
course again *all* the persons in the past are related to you in varying
degrees. I'm clearly related, *historically*, to the people James Holland
held in slavery: my great-great-grandmother grew up with them, that's
a relationship. I'm not responsible for their enslavement, but their enslavement left a trace of consequences. And of course I was already
in a relationship to slavery, in the sense that the economy of the antebellum United States was built on slavery, and American political

ideas were formed by ideas about slavery and freedom. What does it mean to be *related*, and what weight does a biological tie have relative to the weight of history?

And what it might mean to have African ancestors? Would it "cancel out" having slave-owning ancestors? I've spent decades as a musician, playing small-time local gigs sincerely if not especially well, studying the great figures of classic American jazz, who are mostly people with African ancestors. Transcribing the bass lines of Ray Brown or Charles Mingus, playing the chord voicings Wes Montgomery used, puts you deeply in the heads of the people who made that music and, in a very small way, in their community of practice. Would having African ancestors grant me any special entitlement? The answer is clearly "no": just as having Irish ancestors does me no good at all on the flute. Racism's marks on my upbringing took the form of the advantages of whiteness, and anyone can study any form of music and learn its styles and idioms. Musicians often bristle when people talk about "musical talent" because the phrase replaces hours of hard practice and experience with fantasies of magical blood or genetic essence. I was already in a community of practice with jazz: I could claim a meaningful (but certainly not close) relationship to Wayne Shorter by playing his music and reading the interviews he gave, but it would be absurd and grotesque to suddenly claim some sort of racial birthright.

Chapters 1 and 2 told the story of people with mixed European and African ancestry: Mary Holland, murdered over a barking dog, and her sister-in-law, Annie Holland, married to Dempsey Hare. It mentioned elderly Thomas Holland, who remembered life under slavery when asked to testify on Dempsey's behalf. Hare wrote a will about 1870: the three witnesses were all named Holland. Hare's second and final will left his estate to two white men, Dr. Job Holland and Edward Everett Holland. Dr. Job Holland's household included his African American half brother, Solomon Holland. A white undertaker also named Solomon Holland exhumed Hare's corpse and reburied it. Hare's daughter, who he cut out of his will, married a descendant of Axa Holland, the mother of Dempsey's wife, Annie Holland. And here we see two men named James M. Holland, both married to women named Elizabeth. And lo, the records show a *third* James M. Holland, born 1816, living in Nansemond, married to "Metildy."

Are some of these people related "by blood"? The answer *must* be "certainly." In a premodern world, where "rapid transit" meant saddling a horse, the range of people anyone could meet and marry rarely exceeded a day's journey. Ten miles on foot would take roughly three hours on good roads; returning home would mean six hours of your day spent traveling, leaving little time for romance. Religious and civil authorities frowned on first cousins marrying, but historically, having no choice, people married second and third cousins all the time, and so a small number of surnames dominate the record in nearly any locality. Donegal and Nansemond are the same in this sense. And of course this was a society invested in white supremacy and granting entitlement to slave owners. An enslaved woman had no legal right to refuse sexual intercourse.

Careful work can piece together a record of these relationships, but why should we care that James M. Holland and James M. Holland might have been third cousins, twice removed? Which relationship would seem more significant—the relationship of third cousin to the family on the outskirts of the village, or the business relationship with the miller or the grain broker, or the political relationship with the town council? The relationship of teacher and student, or minister and parishioner, or employer and employee? From a historical perspective, the more important relationships are not relations of "blood," which no one chooses at birth, but of association. Put history aside and consider a successful marriage: the person you are closest to in the world is probably not at all related by "blood." The relationship that matters is the one you chose and cultivated. All these Hollands are related in the sense that they all have to navigate the same political economy, the same framework of laws, the same climate; all live in the same time. In a historical sense, they are all different but all related.[7]

That perspective reflects modern ideas: the replacement of clan and kin as signifiers of identity with individualism, which required new systems of governance and the rule of law, and static records of identity. People in the premodern world organized and identified themselves through family and kin. Modern people of course still cherish family, understand themselves in terms of family, and still pass wealth to family, but they also to a much greater extent view themselves as "alienable" from family, community, and culture, capable of self-transformation, individuals navigating a world of other individuals. Paper records of the sort Peter Prentis generated make that world possible.

The paper record on Hester/Esther and her family offers little detail about what would have led Peter Prentis to call her a colored person. That James Holland's household had an eighteen-year-old enslaved woman on the 1860 census is striking, and so is the age of Elizabeth at the birth of her last child, Hester: forty-nine. Could she have given birth at forty-nine? It's certainly possible, although it puts her at the far end of the onset of menopause. She had eleven children, the first at age twenty. It's also possible her age was lower, because records are so imprecise.

There's an obvious question here: Was someone else Hester's mother, someone with African ancestry? Or did James Holland himself have invisible African ancestry "in his blood"? Or did Elizabeth Moore, his wife? If so, Peter Prentis could very well have known, just as judge and jury in 1900 knew about but ignored Dempsey Hare's children by Frances Whitfield. There were in fact two other "Hester Hollands" in Nansemond, both older and both named as having ancestors from Africa. If James Holland had some sort of liaison with a woman of color, it went unrecorded. But all those Hollands of mixed European and African ancestry had to come from somewhere.

Genealogy, on the other hand, very much wants to determine whether Hester Holland was related by blood to, for example, Anne Holland, Dempsey's wife. The blood secret might by law make Hester, and myself, "really black." Here again we might simply say, should such a relationship turn up, that Hester Holland had ancestors from

Europe and Africa. Because I live in a society in which the spells of racecraft have enduring power, I've looked for any biological relationship between Hester's family and Dempsey Hare's family, or any other people with known African ancestors, and have found none.

Spitting in a tube and mailing it off to find out if you have African ancestors shows DNA testing as a form of racecraft. The test results produce what looks like a reassuring certainty. Let us imagine—there is no evidence to support it—Hester was the daughter of James Holland and the woman he held in slavery in 1860. We have no idea what degree of African ancestry *that* woman had. Was it 100 percent? Fifty percent? One-eighth? One-thirty-second? I'm now asking exactly the same questions Virginians asked themselves about their colored neighbors in 1850. What are these people *really*, and how would I know? But scientists who study DNA argue that all people come from Africa, and they can report back on the presence or absence of Neanderthal DNA. So what are these services telling me? At what point would Hester's African ancestry, if she had it, be too insignificant to report?

In figure 5.3, the photo of Hester Holland and Selena White Holland, Dempsey Hare's granddaughter, invites consideration of the question and highlights its absurdity. Are these women related? Does relation lie in the set of their mouths, tight and disciplined; in the high forehead; the narrow jaw; the clear-eyed gaze? There is no documentary evidence these two women are genetically related, but if you were county clerk and wanted to see a family resemblance between the two women, if you grew up in a world where people named Holland came in all shades, you might tell yourself it's there. History gives us fragments, grainy and blurred as these photos. Skin tone, ironically, is harder to judge in black-and-white family snapshots. Time presents us with differences in styles of hair and clothes. But do they look like they could be? It's not that far-fetched: census records called Selena's maternal great-grandmother, Axy Holland, a white woman. They're related by the shared culture of the South and the climate and land of Nansemond. Both were Protestants. They're related by their gender and the different and specific burdens culture and politics

*Figure 5.3. Left,* Hester Holland, about 1900, photo in author's possession. *Right,* Selena White Holland, Dempsey Hare's granddaughter, the child of Ira Ann Hare White and Meredith White, undated, from a Memorial Program commemorating the 150th anniversary of the Mount Sinai Baptist Church. Courtesy of Andre Kearns.

loaded on women: both were related in the duties of motherhood; both women bore eight children. Racecraft served to neutralize those relationships and make them less meaningful than the simple binary of black/white.[8]

Hester certainly had African ancestors: geneticists say we all do, since *Homo sapiens* evolved in Africa, but this only demonstrates that when we talk about "Africa" we reflexively mean "black": producing race from ancestry and endowing it with the appearance of natural fact. DNA test results will explain a person as "23 percent Italian," but historians point out that "Italian" is a socially created thing, not a biological fact. There is no Italy in ancient Rome: the Romans did not regard themselves as "Italian." Italy as a nation was invented in the nineteenth century. Ancestry.com tells me I'm 93 percent Irish and 6 percent Scottish, with no African ancestry, but neither of these identities have clear historical origins. People one thousand years ago didn't think of themselves as Irish or Scottish, and Ireland and Scotland as nations are historically contingent things, powerful ideas but products of the mind, not the body. It took vast amounts of political work to convince warring tribes they were "actually" English, or Vietnamese or Nigerian, and it doesn't always work. DNA results tend to conflate "nation," a political idea, with biological ancestry. In this sense individual ancestral DNA results combine racecraft and statecraft, reinforcing the idea that the political entities Irish and Scottish and Italian are "races."

## A Virginia Gentleman and the Irish Race

Peter Bowdoin Prentis marked both Patrick and Hester colored, so it's worth looking at Mr. Prentis. The photos of Hester Holland and Selena White Holland (figure 5.3) put us in the position of Prentis, whose job required him to engage in racial surveillance every time a couple married. If you looked at the pictures and wondered, then like Prentis you are acting the detective, balancing the few genealogical records he had at hand with personal knowledge of these people's backgrounds and his own judgment of appearance. If he had reason to believe Hester was "colored," did he have reason to believe the Irish were not white?

Prentis, born in Suffolk Town in Nansemond, came from an "old Virginia" family. His father was a lawyer and his grandfather a judge. His uncle, Joseph Prentis, traded slaves from his office in Richmond, one of the largest and most successful slave traders in Virginia, a man who veered between enthusiasm and some degree of shame about his trade. Peter attended Amelia Academy, a boarding school, and later attended the University of Virginia, where he graduated with a degree in modern languages and then studied law for a year. At the time the University of Virginia had a reputation as the welcome home of overly entitled children of the slaveholding aristocracy. While at UVA, in 1839, Prentis took "natural philosophy," a subject including math, astronomy, chemistry, and physics, from William Barton Rogers, himself a slave owner. Peter never missed a class.[9]

Prentis practiced law for a few years and then was elected clerk of

Nansemond County Court in 1852. He served till 1871, then was briefly
Circuit Court judge from 1873 to 1875. After that he resumed the clerk's
job, which he held till he died in 1889. His funeral included a "colored
escort" among whom walked Exum White, likely the brother of Meredith White, who had married Dempsey Hare's daughter and was the
father of Selena, above. Peter's nephew was the judge who instructed
the jury when Ira Ann White, Selena's mother, sued to invalidate her
father's will.[10]

Prentis served as county clerk when the Union occupied Suffolk,
and during the occupation the Yankees arrested him. In May 1863,
he was held in his office "three or four days, then sent to Norfolk city
jail, thence to Fortress Monroe, then to Fort Norfolk," "having been
held, as shown in his diary which the Yankees had stolen from him,
six weeks and one half hour."[11]

The diary of his experience apparently did not survive. One letter to his sister, written after his release, mentions "my old quarters,
Fort Monroe," and in the same letter, he told her "we had another
very short visit on Friday last by the Yankees: a gun-boat with its crew
came up to the wharf about 11 o'clock a.m. An officer, with some 14 or
15 men marched up town and returned in about an hour or less time.
No one was arrested." He added, "the only bad conduct which some
of them displayed was an attempt to secure some of Mrs. Clara Riddick's geese and Mr. Dean's chickens but in this they were foiled, as the
hens were so well acquainted with the smell of a Yank that the geese
took to their wings and the chicks to their heels." He ended that same
letter with a request to be "affectionably remembered of you and Dr.
and Joe and slaves."[12]

Prentis's letters show him as a courtly and unimaginative person,
well educated, inclined to conceal emotion with light banalities. When
running for the position of county clerk in 1875, he gave a speech in
which he insisted, "he did not think that these county offices should
be dragged through the dirty pool of politics," and that "he had always
been a good Conservative at heart," and "he would be found voting as
he had always done with the Conservatives." He added "that he was

born and reared in this county, the people knew him and in his declining years would vote for him as their choice for clerk." His father
had held the office, and Prentis felt entitled to it.[13]

People less personally reserved than Prentis described the occupation of Suffolk differently. "Thank God, I can now write you un-
trammeled, the contemptible, diabolical, rascally Yankees have at last
left us." He added, "many of our people are utterly ruined, houses all
destroyed and negroes all gone. What are they to do? A large majority of our people have not a single negro left. Many of us have not a
darkey on our lots, nor can we get them." He told the reporter, "my
neighbors, Dr. C and Dr. H, say they are so tired of cutting and splitting wood and toting water." No doubt: but it's hard to feel any sympathy at all for people angry at having to do labor they once compelled enslaved people to do. The anonymous citizen sought to vent
his rage on any available brown people, but "most of the free negroes
have left . . . I had very much hoped that some of the most prominent
would have remained, in order that we might have had the satisfaction of hanging them."[14]

The Union soldiers occupying Suffolk included "Corcoran's Legion," also known as "the Irish Brigade." Michael Corcoran, born in
County Sligo, had enlisted his New York state militia in the war effort and been captured at the first Battle of Bull Run. On his release
he raised and combined five regiments of mostly Irish American soldiers from New York. The *Richmond Enquirer* talked to members of
"Corcoran's command, made up of Irish, and blue-bellied Yankees,"
who said "they are for prosecuting this war for fifty years, if so long a
time be necessary, for the suppression of the rebellion." His men took
serious casualties at the Battle of Deserted House, but most of their
time in Suffolk was spent raiding local farms for food or digging fortifications. Irish soldiers were so common that Irish jokes appeared:
for example, one involving "a witty Irishman, Owen Caragher," who
had spent most of his time digging. When rebuked by his general for
having a rusty gun, Caragher replied, "indade, it's a bit rusty for want
of use; but bedad it's mesilf as has a spade down at me tint, bright as
a new shillin', that yez can see yer face in like a lookin' glass."[15]

Suffolk's white citizens tended to see the Irish less as charmingly comic and more as degraded. Commenting on Union plans to enlist African American soldiers, the *Staunton Spectator* claimed the Yankees "have no stomach for the fight themselves. This they long since confessed by hiring Irish and Dutch to do the work for them. They now confess that notwithstanding the twenty odd millions of fire-eating Yankees, flanked and advanced by terrible Irish and Dutch brigades, they are not a match for the rebels. They are obliged to call in an army of negroes to aid them in their undertaking." The editorial imagined a Northern army organized on "the promiscuous principle: the whites and blacks thoroughly intermixed all through the army." Conflating Irish and African Americans was an effective attack. And indeed Corcoran's Irish Union soldiers worked with free people: "the Yankees have employed for some time past a lot of free negroes, who scour the country, tamper with slaves, and use every means to entice them from their owners." An Irishman might have seen some affinity between enslaved people rebelling against owners and their own ancestors back home, truckling under the thumb of landlords.[16]

Prentis was a member by illustrious ancestry of the Southern elite. The family had arrived at Williamsburg in 1715: visitors to Colonial Williamsburg today can shop in the "Prentis store" on Duke of Gloucester Street, where great-grandfather William Prentis got his start and grew wealthy. Peter's grandfather had been speaker of the House of Burgesses. They were not major slaveholders, or plantation grandees, and his uncle Joseph's slave-trading business brought in more money than social prestige. But Peter's nephew ended his career as chief justice of the Virginia Supreme Court. They were wealthy, educated, and accustomed to influence. If soldiers with Irish accents had occupied Prentis's fine house, still standing in Suffolk, and taken food, and held him prisoner; if they had encouraged the "darkies" to leave, forcing his wife and neighbors to do their own work, we could understand why he might be hostile to Patrick Melley, with his Donegal brogue and his foreign ways, charming a local woman.[17]

And Prentis likely would have had little respect for Hester Holland. The Holland family's modest wealth did not survive slavery. In

1885, one year after Patrick and Hester married, James M. Holland (of James) made out his will. He left two dollars to each of his children, including "to my daughter Esther W. Malley, the wife now of Patrick O. Malley the sum of two dollars." Prentis, who had secretly declared Patrick and Esther to be colored, recorded the will and in 1887 certified its legitimacy after James died. Esther's father had to add "of James" to distinguish himself, but Peter Bowdoin Prentis had a name resplendent of Virginia history. Hester had married a common laborer with an Irish accent and skin darkened by the sort of outdoor labor men like Prentis didn't do. She had that sister, Pocahontas, whose marriage Prentis had also certified. So we could imagine a degree of contempt for the couple: Hester of undistinguished and uncertain ancestry; Patrick, reminiscent of those Yankees who jailed him in 1863.[18]

*Figure 5.4.* Peter Bowdoin Prentis, probably around 1860. In Webb–Prentis Family Portraits, circa 1850–90, Accession #4136-g, Albert and Shirley Small Special Collections Library, University of Virginia, Charlottesville.

As an educated man of the elite, Prentis certainly knew Josiah Nott and George Gliddon's *Types of Mankind*. The book, widely advertised in Virginia newspapers, summarized and popularized earlier work aimed at establishing the idea of race and racial hierarchy. The two men drew on the studies of Samuel George Morton, a Philadelphia doctor convinced that cranial capacity—the interior space of the skull—measured fundamental intelligence. Morton, with the help of an international network of scientists, collected over one thousand skulls, which he carefully cleaned, labeled, and then filled with birdshot or mustard seed so he could pour the material back into a graduated cylinder and get a measure of volume. He published the results as *Crania Americana* in 1839. Not surprisingly, Morton found what we would call white people on the top of the hierarchy and Africans on the bottom. Within the category "white people," which he termed "Caucasians," he identified the "Germanic, Celtic, Arabian, Libyan, and Nilotic racial types." Though an Anglo-Irish uncle financed his book, he regarded "Celts" as primitive, especially in Ireland. "In some localities their physical traits, their moral character and their peculiar customs, have undergone little change since the time of Cæsar. It is probable that the most unsophisticated Celts are those of the southwest of Ireland, whose wild look and manner, mud cabins and funereal howlings, recall the memory of a barbarous age." Morton's expensive book did not sell well, but it was the sort of book a young slaveholding Southerner like Prentis, studying natural philosophy at UVA that very year, might have sought out, because it justified slavery.[19]

Nott and Gliddon took Morton's findings and amplified them in *Types of Mankind*. The book used "physical anthropology"—mostly the measurement of skulls—to establish racial differences and hierarchies. Anne Fabian, in her history of skull collecting and race, puts Nott and Gliddon in a network of doctors and scientists who "helped Morton establish a 'natural history' of race that pretended to have 'discovered' the racial differences that it, in fact, had helped to invent." The chart in figure 5.5 asserted that among Caucasians, German and English people (and Anglo-Americans) had the largest

TABLE, *showing the Size of the Brain in cubic inches, as obtained from the measurement of 623 Crania of various Races and Families of Man.*

| RACES AND FAMILIES. | No. of Skulls. | Largest I. C. | Smallest I. C. | Mean. | Mean. |
|---|---|---|---|---|---|
| MODERN CAUCASIAN GROUP. | | | | | |
| *Teutonic Family* — Germans.................. ......... | 18 | 114 | 70 | 90 | ⎫ |
| " " English ...................................... | 5 | 105 | 91 | 96 | ⎬ 92 |
| " " Anglo-Americans................ ......... | 7 | 97 | 82 | 90 | ⎭ |
| *Pelasgic* " Persians ...................................... | ⎫ | | | | |
| " " Armenians ...................... ......... | ⎬ 10 | 94 | 75 | 84 | |
| " " Circassians .............................. | ⎭ | | | | |
| *Celtic* " Native Irish .............................. | 6 | 97 | 78 | 87 | |
| *Indostanic* " Bengalees, &c...................... | 32 | 91 | 67 | 80 | |
| *Semitic* " Arabs ...................................... | 3 | 98 | 84 | 89 | |
| *Nilotic* " Fellahs........................ ......... | 17 | 96 | 66 | 80 | |
| ANCIENT CAUCASIAN GROUP. | | | | | |
| *Pelasgic Family* — Græco-Egyptians (catacombs). | 18 | 97 | 74 | 88 | |
| *Nilotic* " Egyptians (from catacombs).. | 55 | 96 | 68 | 80 | |
| MONGOLIAN GROUP. | | | | | |
| *Chinese Family* .................................................... | 6 | 91 | 70 | 82 | |
| MALAY GROUP. | | | | | |
| *Malayan Family*.................... ....................... | 20 | 97 | 68 | 86 | ⎫ 85 |
| *Polynesian* " .................................................... | 3 | 84 | 82 | 83 | ⎭ |
| AMERICAN GROUP. | | | | | |
| *Toltecan Family* — Peruvians ........................... | 155 | 101 | 58 | 75 | ⎫ |
| " " Mexicans............................ | 22 | 92 | 67 | 79 | | |
| *Barbarous Tribes*—Iroquois ............................ | | | | | ⎬ 79 |
| " " Lenapé....................... ......... | ⎬ 161 | 104 | 70 | 84 | |
| " " Cherokee.............................. | | | | | |
| " " Shoshoné, &c...................... | ⎭ | | | | ⎭ |
| NEGRO GROUP. | | | | | |
| *Native-African Family* ................................... | 62 | 99 | 65 | 83 | ⎫ 83 |
| *American-born Negroes*........ ....................... | 12 | 89 | 73 | 82 | ⎭ |
| *Hottentot Family* .................................................... | 3 | 83 | 68 | 75 | |
| *Alforian Family* — Australians................ ......... | 8 | 83 | 63 | 75 | |

*Figure 5.5.* From Nott and Gliddon, *Types of Mankind*, 450, showing the alleged intelligence of "races" based on extremely small samples of dubiously sourced skulls. Library of Congress.

skulls, while the "native Irish" lagged behind Germans, English, and "Anglo-Americans" This was not a surprise, since the authors noted that "dark-haired, dark-eyed and dark-skinned Irish" still persisted in Ireland. There are all sorts of problems with this: for example, the tiny samples; their indifference to the size and gender of the person the skull had been attached to in life; and the larger problem of cranial capacity as a measure of "intelligence," which would put elephants and whales above everyone on this list.[20]

*Types of Mankind* was a useful book for people committed to hereditary racial slavery. It twice quoted Morton's claim that although "negroes were numerous in Egypt," "their social position, in ancient times, was the same that it is now: that of servants or slaves." And it was just as useful if, after hereditary racial slavery came to its violent end, you wanted justification for white supremacy. Nott and Gliddon embraced "polygeny," the idea that each "race" had its own "Adam and Eve." In this theory, the Christian Bible told only the story of the white Adam and Eve. If Christian lawmakers were uneasy with polygeny, they repeatedly cited the book's claims about natural hierarchy. *Types of Mankind* was not just some quaint nineteenth-century oddity: slaveholders and then advocates of white supremacy cited it repeatedly, well into the twentieth century. If Prentis did not own a copy of *Types of Mankind*, he surely knew about it. His job as clerk required him to assign a race to every person born or married in Nansemond and his term as judge required that he know about the book's claims, because as with Dempsey Hare, the law often had to settle legal questions revolving around race.[21]

## Race and Detection

In the last chapter, we saw that the problem of detection: forensic detection, intersecting with law, was always a central part of racecraft / statecraft. The law compelling free Negroes to register created a legal trace of African ancestry that appearance might conceal. Laws specifying what degree of blood made someone black were partly laws about detecting false appearance, like the Molly Maguires pretending to be ordinary miners or James McParlan posing as a miner so he could pose as a Molly. Witchcraft always involved detecting the presence of the hidden witch: racecraft required looking out for the hidden race. Building a society on presumed racial difference made the detection of individual and racial difference a vital skill.

Nott, a slaveholder, was born in South Carolina but practiced medicine in Mobile, Alabama. He wrote, "I am not sure that I ever saw at the South, one of such adult mixed-bloods so fair that I could not instantaneously trace the Negro type in complexion and feature." He believed that since Europeans and Africans were two different species, mixed people were doomed to die out. This is why he boasted that he could always tell: "the mulattoes, or mixed-breeds, die off before the dark stain can be washed out by amalgamation." He mentioned British geologist Charles Lyell, who "speaks of some mulattoes he met with in North Carolina, whom, he says, he could not distinguish from whites." Nott disagreed: "if any such examples exist, among the multiform crosses between Anglo-Saxons and Negroes, they must be extraordinarily few; because my half century's residence in our slave States should have brought me in contact with many instances." Nott argued a native of Britain "could not become familiarized with these various grades, and therefore his eye might well be deceived."[22]

Nott's interests compelled him to play detective. Enslavers prided themselves on being good judges of the "quality" of a person for sale, the way they might pride themselves on judging horses. Similarly they regarded themselves as experts on the nature of racial difference and wanted to believe, like Nott, that they could always detect African ancestry. In the case of *Hudgins v. Wright*, described in chapter 1, the judge had treated the court to a long speech regarding race and hair: "Nature has stampt upon the African and his descendants" characteristics that persist long after skin color changes. The "woolly head of hair . . . disappears the last of all: and so strong an ingredient in the African constitution is this latter character, that it . . . never fails to betray that the party distinguished by it." This doubtful theory of persistent hair was a large part of why he was willing to free Jackey Wright and her children. He was playing detective, and in 1806 detected no "African hair." The paper registration of free Negroes would have made that job easier.[23]

Seeing yourself as a good detective was central to racecraft. For example, William Ellis was born enslaved in Texas, with ancestors from Europe and Africa, but became a millionaire by passing as, variously Mexican, Cuban, Brazilian, and Hawaiian. He eventually bought a seat on the New York Stock Exchange. Karl Jacoby, in his biography of Ellis, points out that his ability to "pass" depended on other people's sense of themselves as acute judges of character and race, as masters of racecraft. Appearance, class, deportment might all be used to judge race, Jacoby writes, but once someone was assigned to a racial group "it became almost impossible to revisit the decision. Given that race was imagined to be so powerful, how could one have made a mistake earlier?" If you accused a person of having African ancestors, you might face a suit for slander. So "unless one felt that certain that the ancestry of another great-grandparent was provable in a court of law, legal practice discouraged reassessing a racial classification once it had been accepted." If someone accused William Ellis—or Dempsey Hare's illegitimate daughter Ida Ann Bland—of "being black," they also accused everyone who had accepted them of lacking judgment and acuity, of being duped. Paper documents certifying ancestry would answer the question.[24]

Prentis might have regarded the Irish as nonwhite or actually have convinced himself he saw a nonwhite person when he looked at Patrick. Figure 5.6 shows Patrick and family in about 1898, fourteen years after his marriage. He's noticeably darker than everyone else. Is it a trick of the light, or is that how he appeared when he went to the office of Peter Prentis?

All these things might explain why Prentis recorded Patrick and Hester as both white and colored: he wasn't sure, but didn't want to admit it to their faces. He had before him this sun-browned Irish laborer, clearly a member of the marginally white Celtic race, reminiscent of the soldiers who jailed him during the war, and this woman of modest background bearing a name shared equally by people of European and African ancestry. He knew about the sister named "Pocahontas" and maybe the name gave him pause. Maybe Hester looked like some of the people known to be "colored" in Nansemond. A photo of Josephine Hare, Dempsey Hare's niece and granddaughter of Axy

*Figure 5.6.* Patrick and family about 1898. Copy of family photo in author's possession.

Holland, appears on Andre Kearns's blog post "Race and Color Politics Revealed in Family History" (https://andrekearns.medium.com/race -and-color-politics-revealed-in-family-history-115959696a61). She could easily pass for white. Prentis likely knew of both these women, and he might have had doubts. Publicly he attested to Patrick's and Hester's whiteness; privately he expressed his doubt.

Perhaps he simply made a mistake, but everything in the world of Virginia pointed to the serious consequences of racial classification and the high stakes involved. Race, in Nansemond, often had little to do with what people looked like. As Francesca Morgan put it, surprisingly often "race resides in the eye of the beholder to the point that the search for confirmation of someone's race effectively creates their racial status." Neither Hester nor Patrick has any obvious, visible African ancestry in the photo, but did Prentis think Hester or Patrick were "passing"?[25]

## Patrick Reinvents Himself

Of course Patrick himself *was* "passing" at that very moment: passing
as an unmarried man, for one thing, and passing as a Protestant. His
Virginia marriage was illegal, a grave sin and a serious crime, bigamy.
His identity was arguably false: he used a different last name than his
siblings, back in Pennsylvania, who still went by "Melley." He might
have been hiding some relationship to the Molly Maguires. Chapter 1
talked about "runaways": Patrick was secretly a runaway. Along with
class snobbery or scientific racism or memories of "Yankee outrages,"
Prentis might have detected "the odor of mendacity" in Patrick. In
Summit Hill he would have been obviously one of thousands of Irish
immigrants, but here if he shed his old identity, he had a chance to
be something else. Both his individual identity and his racial identity
were unstable and unclear.

In Nansemond he reinvented himself. Patrick and Hester started a
family, and that family entered the historical record. Their first child,
Frederick, enthusiast of blacksmithing, came along in 1885. Family
stories have Fred born in Wakefield, Virginia, well to the north, where
in 1885 men labored building a branch of the Atlantic and Danville
Railroad. When he registered for the draft in WWI and WWII, Fred
gave his birthplace as "Suffolk." But the birth records of Virginia say
"Malley, Fred O," birthplace, Nansemond, list his race as white, and
name Patrick as a farmer. "Hester" has become "Esther": the "H" has
migrated east. A second son, Patrick, also listed as white, came along
in 1887. By then the family was named as "O'Malley." Patrick and Hester had a daughter named Anna, born in Nansemond in 1889, who
died three months later, that same year they named a newborn girl
Anne in her place. On those documents they are described as white
and named "Omalley." In 1892, they had a daughter, Mary. By then,
still listed as white, they were back to "O'Malley," but Patrick's occupation had changed from farmer to "mechanic." A son Joseph, also
termed white, was born in 1894.[26]

In January 1889, "Patrick O. Mally" and "Esther W. Mally" made the

first of several purchases of land, all of it at "Elwood Station" on the Atlantic and Danville line, which ran west to Charlotte County and east
to Portsmouth and the ocean. This was the railway proposed when the
Keileyville colony formed a decade earlier. They bought "the lot of land
on which the said O. Malley now lives," roughly half an acre, thirty-five
by seventy-five yards, fronting on the railroad, for $300, half paid up
front and the rest in installments of $15 a month. This made it very ex-
pensive land indeed: an acre in Keileyville went for $10. But he made
good on it: a month later he returned and bought the land outright.
He then made a series of somewhat complicated transactions, sometimes for parcels of land on the railroad amounting to less than an acre,
sometimes for parcels as large as ninety acres. The shifting names—
"Malley" "Mally," "O. Malley," "O. O'Malley," "Omalley"—show how
modern individualism was still not fully realized. He had an identity as a
property owner, but it wasn't fixed in the way, say, my name is fixed.[27]

Or sort of fixed: a few years ago, when applying for a new driver's
license compliant with the Department of Homeland Security's "Real
ID" regulations, I had to spend several hours trying to reconcile the
fact that some of my identity documents included an apostrophe and
some did not, either because some digital form did not allow for an
apostrophe or the person filling it out hadn't bothered to add it. Now
they all include the apostrophe, but many online forms still will not
allow an apostrophe including, ironically, Aer Lingus, the Irish airline.
But I might also seek to reclaim the Irish spelling: drop the apostrophe and insist on Ó, as in Ó Máille, the correct spelling of the name
in Irish, the spelling erased by colonization. Except Patrick's name in
Ireland was Melley, so I should call myself Mícheál Ó Meallaigh, with
a glorious three *fadas*, the accent mark, if I want to be as accurate as
possible. Except in Patrick's Donegal youth they didn't actually care
all that much about stable surnames, so why would I pretentiously
call on ancestry to insist on a fixed name the ancestors themselves
left behind in Ireland?

The individualism created by documents of identity is thus arti-
ficial, and the identity that the Department of Homeland Security

demanded only dimly reflects the complexities of history. At the same time, it's "natural" in that it's tied to physical individualism: when you reenter the US from Ireland you have to gaze into a facial recognition system. This facial recognition system of course adds metadata for "race" to the information it encodes, and no one who has read this far will be surprised to find that facial recognition systems stumble over racial classification. So we all have a dual personhood: a personhood rooted in the complex and messy legacies of family history and a static individualism severed from history and coded with race.[28]

If Patrick engaged in this sort of navel gazing, it does not show up in the record: Patrick was busy prospering. Trains began running past his house shortly after 1888, which meant easier connections to markets. The tracks, now abandoned, still cross Elwood Road about three miles from Dempsey Hare's house. A business called the Holy Neck Lumber Company ran a mill at Elwood, and in 1894, the "Elwood Manufacturing Company" got a charter to "manufacture barrels, baskets, fruit boxes, butter trays and all other articles made of wood or in which wood may be used." These latter might explain why Patrick was sometimes listed as a "mechanic" on his children's birth certificates. Trains carried cotton, tobacco, lumber, and coal from the west to Norfolk. Family stories suggest Fred, my great-grandfather, remembered his childhood in Virginia fondly. If you walk a few hundred yards west along the tracks from Elwood Road, you come to a bridge over a swampy pond, a place any child would love to play in and around. Judging by his adult passion for blacksmithing, he must have liked the steam and smoke and noise, the smell of burning coal and hot iron, as the locomotives went by. My father has a vague memory, when he was very small, of meeting "the Southern relatives" who made one visit north to Pennsylvania to see Fred: two slightly older kids related to Esther Holland. He never saw them again.[29]

In 1887, Patrick declared his intent to become a citizen, renouncing allegiance to all foreign potentates "especially to Victoria, Queen of Great Britain and Empress of India etc. whose subject he has heretofore been." In 1887, a person seeking naturalized citizenship had to have lived in the US for five years. They had to have a fixed place of residence and declare their intent to become a citizen to the court three years before applying. Applicants for citizenship also needed witnesses who could attest to their good character. An employee of the court, Norman Hayden, witnessed on behalf of Patrick, along with Charles H. Causey Jr., a prominent lawyer in the Hampton Roads area and the grandson of the same Peter Prentis who had secretly declared Patrick colored three years earlier. They swore that since his arrival he "has behaved as a man of good moral character attached to the principles of the Constitution." The assertion that he and Hester were colored seems to have had no impact: Peter Prentis died in 1889, and Judge Wilbur Kilby granted Patrick O'Malley citizenship a year later. But he may have faced a dilemma, because naturalized citizens also had to be white.[30]

In its first statement on citizenship, in 1790, Congress had limited naturalized citizenship to "free white persons of good character." Only white people could move to the US and gain citizenship. But Congress never defined what the term "white" meant—did it refer to skin color? In that case light-skinned people with African ancestors would become white. Or did it refer to "race," in which case persons with light skin might not count as white? The question fell to courts to decide, and between 1870 and the 1920s state and federal courts heard more than fifty cases in which they tried to sort out what "white" meant. Were Syrians, who came from the region of Jesus Christ, white? (sometimes). Were Asian Indians, classified by "racial science" as the first Caucasians, white despite their brown skin? (maybe). Were Japanese and Chinese people, light in color, "white"? (no). The racial classification cases culminated in two Supreme Court cases heard just weeks apart in the early 1920s. Takao Ozawa, born in Japan, applied for citizenship, arguing he had fully assimilated to American life. Ozawa pointed out that Japanese "not exposed to the heat of summer are particularly white-skinned. They are whiter than the average Italian, Spaniard or Portuguese." That is, he was "whiter" than many persons routinely considered white. In *Ozawa v. US* (1922), the court rejected his appeal, insisting that "the color test alone would result in a confused overlapping of races and a gradual merging of one into the other." White did not mean skin color; it meant "race." A few weeks later, it heard from Bhagat Singh Thind, born in Punjab, who argued that he was, according to racial science, an Aryan Caucasian and therefore a white person. The court rejected Thind as well, insisting that while "it may be true that the blond Scandinavian and the brown Hindu have a common ancestor in the dim reaches of antiquity," "the average man knows perfectly well that there are unmistakable and profound differences between them today": that is, the "average man" knows Thind is not white. So the court argued Ozawa was white but not Caucasian, and Thind was Caucasian but not white: neither met the standard for naturalized citizenship, which it held was governed by the general understanding of "the average man."

While "Arabians" and Syrians sometimes failed the test of whiteness, courts never considered if Jews were legally nonwhite, or Italians; interestingly, the one case regarding Mexicans concluded Mexicans were white. And despite the caricatures seen earlier, none of the cases concerned the Irish or made the claim that the Irish were not white. These groups all faced undeniable prejudice and discrimination, sometimes codified in local customs, regulations, or codes, and sometimes in violence. Racial theorists would regularly divide Caucasians into "Mediterranean" or "Latin" or "Semitic" or "Celtic" races. But in federal and state law, at least in terms of citizenship, all these groups sheltered under the umbrella of whiteness. We see here clearly the shoddy foundations supporting the idea of race: the common man "just knows" a Jewish immigrant or a Mexican immigrant counted as white, and that Syrians did not but Italians did. Whiteness might be understood as appearance, but it might be understood as an inward racial essence entirely unrelated to appearance. If Judge Kilby had looked at the Nansemond County register of marriages and seen how Patrick was listed, he might have faced a difficult decision: a colored immigrant was not eligible for naturalized citizenship.[31]

Patrick's marriage was not the only instance of an Irish person being declared colored—chapter 7 discusses other examples—but it seems to have had no effect on his ability to prosper in Virginia. In Pennsylvania's coal fields, Patrick was just another Irish laborer, despised and constrained. Virginia forced that underclass role onto African Americans. Whiteness gave Patrick a competitive advantage, and his prosperity grew from that relative advantage. He worked hard and struggled, nothing came easily, but in Virginia he could belong to a higher caste.

## Relocating to Georgia

But then he left Nansemond behind around 1897, with no explanation. He apparently sold the land in Nansemond and turned up next in Lumber City, in Telfair County, Georgia. Esther may have had relatives there: tax and census records show three men named Holland living in Lumber City in the 1880s. Again, as with Nansemond, he picked a place with no Catholic church and few if any Catholic residents. They had two more children in Georgia, and the 1900 census shows "Patrick O. O'Malley," "iron merchant" owning a substantial house. Family photos, purportedly of the house, show a two-story wood frame building with a one-story kitchen extension off the back, locally referred to as an "I-house." People in overalls pose in the pictures, but no one knows who they are. In a photograph taken in Lumber City, Patrick and Esther are seated, with their six children around them (figure 5.7). Esther wears a shirtwaist dress with mutton sleeves, faultlessly gleaming white and buttoned to the neck. Her hair in a tight bun, she offers the camera a grudging smile and again a look of energetic expectation, eager, it seems, to get this photo over with. Her oldest daughter wears a similarly gleaming white dress with a lace collar buttoned high: her youngest child sits on her lap. The two oldest boys, fourteen and twelve in 1900 and both listed as "day laborers" in the census, look resentful and unhappy in jackets and bow ties.[32]

Patrick, very much the satisfied patriarch, wears a suit and formal tie. He has a dark walrus mustache, is well tanned, and has large,

*Figure 5.7.* Family photo, circa 1900. The boy standing back row center, with the prominent ears, is my great-grandfather Fred.

strong hands, hands that do heavy work. He looks skeptical, as if he thinks the photographer charges too much money. He wears a watch chain across his vest with a Masonic lodge medal attached. In fact he had joined the Lumber City Masonic lodge in July of 1898 and had reached the degree of "Master Mason" by September of that same year. In 1899 and 1900, he served the lodge as "Tyler," a position somewhat like "sergeant at arms" or perhaps doorman.[33]

The photo gives more evidence he abandoned Catholicism. Rome forbid Catholics to join the Masons, threatening them with excommunication. The Masons returned the hostility. The *Mystic Star*, a monthly magazine of Masonry, in 1870 declared that "papacy is the stagnant pool from which arise poisonous exhalations, deadly to life, and producing a desert out of a garden of roses." The Masonic lodge offered

Patrick a male world of fellowship and elaborate nonsense, but joining the Masons, proudly wearing its emblem for posterity to witness, confirms that Patrick had repudiated Catholicism altogether.[34]

Lumber City had a population of about five hundred people. It had benefited from a shift in the national lumber industry from Minnesota and the Great Lakes region to Georgia's white pine forests. "Some of the largest stores in this section of the state are here, and the merchants are as enterprising and as clever a set of gentlemen as can be found anywhere. There are many handsome residences, some of which would do credit to a city of several thousand." The town had "a comfortable and commodious academy" for students but no public school. It had a brass band that competed for prizes against the band in nearby Macon.[35]

## Apartheid and Racial Violence

It also had a darker side. "Lumber City is one of the few towns that has heretofore literally enjoyed a white man's government," wrote a local newspaper approvingly. The town's population was evenly split between white and black people, and "under the present charter of the city," the "mayor and councilman are appointed by the Judge of the superior court." Otherwise "the negroes, by getting a few of the lower class white voters to side with them, will carry an election in the city." Another local newspaper, speaking about Lumber City and its "white man's government," added "we would be glad if the whole state was operated under pretty much the same law." As a consequence of having no political power, the newspaper continued, "the negro population there, which is said to be largely in the majority, has never given the authorities any trouble whatever."[36]

But in 1898, Patrick and family witnessed an attempted lynching. Headlines in the *Macon (GA) Telegraph* described how a "black brute" had murdered a local shopkeeper. Lumber City had a turpentine still, with a commissary and pay office. In an apparent dispute over pay the accused man, Will Williams, killed the commissary clerk, then fled. He was captured near Lumber City, where he allegedly confessed and implicated a white man identified only as "Strickland," who he said paid him to kill the clerk. Both men were put on a train passing through Lumber City to nearby McCrea. "A lynching would certainly have taken place at this town tonight if the people along the line of the Southern road between here and Lumber City could have found any way to be present," wrote the *Telegraph*. "It was thought certain that the crowd would get the two parties and lynch them this afternoon." But "the organization of those who wanted to take the men's lives was not perfected. A large crowd were at the depot when the train rolled in, but nobody seemed inclined to take the lead." Was Patrick in that crowd?[37]

The attempted lynching was a planned event, not a spontaneous action: the *Savannah Morning News* reported, "it was planned by people along the Southern Railroad to-night that the negro should be lynched before midnight, but the effort failed. The crowd did not organize sufficiently to accomplish anything and the lynching, if it occurs at all, will be later." The failure to lynch Will Williams probably had to do with the presence of Strickland, the white man. "Both prisoners were badly scared and crouched close to each other," as they made their way by train through Lumber City, chained together in an empty car. "Strickland is not a man of very high standing in the community, but he will probably be given the benefit of all doubt," the *Telegraph* insisted, "if he can establish his innocence no importance will be attached to the negro's story." "It is thought the white man," wrote the *Savannah Morning News*, "will be allowed to have a fair trial, but the feeling against the negro is very intense." Strickland was probably one of the "lower class whites," mentioned above, who might form an electoral alliance with Lumber City's African American citizens. The lynchers could not figure out how to respond to the mixed pair and their cooperation in crime. In the end Williams went to the gallows after a trial, and Strickland never faced prosecution. The difference in treatment was yet another version of racecraft and statecraft working together, in this case allowing the white man to escape justice altogether.[38]

If Patrick had not joined the mob, he would surely have known of this, heard about it as it happened, and discussed it with his family. They would have talked about it at the Masonic lodge. Patrick brought his family to a place where, in order to "avoid the danger of negro domination," they simply didn't hold elections, and where local newspapers licked their chops at the possibility of a lynching. The newspaper's casual enthusiasm reflects the fact that between 1877 and 1950, 595 people were lynched in Georgia, the overwhelming majority people with African ancestors. Here, very clearly, we see the advantages of being understood as white and how the local power structure used racecraft to frankly and openly maintain inequality.[39]

Virginia, by comparison, had "only" eighty-four lynchings in the same period. But across the South, a new, more virulent form of racist politics came to dominate in the 1890s. Southern politics had once included racial liberals, who believed that people with African ancestors might someday reach full equality and that state governments should encourage and foster that ideal. It also gave voice to racial conservatives, believing that African Americans could never be equal, but a just government should protect their basic civil liberties. Racial *radicals* insisted not just on the unchangeable biological fact of race, but as in Lumber City, on preventing African Americans from having any political power at all.[40]

In the 1890s, the racial radicals gained control in every former Confederate state, and between 1890 and 1905 each of the former Confederate states passed laws designed specifically to disenfranchise African American voters. They also established formal legal segregation. Back in Nansemond, segregation had been customary and informal, but by 1900, it had hardened into law and required signs posted in public places, and every public place demanded you locate yourself racially. And radical racism fostered or ignored terrorist violence like the lynching almost accomplished in Lumber City. Patrick was in the midst of this transition.

Historians have often considered why this turn to radical racism took place. C. Vann Woodward argued that Southern whites—as in the quote about Lumber City's governance above—worried about a political alliance of poor black and white farmers, neighbors who shared the same plight. He pointed out that many of the measures used to disenfranchise African American voters, like the poll taxes and the literacy tests, eliminated poor white voters as well. The "colored" and "white" signs nailed and screwed to the walls of waiting rooms, theaters, and bathrooms were racecraft mixed with statecraft, making people constantly think about race, reinforcing a distinction between people who might make common cause. This is exactly what white people in Lumber City feared, an electoral alliance of African Americans and "lower class whites."[41]

Other historians have suggested that radical racism triumphed because African Americans were undermining racecraft. In Nansemond County, Reverend Israel Cross founded the Mount Sinai Baptist Church in 1869, after the congregants left the brush arbor church on Dempsey Hare's farm. For more than forty years, he routinely ended sermons by telling his flock "buy some land, build a home, get some education." Owning land, prospering, acquiring practical skills and professional degrees, forming and maintaining churches, clubs, newspapers, and schools made for more effective forms of political organization: this determination to remake the meaning of racial difference terrified Euro-Americans committed to white supremacy.[42]

Life in Lumber City highlighted a dramatic moral question, if Patrick was paying attention. People of African descent in the US were very much like the Irish in Ireland: held in poverty by statecraft mingled with racecraft. Which side was Patrick on, the side of the oppressed or the side of the oppressor? He might have asked himself this question in Virginia, but Georgia made the question more vivid.

## *Philadelphia and a Return to the Catholic Church*

The family only stayed in Lumber City for a few years. By early 1901, they had given up the Georgia house and moved to Philadelphia. I'd like to believe that Patrick was troubled by the frank racism, the

aggressive hostility to outsiders, the enthusiasm for extralegal violence. Possibly his business failed, a common enough outcome, or
possibly he missed his Irish family and the faith of his birth.

Family stories say his sisters talked him into coming back. Patrick's
sisters Anna and Bridget had earlier moved to Philadelphia from Summit Hill or Coaldale. For whatever reason, Patrick and Esther headed
north, stopping in Nansemond to pick up Esther's sister Mary Holland.
Every member of the family, including Esther and Mary, was baptized
Catholic in Philadelphia on March 19, 1901, at Saint Agatha's, an impressive gothic church at Thirty-Eighth and Spring Garden Streets.
Patrick's still-valid marriage to Mary Murphy was never mentioned
or discovered—the older sisters, Anna, Bridget, and Mary, kept their
mouths shut. Sponsors at the baptisms, without exception, were the
children of Patrick's sisters. Whatever happened in Georgia made Patrick rejoin the church he had not belonged to for twenty years and set
his children on this new religious path.[43]

They lived at 720 Harmony Street in West Philadelphia, near the
railroad tracks that ran along the Schuylkill River. The neighborhood,
known then as "Corktown" and now as "Mantua," was heavily Irish. In
Corktown he would have heard songs in Irish again, for the first time in
twenty years. The Irish fiddler and composer Ed Reavey lived in Corktown: it had a lively Irish music community. Some of the tunes played
by Irish musicians have multiple names and were played by country
fiddlers across the US. Patrick might have recognized a hornpipe, "The
Little Beggarman," when Virginia or Georgia fiddlers played a tune
they called "The Red Haired Boy" or heard "Miss McCloud's Reel"
in "Did You Ever See the Devil, Uncle Joe?" He might have thought
of the lyrics to "*An Spailpín Fánach*," the lament of the Irish itinerant
farmworker, when someone struck up "The Girl I Left behind Me," a
common tune about a man whose work takes him away from his love.
Those songs, inflected by American playing, might have felt wrong to
him in Virginia and now he could hear them played the "right" way.
Perhaps he missed his family, missed the culture of his birth and the
faith of his youth. Maybe he remembered James Boyle and the miners

vain struggle. He had been unique in Nansemond, and especially in Lumber City, and he had thrown himself into Hester's world, adopted her religion, and lived with her relatives. Maybe it was time his children knew more about their father's world.

It must have been a shock to the family. The church alone would have dazzled, with its stained-glass windows and statuary, its Latin Mass and ornate vestments and incense: all the "papist mummery" scorned back in Nansemond. Philadelphia was the third largest city in the US, with light and heavy industry of all sorts: textile mills, freight and maintenance yards for two major railroads, and a very busy port. It had magnificent department stores and theaters, a zoo, museums, streetcars. It had Irish Catholics, more than two hundred thousand, more Irish-born citizens than any American city other than New York. Fred, now sixteen and eager to go to work, would have heard people who sounded like his father for the first time in his life.

Patrick had enough money to live in the respectable working-class neighborhood of Corktown but not enough for idleness. He took a job as a night watchman at the Adams Express office at the Broad Street Railroad station, and made the newspapers in 1902 when he helped apprehend two thieves by hiding in a box while they went about their work. Two men, John Nagle and William McDermott, went to jail on his testimony. A photo taken of Patrick, probably around the time of the arrest, shows him unsmiling in what might be a uniform and looking sidelong away from the camera, holding a nightstick. He wears a type of hat often worn by police in the US. Family stories, probably based on this photo, suggest he was a policeman in Philadelphia, but no evidence supports this. Any pleasure at appearing in the paper might have been countered by community disapproval of his role in sending two Irishmen to jail.[44]

Philadelphia was not kind to Esther, despite her sister Mary's presence. She had one more child, a daughter Sofia, in 1902, and then in 1903 Esther died at the Harmony Street house at age forty-one, of pneumonia following measles. The family buried her at Holy Cross Catholic Cemetery. Mary Holland continued to live with Fred, her nephew, until she died in 1911 and joined her sister at Holy Cross. Within two years of Hester's death, Patrick had remarried to a much younger woman named Rose Malloy, born like himself in Donegal. In 1906, now working as a janitor at Bell Telephone, he became a father again at age fifty-three. He and Rose had two more children. After 1912, Patrick worked as a "watchman" for Bell, with steady incremental pay increases amounting, by the 1920s, to just over $1,000 a year. At his death in 1928, from stomach cancer, he left Rose a pension equal to about a year's salary: that same year she remarried. His great-grandson, my uncle, worked in management for Bell and retrieved Patrick's records.[45]

In a last photo of Patrick, taken near his death for some official purposes, the fierceness and pride in earlier photos are replaced by a softer and maybe sadder look. He had been through a great deal: emigration, the violence of the anthracite fields, the life of a miner, the life of a farmer, the racial tensions of the Deep South. He had three marriages: he abandoned the first, saw his second wife die, and started a new family at age fifty; he fathered twelve children in total. Now he made nightly rounds in a deserted Center City office building, a long way indeed from a mud cabin in Donegal. If anyone remained in that cabin, if some sibling unknown to history kept trying to wrest a living from the bog, then maybe he, like Patrick, looked in the mirror and wondered if it had been worth it.

By the time of that photo, Patrick's oldest son, Fred, and his wife, Susan Harkin, also born in Donegal, had established the house they would stay in for the rest of their lives, a duplex in Upper Darby, Pennsylvania. It was a common move among Euro-American Philadelphians as African Americans began emigrating to Philadelphia from the South. I remember Susan Harkin's wake at that house in 1974. Fred worked for the Philadelphia Electric Company as a construction supervisor and manager, and generations of O'Malleys got jobs at Philadelphia Electric as a result. He was proud to have run work on the Conowingo dam, still generating electricity in Maryland just south of the Mason-Dixon Line. He told his grandson that he had

*Figure 5.8.* Copy of undated photo of Patrick O'Malley, circa 1925, in author's possession.

gone "as high as a Catholic could go" at Philadelphia Electric, an observation that suggested he remembered a time when he wasn't a Catholic. Though Fred had a reputation in my parent's generation as a grim domestic tyrant, the sort of man who turned the heat down when he left the house and forbid anyone to touch the thermostat, the family lived like other Irish Americans in Philadelphia: regular attendance at Mass, dances at the parish hall, summer trips to the Jersey shore, jobs in Philadelphia's industrial working class, slow generational mobility.

By the time Patrick Melley died, the range of paper records had expanded dramatically, and the kind of radical passing, the self-transformation and escape that he had pulled off in the 1880s, would have been much harder. He left records of his employment, his application for citizenship, his marriage, the births of his children, their baptisms, his wife's death, his death, his funeral, his gravesite. He had a fixed legal name. He appeared in city directories. None of those things had existed for his parents, back in Ireland. None of them existed for Esther's parents either. His children would register for the draft in WWI and get social security cards in the 1930s. If they traveled overseas, they had to apply for passports. His great-grandchildren can take DNA tests to reconcile paper records with ancestry.

The question of why they were listed as colored is unanswered. It might have been that Peter Prentis regarded Irish people as not quite white. Irish people experienced bigotry and were caricatured as ape-like, and scientific authorities often regarded them as a subset of the Caucasian race, as "melanochroi" Caucasians or at worst as "white chimpanzees." He might have remembered with resentment the Yankees with Irish accents who had put him in jail twenty years earlier. Peter would surely have read of the "savagery" of the Molly Maguires and perhaps sensed Patrick was hiding something—a tangential connection to the Molly Maguires or his abandoned wife. Those things, combined with his status as a common laborer in a region where common laborers were usually people of African descent, might have led him to dip his pen and write "colored" in the privacy of his office.

Or he might have looked at Hester and thought about Dempsey Hare, and his wife Anne Holland, and their daughter Ira Ann, light enough to "pass": Prentis had recorded her marriage to Meredith White in 1870. He would have written the name "Anne Holland" in the space reserved for the mother of the bride. He might have seen the two Hester Hollands "of color" living in Nansemond and thought "she's one of them." If so, he did the couple a favor, sparing them the legal punishment that might have come from engaging in a mixed marriage.

A simple mistake remains the least likely explanation. Racecraft was not practiced lightly: it had momentous legal and social consequences. The law insisted "race" mattered and compelled Prentis to be accurate, and he had just seen the couple with his own eyes and written "white" on their actual marriage license. History shows he had planted a bomb: if anyone wished the couple ill, they might have found this record.

It's conceivable, though no evidence exists, that Patrick left Virginia because rumors of this nonwhite identity plagued him. At the time he left Nansemond, Virginia was transitioning into an era of radical racism and increasingly demanding, and finding, ways to police formal segregation. By the time Patrick died, Virginia was the nation's leader in turning eugenical principles into state law. If he left Virginia because of a vague suspicion he was nonwhite, Georgia was the wrong place to go: the state practiced radical racism with a good deal more ferocity. Whispers of nonwhite status might have followed him to Georgia, and in that climate, and Protestantism and membership in the Masons might not have been enough protection.

If Patrick had remained in Virginia, by 1925 his children would not have been legally allowed to marry people regarded as white and likely would have had their schooling constrained by racecraft, thanks to the work of Walter Ashby Plecker, who waged a national crusade to purify "the race" through careful review of "administrative records." Plecker routinely wrote to county clerks and local officials to tell them the couple they had just married, the person they had just buried, the children in their school were *actually* black. Were he alive today he would regard me as a black man, because in his view and by law any "ascertainable trace" of African ancestry made someone black. Peter Prentis established that trace: Hester and Patrick's marriage record, the genealogical record generated by the state, would have been enough.

# SIX

# RICHMOND

*A Terrible Man*

In August of 1940, Dr. Walter Ashby Plecker, registrar of Virginia's Bureau of Vital Statistics, sat at his desk in Richmond, on the seventh floor of the Virginia State Office Building. The window would have been open to catch some air on a warm summer day. Letters, reports, and pamphlets covered Plecker's desk, protected from stray breezes by paperweights. He had a jar of ink for his fountain pen, and a pot of glue for affixing corrections, and boxes of carbon paper. Someone had made a mistake. Plecker lived for moments like this: they were the entire point of his life.

He dictated a letter to Mr. Arthur H. Crismond, clerk of the Circuit Court of Spotsylvania County. Plecker told him, "we have your certificate for the marriage, February 28, 1940, of Philip N. Saure, a native of the Philippine Islands, and Elsie M. Thomas, an Italian born in Pittsburgh, Pennsylvania." Plecker reviewed every marriage in Virginia, it seemed, hunting for signs of racial impropriety. "If we are correct in assuming that this woman is white," he told Crismond, "then under the law of Virginia, you as Clerk were not authorized to issue a marriage license to a person of any of the colored races, including Filipinos," who as "Malays," were "one of the colored races." "I am calling your attention to this matter that you may take such action as you deem advisable."

Plecker wanted Crismond to tell the Saures their marriage was illegal, and he wanted Crismond to know that he, Plecker, was ever

*Figure 6.1.* Plecker in about 1924, from Philip Alexander Bruce, *History of Virginia* (Chicago: American Historical Society, 1924), 5:398.

on the watch for racial subversives. But he offered Crismond a possible resolution:

> The Italians from the Island of Sicily are badly mixed with former negro slaves, and if this woman is from there, it is barely possibly that she herself would have a trace of negro blood and would be eligible for marriage to a Filipino. Proving this would probably be impossible, we are not attempting to trace genealogy outside of Virginia families.

He held out the slim possibility they might stay married if Italians were not white.[1]

From his office in Richmond, Plecker did this sort of thing all the time, practicing racecraft, week after week, for more than thirty years. Starting in 1912, he campaigned for racial segregation and bans on racial intermarriage, and then hectored officials, lectured school superintendents, traced genealogies, and wrote to ordinary people, just to harass them, hoping to prop up the racecraft that his job revolved around.

In April 1924, he wrote to Mrs. Robert Cheatham in Lynchburg. His office had just received a birth certificate for her child, born a year prior, signed by a local midwife, and the midwife had listed mother, father, and child as white. Plecker had records that suggested otherwise. "Dear Madam," he began innocently enough. Plecker told her they had received a correction from the city health department at Lynchburg, "in which they say that the father of this child is a negro." Plecker declared, "this is a mulatto child and you cannot pass it off as white. A new law passed by the last Legislature says that if a child has one drop of negro blood in it, it cannot be counted as white." He continued: "this child is not allowed to mix with white children. It cannot go to white schools and can never marry a white person in Virginia." He closed with "It is an awful thing. Yours very truly, W. A. Plecker, State Registrar."

The awful thing here is Plecker, with his zeal to practice racecraft on Virginia's most vulnerable citizens. Census records from 1900 through 1930 list Robert Herbert Cheatham as a white man. His draft registration for WWI named him as "Caucasian." But Plecker found someone named Robert Cheatham listed as having African ancestors, and so Plecker was sure, so sure that he wrote the midwife, Mary Gildon, saying, "it is a penitentiary offense to willfully state that a child is white when it is colored. You have made yourself liable to very serious trouble by doing this thing. What have you got to say about it?"[2]

If she had anything to say about it, the response does not survive. Plecker's papers, and the full record of his bullying, were apparently destroyed after he died in 1947, struck by a car a year after he finally retired. By 1946, the revelation of the Nazi concentration camps had given Plecker's eugenical enthusiasms a bad name, but Plecker didn't care. He had boasted, during WWII, that "Hitler's genealogical study of the Jews is not more complete" than his study of Virginia's colored people. Even in Virginia in 1947, this sort of statement was embarrassing. The only extant copies of Plecker's letters and memos reside in one small collection kept by the Clerk of Rockbridge County, Virginia, and in samples Plecker sent to his friend John Powell, hoping to impress him. On a copy of his letter to Mrs. Cheatham he scrawled, "Dear Mr. Powell: This is a specimen of our daily troubles and how we are handling them." Even this small sample of more than thirty years' work, roughly two hundred letters, is enough to appall and dismay.[3]

His range was extensive. Public school officials, for example, sometimes had doubts about their students. Mr. C. K. Holsinger wrote to Plecker from Henrico County, asking about "the racial status of three . . . sons of Alexander Morwood Davis and Edith Maria Collins." Plecker told Holsinger that the father appeared to be white, "the mother, however, is of free negro descent as shown in various records." Here he referred to the "free Negro registers" described in chapter 1, still doing their intended work a century later. "This family has been carefully studied, and we have no hesitancy in declaring that the mother is of negro descent. The children, therefore, according to Virginia law, which says that anyone with any ascertainable degree of negro blood will be classified as a negro, can not be permitted to attend white public schools." Who knows what triggered Superintendent Holsinger's concern? The Davis family might have looked "suspicious," or they might have acted in some way that offended Holsinger. Plecker told him, "this family has been especially aggressive in their endeavors to secure classification as white. The fact that the mother secured admittance into the white ward of Memorial Hospital is evidence of this fact." So we know the family looked white enough for admission into a segregated hospital: she was white enough for the hospital, but not white enough for the school. Plecker offered a definitive answer with the force of state authority: he merged racecraft with statecraft.[4]

In 1943, Nancy Hundley, superintendent of public welfare in Cumberland, Virginia, wrote to Plecker about a local woman, "the illegitimate child of a white mother and probably a colored father" then living in Cumberland. He seized on this chance to build records. "The first thing that we desire to know . . . is whether the birth has been reported to our office." They had no record of the child's parents, and "in cases of this sort, we cannot follow our usual methods of establishing race by records already in our office of the ancestors but must depend entirely upon such information as can be secured locally, and upon the appearance of the child itself." Plecker asked her to bring the child to Richmond, "and we will check on it in connection with the birth certificate and also examine the child as to racial characteristics. Psychological examination or blood tests do not show the race. That has to be decided upon what can be seen and learned."[5]

Nine days later he wrote back to Hundley, who rather than bringing the child to Richmond to be inspected sent him more information about "Mattie Murray, the feeble-minded white woman who seems to have given birth to one or two mulatto children." He told her that in the absence of paper records, "you and the sheriff and any other intelligent citizens of your community, are as capable of judging from the appearance of the child as the most learned scientist." He added, "there is absolutely no blood or other test to determine that question—only the appearance of the children and the habits of the mother as to association with negroes." He concluded by telling her that "the proper thing to do without loss of time is to place this woman in the State Colony and have her sterilized." Virginia was second only to California in the number of "eugenic sterilizations" it carried out.[6]

Plecker liked playing detective, and he liked sorting people into what he regarded as their proper place. As in the case of Mattie Murray, he combined flimsy evidence about her intelligence and "association with negroes" in the present with strict attention to genealogy. He made it personal and took pleasure in shaming and intimidating people when he could. When Aileen Hartless wrote to him from Fishersville, Virginia, he told her, "all of the records in your family, and particularly on the Clark side, which have been traced back to the Revolutionary War, show them before the War Between the States as free negroes. After the war until quite recent years, they were called colored, or Mulatto or free issues." It was true, he admitted, that "many of these women have mixed up with white men out of wedlock so that many of them look almost white, and are moving away from home as you, or your family, has done, and are trying to pass as white." Plecker wanted to stop this sort of passing at nearly all costs. "I have no doubt at all but that it is embarrassing for you," he told Mrs. Hartless, but "your parents started out to make false statements about themselves, and their children are suffering." If he had his way, they would suffer more. "Giving of false registration as to race, makes the parents, or whoever wrote it down, liable to one year in the penitentiary . . . it is possible that some of these cases will come into court. We might try this one. It would make a good one, if you continue to try to be what you are not."[7]

Plecker had no authority to initiate prosecutions, but he saw intimidation as a crucial tool in building a more extensive and effective record of racial identity. The Rockingham Poultry Marketing Company in 1945 wrote to Plecker asking about a prospective employee. He told them, "the names of the parents, Floyd and Clark, are those of a large group of mixed breeds striving to pass as white. They have given the race of both parents as white. The law now requires us to verify such apparent errors and to give the correct pedigree of the race from public records. This requires some time and it may be a while before we can furnish you certificates. Do not consider this girl as white unless you secure our endorsement to that effect."

The Rockingham Poultry Marketing Corporation would not hire Dorothy Lucille Floyd if she had African ancestors, but they could not see clear evidence. Plecker seized the chance to investigate her background, make the invisible seem tangible, and produce another definitive account of "race" that he could project forever into Ms. Floyd's future. Dorothy Floyd's job depended on the outcome of Plecker's research. If he pronounced her to be a black person, she wouldn't get the job, and neither could her children, and then she might be added to statistics on unemployment among people with African ancestors. And then white officials might cluck and shake their heads in disapproval of unemployment rates among the lazy black people. Racecraft produced and then justified systematic inequality.[8]

As a state official, Plecker used the past to control the present and the future. He wrote to the superintendent of the Riverview Cemetery in Charlottesville to tell him, "we have a certificate, Volume 1794-6706, for William H. Moon, who died March 15, 1940, at the University Hospital and was buried at Riverview Cemetery March 17, 1940." Plecker's numbered volumes indicate the extent and meticulousness of his record keeping: he mentioned it to intimidate his reader with a vision of vast and precise bureaucracy. "Possibly you are not aware of the fact that this man is of negro ancestry, the record of this man's birth, January 17, 1874, shows his mother as colored. Other records of our office confirm this classification." "There is a mulatto branch of the Moon family of Albemarle County," he continued, "striving in every way possible to secure white recognition." He wanted to put a stop to it and told the superintendent "to take such steps as you may deem necessary. You probably know whether the State law permits the use of a white cemetery by colored people." Statecraft and racecraft merged: Plecker magically turned a white corpse black and then used state authority to compel the cemetery director to move the body.[9]

People from other states heard about Plecker's impressive work and wrote to him. Charles Stokes, executive secretary of the County Welfare Board in La Plata, Maryland, asked Plecker about "the four children of George Hoffman and Ema Smith Hoffman." Plecker eagerly told him, "we had occasion to study this family some time ago when requested by a Washington cemetery for information as to their color. An effort seems to have been made to bury some of them in a white cemetery." He attached a list his office compiled regarding the racial status of the Huffman family:

> You will observe that four of the children are listed as colored or mulatto. Two of the latter ones got by as white. It may be that they are actually of lighter color than the others and according to Mendel's law could succeed in passing as white. By that law, you know that out of four children one would be quite dark, another quite light, with two intermediates. They all, however, bear the negro heritage and are capable of transmitting the negro characteristics to their own children. We do not classify any of these children as white even though two of the six may have been so listed in our office. They are all considered in our office as colored. . . . The Huffman grandparents of these children were married under a colored license on July 30, 1885, in Fauquier County, which they seem to have accepted from the clerk and used without any question.[10]

This is exactly the case, it seems worth noting, with Patrick O'Malley and Hester Holland. Both were recorded as colored in the Nansemond County register of marriages in 1884 and "seem to have accepted it and used it without any question" because they possibly never knew about it. Plecker in 1939 did not have a copy of that marriage register, but he had asked for it, and in 1940 it arrived, part of his statewide campaign to centralize, rationalize, and resurvey the state's practice of racecraft. Plecker often confronted the "problem" of people who looked white but had an African ancestor visible only in a marriage license, a birth certificate, or census record from the distant past. So having obtained a genealogical, administrative record of Patrick and Esther as black people, would he have forbid their children to marry white people?

Correspondents often asked Plecker if there was a blood test to determine race. "There is no dependable blood test by which the race may be determined. Various attempts have been made at that but they are entirely misleading and we make no effort at settling the question in that manner," he told Dr. Samuel Nixon. "The only way is by the genealogical records." In our office, he continued, we have records of "the births, deaths, and marriages, and in the State library are the census reports of 1850 and 1870, and the tax lists by race, which go back to the early part of the last century, all of which show how individuals are listed as to race many years ago before they had secured illegitimate crossing with the white race." These are the very records described earlier, in chapters 1 and 2: those records were materials with which Plecker practiced racecraft. In lieu of a blood test, he sent Dr. Nixon a list of Montgomery County surnames he regarded as suspect.[11]

When Elsie Graham, a public health nurse, asked a similar question about a "blood test" he told her, sadly, "there is no reliable test for such determination, and I know of no court that recognizes any claims of that sort." His response got to one of the central problems of racecraft. "Even if it were possible to distinguish the blood of a true negro from that of a white person, the difficulty would come with the intermediates—the only place where the test is required. Then it would sometimes prove Black and sometimes white, thus making it totally unreliable." Like the judge in *Hudgins v. Wright*, he considered hair: "some effort has been made to determine the race by the hair," but "the hair of a mulatto may have the characteristics of a negro or of a white person, thus making such a test entirely unreliable." As a result, "the only method which we use of determining the race is by the pedigree. In our office we have been able to trace large numbers of mixed families who are now trying to pass as white back to the original negro ancestors through the records in our office and the census office, going back to 1830. If you have any case that is troubling you, it is possible that we have already studied it and can give you information if you will give us, if possible, all of the facts, including the parents and grandparents involved."[12]

A Pennsylvania woman wrote to Plecker asking about the pedigree of someone her daughter was dating. "Clarence Brown is the great great grandson of a negro-man by a white woman, Betsy Catlett," he told her. "Their mulatto child was named Nancy Elizabeth, or 'Sood' [she is shown as white]. This mulatto child afterwards married Bill Ripley Brown, a white man. By this marriage there were three children, Lize, Bettie Lee, George. Lize gave birth to an illegitimate child named Thomas Henry Brown, [listed as white 1900] who married Nora Maupin [also listed as white] and became the father of Clarence Brown." By this complicated and confusing history Clarence had only a very slight trace of African ancestry, but Plecker regarded his records as faultless and clear. "You have the thing straight now," he told Mrs. Quibell, "and we hope that your daughter can see the seriousness of the whole matter and will dismiss this young man without more ado."[13]

The thing was anything but straight. The 1850 census shows the three children of Bill Ripley Brown as white, and the 1900 census shows Thomas Ripley Brown and his wife, Nora Maupin, as white. Clarence Brown's birth certificate shows him as white, but Plecker penciled in the word "over," meaning "see reverse side," near the word "white" and on the back added a typed card saying:

> Clarence Brown is the great great grandson of a white woman and a negro man. His great grandmother was a mulatto and named Nancy Elizabeth or "Sood" Catlett. She married a man said to be white by the name of Bill Ripley Brown and had three children, Lize, Betty Lee and George. Lize had an illegitimate child named Thomas Henry Brown. This Thomas Henry Brown married Nora Maupin of Albemarle County and Clarence is the son of this union.[14]

Plecker eventually issued a "WARNING. — To be attached to the backs of birth or death certificates of those believed to be incorrectly recorded as to color or race." The full page of closely spaced text gave a short history of mixed people in Virginia and would cast suspicion on people when bureaucratic records were lacking or unclear.[15]

Put aside the hounding going on here, the obsessiveness, and it's fascinating to look at how Plecker combined claims to precision with pure assumption and rhetoric designed to sow doubt. For example, "Clarence Brown is the great great grandson of a white woman and a negro man." This "negro man" is not named, and the source of the information not given, but by this piece of racecraft he has magically transformed Nancy Elizabeth Catlett into a person with African ancestors. Bill Ripley Brown was "said to be white," Plecker wrote: said to be white by *exactly the records Plecker liked to rely on*. The 1850 census lists Bill, his parents, and his entire family as white, but "said to be" throws shade, as it were, on Clarence and his family. Bill Ripley Brown and Nancy Catlett did have a daughter, Elizabeth—the 1860 census records call her "Eliza," not "Lize." Calling her "Lize" also serves to make her seem less reputable. The 1860 census lists the entire family as white. Elizabeth married a man named William Staton, listed as white on the 1880 census. But that record transforms Elizabeth from white to "mulatto" and lists Thomas as "step-son," also mulatto. Plecker called Thomas an "illegitimate child," but a stepson is not necessarily illegitimate, and by 1900 the census was calling Thomas Henry Brown a white man. Plecker wanted to cast doubt on Thomas. There was nothing at all straight about the record, but Plecker blended descriptive rhetoric with administrative records, and he insisted that one record showing African ancestry outvoted half a dozen showing only European ancestry. In his view—and according to a law he worked hard to pass—"any ascertainable trace" of African ancestry made someone black. Plecker used the state's records of racecraft to produce the thing he desired to see.[16]

Around 1940, Blanche Cunningham of Hampton, Virginia, started a relationship with a man named Gus Stewart. The local clerk of the court advised her to write to Plecker to have Stewart checked out. "Dear Miss Cunningham," he replied. "I am surprised that one of the

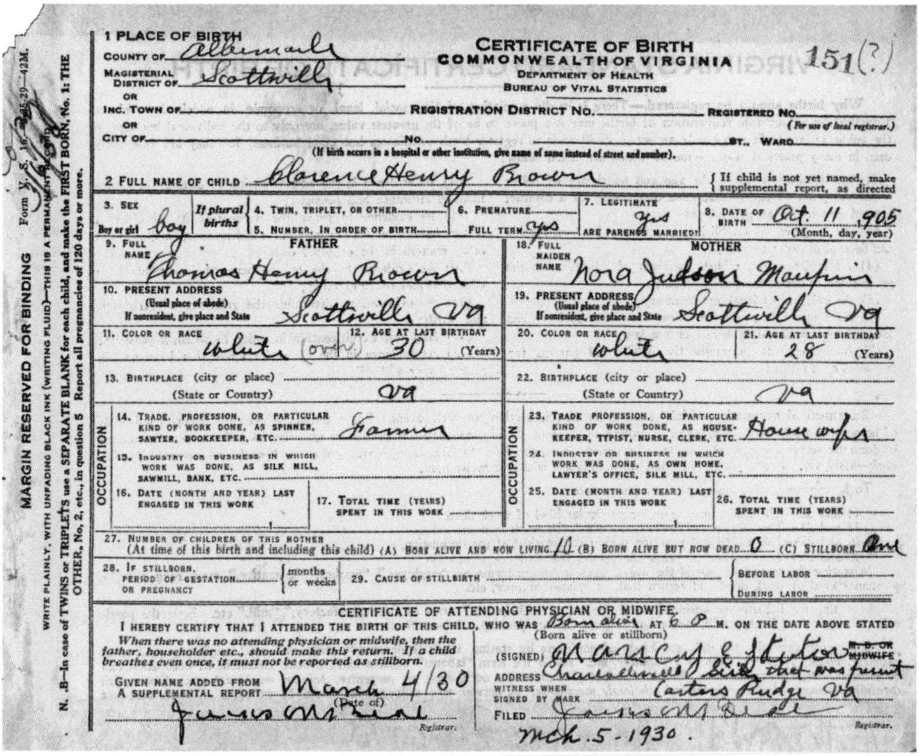

Form V. S. 16 ... 29—42M.

MARGIN RESERVED FOR BINDING

WRITE PLAINLY, WITH UNFADING BLACK INK (WRITING FLUID)—THIS IS A PERMANENT RECORD

N. B.—In case of TWINS or TRIPLETS use a SEPARATE BLANK for each child, and make the FIRST BORN, No. 1; THE OTHER, No. 2, etc., in question 5. Report all pregnancies of 120 days or more.

1 PLACE OF BIRTH
COUNTY OF Albemarle
MAGISTERIAL DISTRICT OF Scottsville
OR INC. TOWN OF
OR CITY OF ... NO. ... ST., WARD
(If birth occurs in a hospital or other institution, give name of same instead of street and number).

CERTIFICATE OF BIRTH
COMMONWEALTH OF VIRGINIA
DEPARTMENT OF HEALTH
BUREAU OF VITAL STATISTICS

151(?)

REGISTRATION DISTRICT NO. ... REGISTERED NO. ... (For use of local registrar.)

2 FULL NAME OF CHILD Clarence Henry Brown
{If child is not yet named, make supplemental report, as directed

3. SEX Boy or girl boy | If plural births | 4. TWIN, TRIPLET, OR OTHER | 5. NUMBER, IN ORDER OF BIRTH | 6. PREMATURE / FULL TERM yes | 7. LEGITIMATE yes / ARE PARENTS MARRIED? | 8. DATE OF BIRTH Oct. 11 1905 (Month, day, year)

FATHER
9. FULL NAME Thomas Henry Brown
10. PRESENT ADDRESS (Usual place of abode) If nonresident, give place and State Scottsville Va
11. COLOR OR RACE white (over)
12. AGE AT LAST BIRTHDAY 30 (Years)
13. BIRTHPLACE (city or place) (State or Country) Va
OCCUPATION
14. TRADE, PROFESSION, OR PARTICULAR KIND OF WORK DONE, AS SPINNER, SAWYER, BOOKKEEPER, ETC. Farmer
15. INDUSTRY OR BUSINESS IN WHICH WORK WAS DONE, AS SILK MILL, SAWMILL, BANK, ETC.
16. DATE (MONTH AND YEAR) LAST ENGAGED IN THIS WORK
17. TOTAL TIME (YEARS) SPENT IN THIS WORK

MOTHER
18. FULL MAIDEN NAME Nora Judson Maupin
19. PRESENT ADDRESS (Usual place of abode) If nonresident, give place and State Scottsville Va
20. COLOR OR RACE white
21. AGE AT LAST BIRTHDAY 28 (Years)
22. BIRTHPLACE (city or place) (State or Country) Va
OCCUPATION
23. TRADE, PROFESSION, OR PARTICULAR KIND OF WORK DONE, AS HOUSEKEEPER, TYPIST, NURSE, CLERK, ETC. Housewife
24. INDUSTRY OR BUSINESS IN WHICH WORK WAS DONE, AS OWN HOME, LAWYER'S OFFICE, SILK MILL, ETC.
25. DATE (MONTH AND YEAR) LAST ENGAGED IN THIS WORK
26. TOTAL TIME (YEARS) SPENT IN THIS WORK

27. NUMBER OF CHILDREN OF THIS MOTHER (At time of this birth and including this child) (A) BORN ALIVE AND NOW LIVING 10 (B) BORN ALIVE BUT NOW DEAD 0 (C) STILLBORN One

28. IF STILLBORN, PERIOD OF GESTATION OR PREGNANCY ... months or weeks | 29. CAUSE OF STILLBIRTH | BEFORE LABOR / DURING LABOR

CERTIFICATE OF ATTENDING PHYSICIAN OR MIDWIFE
I HEREBY CERTIFY THAT I ATTENDED THE BIRTH OF THIS CHILD, WHO WAS Born alive AT 6 P. M. ON THE DATE ABOVE STATED
(Born alive or stillborn)
When there was no attending physician or midwife, then the father, householder etc., should make this return. If a child breathes even once, it must not be reported as stillborn.
(SIGNED) Mary Cuf E. Staton M. D. OR MIDWIFE
ADDRESS Charlottesville Va. that was present
WITNESS WHEN SIGNED BY MARK Carters Ridge Va

GIVEN NAME ADDED FROM A SUPPLEMENTAL REPORT March 4/30 (Date of)
James M. Neal
Registrar.

FILED James M. Neal
Mch. 5-1930.
Registrar.

Clarence Brown is a great great grandson of a white woman and a negro man. His great grandmother was a mulatto and named Nancy Elizabeth or "Sood" Catlett. She married a man said to be white by the name of Bill Ripley Brown and had three children, Lize, Betty Lee and George. Lize had an illegitimate child named Thomas Henry Brown. This Thomas Henry Brown married Nora Maupin of Albemarle County and Clarence is the son of this union.

*Figure 6.2.* Birth certificate of Clarence Henry Brown. *Top*, box 11, see where Plecker's office penciled in "over" so people would look at the back of the certificate and see his correction. *Bottom*, the typed addendum Plecker's office attached to the certificate. Virginia Department of Health, Richmond, Virginia, *Virginia, Births, 1864–2015*. The record is available at Ancestry.com, *Virginia, U.S., Birth Records, 1912–2015, Delayed Birth Records, 1721–1920*.

respectable Cunningham family of Elizabeth City County should ask us about the racial status of one of Gus Stewart's children with a view to obtaining a marriage license." "His family is of negro descent and therefor cannot intermarry into the white race." He warned her that "if a white person insists upon marrying anyone of this family they are both liable to one or two years in the penitentiary." Proud of his office staff, he declared, "we have definitely traced the family tree of Gus Stewart back to a negro woman. Gus Stewart was a child by a white man of Margaret Stewart, a mulatto woman she herself being a daughter of a negro woman, Eliza Harris, by a white man. I trust that will be clear enough and that you will immediately break off entirely with this young mulatto man."[17]

He trusted it would be clear enough because again in Plecker's mind—and by that point in Virginia by law—any evidence at all of African ancestry made someone nonwhite, and no amount of European ancestry could overcome this deficit. Records of Gus Stewart's family are very hard to find: it may have been a nickname, and in this case Plecker seems to have relied on personal experience. "When practicing medicine in Hampton thirty years ago I myself attended the wife of Gus Stewart when one of her children was born. When they reported the birth she stated that she was Indian and colored. You can find that certificate now on record in the county health office. That is one of the very few cases in which the negroes who are trying to pass as Indians have themselves stated that they are colored."[18]

Many historians have written, well and in detail, about Plecker. Most have focused for excellent reasons on his enthusiasm for eugenics, his influence on Virginia law, and his claim that there were no "real" Indians in Virginia, only colored people trying to escape segregation. Though in practice communities might accept some people as Indian, Plecker was determined to stop that practice and treat all people with Indian ancestors as colored people. Plecker is sometimes accused of "bureaucratic genocide" for having altered records so that people who called themselves Indian were listed as colored, an effort to wipe out the historical record of Native people in Virginia. But here

I want to look at Plecker as Virginia's "state genealogist," the man sorting out family and its relationship to law and the state, the man who worked hardest to unite "racecraft" with statecraft. Genealogy was his primary tool in the construction of racial hierarchy. Plecker's work makes the relationship between individualism and racism clear: Plecker used stable paper records of individuals to produce his ideas of racial truth and project it into the future.[19]

## Childhood

Plecker was born in 1861, in Augusta County, Virginia, near Staunton, the county seat. His father, Jacob Plecker, ran a store that sold household goods—furniture, china. The "Plecker building" is still there. The Pleckers came from Switzerland before the Revolutionary War, and Jacob's father, who used the surname "Blaecher," fought in the war of 1812. Jacob grew up in house with people held in slavery, three in 1850. He had a restless side. Jacob applied for a passport in 1850, and as mentioned in chapter 1, by law the application required a physical description. Jacob was five feet and eleven and a half inches, with a forehead "full and round": he had "hazel" eyes, an "oval" face with "regular" features, brown hair, and a "light" complexion.

It's not clear why he needed the passport: he was said to have gone to California for the gold rush of 1849, "returning several years later." In 1854, he married Frances Burton Smoot in Virginia. A year later, he managed to get himself appointed postmaster at "Mount Eutopia" in Augusta County. "He put the gold with the money he inherited from his father's estate and operated a very successful mercantile business [in Staunton] until he retired from business in 1885." In the 1880 census, he is not listed—he must have been away, suggesting again a certain restless streak, but it's odd that the census taker did not ask Frances Plecker about her absent husband. He engaged in several different real estate speculations, one in Jefferson County, Alabama, and one in Rockbridge County, Virginia. At the time of his death in 1890, he was "director and general manager of the Raphine Improvement

Company," which was trying to build a railroad between Raphine and Staunton. He died in a railroad accident in Staunton in 1890, and Walter was at his bedside.[20]

Walter went to school in Staunton at the Hoover Military Academy. The 1880 census shows him working as a clerk at his father's store on North Augusta Street, offering "one of the most extensive and beautiful assortments of holiday goods in the Valley." He graduated in 1881 and went off to the University of Virginia. Although he only attended UVA for a year, he seemed to enjoy his time there, and in 1895 he wrote fondly about "his days of pleasure and profit beneath the arcades" of this "mother of learning." From UVA he went to the University of Maryland medical school in Baltimore, graduating in 1885. After stints in Alabama and Rockbridge County, Virginia, he started a general practice in Hampton, Virginia. He married Kate Houston of Fincastle, Virginia, in 1888. Around 1899, he bought the forty-two-room Augusta Hotel in Hampton, which he oversaw until 1912, when he leased the operation. The 1910 census shows he and Kate living on Queen Street with seventeen boarders, presumably people staying at the hotel.[21]

## A Progressive Career in Public Health

Aside from his medical practice, Plecker served as health officer for Elizabeth City County, at a substantial annual salary of $7,500. He was a prominent figure locally and in the state. In 1905, he served on the city "Commission on Lunacy" in Hampton and examined criminals for mental soundness. That same year, he joined the Board of Directors of the Virginia Sanitarium for Consumptives. He gave public talks explaining the dangers of tuberculosis, typhoid, and alcohol consumption. In 1906, he got a postgraduate degree in obstetrics in New York. He won a citywide chess tournament sponsored by the YMCA, and in 1909 volunteered his services as doctor for the newly formed Virginia State School for Colored Deaf and Blind Students. "A case of diphtheria developed in the school a few days after it opened, but was successfully combated by Dr. Plecker and the school thereby saved from an epidemic."[22]

He participated in a 1910–12 study, funded by the Rockefeller Foundation, of hookworm and its relation to contaminated water and poor sanitary practices, and it brought him statewide notice. In 1912, Virginia created a new State Board of Health, including a Bureau of Vital Statistics, and the position of registrar, charged with enforcing laws regarding the registration of births, marriages, illness, and deaths. By 1914, Plecker held the job of registrar and would hold it for more than thirty years.[23]

Even while Patrick O'Malley was living at Elwood Station, Virginia was intensifying its efforts to track births, deaths, marriages, and illnesses. Starting in the mid-nineteenth century, states began working to establish certificates for all births. As mentioned earlier, Virginia passed a law mandating birth registrations in 1853, partly so that it could track racial identity. By the early twentieth century, states routinely demanded birth certificates, and by 1915, the US had settled on a system still in use, whereby states collected birth data and forwarded it to the federal government. Birth certificates would establish racial identity but also "proof of age for employment or pensions." They represented an expanding idea of state power. "Birth registration made a child known to a state" and offered protection "from being forced to marry, soldier, or work underage; a child who is known belongs to a country and is entitled to its protections and entitlements." A child with a birth certificate could "move freely and return to her country of origin. A child who is registered has legal parents who have legal obligations."[24]

Patrick O'Malley's two oldest sons, Fred and Patrick, were both listed as "day laborers" on the 1900 census, at age fifteen and thirteen, respectively. Child labor laws, then just becoming more common, depended on accurate records of age. In 1915, Pennsylvania established fourteen as the minimum age for work, restricting children to a nine-hour workday. Fred had his first child, my grandfather, in 1911. He went to work as an apprentice to a machinist after he graduated eighth grade, age fourteen. His younger siblings were allowed to finish high school. Philadelphia newspapers in the 1920s and 1930s were full of debate about the ethics of child labor. Birth certificates made it possible to regulate children's labor and "shifted authority from families to documents and from oral to documentary forms of knowledge."[25]

Birth certificates offered protection but also represented only the first step in navigating a web of identity-fixing instruments. The American Bar Association website tells us birth certificates "are necessary to obtain a social security number, apply for a passport, enroll in schools, get a driver's license, gain employment, or apply for other benefits." In other words, they are necessary to acquiring a series of documents that further build and secure identity. The obvious next step would be the replacement of paper records altogether by a single digital identity "card" that could serve as driver's license, birth certificate, passport, social security card, insurance card, credit card. The US has traditionally resisted this kind of measure, but smart phones already serve many of these functions, and as we will see in the case of Ancestry.com, functions that once belonged to the public sector will likely wind up under the administration of the private sector.[26]

The growing interest in birth certificates connected closely to Plecker's emerging field, "public health." Under the rubric of "public health," the state's interest widened. At one time it wanted to know about taxable property and population for apportioning elected representatives. Now it wanted to know about the general state of its population. How healthy were they? How fast was the population growing? How many children were people typically having, and what was the mortality rate among those children?

Michel Foucault described the emergence of what he called "the Malthusian couple" as the state's interest in family grew. Economist Thomas Malthus theorized that population growth would always outstrip growth in the food supply. Malthus made managing population growth an issue of concern to the state. Rather than just a couple having a family, adding labor power to the farm and adding perhaps to a local kin network, the couple by 1900 anchored an agenda of national health and national greatness. Agricultural experts worried about access to land and food production. Criminologists worried about crime and its relationship to family life. Birth certificates coupled to child labor laws showed the states understood education as vital to an effective workforce, while experts in social welfare argued for the importance of childhood as a distinct category of life. Psychologists studied the proper ways to have or not have sex, and the proper relationship of sex as pleasure to sex as the production of children. Economists worried about the rate of population growth and its connection to economic growth, and by 1900, they regularly compared birth rates in different countries. Increasingly, social scientists noticed that people in industrializing nations had fewer children.[27]

## *Race Suicide and Eugenics*

The relationship between industrialization and declining family size seemed like a crisis, a moral panic. No less than Theodore Roosevelt used the term "race suicide" to express the idea that civilization made "advanced" races feeble. Roosevelt's most famous essay, "The Strenuous Life," urged upper-class men to stave off feebleness by hunting and fishing, chopping down trees, and exploring wilderness: to engage in what today might be called "extreme" sports or even better, fighting wars. For women the strenuous life meant "having lots of children," because an invigorated race was going to need soldiers to fight wars of conquest.[28]

Plecker certainly knew about these ideas, well before he was appointed registrar, and he routinely broke down birth and death statistics by race. For example, the *Newport News Daily Press* commented on his report for November 1909. "Thirteen Deaths Occurred among Negroes and Only Six among Whites," it headlined, and then when it looked at the number of babies born that year and compared the numbers by race, happily concluded, "This shows that the colored population is decreasing, while the white is on the increase." The *Daily Press* used Plecker's comparative statistics to refute concerns about "race suicide." Racecraft merges with statecraft: in this example public health as a subject draws and reinforces racial distinctions. Disparities in income that increased mortality among the poor are framed as signs of "race," and the newspaper interprets the higher mortality among colored people as a sign of racial decline.

Plecker closed his report with a complaint. "There are many births, especially white, which have not been reported and physicians and midwives are requested to report at once: Heads of families are asked to aid in having births reported. There have been several requests for copies of birth certificates recently, which could not be furnished, because the information had not been sent to the health officer by the attending physician." Here we see racecraft and statecraft merging: he needs accurate individual records so he can continue to inscribe racial categories into policy. We have already seen the kind of work he made those records do.[29]

In 1924, *the Survey*, a well-known national magazine with progressive political leanings, quoted Plecker saying, "I have watched with much anxiety the steady decrease in the birth rate of our native-born American stock, and the rapid increase of undesirable foreigners." New York, he added, "showed in 1917 a birth-rate of 17 per 1,000 of native born and the marvelous rate of 90 and 91 amongst immigrants from Eastern and Southern Europe." Already some of the New England states, and large American cities, have turned "into foreign settlements." "The Japanese and Chinese are already bringing about the same situation upon the Pacific Coast." "In my humble way, I am doing what I can in connection with my regular work, to create a sentiment in Virginia against any influences that will decrease our white birth-rate, while instructing mothers how to guard the health and lives of the infants they bear."[30]

Plecker was very much a progressive reformer, using the authority of professional credentials and scientific knowledge to reform public policy. "Progressivism" often relied on "racial science": some of the best-known progressives, Woodrow Wilson, for example, were committed to segregation. Plecker's work on hookworm, and his work on infant mortality, certainly did good, and that good extended to "colored" people. But it took place in the context of the radical racism described in chapter 5. Plecker gave his report on hookworm at the 1913 conference of the Southern Medical Association. He and his collaborators reiterated the importance of state records and described the measures people could take to eliminate the problem. "Speakers at tonight's session advocated better living conditions for the negro," newspapers reported: "better sanitation and an extension of education in social hygiene, also urging that landlords of tenement property

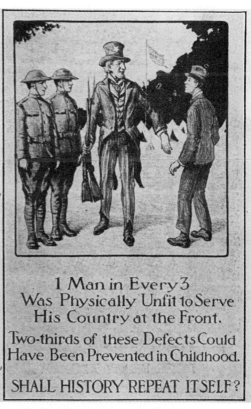

*Figure 6.3.* Front and back cover of a 1924 pamphlet produced by Plecker's office to promote public health. Rockbridge County (VA) Clerk's Correspondence, Library of Virginia, Richmond.

cooperate in such measures as may be undertaken." Further, "the conference went on record as favoring the giving to the negro of every
chance to become a better citizen."

This was not necessarily out of benevolence: Several speakers referred to "the danger of the negro as a servant in the homes of white
people as a carrier of disease." Weighing this danger, "it was urged that
the family physician be called upon to examine the servants as well
as the members of the family." Various speakers pronounced on "the
Negro Problem," and "The Negro as a Public Health Problem." They
then heard from "P. D. Robinson, a negro doctor who curtailed his
remarks when objection was made to hearing him and whose obser-
vations were expunged from the record." They could talk about "the
Negro problem" and profess affection but could not bear hearing from
a doctor with African ancestors.[31]

The meeting also included a paper on eugenics from Memphis doctor Lee Alexander Stone, then hard at work on his 1915 book *Eugenics
and Marriage: A Treatise upon an Important Phase of Social Hygiene*.
"Eugenics and Social Hygiene," Stone announced, "are closely allied,
and one cannot be properly referred to without touching closely upon
the other." Eugenics aimed to "improve the race by inducing young
people to make a more reasonable selection of marriage mates; to fall
in love intelligently," adding that eugenics "includes the control by the
state of the propagation of the mentally incompetent." Earlier in the
chapter, we saw Plecker endorsing this idea by calling for the imme-
diate sterilization of Mattie Murray.

Stone wanted laws that restricted the right to marry. At present, he
lamented, anyone can get a marriage license merely by asking: "even
today, in the majority of states, a lewd, disease-ridden profligate . . .
may go to any County Court Clerk and obtain a marriage license."
"There are no questions asked," he continued, "and even if the clerk
who issues the license knows perfectly well the character of the man
with whom he is dealing, he, on account of our present laws, is pow-
erless to act, and must issue a license." Plecker showed less concern
with disease than with race, but he shared the desire to give county

clerks the power to deny the right to marry, and once he was appointed registrar, he set out to do exactly that.

Citing other prominent eugenicists, Stone declared, "I hold that every man or woman who belongs to the degenerate class, whether criminal, inebriate, beggar, pimp, prostitute, imbecile, moral leper, or pauper, should have their powers of procreation taken from them." He offered a vision Plecker did his best to bring about. "The day is fast approaching when legislation will in every state enact marriage laws which will be strict and will have to be obeyed to their very letter. Before a marriage license is issued both applicants will have to produce certificates of health, signed by an official board composed of reputable physicians, stating that the parties to the proposed marriage are physically and mentally fit to marry and procreate healthy children."[32]

Eugenics is the place where racecraft, science, genealogy, and precise public records of individuals all come together. It is the logical culmination of the record-keeping measures Virginia introduced before the Civil War: individualism and race intertwined. It demands attention to ancestry and relies on bureaucracy to produce the necessary records. It ties the magical thinking of racecraft to individuals and ties both to a scientifically grounded notion of public health, and connects the past to a permanent state of racial being, an identity time can never erase. Stone insisted, "It is the right of all races to be well-born. It is their right to be able to boast of the strength of their ancestry."

In this line of thinking, your children can be more or less valuable to the nation depending on their genetic fitness. Their rate of increase can be charted against the increase in less desirable people. This dogma would be central to the rise of the National Socialist Party in Germany, and Hitler looked to the United States for inspiration as he saw eugenical thinking permeating law. A reinvigorated race of Aryan Germans would need more land for its growing population of superior people. It is not at all unreasonable to conclude that eugenics killed twenty million people in WWII.[33]

## Eugenics and State Law: The Racial Integrity Act

Enthused by eugenics, Plecker set out to modify Virginia's laws. He allied himself with two younger men, Earnest Sevier Cox and John H. Powell, both born around 1880. Cox was a lapsed Methodist minister and the author of *White America* (1923). He took classes at the University of Chicago but did not get a degree. Powell was a gifted musician, a pianist and composer. He studied in Vienna and toured the United States and Europe, giving concerts. He often drew on self-consciously American musical themes. His most celebrated work was the *Rhapsodie Nègre* and his *Virginia Symphony*, both of which included African American motifs. In 1906, he composed *In the South*, which included a "Negro Elegy." The latter sounds a great deal like George Gershwin's "It Ain't Necessarily So" from *Porgy and Bess*. Powell's use of African American themes made him a celebrity in European art-music circles and among Americans anxious for the approval of Europeans. But Powell would later insist there was no African American music, that African Americans had stolen melodies from Europeans. He became obsessed with Anglo-Saxon folk music and founded the White Top Folk Festival in Virginia, where mountain people with European ancestry were urged to perform unfamiliar Morris dances as part of their "Anglo-Saxon" racial heritage, and performers with African ancestors were not allowed.[34]

Powell had high culture credentials and old-family respectability; Cox had spent time in South Africa and was an effective public speaker, while Plecker had medical expertise and a position of authority in public health. The three men founded the "Anglo Saxon Clubs of America," a sort of more genteel version of the KKK that focused on building chapters on college campuses. In 1924, they worked to pass the landmark Racial Integrity Act, Plecker's proudest moment.

The act required all county registrars or clerks recording births or marriages to fill out a form noting "the racial composition of any individual, as Caucasian, negro, Mongolian, American Indian, Asiatic Indian, Malay, or any mixture thereof, or any other non-Caucasic strains, and if there be any mixture." "It shall be a felony for any person willfully or knowingly to make a registration certificate false as to color or race," adding "the willful making of a false registration or birth certificate shall be punished by confinement in the penitentiary for one year." Plecker, as we have seen, regularly cited this law in his letters to Virginia citizens. The act further insisted, "no marriage license shall be granted until the clerk or deputy clerk has reasonable assurance that the statements as to color of both man and woman are correct." If the clerk found "reasonable cause to disbelieve that applicants are of pure white race," the law instructed them to "withhold the granting of the license until satisfactory proof is produced that both applicants are 'white persons' as provided for in this act." This proof required the applicants to produce evidence of "pedigree." They had specifically to prove what they were *not*, but as the act was framed proving whiteness required examining every single ancestor.[35]

The Racial Integrity Act offered the most sweeping definition of "white" to date. It insisted, "the term 'white person' shall apply only to the person who has no trace whatsoever of any blood other than Caucasian." As we have seen, the "trace" did not have to be visible in skin or hair: paper records of ancestry worked just as well. And as we have also seen, paper records varied. Dempsey Hare and his wife Anne Holland were both listed as "white" in the 1880 census. Dempsey's children with his mistress Frances Whitfield appeared as white in records. Patrick and Esther had two records of their marriage, one listing them as white and one listing them as colored. Plecker blustered and threatened local registrars who listed people as white without thoroughly searching their ancestry. His office completed the transition from "ancestry" as something known in family lore and local knowledge to ancestry as a thing held in "400 dusty volumes of records, musty and dog-eared with faded ink marks almost obliterated by time," that resided in Plecker's offices in Richmond. They "hold the answer to a score of legal questions affecting thousands of Virginians." "Let a dispute on bigamy or racial integrity or American citizenship or pension eligibility or a dozen other problems arise, and these volumes constitute the court of last resort from which there is no appeal." Plecker had managed to get himself installed as racecraft's judge and jury, adding the force of administrative bureaucracy and medical expertise to what remained an exercise in wishful thinking.[36]

Plecker resented the Racial Integrity Act's "Pocahontas exemption." He told a New York legislator, "we have a number of excellent white families descended from unions between whites and Indian 'princesses' as far back as 1615, 1644, and 1684. There are probably others unknown to us and in order to protect all of those, we inserted Section 5 (b), which we consider dangerous." Section 5 (b) said that "persons who have one-sixteenth or less of the blood of the American Indian and have no other non-Caucasic blood shall be deemed to be white persons." The exception was solely to flatter elite Virginia elites' desire to root themselves in the state's very distant past without acknowledging the sexual violence of conquest. The "Pocahontas exemption" caused Plecker a great deal of trouble and partly accounts for why he focused his detective interest on people with Indian ancestry.

## Defining White and Indian

Plecker argued, following the work of eugenicist Arthur Estabrook, that because of intermarriage, there were no Indians in Virginia, only the "WIN" (white / Indian / Negro) tribe. In 1925, he wrote an urgent letter to Estabrook, who was then in residence at Cold Spring Harbor on Long Island, home of the Eugenics Record Office, an organization devoted to the study of "experimental evolution." A. T. Shields, clerk of Rockbridge County, had refused to issue a marriage license to James Connor, "a 100% white man," and Dorothy Johns, "on account of a copy of a letter that was written by [Plecker]" stating "that the Johns family of Irish Creek and Amherst County probably have some negro blood in them." The couple's attorney wrote that Dorothy Johns's kin "have always been classed as white and they disclaim the faintest trace of negro blood. . . . If you have sufficient proof that they have negro blood in them, it will mean that they can no longer attend the only school in the Irish Creek neighborhood, as well as the white churches, and numerous of them who have married into absolutely white families under white marriage licenses will have their offsprings classified as negros." Plecker wrote to Estabrook pleading for any evidence that would prove Dorothy Johns was "actually a negro."[37]

Plecker spent a great deal of time and attention on the "Irish Creek" area of Rockbridge County, but there's no evidence it had anything to do with Irish people who may or may not have given the region its name. Instead he focused on people with African and Native ancestors. When the case came to trial, Plecker was able to produce records showing that Dorothy Johns had "colored" ancestors. Her lawyer argued that colored meant "Indian," not African, and so the clerk must issue the certificate. The judge in this case, Henry W. Holt, ruled with Plecker's side, but a few months later heard a similar case, *Atha Sorrells v. A. T. Shields*, from the same area. Plecker wrote to Shields, the Rockbridge County clerk, insisting he must "have the full cooperation of the county officials and citizens of Rockbridge County in keeping the Irish Creek free issue people in their place. That place, as you well know, is not in the white race." But in *Sorrells v. Shields*, the judge ruled in favor of the couple seeking a license.

Holt began by expressing his "cordial sympathy with the general purpose of the statute." White Virginians "look upon ourselves as a sceptered race and stand for its preservation in all its integrity." The problem he found lay in the full scope of "ancestry" and the vagueness of racial categories. "In twenty-five generations one has thirty two millions of grandfathers," Holt wrote. "Some of them were probably hanged and some knighted. Who can tell?" I cannot prove, he insisted, that there was not "some foreign strain" among these dead millions. He also objected to one of the central problems endemic to racecraft: what was the relation of white as a color and white as a "race?" The judge pointed out that according to multiple scientific authorities "all white people are not Caucasians, and all Caucasians are not white people." Holt cited Thomas Huxley, who we saw earlier describing dark-skinned "melanochroi" Caucasians, to assert that "Hungarians are not Caucasians," though white, and Virginia's law "which excluded a Hungarian would not bar an Arab, a North African, a Toda of India, an Ainu of Japan or the Wild Man of Borneo" from marrying a white Virginia woman. Holt seemed to be relying on Augustus Keane's *Man, Past and Present* (1899), which had included photographs of Ainu and Toda men to demonstrate people who confounded racial understandings. The judge's commitment to the "sceptered race" rested on the judgment of what he called "reasonable men" who would look at Atha Sorrells, and at "the evidence in this case which occurs over a period of 130 years," and conclude "that there is no strain present in the applicant of any blood other than white, except Indian, and there is not enough of that to come within the statute."[38]

Judge Holt's list of people who might or might not be considered white or Caucasian, whatever that means, seems similar to the arguments Augustus Keane made in multiple books on ethnography. In figure 6.5, Keane's chart of the various forms of "caucasic" people. Some of these people on the "melanochroi" line, Somalis, for example, or Egyptians, might not read as "white" to the "reasonable man" of 1924. This is effectively the problem the Supreme Court stumbled over in the cases of *Ozawa* and *Thind*, described in the previous chapter. What was the difference between "white" as a skin color and white as a "race?"

Holt advanced a "reasonable man" standard for judging who was and was not white, but Plecker and his friends were anything but reasonable men. Powell, the pianist, was outraged. The judge, he wrote, was not aware of "the catastrophic biologic and social results of the infusion of even an infinitesimal strain of African blood." Powell cited Plecker to claim, "there are at present in Virginia no Indians who do not possess some degree of negro blood. Also, many negroes are claiming the status of Indians as the first step towards 'passing over into white.' Indians are springing up all over the state as if by spontaneous generation." Civilization itself lay in the balance. "We cannot suffer this outrage to continue. The breach in the dike must be stopped. If we are to preserve our civilization, our ideals, the soul of our race, we must call a halt."[39]

1. TODA MAN, S. INDIA.
(Caucasic Type.)

2. TODA MAN, S. INDIA.
(Caucasic Type.)

3. AINU, SAKHALIN I.
(Caucasic Type.)

4. AINU, YEZO I.
(Caucasic Type.)

*Figure 6.4.* From Augustus Keane, *Man, Past and Present,* 1899, facing 558, showing examples of what Judge Holt called "Caucasians who are not white people," among the Ainu of Japan and the Toda of India. Internet Archive.

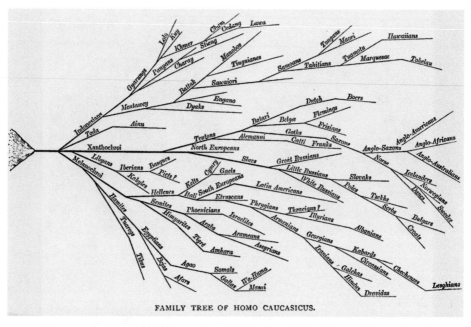

FAMILY TREE OF HOMO CAUCASICUS.

*Figure 6.5.* From Augustus Henry Keane, *Ethnology. In Two Parts: I. Fundamental Ethnical Problems. II. The Primary Ethnical Groups* (Cambridge, 1896), 380. Internet Archive.

But whiteness remained hard to define. As late as 1940, Plecker addressed the question of Asian Indians in an exchange with the Department of Anthropology at UCLA. The original letter had asked about "Hindus" in Virginia under the Racial Integrity Law. Plecker testily replied, "the purpose of this law is to exclude from marriage with a white person any individual of any of the colored races, including Hindus, who are either considered Mongolian or Malay, I am not sure which." "It is barely possible," he grudgingly admitted, "that there are still resident in India descendants of the original Aryan conquerors who have remained unmixed with the native population through the strict enforcement of the caste system." But "for practical purposes we class the Hindu as non-white without permission to intermarry into the white race." This lazy reliance on bigotry disguised as "practical purposes" must have bothered him, because he hastened to add, "our office is endeavoring to enforce the spirit of this law by refusing the classification of near-white mulattoes as white and has made a genealogical study of many large groups and families of these mixed breeds."[40]

Plecker, Powell, and Cox are wearying to read. Their arrogance; their fearfulness; their incoherence; their eagerness to pounce on ordinary citizens who fell in love, rejoiced in a child's birth, shooed their children off to school, or buried a loved one, appalls the spirits of human kindness and decency. They forced people into a rigid racial caste system and told them civilization itself required their subordination. Yet all three men expressed sympathy for Marcus Garvey, the Jamaican advocate of African nationalism, when he argued that persons of African descent should emigrate to Africa because Europeans would never treat them fairly. Cox and Powell visited Garvey when he was jailed for securities fraud. Plecker wrote to Calvin Coolidge urging a pardon for Garvey. Plecker also wrote, in *Eugenics in Relation to the New Family and the Law on Racial Integrity*, "let the young men who read this realize that the future purity of our race is in their keeping, and that the joining of themselves to females of a lower race and fathering children who shall be a curse and a menace to our State and civilization is a crime against society, and against the purity and integrity of their future homes and the happiness of their future loved ones and of themselves." Racecraft has blown up the birth of children into a crisis threatening the foundations of civilization itself.[41]

### The Mythical Faithful Servant

"Civilization" meant a caste system in which "the sceptered race" could express affection for the lesser races who knew their place. Plecker claimed that "those of us who have been reared with the Negroes have attachment for them, at times very warm, even though we know them from every angle." He told readers of *the Survey* about how "as a young child I was largely under the control of a faithful servant who had been born in my mother's family and was early assigned to her as her personal maid, and went with her when she married and established her own home." When this woman, who he names only as Delia, married, "my young sister and I were present as interested witnesses. Just as the preacher was getting well started my little sister broke forth into an outburst of sobbing and was joined by Delia, almost breaking up the wedding."

"Delia," who Plecker did not grant a last name in his story of fond remembrance, was known to her family as Cornelia Strother. The 1870 census shows her living in the Plecker household, age twenty-three, as Delia Strother, a domestic servant. She married French Dixon 1873. By 1880, according to the census, she was living in Rappahannock County with her family, about eighty-five miles away from Staunton. Plecker added that Delia attended his mother on her deathbed in 1915, "and closed her eyes in death," and "when my mother's will was read we found that Delia was remembered, and as executor the first check I drew was for her." This story, meant to be touching, was nonsense. Francis Plecker's will mentions only Walter, his sister Emma Cassell, and the grandchildren of her late daughter Hattie Wayman. It does not mention "Delia," or any other allegedly loyal maid, in any way.

Herbert Seligman, the director of publicity for the National Association for the Advancement of Colored People, wrote a response to Plecker's letter. "When a Southern gentleman writes thus, he composes usually something as absurd as the effusion from W. A. Plecker, M.D." And "of course," Seligman continued, "all the race purity talk of Plecker and his ilk is twaddle." What accounts for Plecker's obsessive dishonesty and his odd combination of scientific fact and romantic Southern fantasy?[42]

His fictional story of Delia is worth a close reading. He could have written "born in my mother's household," for example, but he chose "born in my mother's family," which suggests a relation. "Know them from every angle" is also an interesting phrase in this context, while Plecker saying he was "largely under the control" of Delia suggests a close but not happy relation. Walter and Frances went to Delia's wedding, he said, "as interested witnesses," not as friends or family. Yet his sister burst into hysterical tears, and so, he claimed, did Delia.

Plecker had an older brother named "Othello Smoot Plecker," a very surprising name to find in the family of someone so deeply committed to white supremacy. In Shakespeare's play of the same name, Othello, described as a "Moor," is undeniably "other," and has darker skin, but he comes from a time before the enlightenment idea of "race" existed. Shakespeare uses the adjective "black" to describe him, but as we saw in earlier chapters "black" or "dark" was used to describe Irish people into the nineteenth century. It did not necessarily mean "nonwhite": it indicates "racecraft" at an early, incomplete stage. Shakespeare's character presents much of the ambiguity that drove Walter Plecker to extremes. But Othello Smoot Plecker died in 1863, age six, when Walter was only two years old.

## Genealogy and the Lost Cause

His older sister, Emma Plecker Cassell, lacked the official state position and medical degree but had the same intense enthusiasm for records of family and ancestry. It's Emma who allegedly burst into tears at the wedding of Delia, the mostly fictitiously faithful maid. Emma belonged to the Daughters of the American Revolution and also the Daughters of the Confederacy, and thus was one of the people who put up the monuments to slaveholding generals American have spent the last decade fighting over and taking down.

"From the 1860s to the mid-twentieth century," writes one historian of the practice of genealogy, "the language of race, heredity, and later eugenics invaded the genealogical sphere, helping many white Americans describe themselves self-consciously as Anglo-Saxons and claim racial and social superiority over others." In 1911, the president of the DAR, Mrs. William T. (Julia) Scott, told the annual convention in Washington, DC, that the organization stands for "the purity of our Caucasian blood (applause); the perpetuity of our Anglo-Saxon traditions of liberty, law, and the security and gradual elevation of the white man's standard of living (applause)." Scott insisted, "woman is the divinity of the spring whence flows the stream of humanity—nay, she is the source herself," and "in her hands rests the precious cup, the golden bowl of life." "We must look to the ingredients which are being cast into the cup," she insisted, "we must protect the fountain from pollution." That meant seeing to it that "the sources of our national life are kept undiluted and unpolluted by any unassimilable strains of race and blood. We must see to it that our nation no longer permits" people of lesser blood "to trample the mud of millions of alien feet into our spring (applause)." Scott especially dreaded "the clouding of the purity of the cup with color and character acquired under tropical suns, in the jungle, or in the paradisiacal islands of the sea." She told the convention—which had just been addressed by President William Howard Taft—"we must conserve the source of our race, the Anglo Saxon race, mother of liberty and self-government in the modern world," and to that end "I would rather our census show a lesser population and a greater homogeneity."[43]

Emma Cassell was likely among those applauding. At one meeting of the J. E. B. Stuart chapter of the United Daughters of the Confederacy, Emma "learned that her eligibility to membership in said Chapter had been questioned." She produced a letter from the Department of Confederate Military Records attesting that her father had served as a private and a letter from a fellow veteran who testified, "your father was a gallant soldier and was never known of him to attempt to shirk a single duty that was requested of him." This was rather faint praise and probably made Emma anxious around women who had more illustrious ancestors, but these documents "established for all time her inalienable right" to membership. Administrative individualism conquered time. She also worked for an organization called the Children of the Revolution that aimed to get more children interested in their Revolutionary War ancestors, as long as they were understood as white.[44]

It's especially interesting how many people in Plecker's circle of eugenical racists, people obsessed with ancestry and its meaning, had no children. Emma Cassell had no children, which I suppose might partly explain her obsession with other people's children. Powell and Earnest Cox were both married but had no children. Plecker's office depended heavily on two unmarried, childless women, Eva Kelley and Estelle Marks. Marks served at the Bureau of Vital Statistics for almost as long as Plecker: he suggested she take over the office after he retired. Kelley was Plecker's genealogical researcher. She "has devoted years of study to this problem," he said "and has developed into a racial genealogical expert never equalled." She lived in Richmond with her mother and two sisters. The Pleckers themselves were childless, and it might be worth noting that he seems to have turned toward eugenics early in the twentieth century, around the time he would have realized he would never have children, the very condition eugenicists worried about. Plecker and his circle were in many ways the very problem eugenics aimed to address, falling birth rates among the "higher classes."[45]

Plecker, coworker Russell Booker recalled, "was a man you could sometimes respect and admire, but never love." Booker "grew up in Plecker's neighborhood, delivered his newspaper" and eventually directed the Bureau of Vital Statistics himself, well after Plecker's death. "He was a very rigid man," Booker added. "I don't know of anyone who ever saw him smile." Booker called him "a miserly taskmaster." "You didn't get a new pencil until you turned in your old one, and it better not be longer than an inch and a quarter." Reportedly he never looked before crossing streets, simply stepping out and expecting cars to stop. His home life may have been troubled. Kate Houston Plecker, who married Walter in 1888, committed "suicide by illuminating gas" in 1932. Walter stoically reported her death, as the law required.[46]

In late May of 1946, Plecker wrote to Dr. I. C. Riggin, Virginia's health commissioner, to announce his resignation. "I am laying down this, my chief life work, with mingled feeling of pleasure and regret—regret at relinquishing this branch of health work, in which I have been greatly interested—pleasure in knowing that I will thus find the time to pursue further some ethnological studies in which I am interested." He told Riggin, "in this work I will find need for reference to the valuable racial files which have been for years accumulating in Miss Kelley's office, and which are unequaled for an entire State population anywhere in this or other countries." Eva Kelley seems to have left no record of her work, other than what we see in Plecker's surviving letters, but he told Riggin he "would be glad also for a while to assist Miss Kelley in the great struggle in which she is involved . . . the prevention of illegal racial intermarriage and speedier amalgamation." He could help her with this work, "which at times arouses opposition, even to the point of becoming hazardous." Unable to let go at age eighty-five, he suggested for himself "a new position — 'Ethnologist' — without salary, or at a nominal one of one dollar a year," so he could continue his own research. Riggin's reply was not preserved.[47]

Two days later, Plecker wrote to John Powell to tell him, "today my service as State Registrar of Vital Statistics ends." He was clearly worried about his legacy. "With this bunch of letters," he told him, "your receipt of such copies will likewise end. If you have preserved them, you have a pretty good history of the various racial problems which have come before us since we began sending you these." He was not sure his legacy of harrying and hounding the racially suspect would continue: "As I do not know who my successor will be and whether he is at all interested in that subject and as this correspondence may ultimately be destroyed or lost, your copies would furnish a pretty good outline of the situation." He told Powell he planned to write a book, tentatively titled "The Vanished Race and Other Studies in Virginia Demography," but his sudden encounter with a car on Chamberlayne Avenue ended that plan.[48]

Powell saved at least a representative sample of Plecker's work, but not enough to answer the questions I started with. The roughly two hundred surviving documents from Plecker's office don't show any interest in the Irish as a different race, but they represent only a tiny sample of a thirty-year career. None of them reference Nansemond County. Plecker used the term "caucaisic" to describe white people who were not "Anglo-Saxons," which reflects the kind of racial thinking that Nott and Gliddon advanced. He thought Sicilians were heavily intermarried with people from Africa. But if he had any special bias against the Irish, the record is silent.

The marriage certificate that initiated this book gives the date of Patrick and Hester's marriage as 1884, but says, "date record filed: July 1940." That's Plecker's hand at work: he asked county clerks to copy existing records and forward them to his office for review, so that he could more effectively track people who moved from one county to another. In 1935, he wrote to "the County Clerks of Virginia" and pointed out that "on account of the large number of courthouses which have been destroyed by fire . . . our thought is to provide against that calamity as well as to secure the records promptly." Nansemond County's courthouse had been destroyed by fire, most recently in 1866.[49]

The county clerk of Nansemond, coincidentally also named John H. Powell, made a copy of the original marriage register and delivered it to the Bureau of Vital Statistics in Richmond in 1940. If Plecker had his own clean copies of local records, he could have found out that Frances Whitfield's children with Dempsey Hare were "really black" by the standards of the Racial Integrity Act and demanded the annulment of their marriages or told the local school superintendent to send them to the colored school. He might very well have done so, but the records of his actions in Nansemond did not survive. My grandfather Joseph O'Malley started dating Catherine Cody in the early 1930s, in Philadelphia. If one of her relatives had doubts about Joseph, and knew that Joseph's father Fred had been born and raised in Virginia, a letter to the ever diligent Plecker would have started an investigation. This sort of thing was exactly his passion, and he would have found a "trace" of African ancestry and reported back that "Mr. O'Malley is a negro." We have already seen examples of Plecker doing exactly that. So the question remains: was there some African ancestry in Hester Holland, or was Patrick not considered white?

## Following Plecker's Footsteps

It occurs to me here that the person I resemble most in this book is not Patrick, my paternal ancestor, but Walter Plecker. I don't share any of his enthusiasm for eugenics, or any of his belief in race, but I've spent many hours charting the ancestry of multiple people in Virginia, poring over old records, and asking questions that revolve around racial identity and its relationship to family history. Like Plecker or his assistant Eva Kelley, I've noted the "race" of people not related to me and tried to place them. This research, like Plecker's work, entangles racism and individualism: the two ideas work together. It's disquieting to follow that path. Historians should not just seek answers to questions: we need to understand what asking any question also does. I want this book to treat genealogy as history, rather than biology, and trace the historical movement of persons rather than "races." The book focuses on people who confounded racial categories and blurred the lines, because any intellectual construction reveals itself best at its edges and margins. The falsity of racial claims appear where "common sense" fails.

Why invest so much in ancestry? The question has a double meaning, since much of this research was conducted on Ancestry.com, which charges a hefty annual subscription fee for access to records that once sat in Walter Plecker's office but are now digitized and searchable. I don't share any DNA with Plecker either, but Plecker often lamented the fact that, as he told Dr. Samuel Nixon in 1946, "there is no dependable blood test by which the race may be determined. . . . The only way is by the genealogical records." Now of course there is such a test, promising tell us who we "really are," and I can access it—along with the Nansemond County marriage register, the birth certificates, the death certificates, the census record, all the "genealogical records" Plecker referred to—via Ancestry.com, the subject of the next chapter.

# SEVEN

# SALT LAKE CITY

In the 1930s, Walter Plecker started asking county clerks to send him copies of their local records, to protect them from loss by fire and to bypass local officials who lacked eugenical zeal. In July of 1940, the Nansemond County clerk, also named John H. Powell, sent Plecker a "fair copy" of the original county register of marriages, kept from 1866 to 1899 and shown in the previous chapter. In 1998, the state generated an official paper document of the marriage license from a microfilm of that copy and sent it to my father. He wrote to the Bureau of Vital Records asking if someone had made a mistake in the racial designation of Patrick and Hester. He got a letter back saying, "a second careful search of the microfilm clearly reveals the white columns on both the bride and groom having been left blank, and the 'C' for colored clearly written in the colored columns." Peter Prentis had used a column labeled "remarks" to record—as the law required—the race of the *couple*, not the individuals. In 1884, there was no column for recording the race of each individual. So I knew that Powell's 1940 copy, sent to Plecker, used a different form.[1]

I went to the bureau in Richmond and asked to see that 1940 copy. This request met with snorts of derision and was refused. While I was there, I ordered a new certified copy of the marriage license, which arrived a few weeks later giving the date of marriage as 1834, twenty years before either Patrick or Hester were born. This did not inspire confidence.

I filed a Freedom of Information Act request to see the actual source of the official copy and wrote to the director of the bureau. About a month later, we had a pleasant conversation in which he explained that yes, they had a microfilm of Powell's copy, filed in 1940, but it would contain no different information from the certified copy sent to my father. He suggested the Suffolk Courthouse might have the physical copy Powell made. Suffolk Courthouse was then closed to the public due to COVID. A few months later, this second register, the one I was not allowed to see, appeared on Ancestry.com, photographed, transcribed, and indexed. Figure 7.1 shows the image of the 1940 register as held at Ancestry.com. Under Plecker's grim bureaucratic gaze, John H. Powell in 1940 separately listed both as "C." The official copy sent to my father helpfully spelled out "colored," in place of "C," removing all ambiguity and making their racial designations seem more solid.

This odd chain of documents shows again the contingency and uncertainty around racial designation, and the state's role in making it seem real. Two people asked for a marriage license in 1884: the license, filled out in their sight by county clerk Peter Prentis, shows them as white. But Prentis's 1884 register, filled out in private, names them "colored." Walter Plecker wanted more efficient and centralized control of records, so he asked county clerks to make copies of their records and send them to Richmond. In 1940, the Nansemond

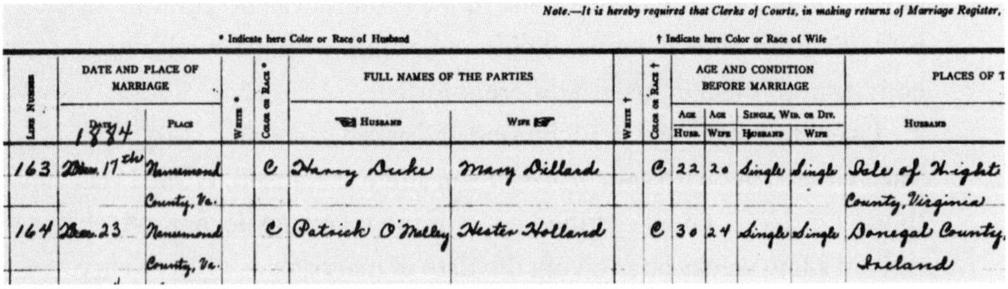

Note.—It is hereby required that Clerks of Courts, in making returns of Marriage Register,

| Line Number | Date (1884) | Place | White * | Color or Race * | Husband | Wife | White † | Color or Race † | Age Husb. | Age Wife | Single, Wid. or Div. Husband | Single, Wid. or Div. Wife | Places of B… Husband |
|---|---|---|---|---|---|---|---|---|---|---|---|---|---|
| 163 | Dec. 17th | Nansemond County, Va. | | C | Harry Duke | Mary Dillard | | C | 22 | 20 | Single | Single | Isle of Wight County, Virginia |
| 164 | Dec. 23 | Nansemond County, Va. | | C | Patrick O'Malley | Hester Holland | | C | 30 | 24 | Single | Single | Donegal County, Ireland |

* Indicate here Color or Race of Husband
† Indicate here Color or Race of Wife

*Figure 7.1.* Marriage of Patrick O'Malley and Hester Holland, copy of the original Nansemond County Register of Marriages, made at Walter Plecker's behest in 1940.

County clerk made a paper copy of Prentis's register, listing both explicitly as "C." That copy, microfilmed, wound up in Richmond and in turn generated, in 1998, a certified, official paper certificate, elaborately bordered and bearing the noble seal of the state of Virginia. It is the *official* copy of what the state deems a "vital" record. The state holds this record securely: you can't actually get to see it. And then in 2021, another certified copy appears, yet more imposing and formal, which has a serial number and instructs me to verify the watermark by holding it to the light, and which again unambiguously lists both as colored, but which gets the date of the marriage wrong by fifty years. And then the 1940 document suddenly appears on Ancestry.com. Statecraft and racecraft combined, exactly as Plecker had hoped, but human error persists, exactly as Plecker feared.[2]

I still have no solid evidence as to why Prentis listed them as "colored," but you can see clearly how the racial designation gained authority over time, for no reason other than the demands of the 1940 form, which require Powell to assign a race to each person. And then it grew more solid still when the Bureau of Vital Statistics spelled out "colored" instead of simply using "c." Individual and racial identity is created by documents.

The other question raised by this elaborate and dry tale is about access and authority, and why I could only see the Plecker-inspired 1940 copy through a subscription to Ancestry.com. In Virginia, ancestry conferred racial status and the right to marry: it determined what school you could attend or where you had to sit in a movie theater or bus. Now the official source for Patrick and Hester's racial status lies in the digital images of Ancestry.com, and an image of the original document awaits anyone willing to pay the annual subscription fee. Having paid, you can view it in the context of your DNA profile, the "blood test" Plecker dreamed of, in a massive privately owned relational database of individual genetic information. Once authority over ancestry lay in the memories of local people, then it moved to county ledgers, and then to central state control in Richmond. If you search for records on the website of the Virginia Department of Health, you will now find a portal designed and maintained by Ancestry.com. State-craft and racecraft, once merged, are coming apart.

## Mormonism and the Value of the Dead

Ancestry.com started in a close relationship to the Church of Jesus Christ of Latter-day Saints, the "LDS," known colloquially as the Mormons. Mormon theology in turn plays a central role in the popularity of online genealogy. *The Book of Mormon* stresses the importance of "proxy baptism," by which the souls of those millions of people who died before Joseph Smith's revelations in the 1820s can be saved if a living Mormon receives baptism in their name. Mormonism casts proxy baptism as a sacred duty, equivalent to going on a mission trip to convert the living.

But Mormonism also stresses family as eternal: instead of being married till "death do you part," you are "sealed" to your spouse for eternity. Similarly, you have the same relatives in heaven as you did on earth. The website of the Church of Jesus Christ of Latter-day Saints asserts, "Church members believe that families are forever," and "they seek to identify generations of relatives through family history work," and further that "a family's importance extends beyond mortal life. We highly value the promise that families can be together forever." Baptizing the deceased increases your level of "exaltation," a state of godhood in the afterlife. On that same website, Church Elder Russell Nelson declared, "any discussion of family responsibilities to prepare for exaltation would be incomplete if we included only mother, father, and children. What about grandparents and other ancestors?" He quoted Joseph Smith's words in Doctrine and Covenants 128 of the *Book of Mormon*: "The Lord has revealed that we cannot become perfect without them; neither can they without us be made perfect." The Latter-day Saints refer to marriages and baptisms as "sealing ordinances," which fix people to each other for eternity. "You live with your family now, and we believe that even after you and your family members pass on, you can live together again in heaven."[3]

You *can*, if the ancestors have been baptized. "Sealing ordinances are essential to exaltation," Elder Nelson continued. "A wife needs to be sealed to her husband; children need to be sealed to their parents; and we all need to be connected with our ancestors." "Let all the records be had in order," Joseph Smith had declared, "that they may be put in the archives of my holy temple, to be held in remembrance from generation to generation, saith the Lord of Hosts." And so the LDS has compiled the most astonishing database of human genealogy ever contemplated, stored in a vault beneath a mountain near Salt Lake City, the source of many of the records to which Ancestry .com sells access.[4]

The records range from fragile books and scrolls, to photos and transcriptions of ancient documents, to tapes of oral genealogies chanted by tribal elders: more than twelve billion names and growing. The church has developed extremely sophisticated hardware and software for recognizing text and sound and converting to digital media. Each source is transcribed and each person named is, ideally, baptized. The Granite Mountain Records Vault contains the single largest organized record of humanity's existence on earth, and if genealogy is history, it amounts to the most detailed history ever attempted, all to facilitate the project of baptizing the dead.[5]

## Other People's Ancestors

In the 1990s, Jewish people doing family history, and using databases compiled by the LDS, began discovering the proxy baptism of ancestors. In 1994, while consulting the online International Genealogical Index, which the LDS began in 1969, Esther Ramon was surprised to find a baptismal record for her grandfather, who had died in a Nazi prison camp. More baptisms of Jewish Nazi victims came to light, including Anne Frank. Pressed on this, the LDS estimated about 380,000 Jewish concentration camp victims had been baptized by 1995. It was soon revealed that other proxy baptisms included "Adolf Hitler, his mistress, Eva Braun; Josef Goebbels and Heinrich

Himmler." According to the Jewish magazine *Forward*, "On at least three occasions since 1993, church members have performed baptism by proxy for Hitler in Mormon temples in Los Angeles, London and Jordan River, Utah." Hitler's parents as well as Joseph Stalin, Benito Mussolini, Lee Harvey Oswald, and John Wilkes Booth all received proxy baptism. A spokesman for the LDS Family History Library in Salt Lake City said "that he had not known that this work was being done," and he added, "It's unthinkable that someone would consciously submit those names for temple ordinance." Clearly someone found it eminently thinkable.[6]

It's important to note that like any large religion, the LDS includes members who differ in their interpretation and their fervor, and also like any religion it has internal and external critics, some of whom have eagerly attacked the practice of proxy baptism by finding the examples above. The LDS has been incredibly fast in collecting names and speed often undermines care. But Mormon beliefs are crucial to understanding the growth and popularity of genealogy as a hobby and the way in which Mormon genealogical practices shift the role of the state.[7]

Although the LDS quickly signed an agreement with Jewish groups declaring they would end the practice of proxy baptizing victims of the Shoah, less than a decade later, researchers found Nazi hunter Simon Wiesenthal had been baptized, along with others including Daniel Pearl, the Jewish American journalist beheaded by jihadists in 2002. Responses ranged from deep anger to laughter. A website, "alldeadmormonsarenowgay.com," offered to convert dead Mormons who died "without knowing the joys of homosexuality." The *New York Times* quoted Rabbi Laura A. Baum, who said, "I don't want to give any credence to anyone who thinks baptizing us matters," but "on the other hand, I don't think it's nice." Other religions and other ethnic groups objected as well. After learning that prominent Catholics including Pope John Paul II had been baptized—and that John Paul had possibly been sealed in a proxy marriage to an equally deceased woman—the Bishop of Kerry in Ireland urged Irish clerics to "protect parish records to ensure they—are not used by Mormons to baptize dead Catholics." The Vatican wrote to Catholic dioceses worldwide, "urging them not to 'cooperate with the erroneous practices of the Church of Jesus Christ of Latter-day Saints' by providing them with parish records." The church further declared that any Mormon who converted to Catholicism would have to be rebaptized, because "the Mormon view of the nature of God was too different" from Catholic doctrine.[8]

Many people might dismiss these concerns. Nonbelievers will roll their eyes at the whole business, while even most religious believers might regard the practice as well intentioned and harmless. The Latter-day Saints insisted that proxy baptism does not forcibly convert the dead, but merely offers them a choice to believe. Historian of religion John Turner thus argued that "when Mormons are immersed in water in an attempt to offer salvation to our deceased ancestors, they do no harm to the living or the dead."[9]

But these arguments, while reasonable, obscure the fact that the LDS is not just offering people the choice to become Mormon: it is enlisting them in a larger project of personal salvation via genealogical records. Mormon practice understands the significance of the dead through their genetic connection to the living: who they *were*, what they did, only matters to the extent that they are someone's blood relatives. This is partly why Mormons could baptize both Hitler and Anne Frank: the content of individual lives matters far less than the simple fact of blood relation. "It's outrageous," Armenian American historian Ruth Thomasian insisted on learning that victims of the Armenian genocide had been baptized. "Proxy baptisms are not what historic documentation is all about, to make people into something they are not. Everybody thinks that this is just a listing of genealogy, when in fact they're making everyone into Mormons. It's total disrespect." Other Armenian American genealogists were less concerned. The practice of proxy baptisms "has no meaning because I don't recognize it. I don't have a problem with it." "I think it's harmless," another declared. But the president of the Knights of Vartan, an Armenian American fraternal organization, echoed Thomasian when he called it, "the theft of somebody's history and past identity. . . . It's killing the history of the dead."[10]

His comments, like the comments of Jewish Americans angered by the practice, raised a central point about the difference between history and genealogy. Genealogy locates significance in blood relations with the dead, while history looks more at how the person lived. The afterlife can't be footnoted, for one thing, but beyond that, Patrick and Hester O'Malley's significance lies not in their biological relation to me, but in the ways they negotiated identity, and the lives they built, in the face of political and cultural constraints. Patrick left his childhood faith, then returned to it and brought his family with him. Hester's grandchildren, my grandparent's generation, went to Mass and confession; they baptized their children and went in turn to the baptisms, communions, and confirmations of my generation. They had statues of Saint Francis in the garden and the Infant of Prague in the house; they prayed the rosary, ate meals in the parish hall; they sent their sons off to be altar boys and told them to behave themselves at church dances. My grandmother told all her nine male grandchildren she had a box of silver dollars saved for the first to become a priest (no one took her up on the offer). Baptizing them in death treats this daily *practice*, the moral and ethical anchor of their lives, as meaningless. Like so much of genealogy, it ignores the habits, choices, and accomplishments by which every person makes their lives meaningful. It was the story of Dempsey Hare's family, in which their slight African ancestry was always held more important than what they accomplished. In this sense the problem with genealogy is the problem with racecraft: it reduces people to an essential biological identity.

### Property in the Dead

Baptizing the dead also represents a kind of claiming, an assertion of what we might call property in ancestry. Jews have historically been persecuted: claiming the Jewish dead as members of some other religion seems to use ancestral history to extend that persecution backward in time. The Jewish and Armenian and Catholic dead are made to do the work of the living, growing a religious community and serving as the building blocks of a robust afterlife.[11]

Genealogy also stresses, as Francesca Morgan has pointed out, biological relations "over chosen forms of relatedness, such as those created by marriage or adoption." Commercial genealogy services "threw their weight behind definitions of family that treasured pro- creation within heterosexual marriage at a time when same-sex, child- less, and unmarried family formations were on the rise." If you try to make a family tree within Ancestry.com or family search.org, you can easily account for heterosexual marriage that produces children, but you will have to go well out of your way to indicate an adopted child, who genealogy wants to understand solely in terms of birth parents. You cannot easily list biological parents *and* adoptive parents, for ex- ample. You have no way to account for people raised by relatives in the absence of parents, or by foster parents, or kind neighbors who nurtured a child in need: such relationships simply don't matter.

Baptizing distantly dead relatives also raises the odd question of who ancestors belong to, and that question again puts biology in ten- sion with history. A twenty-first-century Mormon could very well find a Jewish ten-times-great-grandparent, someone living in the Nether- lands in the 1600s perhaps, who in turn had a descendant murdered by the Nazis as well as a descendant who survived the Nazis and lived in Israel, and a third descendant who left Judaism, settled in Missouri, and joined the Latter-day Saints on their trek to Utah. Who would have the higher claim to that ancestor? Jewishness itself is sometimes understood as racial, as matrilineal descent, and sometimes under- stood as ethnicity, a set of cultural practices, and also as a religion. If the Dutch ancestor's European descendants practiced Judaism, lived out its tenets, and some were killed for being Jewish, then it would seem living Jewish descendants have a superior claim: the proxy bap- tism ignores the continuity of their faith. But genetics doesn't care how observant you were, and alternatively genetics might resolve ownership questions. The descendant who made the trip to Salt Lake in 1847 might have more DNA of the original ancestor in Amsterdam than the person killed by the Nazis, which would seem to grant *that* person a more substantial right.[12]

Property in the dead may seem like an absurd idea, but family history has always figured in property claims. Cases of inheritance spell out ancestry. As we've seen, African ancestry enabled property in slavery. Discovering an African ancestor prevented people from buying a house in some neighborhoods. Uniformly European ancestry granted a set of legal and property rights. Walter Plecker's whole career was about policing property rights in ancestry, making sure that, as we've seen, a person with African ancestors could not own a gravesite in a white cemetery or earn a degree from a white school. Ancestry figures as property in claims to land—in Palestine, in Northern Ireland, or in the United States where indigenous Americans assert ancestral rights. All these iterations of property in the dead intersect with the government's role overseeing property transfer. Mormon sealing ordinances assert a property in ancestry—ancestors belong to one particular family—which people who object to proxy baptism resist. And of course property in ancestry is what Ancestry.com sells: to you, the customers, and sells to medical researchers who want aggregated data about DNA. Seen this way, proxy baptism is not trivial at all, but rather part of a larger set of relations of ancestry as property, a set of relations in which the role of the state is shifting.

*Secure Storage*

Today nearly any argument about descent, or any claim of property in ancestry, will likely involve the Granite Mountain Records Vault. The vault was built by the LDS in the 1960s, during the Cold War. It has two fourteen-ton steel outer doors designed to withstand a nuclear blast and two nine-ton inner doors for extra security. The designers aimed for a structure that would last one thousand years. Round hallway tunnels made of corrugated steel lead to the records and to a six-thousand-gallon water reservoir. It has its own generator:

temperatures are kept at a constant fifty-seven degrees, and humidity carefully monitored. The public is not allowed to enter—they would bring unwanted dust, lint, and humidity—and those who do get a tour may not take pictures.[13]

The mountain tunnels, the blast doors, the secrecy, all recall government facilities—bomb shelters, Fort Knox, or the once-secret underground bunker at the Greenbrier resort in West Virginia, reserved for members of Congress in the event of a nuclear attack. The collection is government-like in that it "consists primarily of birth, marriage, and death registers; wills and probates; census reports; and other documents that can be used to establish individual identities": that is, mostly the records assembled by state and local governments.[14]

Alternatively, the Granite Mountain vault might remind someone of the villain's secret lair in any number of James Bond films, which invariably pit government agents against sinister actors with government-like powers; uniformed minions, and the desire to control the world. Granite Mountain has more and more of the world's genealogical records every month and is indeed run by a religious organization that actively seeks to convert the entire globe and everyone who ever lived upon it.

This is a gross overstatement, yet at the same time the vault *is* like that: it comes from the same era as James Bond films and secret government bunkers under mountains. It contains a vast array of documents originally generated by state and national governments to track citizens, determine their legal rights, establish their social and racial status, and secure property. It stresses security. Just a mile down the road from the Granite Mountain Records Vault is the similar vault of Perpetual Storage Inc., which stores nearly anything people want to store: "the proprietors insist neither earthquake, fire, flood nor the most James Bond–inspired thief could penetrate its security. The vault is protected and safe from 'any force known to man,' they say, even a nuclear blast." Perpetual Storage began construction in 1968, just four years after the Granite Mountain Records Vault opened.[15]

Here under tons of rock we have the conjunction of the public and private sector, of religion and the state, of racecraft in genealogy. The cool tunnels preserve obsession with property, security, and access, as well as an effort to locate people in relation to their family's past, secure their identity, and save the past from the future's vagaries. So while the Catholic Church, on the one hand, objected to the baptism of the Catholic dead and urged parishes to restrict access to records, the website of FamilySearch.org links to a testimonial from Venezuelan cardinal Baltazar Porras Cardozo, about preserving Catholic records with FamilySearch's commercial data archiving services. The cardinal praises the sincerity and transparency of the LDS and argues for the records as documents of history, not just genealogy. Plecker would have loved the vault. Had it existed during his reign, under the Blue Ridge Mountains, he might have never seen daylight again, an outcome the present might applaud. But he would have been horrified by the degree of public access to the documents and by the relative decline of state authority they represent.[16]

## *The LDS and Digital Genealogy*

The LDS has made these records widely available through its genealogy-focused website FamilySearch.org. FamilySearch started in 1894, as the Genealogical Society of Utah. The society eagerly collected genealogical records, copying and indexing them or purchasing them outright, and started microfilming the moment the technology appeared. It was renamed "FamilySearch" when it built its first website in 1999. The site contains, at no cost, a truly astonishing array of digitized records. But searching both Ancestry.com and FamilySearch.org for the same person will turn up different results. The search algorithms used are different, the search parameters are different, and Ancestry.com includes records not available to the general public through Family-Search. The site is a boon to people interested in genealogy. But it's problematic for people interested in history, in multiple ways.

For example, Patrick and Hester's 1884 marriage shows up readily in FamilySearch.org if you search for their names, the place, and the date. But the website shows only a partial transcription, and the results don't include their race or his status as a laborer. Where you would click to see the image of the original document it says, "image unavailable." And the results don't explain what source they draw on. FamilySearch cites the record as "Virginia Marriages, 1785–1940', database, FamilySearch (https://FamilySearch.org/ark:/61903/1:1:XRFL -NZB: 29 January 2020), Patrick O'Malley, 1884." But that citation is *historically* useless: is it citing the original marriage license, on which they were declared white, or the 1884 marriage register, or the 1940 copy of the 1884 register, both of which listed them as colored? The citation locates the source in the Granite Mountain Records Vault, or somewhere in the digital cloud, not in Nansemond County or in Plecker's files. What we see is a change in the location of authority, and consequently a change in what results we find.

As history, the records are not reliable unless the original source is provided and the transcription verified. For example, on FamilySearch .org you can cobble together a search of all Virginia marriages between 1800 and 1900, specify the birthplace of one of the parties as Ireland, and then specify race by making a choice from a pull-down menu, including "white" or "w," or "negro" or "colored" or "col" or "C." Searching for Irish-born people who married and specifying "race" as "C" finds over 2,400 entries, the record of roughly four hundred individual marriages. Looking at the first one hundred reveals, in cases where images of the original documents are available, that they are nearly all errors in which the transcriber wrote down the birthplace of the person above the line they were transcribing. Refining that same search for the last name "O'Malley" does not turn up Patrick and Hester, and none of the sixteen names that it returns appear to be listed as colored on any original documents, so the search results are simply puzzling. FamilySearch is not concerned with *historical* questions, only with biological ancestry.[17]

The odd list of choices on the pull-down menu brings racecraft into practice again. All those terms appeared as descriptors for "race" in the past. But in searching you cannot apply the umbrella term "black" and have it include "cold" or col'd," even though the terms were often synonymous. And perhaps because of sensitivity to the word's pejorative origins, FamilySearch.org offers no possibility of searching for "mulatto," which as we've seen was very widely used, both to indicate mixed ancestry and to mean "black." My interest in tracing ancestry for this book made me feel uncomfortably like Walter Plecker, charting "race mixing," but FamilySearch has gone in the other direction and eliminated evidence of mixed ancestry. We might applaud FamilySearch for refusing to accept the terms of racecraft, but not including terms like "mulatto" ignores the reason the information was recorded in the first place: to map and track race.

## Digital Genealogy and the Records of Race

Just clicking on the search category "race" calls up a warning: "Sensitive Terms and Content: The language and content used on the FamilySearch records have been copied directly as they were documented by the creators of the historical records. The content is neither created nor endorsed by FamilySearch." The LDS has certainly cared about race in the past. Like many other Christian denominations, the Latter-day Saints understood persons with dark skin as cursed by God, the children of Ham. In heaven, dark-skinned persons would become white, Joseph Smith declared. As John Turner put it, "a church that emphasized forging links between the generations and eternal sealings between its members [did] not find it easy to incorporate black Americans within this ecclesial family." Until 1978, persons with African ancestry could not be priests of the faith or attain the highest level of salvation. The LDS is quite frank about its past struggles with racism: FamilySearch now omits race altogether from Patrick and Hester's record.[18]

The interface at FamilySearch.org changes depending on which collections you search. If you search *all* United States records for *all* persons born in Ireland between 1850 and 1860, you can then filter the results by "race" by clicking a button and choosing "black." That search returns over five hundred results. The first nine on the list show up as black people born in County Mayo, Ireland. But the original source, a register of births kept in Patrick County, Virginia, shows them living in "North Mayo" or "Mayo River," referring to the North Mayo River flowing in central Virginia near the North Carolina border. "Jefferson," son of "Kizziah," was probably not born in County Mayo, Ireland. In many other cases, the names don't appear to be Irish, suggesting an error, or for people with Irish surnames a photo of the original document isn't online and can't be checked for error. But in at least seven cases, photos of the original source clearly showed Irish-born people listed as "black." For example, Missouri's census in 1910 described the entire family of Michael and Ellen Regan, born in Ireland, as "B" for "black." In 1912, Philadelphia recorded the death of Isabella McGale, fifty-seven, in the city hospital for the insane. Birth in Ireland did not prevent her from being described as "black." And in 1920, the Connecticut census listed Mary McKeane and her two children as "N" for "Negro" although Mary too was born in Ireland.

Searching for Patrick and Hester's marriage on Ancestry.com, on the other hand, turns up their listing as colored and offers an image of the 1940 "fair copy" sent to Walter Plecker in Richmond. You can search Ancestry.com's US-only records for persons born around 1855, when Patrick was born, and specify birthplace "Ireland (exact)" and "race" as "colored (exact)," and get 186 results. Of these results most are transcription errors related to handwriting or misreadings of adjacent lines. A significant number can't be traced via Ancestry.com, because again there are no links to the original source. But they also showed at least thirteen solid instances of people born in Ireland being declared colored.

For example, according to the census taker, Jacob Flynn, a nine-year-old orphan, was born in Ireland but was black in 1860. Irish-born Patrick Donovan died in 1876 in Massachusetts, which listed him as "col'd" in the official register of deaths. Jacob Downey, laborer, died "suddenly" in June of 1880. The commissioner of revenue for Alexandria, Virginia, wrote that Jacob was born in Ireland but checked the column for "colored" after his name. John Parish, a clerk born in Ireland, died in 1882: Massachusetts officials wrote "cold" next to his name. Two years later, when Irish-born Louisa Cook died in Boston, the clerk again saw fit to write "cold" next to her name.

James Garvan worked as a gardener in Philadelphia in 1900: the census listed him as black. Margaret McConvill left Ireland with her parents and married a Pennsylvania man named Gese or Gesse. When she died in 1906, in Tyrone, Pennsylvania, the medical examiner named her colored. Charles McBride was born in Ireland and died in Philadelphia in 1916, at fifty-nine: the death certificate lists his parents' names and says they were also born in Ireland, but gives his race as "colored." The death certificate of Annie Murphy, Philadelphia, filled out in 1921, lists her as born in Ireland and also as colored. She was buried in Holy Cross Cemetery, the same place where Patrick and Hester reside. Mary Healy left Ireland with her parents and married a man named Simmons in Pittsburgh: the medical examiner certified she was colored when she died in 1921. Allegheny County, Pennsylvania, discharged Patrick O'Malley, age eighteen and no known relation, from prison in July of 1928, but not before adding a check after his name in the column for "black."

These records are startling, and the original sources, not all of which are available online, may well show more instances of Irish people being declared "colored" among those 186 names. Most of those records clearly show poor people, more vulnerable to class contempt and less able to contest the official's whims. Jacob Flynn was an orphan. Charles McBride was a single laborer, living in a boarding house. Mary King lived in Rodman Street in Philadelphia, and all her neighbors were listed as "C" for "colored." A census taker might have associated her with her neighbors or, in a hurry, simply filled in a whole column of people as "C."

But a death certificate, especially after 1900, took time to fill out. The account of someone's death carries a gravity and seriousness the census taker, with possibly hundreds of people to record, might not feel. It required statements from the person who reported the death

and an account of the cause. It involved trained medical profession-
als, like Walter Plecker, with an interest in objective public health
statistics. Death certificates typically show a combination of handwritten and typed entries, suggesting that multiple people worked to
fill them out. As late as 1936, Dr. Otto Fleisher Friedman, fifty-seven,
a doctor practicing in North Philadelphia, gave precise explanations
for the death of Julia Madison, born in Galway. Based on clinical evidence, he wrote "myocarditis endocarditis" with arteriosclerosis "contributory." She had suffered from these things for two years and two
months, Friedman noted. Julia's daughter Agnes reported her death.
Agnes lived just over a mile away from Friedman and on the same
block as her mother. Friedman wrote that he attended Julia from August 26 through the 30, the last day he saw her alive. These things suggest Friedman was the family doctor, who might have known them
well. So why did he list Julia as "colored?"

The certificate (figure 7.2) shows how record keeping had changed
by the mid-twentieth century. Walter Plecker was only part of a wider
national system of intersecting disciplines that claimed a right to know
about someone's death. Instructions on the left margin insist, in em-
phatic capitals, "WRITE PLAINLY WITH UNFADING INK—THIS IS
A PERMANENT RECORD." Dr. Friedman was further instructed that
"every item of information should be carefully supplied." "AGE should
be stated EXACTLY," the instructions continued, and "PHYSICIANS
should state CAUSE OF DEATH in plain terms, so that it may be properly classified. Exact Statement of OCCUPATION is very important."
Was the death by violent means, it asked? Was there evidence of
crime? Sociology and economics had a hand in Julia's death: the exact
occupation was "very important." The form demanded the deceased's
trade and employer. Her religion was not stated but could be inferred
from the requirement for "place of burial, cremation, or removal."
Public health administrators wanted to know the exact cause of death,
how long the cause had plagued her, and if she'd gone to a hospital,
and if so, which one? Had a medical operation preceded the death?
Where had the disease been contracted? Public administration has

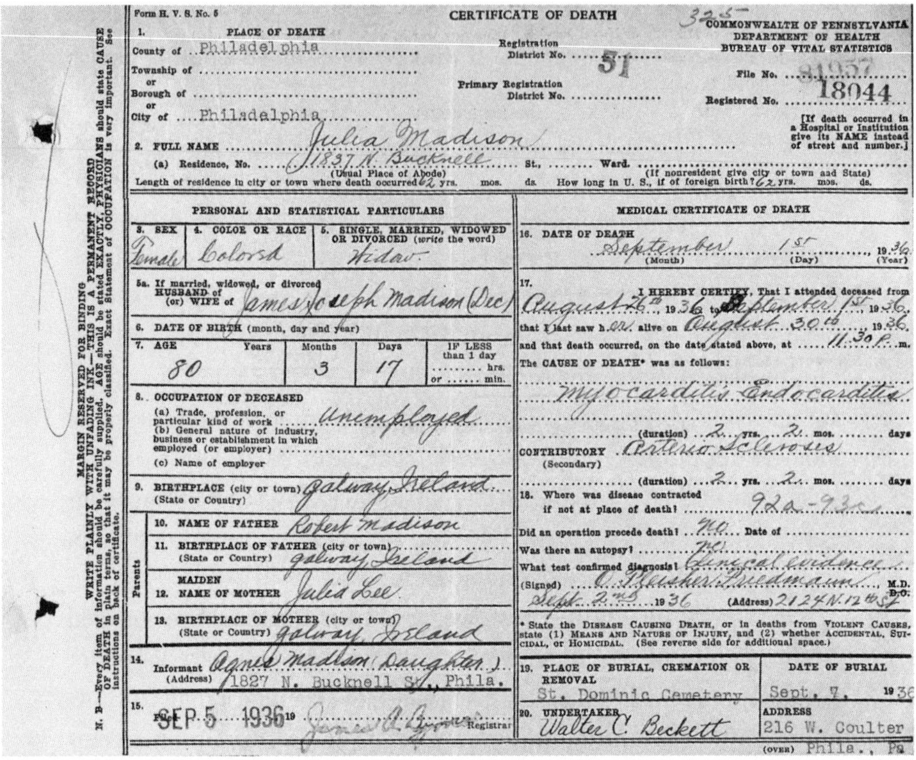

N. B.—Every item of information should be carefully supplied. AGE should be stated EXACTLY. PHYSICIANS should state CAUSE OF DEATH in plain terms, so that it may be properly classified. Exact Statement of OCCUPATION is very important. See instructions on back of certificate.

WRITE PLAINLY WITH UNFADING INK—THIS IS A PERMANENT RECORD

MARGIN RESERVED FOR BINDING

Form H. V. S. No. 5

CERTIFICATE OF DEATH

325

COMMONWEALTH OF PENNSYLVANIA
DEPARTMENT OF HEALTH
BUREAU OF VITAL STATISTICS

1. PLACE OF DEATH

County of Philadelphia

Township of
or
Borough of
or
City of Philadelphia

Registration District No. 51

Primary Registration District No.

File No. 81957

Registered No. 18044

[If death occurred in a Hospital or Institution give its NAME instead of street and number.]

2. FULL NAME Julia Madison

(a) Residence, No. 1837 N. Bucknell St., Ward.
(Usual Place of Abode) (If nonresident give city or town and State)

Length of residence in city or town where death occurred 62 yrs. mos. ds. How long in U. S., if of foreign birth? 62 yrs. mos. ds.

PERSONAL AND STATISTICAL PARTICULARS

| 3. SEX | 4. COLOR OR RACE | 5. SINGLE, MARRIED, WIDOWED OR DIVORCED (write the word) |
|---|---|---|
| Female | Colored | Widow |

5a. If married, widowed, or divorced HUSBAND of (or) WIFE of James Joseph Madison (Dec)

6. DATE OF BIRTH (month, day and year)

| 7. AGE Years | Months | Days | IF LESS than 1 day ... hrs. or ... min. |
|---|---|---|---|
| 80 | 3 | 17 | |

8. OCCUPATION OF DECEASED
(a) Trade, profession, or particular kind of work Unemployed
(b) General nature of industry, business or establishment in which employed (or employer)
(c) Name of employer

9. BIRTHPLACE (city or town) (State or Country) Galway, Ireland

Parents

10. NAME OF FATHER Robert Madison

11. BIRTHPLACE OF FATHER (city or town) (State or Country) Galway, Ireland

12. MAIDEN NAME OF MOTHER Julia Lee

13. BIRTHPLACE OF MOTHER (city or town) (State or Country) Galway, Ireland

14. Informant Agnes Madison (Daughter.)
(Address) 1827 N. Bucknell St., Phila.

15. Filed SEP 5 1936 19 ... Registrar

MEDICAL CERTIFICATE OF DEATH

16. DATE OF DEATH September 1st, 1936
(Month) (Day) (Year)

17. I HEREBY CERTIFY, That I attended deceased from August 26th, 1936 to September 1st, 1936, that I last saw her alive on August 30th, 1936, and that death occurred, on the date stated above, at 11:30 P.m.

The CAUSE OF DEATH* was as follows:

Myocarditis Endocarditis

(duration) 2 yrs. 2 mos. days

CONTRIBUTORY (Secondary) Arterio Sclerosis

(duration) 2 yrs. 2 mos. days

18. Where was disease contracted if not at place of death? 92a-93c

Did an operation precede death? No Date of

Was there an autopsy? No

What test confirmed diagnosis? Clinical evidence

(Signed) O. Pleasher Friedmann, M.D. D.O.

Sept. 2nd, 1936 (Address) 2124 N. 12th St.

* State the DISEASE CAUSING DEATH, or in deaths from VIOLENT CAUSES, state (1) MEANS AND NATURE OF INJURY, and (2) whether ACCIDENTAL, SUICIDAL, or HOMICIDAL. (See reverse side for additional space.)

| 19. PLACE OF BURIAL, CREMATION OR REMOVAL | DATE OF BURIAL |
|---|---|
| St. Dominic Cemetery | Sept. 7, 1936 |
| 20. UNDERTAKER | ADDRESS |
| Walter C. Beckett | 216 W. Coulter Phila., Pa |

(over)

*Figure 7.2.* Death Certificate of Julia Madison, 1936. Courtesy of Pennsylvania State Archives.

been formalized: the certificate instructs that the left margin must be kept blank "for binding," and the certificate has two number stamps, a "file number" and a "registered number." Friedman could answer the question about where the disease "had been contracted, if not at place of death," with a standardized response, "92a-93c." The state, which manifests here as a legal and administrative system and a set of interrelated disciplines, wants to know the name and address of the undertaker.

These multiple disciplines and systems of knowing all claim a property in Julia Madison, a right to use her life and death to draw comparative conclusions and police the social order. Society would surely want to know if someone murdered Julia Madison: to convict the guilty we might want to question the undertaker who prepared the body. We would want to know if there was a relationship between anyone's occupation and their death or if their local environment was unhealthy. Public health officials would want to know what diseases were most common. Did men and women die of different things and at different ages? All these things would be useful to know, and the state also wants to know the ethnicity and race of the deceased: did people with African or Irish ancestors die differently? But anyone using death certificates to draw conclusions about, say, the relative susceptibility of African-descended people to myocarditis would be adding Galway native Julia Madison to the data set. And so we are still left wondering why Dr. Friedman listed a woman born in Galway as colored.

A clue lies in the name of her late husband, James Joseph Madison. The 1910 census found a James J. Matison living in Bensalem, Pennsylvania, just over the northeast Philadelphia border, with his wife, Julia, and their daughter, Agnes. The census taker called James, born in Virginia, "mulatto," but named Julia as Irish and as white. Agnes, then age twenty-three, was listed as mulatto as well. Julia's marriage to a man with African ancestry made her African in the eyes of her neighbor, the doctor. His decision echoes the case of Ira Ann White. By choosing to marry a man with African ancestors, Julia Madison magically acquired African ancestry herself. As we saw earlier, individualizing people was instrumental to racializing them.

Julia Madison's case, and the other instances mentioned above, show that Patrick and Hester's classification as colored was not unique, and that there were clearly other instances in which Irish-born people were declared nonwhite. But it's important to note that if you search the United States, via Ancestry.com, for people born in Ireland around 1855, and eliminate the search term "colored," you turn up 5,491,065 names. One hundred and eighty-six is a statistically insignificant number in comparison to over five million. These results are not simply mistakes, but there are too few to regard them as "typical" in any way.

The goal here is not quantifying disadvantage, or claiming Irish

people were more oppressed than other people, using Irish suffering as a political cudgel. Suffering is general in history, and it takes
infinite forms. What we see here is racecraft at work, racecraft expressed in documents collected by the state and now aggregated by
a partnership between state archives, the LDS, and commercial genealogy companies.

But it's important to point out how these results decouple "race"
from ancestry. As we've seen, you did not need visible African ancestors to be classed as black, nor did having African ancestors prevent
some people from being classed as white: Dempsey Hare's children
with Frances Whitfield, for example. Decoupling race from ancestry
is vital to escaping the hold of "race" on the imagination. But here
we see local officials whimsically declaring whatever race they feel
appropriate.

It's also important to note that you can't easily run this kind of
search. Most results on both FamilySearch.com and Ancestry.com
are glaring transcription errors. And while it's marvelous to easily
find James Matison's family in the 1910 census, a data-minded historian would like to download the entire corpus of digitized information and search across categories for education, occupation, literacy
or illiteracy, race, age of work, age of death, age of marriage, occupation by ethnicity: there are almost limitless ways a historian might
use this data in digital form. If I had access to the data, I could craft
my own topic models for searching. I could see whether other immigrants were classed as nonwhite at the same rate or under the same
conditions. These records might give clear evidence of a connection to
racial status and poverty or geography. More importantly, they would
show the arbitrariness of ancestry's relation to race.

Subscribers can do some of this work. Searching Ancestry.com
for persons born in Italy in 1880 and listed as "colored" in US records
turns up 256 names. Many of these are again egregious transcription
errors, for example, an Alexander Hamilton, born in Rome, Georgia,
listed as Italian. At least thirty-two other times whoever transcribed
Tennessee death records made the same mistake. Thula Panipinto

shows up as a black person in Indiana death records, but for no clear reason: the actual death certificate explicitly lists her as white. So too Domenico Tedesco, who died in Philadelphia in 1920: Ancestry.com finds him as colored, but it's not clear why, because the actual death certificate clearly marked him as white. Still, Umberto Guarro, born in Italy, was named as colored on his Philadelphia death certificate in 1965, and so was Angela Ciabattoni, housewife, and Michael Susca, who died in 1962. Three different doctors saw them as colored as they lay before them in death.

We might conclude that Italians tend to be darker than Irish, and so it makes a kind of racial "common sense." Walter Plecker thought Sicilians were "heavily intermarried" with Africans. But skin color is not the issue here: instead we see officials using records of individualism to wish "race" into being. Michael Susca registered for the draft in 1942, giving his birthplace as Naples, Italy. The draft card lists him as "white" and further describes his complexion as "light." But he also made a mark rather than signing: he was illiterate. These results show again how arbitrary racecraft could be. Personal prejudice could change someone's racial designation, and in thousands of cases, as with Dempsey Hare and his daughter, racial designation might bear little or no relation to what people actually looked like. African ancestry might be invisible, or it might float in and out of visibility or simply emerge from the imagination, depending on class and context. Despite the precision death records demanded, officials could randomly designate people whatever "race" they thought right.[19]

### *Who Owns Family History?*

Historians like me would also like to claim a property in the dead, and the right to use the dead to make meaning and in this case gain a better understanding of how racecraft worked. The data aggregated by Ancestry and FamilySearch is extraordinary. Before about 2010, it would have taken *decades* to manually perform the searches I just described. Full access to the data assembled by FamilySearch and

Ancestry would allow a historian to correlate racial designation to geography, or age, or sex, or occupation. If historians had access to the data, in addition to correcting obvious errors we could add metadata categories. For example, where the death certificate names the cemetery, we might add "religion" as a searchable term. Historians would also like to claim a property in the past. But as Katherina Hering has noted, Ancestry.com, like FamilySearch.org, does not have an interface that can address most historical questions.[20]

What gives me a right to claim this database and make it work the way I'd like it to? You might accept the idea that you "own" your specific ancestors, via family culture or a genetic link, but "the past" is everyone's inheritance. Just as a tyrant can stop people from speaking but can't prevent them from having an opinion, access to the past can be foreclosed, but the past will still have happened, independent of anyone's political desires or profit motive. The past conspired to put you where you sit reading this book. Slavery famously produced "social death," severing people from home, kin, family, and tribe: the voyage across the Atlantic and into enslavement made tracing people incredibly difficult, but the past still happened; the horrific voyage took place. If individuals are hard to track, then we look to recreate the context of the past—as with Patrick Melley, who vanishes into the bogs of Donegal—from other multiple sources. We accept that access to the materials of the past, fragile and easily damaged, can be limited. But in general "the past" is the buried foundation all of us are built on, and it's difficult to see how any one person or corporate person can own it. In the case of US history, the genealogical data in the Granite Mountain vault was originally collected almost entirely at taxpayer expense and belongs to the taxpayers. But the digitization was done by the labor of dedicated members of the LDS, or by contract employees hired by Ancestry, some of whom worked for FamilySearch. Ancestry now owns the aggregate digital records of, for example, the 5.4 million Irish people born around 1855 who emigrated to the US, and the DNA of millions of people, like myself, who mailed them saliva in a tube for testing.

## Ancestry.com and the Latter-day Saints

Julia Creet and Francesca Morgan have recently written about the history of Ancestry.com and its relation to FamilySearch, as well as about Ancestry's move into genetic testing. As we've seen, Americans had long been interested in genealogy as a tool of statecraft, as a badge of social and political authority, and as a roadmap to property transfer. Family history worked with law to determine which people could be property. Genealogical societies like those Emma Plecker joined conferred social status. A spotless genealogy conferred the benefits of whiteness. Mormons draped those interests in sacred robes.[21]

The LDS began digitizing records as soon as it was feasible, offering them at terminals and then on laser disks and CD-ROM. Ancestry .com started as two Brigham Young University students, Dan Taggart and Paul B. Allen, selling CD-ROMs of publicly available data out of the trunk of a car. They very quickly realized the CDs were a dead end and began putting data online in 1996. "In 1998, Ancestry Inc. launched MyFamily.com and the site accumulated over one million users in a matter of half a year." A year later they changed the name to Ancestry.com.

The company always had a symbiotic relationship with Family-Search. As online pioneers, Ancestry offered to digitize and transcribe records held by the LDS in the Granite Mountain vault, and the church eagerly cooperated. If non-Mormons using Ancestry.com began finding ancestors and building family trees, it only augmented the work of the church. As Morgan put it, "the more people—Mormon or not—engaged in genealogy, the closer everyone drew to fulfilling God's plan." By 2010, FamilySearch had established its own online presence and announced in April of that year that it had added 300 million names to its online records. By then Ancestry had been bought by a UK equity firm, Permira. "In August of 2020, in the midst of the pandemic, the private-equity firm the Blackstone Group bought the company for $4.7 billion, nearly triple the amount of its purchase price in 2012."[22]

In September 2013, the two organizations entered into a formal partnership to gather and digitize more records. Ancestry.com CEO Tim Sullivan said, "his company planned to pour more than $60 million into the effort over the next five years." "To have the two, I guess one could say, largest and most important organizations in the family history space working together to bring over a billion records online over the next several years is just a fantastic thing," he added. Ancestry.com by then had more than 2.7 million paid subscribers. Members of the LDS church got free membership to Ancestry.com, and Ancestry got access to the Granite Mountain vault. A year later, Ancestry announced it had added "about 1 billion more digitized family records" to its database, which in turn encouraged $2.6 billion in additional investment, which enabled it to ramp up its processes for "keying in" data.[23]

"We used four vendors to key the 1940 Census," said Todd Jensen of Ancestry in 2012. "Two were located in China . . . another was located in Bangladesh and the fourth in the Philippines." Information was "double keyed." Two different people would key in the same information, and then a third would compare the two for errors. The people doing the keying "probably didn't speak English," admitted Dan Taggart, one of Ancestry's cofounders, which might account for mistaking Rome, Georgia, as the capital of Italy or locating Virginia's North Mayo River in Ireland's Connacht province. Still, FamilySearch was impressed with the speed and contracted some of its own keying-in to Ancestry. "We began digitizing their records and scanning the images of those records," Taggert said, "with the understanding that we would make them available to the church to offer through the Family History Departments and Family History Centers throughout the world, and especially throughout the United States, for free to their members." Shipley Munson, then vice president for marketing for FamilySearch, told Creet that in return, "in many cases, we have chosen not to publish collections that are only available on Ancestry, because they need oxygen to breathe. And at some point, those collections will be made public, and at some point, those records will be commoditized so that they can be available to all the world." All the world with an internet connection and the ability to pay.[24]

The symbiotic relationship was often strained, because the LDS would cooperate with any organization doing the work of digitization and transcription. And Mormons who indexed records out of a sense of sacred duty resented seeing their work packaged and sold to subscribers. But cooperation made sense for both parties, and it made a kind of sense for the third parties holding records: for example, the National Archives and Record Administration (NARA).[25]

## Public Records and Private Property

Ancestry first "partnered" alone with NARA in 2008. Later it moved into a formal partnership with FamilySearch, which held microfilm reels of the federal census returns from 1790 through 1940. They gave these microfilms to Ancestry, which digitized them and merged them with their own indexes of the census, keyed overseas by non-English speakers. NARA in exchange would be allowed to make the indexed images available for free in its reading rooms, via terminals using Ancestry.com's website, while Ancestry would make them available online to subscribers.[26]

Like the 2008 agreement, the 2013 partnership agreement between NARA and Ancestry, available at the NARA website, specifies an "embargo period" of five years, during which Ancestry would have exclusive online rights. "Ancestry will provide free online access to those Digital Materials in all NARA locations to which NARA provides Ancestry with the applicable IP address. . . . This free access will continue as long as the Digital Materials are on the Ancestry Network," the contract stated. It further specified that "after the expiration of the Embargo Period, NARA will have full and unrestricted rights to use the Digital Materials donated by Ancestry, including the right to sell, make available for downloading, or otherwise provide in electronic form, the entire contents of the Digital Materials or segments of them."[27]

NARA published this contract for public comment, and multiple users testified to their frustration with the agreement. Users complained about the poor quality of the images, which did not meet archival standards for online documents. They pointed to the many, many egregious transcription errors, some of which we've seen.

But most expressed resentment that they would have to pay a subscription fee to access records their taxes funded. "Why should we need to pay for information collected by the U.S. Government?" one anonymous commenter asked. "What is the point of privatizing information that should be free? . . . I resent having to pay for information that my taxes paid to collect." While recognizing that "digitization is an expensive operation, and the funds must come from somewhere," Larry Parker asked why "private equity groups" get "a benefit from the United States government," which in turn "increase[s] the value of their companies, so they can sell them for an increased price to the next private equity group or groups." It amounted, Bonnie Schrack wrote, to "a shameful giveaway of extremely valuable public records to Ancestry.com."

Multiple comments pointed out that NARA had failed to make digitized records available or had made them hard to find. Indeed, a decade later, well after the end of the "embargo" period, NARA does not include digitized census records on its website. Instead, it simply links researchers to Ancestry.com, Familysearch.org, and Fold3.com, an expensive subsidiary of Ancestry specializing in records of military service. The National Archives still holds these records, but it directs users to the commercial sites.

Comments on NARA's contract with Ancestry often asked about the Civil War Widows' Pension records. These 1.28 million files, each typically containing at least ten pages and often one hundred or more, describe the soldier, his widow, and their children and offer an extremely rich account of how people came to terms with the loss of war and how they interacted with the government. In 2005, the National Archives had launched the Civil War Widows' Pension Digitization Project. It aimed to digitize the paper case files, originally housed in the Pension Building, described in chapter 2. A press release accompanying the project said the process of digitization utilized "citizen archivists" and mentioned only that someday the records would appear online. NARA publicized their work seven years later, in 2012, with a video that included interviews with the volunteer "citizen archivists" and accounts of the rewards and difficulties of the work. A press release accompanying the video makes clear that by 2012 the index and images were already "available at www.Fold3.com, a research website in partnership with the National Archives" and that "a second partner, FamilySearch, provides volunteers who create the digital images." In other words, these were not simply random history-loving "citizen archivists," but volunteer workers at the behest of the LDS, which then handed the information to Fold3.com for sale to subscribers. The National Archives, nearly twenty years later, has still not made these records available online.

"Can you give us a link to those early Civil War widows' pensions?" asked Peggy Reeves. "It is easy for NARA to say that things are being put on there, but none of us can find those 'customer-driven' high demand records, the widow's pensions being the records that are in highest demand." NARA's website is in fact very hard to navigate, and you cannot easily find records that should, by contract, have escaped "embargo" long ago. Having read these comments, in March of 2023 I spent a good deal of time trying to find these exact Widows' Pension records on the National Archives website and had no luck whatsoever. It's difficult just to find the catalog listing of the actual paper records. When you do, a highlighted text box tells you, "this Series has been digitized and is now fully available online." And indeed they are, at Fold3.com, which costs an additional fee if bundled along with Ancestry's annual subscription: as of this writing the cost is $600 per year.

"NARA's mission is to safeguard the papers and history of the United States for the people of this country. Ancestry's is to line its own pockets," commented P. J. Achramowicz. Indeed, yet building and maintaining a searchable database, with accurate metadata and images of documents in multiple resolutions, takes money for IT support, server space, and regular maintenance. Maintaining a searchable database, equally effective on multiple platforms, with tech support for users and a program for continual updates, strains budgets. It is easier and cheaper to outsource the entire operation to Ancestry.com and load the cost onto individual subscribers. But the result relocates authority over public records into private hands.[28]

Scholars concerned with public access to government records have been pointing this out since at least 2008, when James A. Jacobs warned that "short term, limited gains result in long-term *net losses* to free public access to public information." But Ancestry has continued to work aggressively to engross federal and state records.[29]

### Virginia Gives Its Records Away

In 2015, Virginia entered into a similar agreement with Ancestry.com, and similarly the general public got very little in return. The initial contract was between the Virginia Department of Health, Ancestry, and FamilySearch: a year later it was amended to describe FamilySearch explicitly as a subcontractor employed by Ancestry. The contract and supporting documents stressed that "Ancestry's subcontractor, FamilySearch, has a workforce of over 200,000 volunteers supporting its indexing efforts." That is, FamilySearch organizes the labor of LDS members, merging service to God with service to Ancestry.com. According to the contract, Ancestry would begin photographing, digitizing, transcribing, and indexing "vital" records old enough to make publicly available. Those records include the 1940 marriage register described at the start of this chapter, which appeared miraculously a few months after I was told seeing it was impossible. In return the State of Virginia got the right to make the records available via free access to Ancestry.com at terminals at the Library of Virginia in Richmond. Press releases claimed that the records—more than sixteen million as of 2015—would also be made available online at the website of the Virginia Department of Health. Extremely diligent searching will find only a link that takes you to Ancestry.com.[30]

"This public-private project demonstrates Virginia's continued commitment to innovation, efficiency and leveraging information technology to the benefit of all," Governor Terry McAullife proclaimed in 2015. "Having all Virginia vital records digitized means millions of public birth, death, marriage and divorce records are now more easily accessed for genealogy and family history research." These records are only more easily accessed if you travel to the Library of Virginia in Richmond, or subscribe to Ancestry, or use FamilySearch.org., which as we have seen grants full access to some but not all records to Ancestry.com or its subsidiaries.

McAuliffe added, "this project also provides a long-term conservation solution for preserving the rich history of Virginia's people." This clearly implies that Ancestry is now in charge of storing and conserving these records. Unless the records are recent, and by law can't be digitized and released yet, employees of the Bureau of Health now consult Ancestry.com in order to find them. McAuliffe's generous use of buzzwords like "innovation" and "leveraged" does not conceal the giveaway. "Long-term conservation solution" suggests Virginia has handed control over these documents to commercial firms and the Church of Jesus Christ of Latter-day Saints, which—as with the 1940 marriage register of Patrick and Hester—makes them available in full or partial form, or not at all, at its pleasure. Innovative indeed. The Department of Health still maintains these records unless by agreement they have moved to the Library of Virginia, but as with NARA the physical records become meaningless as users understandably switch to the digitized records available via Ancestry.[31]

To publish a book you need to get permission for any images you want to include. In October of 2023, I wrote to the Bureau of Vital Records in Virginia and requested permission to publish the image of the 1940 register that opened this chapter and the birth certificate of Clarence Brown shown in chapter 6. These images were both digitized by Ancestry.com. I got this response: "I'll have to check with our legal representatives about the request. I don't know if we have the authority to provide permission to publish those images found on Ancestry."

This clearly makes the point that ownership of vital records is being shifted into private hands. The University of Chicago Press looked at Ancestry's terms and conditions and concluded that the use of two images did not violate any restrictions and could be included, but this again only confirms that possession has shifted into private hands.[32]

This book has shown the immense power genealogical records held, for good and for ill. Genealogical records were the backbone of slavery and, later, of segregation. They could determine someone's spouse, or their neighborhood, or whether or not they could get a job. They could help the state sterilize the "feebleminded." But administrative records could also attest to free status or provide the enslaved with a means of escape. By securing individual identity, they certified citizenship, protected property, or helped keep children out of mines, mills and factories. By the early twentieth century, a range of reforms "delimited access to rights and protections by chronological age, from compulsory schooling and the juvenile court to age of consent and eligibility for benefits under workmen's compensation and mother's pension programs." But these forms of individualism nearly always served to produce "race," even to the extent of declaring Irish-born or Italian-born, white-looking people to be black, or insisting on the unambiguous blackness of people, like Julia Madison's husband, with mixed ancestry.[33]

## State versus Private Authority

Shifting these records of individual identity into private hands changes the role and force of state authority. This may be good or it may be bad, but at the least it begins to create a sort of vacuum that other forms of power will seek to fill. Administrative records were a response to the problems individualism raised. The need to understand people distinct from community; the need to authenticate identities and prevent fraud: these things gave rise to a record-keeping state. The idea of a "public domain" also served to manage some of the challenges individualism posed. "The public domain" established realms of culture or bodies of knowledge that can't be owned, that "belong to everybody." That might be because the government generated them at public expense or because they represent traditional practices, like folk songs or crafts. The idea of the public domain modifies strict individualism. Things in the public domain don't have individualized property rights. There is no "author," no fixed possession, no one to buy from.

No money changed hands in the Virginia's contract with Ancestry, a further sign of the ambiguity of the deal. The records of history for the most part belong to the public sphere, the public domain, but both these things are eroded by the kind of public-private "leveraging" McAuliffe promoted. Do you have a right to see documents pertaining to your family's history, or merely a privilege granted for a fee? Historians have seen more and more of the public domain enclosed behind paywalls. Nineteenth-century newspapers, for example, are beyond copyright and free to use in any library that housed them in paper or on microfilm. But today most historians, and most ordinary people, will access historical sources through commercial databases like Proquest Historical Newspapers, or Newspapers.com, which Ancestry owns. In many cases the originals are no longer available, making digital subscription services the only source.

This is a form of enclosure, like the "striping and squaring" of fields in Donegal, and like that enclosure it disrupts older systems of power. There are certainly enormous advantages to having digitized records available through a single portal. Much of the research for this book took place on a laptop instead of in visits to state and federal archives. It would be easy to imagine federal and state governments themselves digitizing documents and putting them online. It would be expensive, and many taxpayers would surely balk, but if we accept paying a fee for an official copy of a birth certificate, we could certainly accept a per-use charge for access to the public records. A database assembled by professional archivists with an eye to history, rather than genealogy alone, would look very different than a database assembled by a mix of religiously motivated volunteers and overseas workers who don't speak English and know nothing of the history and geography around the records they key in, directed by an organization with a theological imperative to baptize dead relatives. Virginia's contract with Ancestry suggests the prospect of public ownership of digital archives has been permanently foreclosed, since it gives Ancestry ownership of digital data.

Describing that contract, state health commissioner Marissa Levine noted that "through this project, people can more easily explore their ancestors' lives and possibly identify family health conditions or hereditary risk factors. This information is empowering and takes us one step closer to our goal of becoming the healthiest state in the nation." Her comments return us to Walter Plecker and to the subject of genetic testing.[34]

## Genealogy and DNA

Ancestry.com's corporate value comes not from its genealogical records, but from the coupling of genealogical records to the world's largest DNA database. In 2022, AncestryDNA had "over 20 million customers in its [DNA] database, dwarfing its number of subscribers for family history services (3 million)." Ancestry sees itself primarily as a biotechnology company, not a genealogical records company. The massive accumulation of genealogical records is a stalking horse for the accumulation of DNA: the presentation of your percentages of African or European native or Asian ancestry is entertaining and maybe even revelatory, but it's also a stalking horse for the accumulation of genetic information.[35]

AncestryDNA originated in the pet project of a Utah biotech billionaire, James Sorenson. A Mormon himself, Sorenson had done family history temple work and was intrigued by the idea of linking genealogical research to DNA. While trying to trace Norwegian ancestors, Sorenson began wondering if he could trace the Ancestry of everyone in Norway via their DNA. In 2002, Sorenson, Scott Woodward, and Joel Myres filed a patent, in the name of the Sorenson Molecular Genealogy Foundation, for a method of joining DNA evidence to genealogical records. "Molecular genealogy," the patent application read, "merges the science of genetics with the study of genealogy and provides an alternative method of identifying genealogical information." Their approach focused on family genetics, not on health or the heritability of physical traits. Sorenson was given to imagining "molecular genealogy" as a force for world peace, uniting all people in a knowledge of their shared heritage. But idealism didn't make him a billionaire: in 2012, Ancestry.com bought the DNA database, then consisting of about one hundred thousand records, and formed its own DNA wing, AncestryDNA.[36]

If you send a sample to AncestryDNA, they in turn send it to Quest Diagnostics, a commercial clinical laboratory. When Ancestry gets the results, it offers them to customers as an "ethnicity estimate" that describes you in terms of ethnic or national percentages. Pie charts appear, typically presenting national identities: in my case 96 percent Irish, 3 percent Scottish, and 1 percent Danish or Scandinavian. The results are simply evidence that you share a lot of DNA with people from a specific geographic place. Making them into national identities—calling them "Irish" or "Scottish"—imposes political designations rooted in history, and ideology, not genetics. As Catherine Nash argues, "Any naming of a location or region as a place of ancestral origin" implies that "that place and the people there can be characterized in terms of genetic distinctiveness. . . . Saying that bits of genetic material come from somewhere evokes an imaginative geography of bounded genetic distinctiveness." That is, they imply a timeless, static place and a kind of genetic purity. Alondra Nelson points out that DNA test results suggest "that at one time we were 100 percent. So there were populations that were 100 percent Subsaharan African, purely so, 100 percent East Asian, purely so, and that we can give contemporary people proportions of who they are today. And that really flies in the face of everything we know about human behavior and also what we know in anthropology about human migration. We've been mixtures for a very long time."[37]

Both historians and geneticists agree that purity is not the default: human populations move and migrate; invaders and settlers intermarry. Ancestry's test might call you a certain percentage Irish. The historical question is, "Irish, starting when?" Before or after the Vikings invaded Ireland, or the Normans, or the English? Irish mythology records successive peoples settling the island before the Christian era. Does Ancestry include these possibly mythical people? All people, geneticists tell us, originated in Africa. So when did those primal Africans become Irish? People in Donegal and Antrim share significant amounts of DNA, but the people living there did not spring from the soil after the ice sheets receded. Ignoring history, refusing to put any sort of dates on the estimates, makes the national designations like Italian or French or Irish seem like natural facts: it makes them seem like "races."

Scholars who have written about genetic genealogy see the problems and strengths similarly. On the one hand, genetic genealogy clearly recapitulates some of the eugenical logic of the nineteenth and twentieth centuries. It is quite literally Walter Plecker's dream come true, individualism united with racism. The history of racism as a tool of oppression and violence, its close connection to exterminatory eugenics, should make us *extremely* wary of genetic databases as a tool of oppression.

### Scientific Research and Race

Reflecting that concern, in 2023 the National Academies of Sciences, Engineering, and Medicine published *Using Population Descriptors in Genetics and Genomics Research: A New Framework for an Evolving Field*, which argued for dropping the term "race" altogether in genetic research, insisting: "it is time for us to reshape how genetics studies are conceptualized, conducted, and interpreted." It critiques "the long-standing use of race, and more recently ethnicity," as a shorthand for "the continuous and complex patterns of human genetic variation across the globe." In humans, "race is a socially constructed designation, a misleading and harmful surrogate for population genetic differences."

The authors point out that human genetic variation results from repeated population mixing and movements across time, "yet the misconception that human beings can be naturally divided into biologically distinguishable races has been extremely resilient and has become embedded in scientific research, medical practice and technologies, and formal education." This is the spell racecraft casts. Societies organized around belief in witches cannot imagine causes other than witchcraft. Societies organized around belief in race find it almost impossible to abandon the fantasy of race. The authors distinguish "race" from ethnicity and ancestry, which they define as "a person's origin or descent, lineage, 'roots,' or heritage, including kinship." Ethnicity as cultural practices is not the same as what might be understood as genetic ethnicity: lineage may be a record of consistency in ethnicity or it might show repeated "mixing." Heritage might include kinship, biological relatives, or practice in community: a person adopted from China who grew up in Kentucky, playing Appalachian fiddle music, might certainly talk about the music as part of their heritage.

The committee warned against casual use of the "typological categories, such as the racial and ethnic categories established by the US Office of Management and Budget (OMB)," described in the epilogue, because "the fundamentally sociopolitical origins of these categories make them a poor fit for capturing human biological diversity and as analytical tools in human genomics research." As the epilogue discusses, racecraft demands categories that can't describe the complexity of human experience. One of the study's key recommendations says, "researchers should not use the term 'Caucasian,'" "often mistakenly interpreted today as a 'scientific' term," or refer to a "'black race' because it wrongly implies the existence of a discrete group of human beings, or race, who could be objectively identified as 'black.'" The Hollands of Nansemond County came in a wide range of skin colors, with a wide range of ancestors from Europe and Africa. Virginia struggled to convince itself that these people could be classified by race.[38]

The apparent scientific objectivity of DNA records is a key selling point. Aside from the potential medical benefits, which are vast and beyond the scope of this book, people can recover a sense of family otherwise lost to the record. If your ancestors were marginalized or excluded from the historical record, as most enslaved people were, evidence of relation can emerge from DNA tests. Ordinary people regularly discover—sometimes to their dismay—relatives they never knew they had. DNA records are full of meaning, but exactly what they mean socially is less clear. Finding an unknown ancestor is a powerful experience, and in television programs or online it often comes as a big surprising "reveal," but the farther back one goes, the less meaningful a genetic connection becomes.

DNA evidence, as Jerome De Groot points out, often appears to have a kind of magic truth power: it enters popular culture hailed both as miraculous science and as something that reveals your individual essence in some fundamental way. "Genetic knowledge" is framed as "a special type of information that can challenge and change received understanding of the past." Partly this comes from its use in criminal investigations, but in family history DNA results are often taken to reveal something fundamental about you, even distant connections you knew nothing about. Programs like Henry Louis Gates's *Finding Your Roots* offer "a kind of genomic literalism, suggesting that genetic ethnic background can change contemporary identity." In an example, Gates's team discovered singer Rosanne Cash, daughter of Johnny Cash, had an enslaved person in her maternal line. In 1965, the KKK had accused Cash's mother, born Vivian Liberto with ancestors from Sicily, of being "a negress." Roseanne's father denied the charge and insisted she was white, but Gates's research revealed she had 3.3 percent sub-Saharan African ancestry, what Gates termed "full African ancestry." This would have vindicated the KKK's charge. On the show, the DNA results claim a power that the lived experience of Roseanne Cash belies.[39]

Geneticist Bryan Sykes wrote, "our DNA does not fade like an ancient parchment; it does not rust in the ground like the sword of a warrior long dead. It is not eroded by wind or rain, nor reduced to ruin by fire and earthquake." DNA, Sykes argued, contains "the whole history of the human race." Like the Gates program, Sykes presents DNA as a magic box containing truth.

DNA evidence is certainly valuable material for historical understanding, but the raw materials of history—a rusty sword, an ancient parchment, or DNA—are not history itself any more than the alphabet is a novel or a pile of bricks is a house. None of these things speak for themselves: meaning always has to be built out. Someone forged the sword, and lost it; someone wrote the ancient parchment, just as someone dug the clay and molded bricks and fired them, the technology of brick-making. Then someone with a blueprint mortared them into a wall and a house. Clay is a fact, a brick is a rough and solid fact, but bricks don't make themselves into a house. DNA similarly is a fact but does not express its own meaning: its meaning is produced by human interpretation. AncestryDNA, with its pie charts and ethnic percentages, builds out a possible meaning for genetic evidence, and those meanings reflect the history of racecraft.[40]

## Genetic Data and Privacy

Genetic genealogy is often framed in terms of "loss of privacy," but this also misses the historic relationship between genealogy and the state. Any society that makes "individualism" a foundation of politics already gave up privacy. Consider young Patrick Melley, living in Madavagh in 1860. He had no birth certificate, no baptismal record, appears on no census records, left no accounts of his family's tenancy. He had near total privacy because he was not individualized in any way. He didn't even have a stable surname. He existed as a person, in a community, but he did not exist as an *individual* till he stepped off the boat in America and the country committed to individualism started to generate documents about him. Those records were incomplete, and he managed to reinvent himself in several ways, but at the end of his life, he had documents attesting to his now-fixed name, his birth, his date of arrival, his marriage, the births of his children, the death

of Hester, and his ownership of property. After 1913, he paid the federal graduated income tax as an individual, known to the state. His
employer kept a record of his labor, year by year, so they could pay a
pension to his widow. When he died his death certificate, file number
23549, register number 5201, was signed and dated and bound into a
volume between Cecelia O'Donnell and John Osborne and thousands
of others, each equally individualized, each assigned a race, and each
equally subject to scrutiny by the state, their private information part
of a paper database. All the available documents on Patrick, or Julia
Madison, or Michael Susca, intruded into private life and made that
life subject to the interests of not just the state, but a range of other
disciplines including the "science" of race and the discipline of history. I doubt Patrick and Hester would have been pleased to see their
description as colored made the subject of a book.

Individualism *is* the loss of privacy: it's the creation of an idea of
privacy *and* at the same time, the instruments to invade it. Plecker
continually invaded people's privacy in order to assign them a race.
The loss of privacy in genetic genealogy is not new: the death certificate, owned by the state, is philosophically a close cousin to the Mormon obsession with identifying *individuals* among the dead, baptizing
them in the solitude of the grave, and keeping a record of the baptisms.
Loss of privacy was what made the free Negro registers powerful tools
for gaining or securing free status.

Francis Galton, the inventor of both the term "eugenics" and of
fingerprinting as a tool of identity, hoped an individual's fingerprints
would reveal a person's racial or ethnic background: "I thought that
any hereditary peculiarities would almost of necessity vary in different races, and that so fundamental and enduring a feature as the finger markings must in some way be correlated with temperament,"
he wrote. He included a table of the frequency of arches in the right
"fore-finger" for "English, Welsh; Hebrew, and Negro" persons in his
1892 book *Finger Prints*. He was sorry to discover fingerprints did
not correlate to race, just as Plecker was sorry he had no solid test for
race. But into the 1920s, Americans could read, in the *New York Times*,

claims that "life insurance companies can tell from fingerprints what will be the insured's career."[41]

DNA testing is not the same as fingerprinting, but they share a lineage with the detective impulse, an aspiration to turn biology to destiny. DNA records individualize in the same way as fingerprints. A newborn, footprinted in birth records, is individualized to the state in the same way but not to the same degree as a newborn in a DNA database. Focusing on loss of privacy as a novel effect of genetic genealogy avoids examining individualism as an idea at all: you can't have individuals in history without loss of privacy.

The focus on loss of privacy can be seen instead as part of the decline of the public domain or the idea of shared, common culture in favor of individualized ownership. Genetic genealogy stands at some distance from history because it puts individual biological relation first, rather than social or community relations. It uses biological family to negate community.

Critics frequently point out that DNA testing turns your ancestry into Ancestry's property, and that genealogy websites like Ancestry .com effectively charge you to compile the product they sell. Here again though this isn't exactly new. Walter Plecker built on Virginia's existing data-collection practices to assert his ownership of family history. When people claimed to be white or Native, he would use his collections of their private data to deny them, even if local communities accepted them. Ancestry.com is of a piece with most social media sites or with Google itself, which is monetizing you while you search, but we can clearly see antecedents in newspapers, for which you paid a nickel so advertisers could get access to your eyeballs. Focusing on technological novelty, or seeing DNA testing as the blood test Plecker wished for, makes it easy to overlook more fundamental questions about the relationship between identity, authority, and history.

Genetic genealogy then is less a transcendently new innovation than an expression of long-standing desires: for information, for control, for avenues of commodification, for a stable sense of what the past might mean. Merged with genealogical services, it has the potential to undermine government's authority over these things. But as we've seen, government was as often a force for bad as for good; it's an imperfect vessel, frequently blown off course, easily commandeered and needing constant maintenance. But if we want to assert rights to our data, or place limits on its use, or require public ownership of what the public creates, what other instrument for doing so is available?

# ALEXANDRIA

In September 2019, three Virginia couples walked into courthouses in Arlington and Rockbridge Counties, and each couple applied for a marriage license. Brandyn Churchill and Sophie Rogers in Rockbridge and Ashley Ramkishun and Samuel Sarfo and Amelia Spencer and Kendall Poole in Arlington each filled out a computerized form with their vital statistics: full legal name, birthdate, place of birth, address. They had to give a telephone number and specify their level of education, and by law they had to specify their race.[1]

The Rockbridge County clerk showed Churchill and Rogers a list of 230 "Race Codes" they could pick from, thick with incoherence. Choices included "quadroon" and "octoroon" as well as our old acquaintance "mulatto," also available as "mixed" and "bi-racial." The stubbornly durable "Caucasian" made an appearance, along with its sinister twin "Aryan." The remarkably broad list included nationalities like Irish or Italian, but also modifiers like "Sicilian" or the politically explosive "English-Irish." You could be Basque or Bavarian, Brazilian or Belizean or Bilalian or "Bravo (Brava)," Cajun or Creole, a Muslim or a Mohammedan or just "Islamic." You could even choose "Cosmopolitan" and drape yourself in an aura of international sophistication. Some of these identities are national, some describe something more like ethnicity: "Mohammedan" is an antiquated term for Muslim, but both describe a religion, not anything like a race or an ethnicity. The list was long and broad but still hopelessly incomplete.

You could be Sicilian but not Calabrian, Bavarian and Bohemian but not Swabian, "Crucian" but not Christian. The list includes identities that have winked in and out of sight over historical time. It also reflects a fundamental irony of American life: the constant demand for "race" and the impossibility of defining it with any precision at all.

The Rockbridge County list of 230 "race codes" appears on the websites of the Center for Disease Control and the National Institute of Health, as well as the Department of Transportation, where you can find it as part of a manual for reporting traffic fatalities. It appears in the State of Tennessee's *Funeral Director's Handbook for Vital Records Registration*. The list seems to have originated in the 1970s, in a Department of Health, Education, and Welfare publication, *Instruction Manual: Demographic Classification and Coding Instructions for Death Records*. Whoever compiled that list clearly wanted to give people a wide range of choices, but it would be hard to know if the deceased was, for example, "Bavarian" unless she was wearing a *dirndl* at time of death. It's also virtually impossible to provide everyone with an accurate choice and, of course, there would inevitably be people like Ashley Ramkishun, standing before the clerk in the Arlington Courthouse with "Guyanese and Asian Indian roots" and what her attorney called "dark-brown skin," or Amelia Spencer, of Irish, English, German, Scottish, and Scandinavian ancestry with "peach pink skin," or her fiancé Kendall Poole, of African and European ancestry and "medium brown."[2]

In Arlington, the couples confronted a pull-down menu offering choices most readers have probably encountered on forms and applications: "American Indian / Alaska Native; African American / Black; Asian; Caucasian; Hispanic / Latino; Pacific Islander; White; Other." These choices came from the federal OMB's "Statistical Policy Directive 15," formulated in 1977 to provide "a minimum set of categories that Federal agencies must use if they intend to collect information on race and ethnicity." It was revised in 1997, to more or less the choices Arlington presented in 2019. This is the very list, described in chapter 7, which the National Academies of Sciences asked researchers to stop using in March of 2023. A year earlier the federal government undertook a review of that list, noting "many respondents have long been dissatisfied with the identity options compared to their lived experiences." The US has "increasing racial and ethnic diversity," it added, and "a growing number of people who identify as more than one race and/or ethnicity."[3]

Each couple saw the lists as ridiculous. Why does Virginia require people to have a "race" at all, while also providing them with manifestly incoherent categories for expressing it? Ramkishun particularly objected to declaring herself "other." They all refused to answer, so by law the clerks could not issue a marriage license. The three couples knew this would happen, and on September 5, 2019, they joined a lawsuit aimed at banning the practice, led by attorney Victor Glasberg.[4]

Virginians had tried to eliminate the "race" requirement for marriage licenses earlier. In 2003, state legislator Marian Van Landingham, Democrat of Alexandria, had introduced a bill striking it. The bill passed, but two years later Republican delegate Harry Blevins, representing Chesapeake, adjoining Nansemond County, had the race question reinstated. In September of 2019, shortly after the three couples brought their suit, delegate Mark Levine of Alexandria announced that he would introduce a bill to eliminate the race question in the next session. He enjoyed the support of Virginia attorney general Mark Herring, who issued a directive that county clerks should let applicants ignore it. But at least in Arlington, software would not allow applicants to leave the "race" question unanswered: they had to choose. Glasberg's lawsuit would settle the issue.[5]

Glasberg had started his career working on *Loving v. Virginia*, 1967, in which the Supreme Court struck down both Plecker's 1924 Racial Integrity Act and bans on interracial marriage nationally. Mildred Loving was born Mildred Jeter in Center Point, Virginia. She had Rappahannock ancestors and at times regarded herself as Indian, not African. On the Washington, DC, marriage license she and Richard Loving were granted, she named herself as "Indian." But when she filled out her application for social security, in 1957, she listed herself

as "Negro," which made sense in that Virginia, thanks to Plecker, did
not recognize the existence of Native people as a distinct "race." After
the couple were arrested for violating Virginia's Racial Integrity Act,
she wrote to the American Civil Liberties Union and described herself as "part negro and part indian." Accounts of the case in the media
described her unambiguously as African American.

In 1884, when Patrick and Hester married, county clerks had full
authority over racial designation—you were whatever the clerk decided. In 2019, the state still demanded a racial identity, but gave
people choices still not adequate to the complexity of the job. Glasberg's argument to Judge Rossie Alston, at the US District Court for
the Eastern District of Virginia in Alexandria, followed the argument
used in *Loving*. It depicted the race questions on marriage licenses as
"a malignant statutory scheme working to the detriment of non-white
persons." The complaint in *Rogers v. State Registrar* gave a history of
American racial law, focusing on Plecker's work.[6]

In his opinion, Judge Alston, an African American and a conservative appointed by Donald Trump, laid the race requirement at
Plecker's feet, "a vestige of the nation's and of Virginia's history of codified racialization." Alston ruled that Attorney General Herring's directive was not sufficient, because any subsequent attorney general might
reinstate the race question: the question itself "denies Plaintiffs their
rights to due process under the Fourteenth Amendment of the United
States Constitution." Alston enjoined further enforcement of the law.[7]

The Fourteenth Amendment says among other things that "no
State shall make or enforce any law which shall abridge the privileges
or immunities of citizens of the United States; nor shall any State de-
prive any person of life, liberty, or property, without due process of
law; nor deny to any person within its jurisdiction the equal protection of the laws." Virginia's marriage license requirement denied due
process of law—a marriage license—to people who chose not to declare a race or call themselves "other."

In this book we've seen how laws demanding formal records of
"race," linked to administrative individualism, worked to keep people

down and also to secure their rights. The "free Negro registers," for example, confined individualized people in a racial identity while protecting free status and opening a covert path for escaping slavery. Within the structures these documents enforced, people made culture: they farmed, raised families, worshipped and sang, and organized politically and socially. Administrative records originally designed to deny people full citizenship now help people reclaim their family's history. Families and persons are more than just biological, genetic connection: they are *historical* relations, relations of custom and habit and practice, part of larger notions of relatedness and engagement with the broader society in which families live. The three couples who sued Virginia were not rejecting ancestry, or nationality or ethnicity, or biological family: they were objecting to the demand for static definitions of race that disregarded their own historical complexities.

In June of 2023, the US Supreme Court ruled on consideration of race as a factor in college admissions. *Students for Fair Admissions, Inc. v. President and Fellows of Harvard College* was two cases, heard as one, involving Harvard University and the University of North Carolina. Both used "race" as one of the factors they considered when reviewing applicants. In the majority opinion, John Roberts acknowledged the history of racial injustice in the US and the need to overturn specifically discriminatory laws. But he declared that work accomplished and insisted that considering race as one of multiple factors in college admissions now amounted to another example of racial discrimination. "Eliminating racial discrimination means eliminating all of it," Roberts wrote.[8]

The ironies of affirmative action have always been apparent: it uses the idea of race to combat the structural inequalities the idea of race produced. Both Harvard and the University of North Carolina saw general diversity in their student body as a positive good, but from the majority's point of view, affirmative action is itself racist: it reinscribes racial categories it seeks to undermine. Throughout this book I've been aware of following in Walter Plecker's footsteps, studying people's ancestry to examine the problem of race. So it's important to consider what the court asserted. Does writing about the history of administering race, taking race into account, reinforce the odious ideas it documents, in the same way that the Roberts court imagined that considering race perpetuated racism?

Roberts smugly declared a lofty-seeming principle of nondiscrimination, but only around the subject of race. Discrimination is of course the entire point of college admissions. Colleges discriminate on the basis of grades and scores but also extracurricular activities, geographical origins, class, or family "legacy." Colleges can build their incoming classes by adding the children of Nebraska farmers or Maine fishermen or Tennessee Baptist preachers, each of whom unpacks a distinctive family history and culture when they move into the dorm. Roberts argues they cannot consider race, on principle, the principles of antiracism implied in the Fourteenth Amendment.

Inflexible principles are dangerous things. Walter Plecker, after all, was a man of fixed, inflexible principles and ideals. Like Roberts he confronted the gap between his highly principled wishful thinking and the complex ways historical experience inflected the present. This book has charted the history of race while simultaneously insisting on its incoherence, and offering instead the messy, less than ideal complications of family history as an alternative. But family history in the US is saturated with racecraft. The law, backed by its expanding web of administrative tools, forced people into racial identities that simplified or denied their complex ancestry and constrained the meaning of their lives. The racial identities people were forced to inhabit imposed long-term costs but also produced shared practices of community and meaning. It would be grotesque to require people to abandon their own family history, or to disregard it as a factor in college admissions simply because talk about the meaning of history makes some people uncomfortable. Roberts relied on a desire to treat people as individuals, but throughout this book treating people as individuals has always been linked to grouping them into races. Individualism is not the antidote to racism: individualism is racism's fellow traveler.

We can take "race" not as a biological fact but as a historical artifact or concept, much as we might understand individualism as a historical idea. Not talking about a historical concept does not make its legacy go away. Imagine, for example, that having decided to abolish the idea of hereditary monarchy, we would deal with it by never talking about it or never recognizing the legacy of hereditary monarchy in law. The power of hereditary monarchy brought Africans to the New World in chains; the power of hereditary monarchy drove Hester Holland's ancestors from Scotland to Ulster to Virginia, a state named after Elizabeth, England's allegedly virgin queen. Hereditary monarchy drove Patrick Melley's ancestors off the land and into debt peonage. When he escaped via American citizenship, he had to specifically renounce "allegiance to all foreign potentates . . . especially to Victoria, Queen of Great Britain and Empress of India etc. whose subject he has heretofore been."

The US threw off monarchism by violent action and by a system of laws designed specifically to repudiate it, and the US frequently refers to itself as an individualistic society, but aside from the historical commitment to racism, we still find people, theorists of "the dark enlightenment" at the most extreme end, arguing for a return to monarchy or eager to treat presidents as monarchs. More than two hundred years of explicitly repudiating monarchy in law has not made the impulse to authoritarian monarchism any less attractive to the growing company of the weak-minded. And many of the same people arguing for right-wing authoritarianism flirt with or openly embrace racial nationalism. It's easy to argue that failure to actually think through or understand the objection to monarchy, to take its abolition for granted, paves the way for its return, in the same way that failing to think through and address the legacy of racism paves the way for its return.[9]

The demand for "race" on marriage licenses grew first out of Virginia's need to police slavery, and then out of an interest in public health closely linked to eugenics. But at every point, gathering more and more information about population served and still serves other purposes. Public health is obviously a serious concern, and if one specific set of people suffers disproportionate harms, the state, with its obligation to justice, equality, and fairness, should know about it. It must have a way to identify that set. A state committed to individualism *must* track people as individuals, but historically people have also been forced into, or chosen, racial identities. Group identities rooted in history, like Irish American or African American or "Southern," shouldn't be lightly disregarded any more than history itself can be lightly disregarded. These identities don't mean only one thing, but why would we toss the meaning away in the interest of abstract principle?[10]

The plaintiffs in *Rogers v. State Registrar* objected to the racial requirement and insisted that either the categories did not fit them or they wanted no part of categories rooted in racist beliefs. It's tempting to applaud this as a step toward a "race blind" society and imagine, as Chief Justice Roberts did, that the United States has always been committed to seeing its citizens as individuals, not as members of races. "At the heart of the Constitution's guarantee of equal protection," Roberts wrote, quoting Sandra Day O'Connor, "lies the simple command that the Government must treat citizens as individuals, not as simply components of a racial, religious, sexual or national class." The guarantee of equal protection came only as a result of the Civil War and the violent overthrow of slavery, and within a generation of the Fourteenth Amendment's passage, the same Supreme Court was enshrining the legal segregation, disenfranchisement, and racial violence Patrick O'Malley saw in Georgia. But Roberts, undeterred, continued in this vein, writing, "the student must be treated based on his or her experiences as an individual—not on the basis of race. Many universities have for too long done just the opposite. And in doing so, they have concluded, wrongly, that the touchstone of an individual's identity is not challenges bested, skills built, or lessons learned but the color of their skin. Our constitutional history does not tolerate that choice."[11]

The stories told in this book make the absurdity of this claim clear: our constitutional history has not just tolerated but insisted on that choice. In Virginia, the main reason for the state's interest in individuals was *precisely* so that it could place them into races, and secure that racial identity, making it nonnegotiable across space and time. The story of Dempsey Hare makes this clear: at every point, individualism worked to fix a racial identity. In the twentieth century, that same impulse to individualize led men like Plecker to the science of eugenics, again individualism and genetic group identity intertwined. Roberts poses individualism as the alternative to racism, but individualism and racism evolved together, coterminous, mutually reinforcing. Walter Plecker saw no contradiction at all in using records of individual identity to assign people a race: records of individuals were his primary tool. DNA databases now use your individual genetic fingerprint to tell you your racial makeup. There is no good reason to deny the meaning of any individual's family history, and to treat individuals as if they magically produced themselves independently of their history, simply to preserve the court's desire for simplicity.

It should be clear to any reader of this book that ancestry is not "race." We can account for the specific history of our ancestry, with all its triumphs and sorrows, without reinforcing the notion of race. The spells of racecraft, in the hands of the people with the power to make laws, have worked to make ancestry seem like race, to make historical outcomes seem like natural facts. Justice Roberts might agree with this point and argue that considering race in college admission does exactly that. But the National Academies of Sciences, in the 2023 report reconsidering population descriptors in genetic research, stressed their focus on DNA and RNA research but also that "knowledge from many other sources (oral, archaeological, traditional, community, etc.) serve to inform our identities, history, relationships to other humans and our traits and diseases" and emphasized that *"it is time for us to reshape how genetics studies are conceptualized, conducted, and interpreted."* They agree that ancestry, considered historically, is a better alternative than either genetic determinism or simplistic clichés about individualism that pretend history is over.[12]

People engaged in family history, or looking at the popularity of genealogy as a hobby, often urge historians to take genealogy and family history seriously. This book has done that, following the histories of multiple families as their histories intersect in law, in the technologies of record keeping, and in modern genetic technologies. Genealogists in turn should take history seriously and not reduce history to biological descent. We might, as Barbara Fields suggests, simply stop talking about race and talk instead about ancestry: we could say someone has ancestors from Africa and Europe or has ancestors from the Middle East and South Asia, rather than being black or Asian or white. Thinking this way highlights movement in history rather than the idea of static identities: thinking about change over time rather than imagining a timeless racial constant. Identity is not a thing: it's an endless process of engagement with one's past and with the constraints the present imposes.

# ACKNOWLEDGMENTS

My father, Jeff O'Malley, and my uncle, Larry O'Malley, uncovered most of the details of Patrick O'Malley's life, through hard research in the days before the internet and via interviews with then living relatives. Andre Kearns introduced me to the Dempsey Hare story through his marvelous, insightful, and moving blog on Medium. His family comes from Nansemond, and Hare is a distant relative; his sharp insights into the meaning of family history made this a better book. Warren Milteer, a historian with roots in Nansemond, shared his knowledge of the county along with suggestions for the possible location of Dempsey Hare's grave. His work is cited often. My cousin Tery O'Malley shared his own research into the Virginia ancestors. I'm deeply indebted to Marta Cook, Deborah Kaplan, Francesca Morgan, and Kathleen Trainor for their review of the manuscript. I benefited enormously from exchanges with Charlie McGovern.

Kevin Kenny encouraged me to explore the connection between Patrick Melley and the Molly Maguires. Breandán Mac Suibhne graciously invited me to give a paper on Patrick Melley at a conference he organized in Derry, on emigration from Ulster. Comments from Breandán and from Patrick Griffin, David Dickson, and Kerby Miller were especially useful. Deirdre Ní Chonghaile shared her findings in the Daniel Murphy Collection at University College Galway. Mícheál Ó Meallaigh shared his knowledge of Donegal Mellys, as did Margaret Beninati. In early stages of the project, I was helped by conversations with Susan McKinnon, Catherine Nash, J. Douglas Smith, Lester Feder, and Sam Golter as well as John Torpey, Kari Winter, and Francesca Morgan. Janet Rainey, formerly state registrar at the Bureau of Vital Statistics, and Seth Austin, director of the Bureau of Vital Statistics, both helped clarify the details of Ancestry.com's contract with Virginia at the gentle urging of Mary Dooley, legislative assistant in the office of my state delegate, Patrick Hope. Edith Jeter, archivist at the Catholic Diocese of Richmond, kindly sent me details on the makeup of Keileyville, Virginia. Brandy Roberts, deputy clerk of the Staunton Circuit Court, sent me a copy of the will of Walter Plecker's mother. Brian Brown, who eloquently documents "Vanishing Georgia" in photographs online, explained housing styles in Georgia. Thanks to Kevin Shupe for help in navigating the Library of Virginia in Richmond, and thanks to Cindy E. Roberston, chief deputy clerk, and Sarah Knight, senior deputy clerk, for their gracious assistance with the records of the Suffolk Circuit Court.

# NOTES

## Introduction

1. June Purcell Guild, *Black Laws of Virginia: A Summary of the Legislative Acts of Virginia concerning Negroes from Earliest Times to the Present* (New York: Negro Universities Press, 1969), 35.

2. Noel Ignatiev, *How the Irish Became White* (New York: Routledge, 1995); David R. Roediger, *The Wages of Whiteness: Race and the Making of the American Working Class* (London: Verso, 1991); Theodore Allen, *The Invention of the White Race* (London: Verso, 1999); Matthew Frye Jacobson, *Whiteness of a Different Color: European Immigrants and the Alchemy of Race* (Cambridge, MA: Harvard University Press, 1998), *Barbarian Virtues: The United States Encounters Foreign Peoples at Home and Abroad, 1876–1917* (New York, 2000), and *Roots Too: White Ethnic Revival in Post–Civil Rights America* (Cambridge, MA: Harvard University Press, 2009); Nell Irvin Painter, *The History of White People* (New York: W. W. Norton, 2010). For a recent survey of the subject, see Patrick R. O'Malley, "Irish Whiteness and the Nineteenth-Century Construction of Race," *Victorian Literature and Culture* 51, no. 2 (June 2023): 167–98.

3. Roy Rosenzweig, beloved colleague and friend, was one of the few historians to argue for taking genealogy seriously in his book with David Thelen, *The Presence of the Past: Popular Uses of History in American Life* (New York: Columbia University Press, 1998). Recent studies looking at genealogy include François Weil, *Family Trees a History of Genealogy in America* (Cambridge, MA: Harvard University Press, 2013); Francesca Morgan, *A Nation of Descendants: Politics and the Practice of Genealogy in U.S. History* (Chapel Hill: University of North Carolina Press, 2021); Nadia Abu El-Haj, *The Genealogical Science: The Search for Jewish Origins and the Politics of Epistemology* (Chicago: University of Chicago Press, 2012); Catherine Nash, *Genetic Geographies: The Trouble with Ancestry* (Minneapolis: University of Minnesota Press, 2015); Catherine Lee, Alondra Nelson, and Keith Wailoo, *Genetics and the Unsettled Past: The Collision of DNA, Race, and History* (New Brunswick, NJ: Rutgers

University Press, 2012); Alondra Nelson, *The Social Life of DNA: Race, Reparations, and Reconciliation after the Genome* (Boston: Beacon Press, 2016). For an example of a historian grappling with the meaning of family history, see Kendra T. Field, "The Privilege of Family History," *American Historical Review* 127, no. 2 (2022): 600–633.

4. Bill Thomas, "Last Soldier Buried in Tomb of the Unknowns Wasn't Unknown," *Washington Post*, November 8, 2012, sec. Magazine. The argument about the Tomb of the Unknown Soldier draws on Benedict Anderson's argument in *Imagined Communities: Reflections on the Origin and Spread of Nationalism*, rev. ed. (London: Verso, 2006).

5. Virginia's particularly ferocious demands for binary understandings of race are discussed in Arica L. Coleman, *That the Blood Stay Pure: African Americans, Native Americans, and the Predicament of Race and Identity in Virginia* (Bloomington: Indiana University Press, 2013); J. Douglas Smith, *Managing White Supremacy: Race, Politics, and Citizenship in Jim Crow Virginia* (Chapel Hill: University of North Carolina Press, 2002); Helen C. Rountree, *Pocahontas's People: The Powhatan Indians of Virginia through Four Centuries* (Norman: University of Oklahoma Press, 1996). The intersection of racial binaries with individual record keeping is discussed in Susan J. Pearson, *The Birth Certificate: An American History* (Chapel Hill: University of North Carolina Press, 2021), which covers similar ground to this book. On Walter Plecker as a eugenicist, see Edwin Black, *War against the Weak: Eugenics and America's Campaign to Create a Master Race* (New York: Four Walls Eight Windows, 2003).

## Chapter One

1. *Virginian Pilot*, January 30, 1901, 6; *Baltimore Sun*, December 3, 1901, 7; weather described as "inclement."

2. *Norfolk Virginian*, September 15, 1897; *Colored American*, February 9, 1901.

3. *Baltimore Sun*, December 31, 1901, 7; *Boston Evening Transcript*, January 3, 1901; *Evening Republican* (Meadville, PA), January 31, 1901; *Fort Worth Record and Register*, February 6, 1901, 8; *Norfolk (NE) Weekly News-Journal*, February 1, 1901, 2; *Buffalo Enquirer*, January 30, 1901, 10.

4. *Baltimore Sun*, February 1, 1901, 10; *Buffalo Enquirer*, February 19, 1901, 5; *Wilkes-Barre Times Leader*, February 4, 1901.

5. Ross W. Jamieson, "Material Culture and Social Death: African-American Burial Practices," *Historical Archaeology* 29, no. 4 (2016): 39–58; Jerome S. Handler, "A Prone Burial from a Plantation Slave Cemetery in Barbados, West Indies: Possible Evidence for an African-Type Witch or Other Negatively Viewed Person," *Historical Archaeology* 30, no. 3 (1996): 76–86; Amelie Alterauge et al., "Between Belief and Fear—Reinterpreting Prone Burials during the Middle Ages and Early Modern Period in German-Speaking Europe," *PloS*

*One* 15, no. 8 (2020): e0238439–e0238439; Ja Young Lee et al., "Prone Burials and Evidence of Interpersonal Violence: A Case Study from Early Medieval Bavaria, Germany," *International Journal of Osteoarchaeology* 32, no. 4 (2022): 904–9.

6. See the essays in Barbara J. Fields and Karen Fields, *Racecraft: The Soul of Inequality in American Life* (London: Verso, 2012), and Barbara J. Fields, "Whiteness, Racism, and Identity," *International Labor and Working Class History* 60, no. 60 (2001): 48–56, and "Of Rogues and Geldings," *American Historical Review* 108, no. 5 (2003): 1397–1405. For a review of the idea of "racecraft," see Walter Benn Michaels, "Believing in Unicorns," *London Review of Books* 35, no. 3 (February 7, 2013), and Ruha Benjamin, "Conjuring Difference, Concealing Inequality: A Brief Tour of Racecraft," *Theory and Society* 43, no. 6 (2014): 683–88.

7. The story of "prone burial" may not have been true. The *Virginian Pilot* on February 2, 1901, 6, wrote, "Undertaker S W Holland of the town of Holland called up this office tonight and said there was one mistake in an item about the reinterment of Dempsey Hare. He says the head was pointed the wrong way and the body was exhumed and fixed right as stated but that the face was not buried downward." My argument here is that people were eager to believe this for the reasons stated in the paragraph: Hare's story dramatized the workings of racecraft.

8. Will of Dempsey Hare, *Will Records, 1807–1964, and Cross Index, 1779–1964*; Author: *Gates County (North Carolina). Superior Court Clerk*; Probate Place: *Gates, North Carolina*, 16–17. Will Records, Book 6–7, 1915–64.

9. *Dempsey Hare v. Elisha Darden*, No. 1889-005 (Chancery, Nansemond County, July 4, 1887). The full record of the case is online, and testimony appears on a series of numbered PDF files. The location is described in numbers 20–21, 27, 57, and elsewhere, http://www.virginiamemory.com/collections/chancery/?_ga =2.226266076.790955526.1594489621-1700126139.1594489621. The brush arbor church is described on Mount Sinai's successful application for designation on the National Register of Historic Places, https://www.dhr.virginia.gov /wp-content/uploads/2018/04/133-5249_MtSinaiChurch_2006_NRfinal.pdf.

10. Joseph Bragg Dunn, *The History of Nansemond County, Virginia* (Suffolk, VA: n.p., 1907), 61.

11. Harriet Beecher Stowe, *Dred: A Tale of the Great Dismal Swamp* (Chapel Hill: University of North Carolina Press, 2006); Warren E. Milteer, "Life in a Great Dismal Swamp Community: Free People of Color in Pre–Civil War Gates County, North Carolina," *North Carolina Historical Review* 91, no. 2 (2014): 144–70; and Daniel O. Sayers, *A Desolate Place for a Defiant People: The Archaeology of Maroons, Indigenous Americans, and Enslaved Laborers in the Great Dismal Swamp* (Gainesville: University of Florida Press, 2014).

12. See Edmund S. Morgan, *American Slavery, American Freedom: The Ordeal of*

*Colonial Virginia* (New York: Norton, 1995); T. H. Breen, *Myne Owne Ground: Race and Freedom on Virginia's Eastern Shore, 1640–1676* (New York: Oxford University Press, 1980); Kathleen M. Brown, *Good Wives, Nasty Wenches, and Anxious Patriarchs: Gender, Race, and Power in Colonial Virginia* (Chapel Hill: University of North Carolina Press, 1996); Philip D. Morgan, *Slave Counterpoint: Black Culture in the Eighteenth-Century Chesapeake and Lowcountry* (Chapel Hill: University of North Carolina Press, 1998).

13. *Connecticut Gazette* quoted in Ariela Julie Gross, *What Blood Won't Tell: A History of Race on Trial in America* (Cambridge, MA: Harvard University Press, 2008); *Pennsylvania Gazette*, June 29 1738; Liam Hogan, librarian and scholar in Ireland, has closely examined claims of Irish slavery in essays at https://hcommons.org/members/liamhogan/.

14. For an account of the centrality of runaways and runaway advertisements, see David Waldstreicher, "Reading the Runaways: Self-Fashioning, Print Culture, and Confidence in Slavery in the Eighteenth-Century Mid-Atlantic," *William and Mary Quarterly* 56, no. 2 (1999): 243–72, and *Runaway America: Benjamin Franklin, Slavery, and the American Revolution* (New York: Hill and Wang, 2004).

15. *Pennsylvania Gazette*, April 5, 1729.

16. https://home.chicagopolice.org/about/contact-us/how-to-describe-a-suspect/. It should come as no surprise to find facial recognition software as "racecraft," recapitulating broader ideas about race: having trouble with "black" or Asian faces; for example, see Salem Hamed Abdurrahim, Salina Abdul Samad, and Aqilah Baseri Huddin, "Review on the Effects of Age, Gender, and Race Demographics on Automatic Face Recognition," *Visual Computer* 34, no. 11 (2017): 1617–30; James Coe and Mustafa Atay, "Evaluating Impact of Race in Facial Recognition across Machine Learning and Deep Learning Algorithms," *Computers (Basel)* 10, no. 9 (2021): 113, and Fabio Bacchini and Ludovica Lorusso, "Race, Again: How Face Recognition Technology Reinforces Racial Discrimination," *Journal of Information, Communication & Ethics in Society (Online)* 17, no. 3 (2019): 321–35.

17. *Pennsylvania Gazette*, October 2, 1729.

18. All ads from the *Pennsylvania Gazette*: Meshefrey, April 7, 1768; Downing, April 6, 1738; McCarter, July 16, 1772; O'Cannon, August 7, 1776.

19. *Pennsylvania Gazette*, August 31, 1785. This unusual ad gives much more physical detail, and examples of behavior, than is common. It mentions an enslaved Indian grandmother but says nothing of the mother, and if the children spoke with Irish accents or spoke Irish, then clearly either Mr. Mullon raised them or they had an Irish mother.

20. *Pennsylvania Gazette*, June 5, 1766.

21. Louis Albert Fischer, *History of Standard Weights and Measures of the United States* (Washington, DC, 1905). On the history of the birth certificate, see

Susan J. Pearson, *The Birth Certificate: An American History* (Chapel Hill: University of North Carolina Press, 2021).

22. Dunn, *History of Nansemond County*, 48; John H. Russell, *The Free Negro in Virginia, 1619–1865* (1913; reprint ed., New York, 1969), 15; *Dempsey Hare v. Elisha Darden* (Chancery, Nansemond County 1887), online at https://www .lva.virginia.gov/chancery/case_detail.asp?CFN=901-1889-005, testimony of Washington Copeland. On the lives of free people in the region and the South generally, see Warren E. Milteer, *North Carolina's Free People of Color, 1715– 1885* (Baton Rouge: University of Louisiana Press, 2020), and *Beyond Slavery's Shadow: Free People of Color in the South* (Chapel Hill: University of North Carolina Press, 2021).

23. Federal Writers' Project: Slave Narrative Project, Vol. 2, Arkansas, Part 1, Abbott-Byrd, online text, *Library of Congress, Washington, D.C. 20540*, http:// hdl.loc.gov/loc.mss/mesn.021.

24. *Virginia Gazette*, November 15, 1775.

25. *Virginia Gazette*, April, 26, 1785.

26. Boone quoted in Federal Writers' Project: *Slave Narrative Project*; Milteer, *Beyond Slavery's Shadow*, 41.

27. George Carrington Mason, "The Colonial Churches of Nansemond County, Virginia," *William and Mary Quarterly* 21, no. 1 (1941): 51–52; W. E. MacClenny, *The Life of Rev. James O'Kelly and the Early History of the Christian Church in the South* (Raleigh, NC, 1910).

28. Guild, *Black Laws of Virginia*, 95; Milteer, *Beyond Slavery's Shadow*, 89.

29. Paul A. Gilje, *Free Trade and Sailors' Rights in the War of 1812* (Cambridge, MA: Harvard University Press, 2013), 112–15, and Kathryn Mudgett et al., "Contested Allegiances: Becoming American in the Age of Sail," *Early American Literature* 52, no. 2 (2017): 461–72.

30. On the history of the passport, see John Torpey, *Invention of the Passport* (Cambridge: Cambridge University Press, 2009), and Jane Caplan and John Torpey, *Documenting Individual Identity: The Development of State Practices in the Modern World* (Princeton, NJ: Princeton University Press, 2018).

31. On the particularities of the passport in the US and the relation to race, see Craig Robertson, *The Passport in America* (New York: Oxford University Press, 2010), 253 and part 2.

32. James C. Scott, *Seeing Like a State: How Certain Schemes to Improve the Human Condition Have Failed* (New Haven, CT: Yale University Press, 1998); Michel Foucault, *Discipline and Punish: The Birth of the Prison* (New York: Vintage Books, 1975), and, *The History of Sexuality*, vol. 1 (New York: Vintage Books, 1988).

33. Frederick Douglass, *Life and Times of Frederick Douglass* (Hartford, CT, 1888), chap. 1.

34. *Richmond Enquirer*, June 17, 1833.

35. *Richmond Enquirer* June 19, 1829.

36. Benjamin Franklin, *Autobiography of Benjamin Franklin*, Project Gutenberg online version, https://www.gutenberg.org/files/20203/20203-h/20203 -h.htm.

37. "Free Black Registers, Albemarle County," http://www2.vcdh.virginia.edu /fbr/person-search.php?any=johnson&a=&b=&go=1&submit.x=44& submit.y=5.

38. Johnson Smith, free Negro, appears on county tax roles, sometimes with a taxable horse. Charlottesville, Virginia, is the capital of Albemarle County. On Court Square, where slave auctions once took place, a marker names Johnson Smith as a Revolutionary War veteran. Revolutionary War military records show a Johnson Smith of Albemarle but don't assign that person a race. We can't be sure it's the same person, but Smith's scars may have come in the service of the Revolution.

39. Milteer, *Beyond Slavery's Shadow*, 4.

40. Joshua D. Rothman, *Notorious in the Neighborhood: Sex and Families across the Color Line in Virginia, 1787–1861* (Chapel Hill: University of North Carolina Press, 2003), 173. Rothman suggest this law may have been intended to prevent political unrest among the free colored population.

41. Milteer, *Beyond Slavery's Shadow*, 151, 155.

42. Milteer, 9; Rothman, *Notorious in the Neighborhood*, 173.

43. *Jenkins v. Tom*, 1 Va. 123, 1 Wash. 123 (1792), https://cite.case.law/va/1/123/.

44. *Pegram v. Isabell*, 12 Va. 193, 2 Hen. & M. 193 (1808), https://cite.case.law /va/12/193/. The case was tried twice: the first instance can be found at *Pegram v. Isabell*, 11 Va. 387, 1 Hen. & M. 387 (1807), https://cite.case.law/va/11/387/. Edward A. Wyatt, "George Keith Taylor, 1769–1815, Virginia Federalist and Humanitarian," *William and Mary Quarterly* 16, no. 1 (1936): 2–18.

45. 11 Va. (1 Hen. & Mun.) 134 (1806), the Richmond District case record in St. George Tucker, "*Hudgins v. Wright* Case Material" (1806), at https:// digitalarchive.wm.edu/xmlui/handle/10288/16635. H. Jefferson Powell, *A Community Built on Words: The Constitution in History and Politics* (Chicago: University of Chicago Press, 2002), chap. 10.

46. Gross, *What Blood Won't Tell*, 3; Milteer, *Beyond Slavery's Shadow*, 46. See also Peggy Pascoe, *What Comes Naturally: Miscegenation Law and the Making of Race in America* (Oxford: Oxford University Press, 2009); Martha Elizabeth Hodes, *Sex, Love, Race: Crossing Boundaries in North American History* (New York: New York University Press, 1999). On "Certain parties named Wharton," see Guild, *Black Laws of Virginia*, 32.

47. See chapter 2.

48. Guild, *Black Laws*, 32–33.

49. North Carolina, US, Marriage Records, 1741–2011, at Ancestry.com.

50. Virginia, Freedmen's Bureau Field Office Records, 1865–72, Roll 176, Letters

sent, August 1867–December 1868; image 13 of 78; NARA microfilm publication M1913 (College Park, MD: National Archives and Records Administration, n.d.).

## Chapter Two

1. Virginia, Freedmen's Bureau Field Office Records, 1865–72, Roll 176, Letters sent, August 1867–December 1868; image 13 of 78; NARA microfilm publication M1913 (College Park, MD: National Archives and Records Administration, n.d.).
2. "Virginia Marriages, 1785–1940," database, FamilySearch (https://familysearch .org/ark:/61903/1:1:HVSJ-966Z: January 29, 2020), Dawson C. Parker in entry for William E. Costen, 1882.
3. *Richmond Daily Dispatch*, August 4, 1862.
4. Brian Steel Wills, *The War Hits Home: The Civil War in Southeastern Virginia* (Charlottesville: University of Virginia Press, 2017), 125, 167, 169.
5. Wills, 124, 3. Personal correspondence about Nansemond County with genealogist Andre Kearns, July 13, 2020. Freeman receipts in Confederate Papers Relating to Citizens or Business Firms, compiled 1874–99, documenting the period 1861–65, National Archives, catalog ID 2133274.
6. *Richmond Daily Dispatch*, August 4, 1862; Boone quoted in "Federal Writers' Project: Slave Narrative Project, Vol. 2, Arkansas, Part 1, Abbott-Byrd," online text, Library of Congress, Washington, DC.
7. *Philadelphia Inquirer*, August 6, 1862, 1, May 21, 1862, 1; *Chicago Tribune*, May 21, 1862, 1; *Daily Progress*, November 18, 1862, 2; *Athens Post*, April 24, 1863, 2.
8. Boone quoted in "Federal Writers' Project: Slave Narrative Project."
9. The register of deaths for 1858 records the death of "Eliza" belonging to Richard B. Freeman.
10. In 1862, Freeman had enlisted, or been drafted, for six months service in the Fifty-Ninth Virginia Militia and was promoted once, to first corporal. The entire unit, most likely a home defense unit, was disbanded, apparently in May of that year, and those men eligible for conscription sent off elsewhere. "Virginia, Civil War Service Records of Confederate Soldiers, 1861–1865," database, FamilySearch (https://familysearch.org/ark:/61903/1:1:J3WB-DQ7: December 5, 2014), Richard B. Freeman, 1862; from "Compiled Service Records of Confederate Soldiers Who Served in Organizations from the State of Virginia," database, Fold3.com (http://www.fold3.com: n.d.); citing military unit Fifty-Ninth Infantry (Second Regiment, Infantry, Wise Legion); Fifty-Ninth Militia, NARA microfilm publication M324 (Washington, DC: National Archives and Records Administration, 1961), roll 1010.
11. Records of the Field Offices for the State of Virginia, Bureau of Refugees,

Freedmen, and Abandoned Lands, 1865–72, accessed September 13, 2022, https://sova.si.edu/record/NMAAHC.FB.M1913.

12. Brandi Clay Brimmer, *Claiming Union Widowhood: Race, Respectability, and Poverty in the Post-Emancipation South* (Durham, NC: Duke University Press, 2020).

13. William C. Dickinson et al., eds., *Montgomery C. Meigs and the Building of the Nation's Capital*, Perspectives on the Art and Architectural History of the United States Capitol (Athens: Ohio University Press, 2001), 111. On the eth-nological department of the Smithsonian, see Jacqueline Fear-Segal and Re-becca Tillett, *Indigenous Bodies: Reviewing, Relocating, Reclaiming* (Albany: State University of New York Press, 2013). Thirty-three sculptures copied from these "ethnological heads" today adorn the exterior of the Jefferson Building of the Library of Congress.

14. Report of Brevet Major J. K. Stone to Office of the Assistant Commissioner, Bureau of Refugees, Freedmen, and Abandoned Lands, in US Congress, House, *House Documents, Otherwise Publ. as Executive Documents: 13th Con-gress, 2d Session–49th Congress, 1st Session*, 1866, 220–21. On the burning of the school, see Virginia, Freedmen's Bureau Field Office Records, Roll 176, Letters received, vols. 1–2, March 1867–December 1868, image 13 of 99; citing NARA microfilm publication M1913 (College Park, MD: National Archives and Records Administration, n.d.). The men's case was brought to Barnes, above, and he was directed to charge them in civil court.

15. Virginia, Freedmen's Bureau Field Office Records, 1865–72, Roll 136, images 753, 767.

16. *Alexandria Gazette*, November 4, 1867, 2.

17. William Archibald Dunning, *Essays on the Civil War and Reconstruction* (New York: Macmillan, 1898); Kenneth M. Stampp, *Reconstruction: An Anthology of Revisionist Writings* (Baton Rouge: Louisiana State University Press, 1969); William Edward Burghardt DuBois, Henry Louis Gates, and David Levering Lewis, *Black Reconstruction in America: An Essay toward a History of the Part Which Black Folk Played in the Attempt to Reconstruct Democracy in America, 1860–1880* (New York: Free Press, 2007); Eric Foner, *Reconstruction: Amer-ica's Unfinished Revolution, 1863–1877* (New York: Harper Perennial, 1988). The historiography of Reconstruction is described in a forum, "Eric Foner's Reconstruction at Twenty Five," in *Journal of the Gilded Age and Progressive Era* 14, no. 1 (2015): 13–27.

18. *Daily State Journal*, October 12, 1871, 2; Luther Porter Jackson, "The Virginia Free Negro Farmer and Property Owner, 1830–1860," *Journal of Negro His-tory* 24, no. 4 (1939), 310–431; Sarah S. Hughes, "Farming in Lower Tidewa-ter," in *Readings in Black and White: Lower Tidewater Virginia*, ed. Tommy Bogger and Jane H. Kobelski (Portsmouth, VA: Portsmouth Public Library, 1982), 28. The account of the brush arbor church on Hare's land comes from

the website of the Mount Sinai Baptist Church on Holy Neck Road, and the church's successful application for inclusion in the National Register of Historic Places, available online at https://www.dhr.virginia.gov/wp-content /uploads/2018/04/133-5249_Mt. SinaiChurch_2006_NRfinal.pdf.

19. The Freedmen's Bureau records show many receipts for payment of rent to Hare. For the dimensions of the school, see Freedmen's Bureau Field Office Records, 1865–72, Roll 176, Letters sent, August 1867–December 1868, image 12 of 78; NARA microfilm publication M1913 (College Park, MD: National Archives and Records Administration). Reports on the school and feelings toward colored schools in Roll 177, School reports, February–December 1868, image 142 of 213; NARA microfilm publication M1913, image 146 of 213, in that same roll shows the school closing.

20. James Kemper, address to the legislature quoted in Virginia General Assembly, *Journal of the House of Delegates of the Commonwealth of Virginia*, Commonwealth of Virginia, 1874, 25.

21. Steven Hahn, *A Nation under Our Feet: Black Political Struggles in the Rural South, from Slavery to the Great Migration* (Cambridge, MA: Harvard University Press, 2003), 365.

22. *Norfolk Landmark*, April 13, 1897, 4, shows Hare buying eight acres of land from a J. E. Holland in Holy Neck district for seventy dollars; the evidence in the case of *Hare v. Darden*, below, includes two deeds in which Dempsey bought two separate parcels of land from his siblings.

23. *Dempsey Hare v. Elisha Darden* (Chancery, Nansemond County, 1887), Virginia Chancery Court Records, Index Number 1889-005. Documents in the case file are not paginated, but individual PDF files of the pages have sequential numbers. The records can be accessed via the Chancery records index at https://www.virginiamemory.com.

24. *Hare v. Darden*, testimony of Washington Copeland, PDF 901 1889 005 0030– 0032.

25. *Richmond Daily Dispatch*, January 22, 1858.

26. *Have v. Darden*, Testimony of Washington Copeland, PDF 901 1889 005 0030– 0032; Thomas Holland PDF 901 1889 005 0020–21.

27. The 1830 census shows Howell's household including two adult white males between twenty and thirty years old, two "free colored" girls under ten, one free colored woman aged twenty-five, one male slave under ten, three male slaves between ten and twenty-three, one male slave twenty-four to thirty-five, another aged thirty-six to fifty-four, and finally a male slave older than fifty-five. It's possible Sophia Hare's children were mistaken for slaves by the census taker. Washington Copeland's sister might have lived among them at some point; Thomas Holland's kin lived there. That list does not include Sophia Hare's children, who would have been born free. On the denial of family and its persistence, see Kendra T. Field, "The Privilege of Family History,"

*American Historical Review* 127, no. 2 (2022): 605–8; Steven Deyle, *Carry Me Back: The Domestic Slave Trade in American Life* (New York: Oxford University Press, 2005); Daina Ramey Berry, *The Price for Their Pound of Flesh: The Value of the Enslaved, from Womb to Grave, in the Building of a Nation* (Boston: Beacon Press, 2017); Kari J. Winter, *The American Dreams of John B. Prentis, Slave Trader* (Athens: University of Georgia Press, 2011).

28. https://andrekearns.medium.com/ contains his account of Dempsey Hare and his own efforts to trace ancestry using DNA where administrative records fail. Alondra Nelson, *The Social Life of DNA: Race, Reparations, and Reconciliation after the Genome* (Boston: Beacon Press, 2016), 7; Kim TallBear, *Native American DNA: Tribal Belonging and the False Promise of Genetic Science* (Minneapolis: University of Minnesota Press, 2013), Kindle ed., location 231.

29. *Hare v. Darden*, PDF 901 1889 005 0092; testimony of Langston PDF 901 1889 005 0024–27.

30. Martha Elizabeth Hodes, *White Women, Black Men: Illicit Sex in the Nineteenth-Century South* (New Haven, CT: Yale University Press, 1997), and the essays collected in Hodes, *Sex, Love, Race: Crossing Boundaries in North American History* (New York: New York University Press, 1999).

31. *Have v. Darden*, testimony of Dempsey Hare, PDF 901 1889 005 0087–90, 94.

32. *Hare v. Darden*, testimony of testimony of Jones PDF 901 1889 005 0082.

33. Quotes from the blog of genealogist Andre Kearns, "Race and Color Politics Revealed in Family History," at https://andrekearns.medium.com/race-and-color-politics-revealed-in-family-history-115959696a61.

34. *Hare v. Darden*, PDF 901 1889 005 0121; also see *Hare v. Darden* (1889) in the common law order book reel of Nansemond County at the Library of Virginia, in which Hare's injunction against Darden, preventing him from setting foot on the land, was dissolved.

35. *White v. Hare* (Nansemond County Circuit Court 1893). Common law order books, Book 2, reel 7, Library of Virginia, Richmond. Land sale in the *Norfolk Landmark*, April 13, 1897, 4.

36. *Virginian-Pilot*, December 10, 1901, 6; *Baltimore Sun*, December 10, 1901, 10; *Richmond Times*, December 10, 1901, 3; *Raleigh News & Observer*, October 17, 1901, 3.

37. Glenda Elizabeth Gilmore, *Gender and Jim Crow: Women and the Politics of White Supremacy in North Carolina, 1896–1920* (Chapel Hill: University of North Carolina Press, 1996).

38. Lester Daughtry was a near neighbor, a white man born in the Holy Neck region in 1877. He acceded to what I assume was Hare's demand to cross out the "B" but did not add a "W" in its place.

39. *Baltimore Sun*, January 30, 1901, 8.

40. *Baltimore Sun*, December 31, 1901, 7; *Richmond Times*, December 5, 1901, 10; *Richmond Dispatch*, December 10, 1901, 9.

41. *Baltimore Sun*, February 1, 1901, 10.
42. *Richmond Times*, December 5, 1901, 10.
43. *Baltimore Sun*, December 10, 1901, 10.
44. Guild, *Black Laws of Virginia*, 33.
45. Guild, 25, 30, 34.
46. *Richmond Dispatch*, December 10, 1901, 9.
47. *White v. Edward E. Holland et al.* (Chancery Court, Nansemond County, 1902). Hare's second will is in the record of the case, 35–36 of the digitized version at https://www.lva.virginia.gov/chancery/case_detail.asp?CFN=901-1902-011.
48. *White v. Holland*, 109.
49. *White v. Holland*, 24.
50. *White v. Holland*, the judge's instructions, 108–23, quote 111.
51. Walter Benn Michaels, "Believing in Unicorns," *London Review of Books*, February 7, 2013, https://www.lrb.co.uk/the-paper/v35/n03/walter-benn-michaels/believing-in-unicorns.
52. Michaels, 113.
53. Michaels, 117.
54. *Norfolk Landmark*, December 13, 1901, 5.
55. *Norfolk Virginian Pilot*, November 11, 1902; October 15, 1903, 7.
56. American Historical Society, *History of Virginia* (American Historical Society, 1924), 524; https://www.dhr.virginia.gov/VLR_to_transfer/PDFNoms/133-0691_Holland_HD_1995_Final_Nomination.pdf.

## Chapter Three

1. "Ireland Civil Registration Indexes, 1845–1958," database, FamilySearch (https://familysearch.org/ark:/61903/1:1:FRPQ-L6F: March 10, 2018), Deaths entry for Farrigle Mellay; citing Glenties, 1865, vol. 12, 64, General Registry, Custom House, Dublin; FHL microfilm 101,582.
2. Breandán Mac Suibhne, *The End of Outrage: Post-Famine Adjustment in Rural Ireland* (Oxford: Oxford University Press, 2017), 100; William Anthony Smyth, "Sir Richard Griffith's Three Valuations of Ireland, 1826–1864," *Irish Economic and Social History* 37 (2010): 129.
3. For a good review of Irish language words for landscape, see Manchán Magan, *Thirty-Two Words for Field: Lost Words of the Irish Landscape* (Dublin: Gill Books, 2020). I live a few miles from the Potomac River, a similar anglicization of an indigenous word, the exact Algonquian word is now lost, but John Smith named it "Patowomeck" in 1612.
4. Hugh Dorian, Breandán Mac Suibhne, and David Dickson *The Outer Edge of Ulster* (Dublin: Lilliput Press, 2001), Kindle ed., location 1612; Mícheál Ó Meallaigh, email to the author, October 3, 2021. Ancestry.com says Mr. Ó Meallaigh and I are related though neither of us knows how.

5. Griffith's valuation was first published as *General Valuation of Rateable Property in Ireland* (Dublin, 1849) and then in subsequent volumes as completed. It is searchable at https://www.askaboutireland.ie/griffith-valuation/ and at Ancestry.com.

6. Margo J. Anderson, *The American Census: A Social History*, 2nd ed. (New Haven, CT: Yale University Press, 2015).

7. "Donegal Workhouses Registers and Minute Books Image / Findmypast.Com," accessed August 21, 2021, https://search.findmypast.com/record?id=IRE%2FDONEGAL%2FBG_92_3_1-3%2F00154&parentid=IRE%2FDONEGAL%2FWORKHOUSES%2F2%2F0073182.

8. Phil Chevron and the Pogues, "Thousands Are Sailing," from *If I Should Fall from Grace with God* (Island Records, 1988). The best line in that song for my purposes comes when the singer asks, "Did you work upon the railroad? / Did you rid the streets of crime?" Patrick Melley worked on the railroad and later worked as a security guard.

9. Douglass quoted in Christine Kinealy, *Frederick Douglass and Ireland: In His Own Words* (New York: Routledge, 2018), 48.

10. For examples, see "Debunking a Myth: The Irish Were Not Slaves, Too," *New York Times*, March 17, 2017. For Hogan's research, see https://libcom.org/article/debunking-myth-irish-slaves.

11. Mac Suibhne, *The End of Outrage*, 90.

12. Thomas Campbell Foster, *Letters on the Condition of the People of Ireland . . . Reprinted . . . with Additions and Copious Notes, from "The Times" Newspaper* (London: Chapman & Hall, 1846), 103.

13. Conyngham Papers, 1614–1935, MS 35, 34 (2), National Library of Ireland, Dublin. As late as 1892, Conyngham's Donegal estates produced an income of more than two million pounds.

14. Nassau Forster, "A Return of Proceedings Had against Several of the Rosses Tenants for the Recovery of Rent," Conyngham Papers, 1820–21, 35 397 (2); Forster to Conyngham, April 22, 1821; March 12, 1821, Conyngham Papers, 35 392 (14).

15. Foster, *Letters on the Condition of the People of Ireland*, 103.

16. Dorian, *Outer Edge of Ulster*, locations 1150, 4446.

17. Foster, *Letters on the Condition of the People of Ireland*, 105.

18. Dorian, *Outer Edge of Ulster*, location 210; Thomas Price, *An Essay on the Physiognomy and Physiology of the Present Inhabitants of Britain, with Reference to Their Origin, as Goths and Celts* (London, 1829), 105.

19. Dorian, *Outer Edge of Ulster*; Alexis de Tocqueville, *Alexis de Tocqueville's Journey in Ireland, July–August, 1835* (Washington, DC: Catholic University Press, 1990), 29.

20. Gustave de Beaumont, *Ireland: Social, Political, and Religious* (Cambridge, MA: Harvard University Press, 2006) 128; de Tocqueville, *De Tocqueville's Journey in Ireland*, 3, 7–8, 79.

21. Christine Kinealy, *Frederick Douglass and Ireland*, 79–81.

22. De Beaumont, *Ireland: Social, Political, and Religious*, 128–29.

23. Foster, *Letters on the Condition of the People of Ireland*, 106.

24. De Tocqueville, *De Tocqueville's Journey in Ireland*, 7; Douglass quoted in Peter D. O'Neill, *Famine Irish and the American Racial State* (New York: Routledge, 2017), 46.

25. De Beaumont, *Ireland: Social, Political, and Religious*, 130; *Illustrated London News*, August 12, 1843, 101.

26. De Beaumont, *Ireland: Social, Political, and Religious*, 128.

27. James E. Doan, "'An Island in the Virginian Sea': Native Americans and the Irish in English Discourse, 1585–1640," *New Hibernia Review* 1, no. 1 (1997): 79; Nicholas P. Canny, "The Ideology of English Colonization: From Ireland to America," *William and Mary Quarterly* 30, no. 4 (1973): 587. See also Peter Rhoads Silver, *Our Savage Neighbors: How Indian War Transformed Early America* (New York: W. W. Norton, 2008).

28. David B. Quinn, *The Elizabethans and the Irish* (Ithaca, NY: Cornell University Press, 1966), 23–24; Matthew Frye Jacobson, *Whiteness of a Different Color: European Immigrants and the Alchemy of Race* (Cambridge, MA: Harvard University Press, 1999), 38; Rebecca Solnit, *A Book of Migrations: Some Passages in Ireland*, rev. ed. (London: Verso, 2011), 132; Bruce Nelson, *Irish Nationalists and the Making of the Irish Race* (Princeton, NJ: Princeton University Press, 2012), 6.

29. Richard McMahon, *The Races of Europe: Construction of National Identities in the Social Sciences, 1839–1939* (London: Palgrave Macmillan, 2016), esp. chap. 5, which summarizes one hundred years of thinking on the subject. See also Mairéad Carew, *The Quest for the Irish Celt: The Harvard Archaeological Mission to Ireland, 1932–1936* (Newbridge, Co. Kildare: Irish Academic Press, 2018).

30. J. P. Mallory, *The Origins of the Irish* (London: Thames & Hudson, 2017), 336. On the ancient Celts, see Barry W. Cunliffe and John T. Koch, eds., *Exploring Celtic Origins: New Ways Forward in Archaeology, Linguistics, and Genetics* (Oxford: Oxford University Press, 2019); Simon James, *The Atlantic Celts: Ancient People or Modern Invention?* (Madison: University of Wisconsin Press, 1999); John Haywood, *The Celts: Bronze Age to New Age* (New York: Routledge, 2004); John Collis, *The Celts: Origins, Myths and Inventions* (London: tempus, 2003); and Melanie Giles, review of Haywood in *Archaeological Journal* 161, no. 1 (2004): 242–43.

31. Disraeli quoted in Nelson, *Irish Nationalists*, 6.

32. De Beaumont, *Ireland: Social, Political, and Religious*, 193; de Tocqueville, *De Tocqueville's Journey in Ireland*, 49.

33. S. J. Connolly, *Priests and People in Pre-Famine Ireland, 1780–1845*, 2nd ed. (Dublin: Four Courts Press, 2001); and Cara Delay, "The Devotional

Revolution on the Local Level: Parish Life in Post-Famine Ireland," *U.S. Catholic Historian* 22, no. 3 (2004): 41–60; Mac Suibhne, *End of Outrage*, 2; de Tocqueville, *De Tocqueville's Journey in Ireland*, 72, 81.

34. John Campbell Colquhoun, *Ireland; Popery and Priestcraft the Cause of Her Misery and Crime* (Glasgow, 1835), 18, 23; *The Harbinger, Or, New Magazine of the Countess of Huntingdon's Connexion* (London: Ward and Company, 1852), 41.

35. For an overview, see James S. Donnelly and James S. Donnelly Jr., *The Land and the People of Nineteenth-Century Cork: The Rural Economy and the Land Question* (New York: Routledge, 2017).

36. Colquhoun, *Ireland; Popery and Priestcraft*, 5.

37. Colquhoun, 5, 7.

38. "A Scene From Ireland," *Harper's New Monthly Magazine*, November 1851, 833, and Jacobson, *Whiteness of a Different Color*, 48. Brawl in Congress from *New York Weekly Tribune*, February 13, 1859. For examples of racializing the Irish, see Nell Irvin Painter, *The History of White People* (New York: W. W. Norton, 2010); Dale T. Knobel, *Paddy and the Republic: Ethnicity and Nationality in Antebellum America*, 1st ed. (Middletown, CT: Wesleyan University Press, 1986); and the excellent survey of US immigration policy regarding the Irish in Hidetaka Hirota, *Expelling the Poor: Atlantic Seaboard States and the Nineteenth-Century Origins of American Immigration Policy* (New York: Oxford University Press, 2017). See also Martha Hodes, "The Mercurial Nature and Abiding Power of Race: A Transnational Family Story," *American Historical Review* 108, no. 1 (2003): 84–118.

39. The full series is available at the website of the National Library of Ireland, at https://catalogue.nli.ie/Record/vtls000566168. Information on the photographers is limited: see Tom Kennedy, *Victorian Dublin* (Dublin, 1980), http://archive.org/details/victoriandublin00kenn; Edward Chandler, *Photography in Ireland: The Nineteenth Century* (Dublin: Edmund Burke, 2001); Peter Somerville-Large and Mark Fiennes, *The Grand Irish Tour* (London: Hamilton, 1982); Sarah Rouse, *Into the Light: An Illustrated Guide to the Photograph Collections in the National Library of Ireland* (Dublin: National Library of Ireland, 1998); Kevin J. James, *Tourism, Land, and Landscape in Ireland: The Commodification of Culture* (New York: Routledge, 2014).

40. On photography and tourism in Ireland, see Chandler, *Photography in Ireland*; Rouse, *Into the Light*. Quotes from Somerville-Large and Fiennes, *The Grand Irish Tour*, 20; Gail Baylis, "Exchanging Looks: Gap Girls and Colleens in Early Irish Tourist Photography," *Early Popular Visual Culture* 10, no. 4 (2012): 325–43; Julian Campbell, "Double Vision," *Irish Arts Review (2002–)* 37, no. 2 (2020): 118–21.

41. Price, *Essay on the Physiognomy and Physiology*, 11.

42. The literature on the Irish famine is vast. Exact figures on population loss in

Ireland are hard to come by, due to relatively poor record keeping. The figure of roughly a million deaths between 1847 and 1851 appears often, followed
by as many emigrations in the same five-year period. See Kevin Kenny, *The
American Irish* (New York: Routledge, 2000); Kerby A. Miller, *Emigrants and
Exiles: Ireland and the Irish Exodus to North America* (New York: Oxford University Press, 2010), 280–344; Cormac Ó Gráda, *Black 47 and Beyond: The
Great Irish Famine* (Princeton, NJ: Princeton University Press, 1999), chap. 7;
and John Crowley, William I. Smyth, and Mike Murphy, eds., *Atlas of the Great
Irish Famine* (New York: New York University Press, 2012), passim. For a skep-
tical account of the famine's relative magnitude, see Liam Kennedy, *Unhappy
the Land: The Most Oppressed People Ever, the Irish?* (Newbridge, Co. Kildare:
Irish Academic Press, 2016) chap. 1. For a concise and powerful general ac-
count of the demoralization of the famine, the way it deranged empathy, see
Breandán Mac Suibhne, *Subjects Lacking Words? The Gray Zone of the Great
Famine* (Hamden, CT: Quinnipiac University Press, 2017).

43. Robert Torrens, *A Letter to . . . Lord John Russell on the Ministerial Measure
for Establishing Poor Laws in Ireland* (London: Longman, Orme, Brown and
Green, 1838), 56–57; William Bence Jones, *The Life's Work in Ireland of a Landlord Who Tried to Do His Duty* (New York, 1880), 102.

44. Charles Kingsley, *Charles Kingsley: His Letters and Memories of His Life* (London: C. K. Paul, 1878), 107.

45. *Kingsley,* 107, 243–44.

46. *Punch,* October 4, 1862, 138; October 18, 1862, 165. There are countless ex-
amples in *Punch* from this era: see, e.g., December 21, 1861, 245, in which at an
Irish political meeting, "Orations . . . were delivered by MR. O'RANGOUTANG,
MR. G. O'RILLA."

47. Mac Suibhne, *The End of Outrage,* 131. Note the British conducted a census
every ten years, but before 1891 they summarized the findings and destroyed
the original records. Michael C. Coleman, "'Eyes Big as Bowls with Fear and
Wonder': Children's Responses to the Irish National Schools, 1850–1922,"
*Proceedings of the Royal Irish Academy: Archaeology, Celtic Studies, History,
Linguistics, Literature* 98C, no. 5 (1998): 177, 180, 183; John Coolahan, "Education and Ethnicity," *Paedagogica Historica* 37, no. 1 (2001): 22; Charles Mc-
Glinchey and Brian Friel, *The Last of the Name* (Nashville, TN: J. S. Sanders,
1999), 7.

48. On Rundale generally, see Eoin Flaherty, "Rundale and 19th Century Irish
Settlement: System, Space, and Genealogy," *Irish Geography* 48, no. 2 (Octo-
ber 19, 2016): 3–38; Tom Yager, "What Was Rundale and Where Did It Come
From?," *Béaloideas* 70 (2002): 153–86.

49. On Rundale in Donegal, see Mac Suibhne, *The End of Outrage,* 14, 85, and
passim. See also the indispensable account of Irish land reform in Kerby A.
Miller, *Emigrants and Exiles: Ireland and the Irish Exodus to North America*

(New York: Oxford University Press, 1985), chaps. 1–2; on postfamine emigration, see chap. 8.

50. Dorian, *The Outer Edge of Ulster*, location 4287.

51. Mac Suibhne, *The End of Outrage*, 25.

52. Trench quoted in Mark Bulik, *The Sons of Molly Maguire: The Irish Roots of
    America's First Labor War* (New York: Fordham University Press, 2015), 74;
    Mac Suibhne, *End of Outrage*, 130, 15.

53. Finlay Dun, *Landlords and Tenants in Ireland* (London, 1881), 172; Thomas
    Conolly and Nelson D. Lankford, *An Irishman in Dixie: Thomas Conolly's Di-
    ary of the Fall of the Confederacy*, 1st ed. (Columbia: University of South Car-
    olina Press, 1988), 45.

54. Conolly, *An Irishman in Dixie*, 132; Dun, *Landlords and Tenants*, 173.

55. I did not find the surname "Melley" or any close variant in the Conyngham
    Papers, which are extensive but not consistent—there are many gaps where
    no reports of rent survived. The papers of the Conolly family are scattered
    and don't include the names of individual tenants. See William Conolly,
    Patrick Walsh, and A. P. W. Malcomson, *The Conolly Archive* (Dublin: Irish
    Manuscripts Commission, 2010); and "Introduction to the Conolly Papers/
    Nidirect," December 2, 2015, https://www.nidirect.gov.uk/publications
    /introduction-conolly-papers.

56. Mac Suibhne, *The End of Outrage*, 254.

57. Patrick Walsh, *The Making of the Irish Protestant Ascendancy: The Life of Wil-
    liam Conolly, 1661–1729* (Rochester, NY: Boydell and Brewer, 2010), 14.

58. Silver, *Our Savage Neighbors*, 11.

59. Pennsylvania Scotch-Irish Society, Annual Meeting and Banquet of the Penn-
    sylvania Scotch-Irish Society (Philadelphia: Press of Allen, Lane & Scott,
    1890), 10; Thomas Dixon, *The Clansman: An Historical Romance of the Ku Klux
    Klan* (New York: A. Wessels, 1905), introduction; James Webb, *Born Fighting:
    How the Scots-Irish Shaped America*, 1st ed. (New York: Crown, 2004), 15.

## Chapter Four

1. *New York Daily Herald*, June 12, 1871, 2; *Liverpool Mercury*, May 10, 1871, 4;
   US Bureau of Statistics, *Information for Immigrants Relative to the Prices and
   Rentals of Land . . .* (Philadelphia: S. D. Burlock & Company, 1871), front mat-
   ter, n.p.

2. *Annual Report of the Commissioners of Emigration of the State of New York, for
   the Year Ending . . . , 1870* (New York: n.p, 1871), 26.

3. *Harper's Weekly*, May 16, 1874, 425.

4. Ancestry.com, *New York, US, Arriving Passenger and Crew Lists (including Castle Garden and Ellis Island), 1820–1957* (database online) (Lehi, UT:
   Ancestry.com Operations, Inc., 2010).

5. *Annual Report of the Commissioners of Emigration*, 4; New York (State) Legislative Assembly, *Documents of the Assembly of the State of New York* (Albany, NY: E. Croswell, 1870), 4.

6. *Documents of the Assembly of the State of New York*, 30.

7. Joseph Simms, *Nature's Revelations of Character; Or, the Mental, Moral and Volitive Dispositions of Mankind, as Manifested in the Human Form and Countenance . . . Illustrated, Etc.* (London: L. N. Fowler, 1873).

8. Samuel Roberts Wells, *New Physiognomy, or Signs of Character, as Manifested through Temperament and External Forms and Especially in "the Human Face Divine"* (New York: Fowler & Wel, 1871) 537, 28.

9. Charles Henry Pullen, *Miss Columbia's Public School, Or, Will It Blow Over?* (New York: Francis B. Felt & Company, 1871), 18.

10. *Pennsylvania Gazette* searched for terms "runaway" and "Irish" between 1730 and 1797. Nell Irvin Painter, *The History of White People* (New York, 2011), 204; Henry David Thoreau, *Walden, or Life in the Woods*, https://www.gutenberg .org/files/205/205-h/205-h.htm.

11. T. H. Huxley, "On the Geographical Distribution of the Chief Modifications of Mankind," *Journal of the Ethnological Society of London* (1870): 406–7.

12. David Goodman Croly, *Miscegenation: The Theory of the Blending of the Races, Applied to the American White Man and Negro* (New York: H. Dexter, Hamilton & Company, 1864), 30–31.

13. Michael O'Malley, *The Beat Cop: Chicago's Chief O'Neill and the Creation of Irish Music* (Chicago: University of Chicago Press, 2022); chap. 2; Christopher J. Smith, *The Creolization of American Culture: William Sidney Mount and the Roots of Blackface Minstrelsy* (Champaign: University of Illinois Press, 2014); April Masten, "The Challenge Dance: Black-Irish Exchange in Antebellum America," in *Cultures in Motion*, ed. Daniel T. Rodgers, Bhavani Raman, and Helmut Reimitz (Princeton, NJ: Princeton University Press, 2017); Noel Ignatiev, *How the Irish Became White* (New York: Routledge, 1995); and David R. Roediger, *The Wages of Whiteness: Race and the Making of the American Working Class* (London: Verso, 1991).

14. "A Visit to Niagara" (1871), in Mark Twain, *Mark Twain's Sketches, New and Old: Now First Published in Complete Form* (Hartford, CT: American Publishing Company, 1893), 63–71.

15. Matthew Frye Jacobson, *Whiteness of a Different Color: European Immigrants and the Alchemy of Race* (Cambridge, MA: Harvard University Press, 1998), 48. For examples of racializing the Irish, see Nell Irvin Painter, *The History of White People* (New York: W. W. Norton, 2010); Dale T. Knobel, *Paddy and the Republic: Ethnicity and Nationality in Antebellum America*, 1st ed. (Middletown, CT: Wesleyan University Press, 1986); Martha Hodes, "The Mercurial Nature and Abiding Power of Race: A Transnational Family Story," *American Historical Review* 108, no. 1 (2003): 84–118.

16. James Dawson Burn, *Three Years among the Working-Classes in the United States during the War* (London: Smith, Elder and Company, 1865), 15.

17. *Chicago Tribune*, October 26, 1873, 6; *Morning Star and Catholic Messenger*, September 21, 1873, 3; *Philadelphia Inquirer*, May 3, 1875, 5; *New York Daily Herald*, December 27, 1865, 8.

18. *Annual Report of the Commissioners of Emigration of the State of New York, for the Year Ending . . . , 1870*, 24–25; *Documents of the Assembly of the State of New York*, 7.

19. Robert Russell to Conyngham, "Boylagh, Account Current for the Year Ending May 1860," Conyngham Papers, National Library of Ireland, MS 35 394 (15). Irish immigrants were often described as destitute and targeted for exclusion based on destitution, but in fact it took some means to buy passage, especially before the famine of 1848. Kerby Miller argues that "many emigrants only appeared destitute after long ocean voyages." See Kerby A. Miller, *Emigrants and Exiles: Ireland and the Irish Exodus to North America* (New York: Oxford University Press, 1985), 200; Hidetaka Hirota, *Expelling the Poor: Atlantic Seaboard States and the Nineteenth-Century Origins of American Immigration Policy* (New York: Oxford University Press, 2017), 2–25; and on assisted emigration, see Gerard Moran, *Sending Out Ireland's Poor: Assisted Emigration to North America in the Nineteenth Century* (Dublin: Four Courts Press, 2004).

20. Nathan Shaler, "The Summer's Journey of a Naturalist," *Atlantic Monthly*, August 1873, 185–86.

21. Lee Mantz, *Summit Hill* (New York: Arcadia, 2009), 73–90, describes the Switchback Railroad and the burning mine. The Library of Congress Prints and Photographs Division had stereopticon slides of Summit Hill, Mauch Chunk, and the Switchback Railroad.

22. An excellent account of mining and mine communities in the anthracite region remains Anthony F. C. Wallace, *St. Clair: A Nineteenth-Century Coal Town's Experience with a Disaster-Prone Industry* (Ithaca, NY: Cornell University Press, 1987), and Grace Palladino, *Another Civil War: Labor, Capital, and the State in the Anthracite Regions of Pennsylvania, 1840–68* (New York: Fordham University Press, 2006).

23. Bulik, *The Sons of Molly Maguire*, 143. The Reverend Daniel J. Murphy Collection is not yet available for general research. Deirdre Ní Chonghaile, who has done work in the Murphy Collection, told me that Murphy found three people named "Melly" singing in Irish in the Coaldale regions. "In Coaldale, there's a Micheál Mór Ó Máille aka Michael Melley from Tuaim / Raithnigh in the parish of Leitir Mhic an Bhaird / Lettermacaward, the same parish as the townland of Maigh Dabhcha / Madavagh. Also in Coaldale there's a Mrs. Melly *née* Peggy Callaghan, who may be from Mín an Chairn [Mín a Chárain = alternative spelling in MS; Meenacarn in English], which is also in the parish of Leitir Mhic an Bhaird. Michael and Peggy may well be husband and wife. And

there's a Mrs. Johnson *née* Mary Melly from 'Glenties,' which may represent a reference to the Poor Law Union, the electoral division, or the townland itself to which that placename can apply." Email to the author, May 4, 2021.

24. Bulik, *The Sons of Molly Maguire*, 149.

25. Records of marriages from Saint Joseph's Church, 462 W. Ludlow St., Summit Hill, PA 18250.

26. The best history of the Molly Maguires remains Kevin Kenny, *Making Sense of the Molly Maguires* (New York: Oxford University Press, 1998), and Bulik, *The Sons of Molly Maguire*. On George Smith see Bulik, *The Sons of Molly Maguire*, 20; on Morgan Powell and John Jones, see Kenny, *Making Sense of the Molly Maguires*, 118–19, 196–97; *Philadelphia Inquirer* November 21, 1874, 3; on the strike and foraging, see Bulik, *The Sons of Molly Maguire*, 275.

27. Kenny, *Making Sense of the Molly Maguires*, 5, 14; Allan Pinkerton, *The Molly Maguires and the Detectives* (New York: G. W. Carleton & Company, 1878), 166; *Harper's Weekly*, March 4, 1876, 194. The Molly Maguire story shows evidence of both cynical pragmatic manipulation by mine owners and a "moral panic," a generalized anxiety about threats to order that exaggerates slim evidence into a full-blown menace.

28. Henry George, "Labor in Pennsylvania," *North American Review*, September 1886, 273.

29. Stephen P. O'Hara, *Inventing the Pinkertons; or, Spies, Sleuths, Mercenaries, and Thugs: Being a Story of the Nation's Most Famous (and Infamous) Detective Agency* (Baltimore, MD: Johns Hopkins University Press, 2016).

30. There is no good history of the rise of the detective story, but a substantial literature in US history examines the problem of imposture and the confidence man. Neil Harris, *Humbug: The Art of P. T. Barnum* (Chicago: University of Chicago Press, 1973), coined the term "operational aesthetic" to describe the fascination with seeing how things work: he noted how P. T. Barnum presented people with dubious claims and asked them to play detective. James W. Cook, *The Arts of Deception: Playing with Fraud in the Age of Barnum* (Cambridge, MA: Harvard University Press, 2001), elaborates on that theme, looking at Barnum's racial and biological "humbugs." Karen Halttunen, *Confidence Men and Painted Women: A Study of Middle-Class Culture in America, 1830–1870* (New Haven, CT: Yale University Press, 1982), documented a generalized cultural anxiety between commercial accounts of correct behavior and the fact that bad people could imitate them and thereby "pass." Miles Orvell, *The Real Thing: Imitation and Authenticity in American Culture, 1880–1940* (Chapel Hill: University of North Carolina Press, 1989), looks at the general fascination with imitation and authenticity. Michael O'Malley, *Face Value: The Entwined Histories of Money and Race in America* (Chicago: University of Chicago Press, 2012), looks at the connection between racial passing and the passing of counterfeit money.

31. Pinkerton, *The Molly Maguires and the Detectives*, 28–29.

32. Pinkerton, 15, 332.

33. Membership lists of the AOH can be seen in the Reading Company records (Accession #1520), Manuscripts and Archives Department, Hagley Museum and Library, Wilmington, DE 19807, and online at https://digital.hagley.org/molly_m_015.

34. *Philadelphia Inquirer*, February 3, 1876, 2; *Lancaster Daily Evening Express*, February 3, 1876, 2.

35. Joseph O'Malley, personal correspondence with the author; Records of Saint Joseph's Church, Summit Hill, PA.

36. Kenny, *Making Sense of the Molly Maguires*, 217–19.

37. The marriage date is inferred: the 1900 census shows Mary Murphy married to John Black and their oldest child as nineteen, suggesting marriage and conception in 1880.

38. Multiple newspapers carried mention of Father Brehony accompanying Alexander Campbell to the gallows. See *Northumberland (PA) Public Press*, June 29, 1877, 2; *Valley Sentinel*, June 29, 1877, 8; *Wellsboro Gazette Combined with Mansfield Advertiser*, June 29, 1877, 2; Quotes on the colony from *Reading Times*, February 7, 1877, 1; *New Orleans Morning Star and Catholic Messenger*, June 10, 1877, 8. See also the many mentions in the *Boston Pilot* in the late 1870s, online via Boston College Libraries (https://newspapers.bc.edu/?a=q&r=1&results=1&puq=pilot&e=-------en-20--1--txt-txIN-brehony------).

39. Quotes on Edina from *Boston Pilot*, April 4, 1864, October 1, 1864. For background on the Catholic colonization movement, see James P. Shannon, *Catholic Colonization on the Western Frontier* (New Haven, CT: Yale University Press, 1957).

40. *Boston Pilot*, April 4, 1864, October 1, 1864; *New Orleans Morning Star and Catholic Messenger*, June 10, 1877, 8. Irish immigrant Francis O'Neill, then a twenty-year-old single laborer in Erie, Pennsylvania, read the advertisements in the *Pilot* and made the trip to Edina alone. He stayed for a year, and though he reported very favorably on life on the prairie he left for Chicago, joined the police force, and eventually rose to chief of police. It was not implausible that Patrick would have made the same kind of choice a few years later. O'Malley, *The Beat Cop*, chap. 3.

41. Shannon, *Catholic Colonization*, 220–33, discusses the Keileyville colony in some depth. *Norfolk Virginian*, January 22, 1878, 2.

42. *Boston Pilot*, April 5, 1879.

43. *Norfolk Landmark*, July 20, 1880, 1; Shannon, *Catholic Colonization*, 227.

44. *Norfolk Landmark*, June 20, 1880. Besides attempts by Plumadore to start a colony in North Carolina, newspaper accounts hint at other colonies either in existence or planned in the late 1870s, one in Mecklenburg County, Virginia, and one in Sussex County: *Norfolk Virginian*, September 23, 1879, 1.

The Mecklenburg scheme ended when the ICBU defaulted on tax payments: the subsequent buyer, claiming he had no idea the land was encumbered with tax obligations, petitioned the Virginia legislature for relief. *Acts Passed at a General Assembly of the Commonwealth of Virginia*, 1888, 226.

45. Smithing is of course a noble profession: it just does not offer as many opportunities. Gerald Gilliam, "The Catholic Colony at Barnesville," *Southsider: Local History and Genealogy of Southside Virginia*, no. 2, 1993; *Boston Pilot*, July 12, 1879.

46. *Norfolk Virginian*, October 31, 1882, 1; "Map Showing the Location of the Virginias Railway across the Grand Divisions of West Virginia and Virginia from the Ohio to Hampton Roads," Library of Congress, Washington, DC, https://hdl.loc.gov/loc.gmd/g3891p.ct009425.

## Chapter Five

1. Elon University, "Report and Recommendations of the Committee on Elon History and Memory," October 2020, https://eloncdn.blob.core.windows.net/eu3/sites/1018/2020/11/MemoryReport_FINAL-wLinksUpdated.pdf. Holland built a submarine designed, in the 1870s, to attack British shipping on the Great Lakes. The "Fenian Ram" is on display in Paterson, New Jersey. Lawrence Goldstone, *Going Deep: John Philip Holland and the Invention of the Attack Submarine* (New York: Simon and Schuster, 2017). Fans of Irish traditional music likely have heard Micho Russell singing a song about Holland: https://youtu.be/FaGVFp3z8Yc?si=2Scgr_e5qjYHmUlM.

2. Bruce S. Allardice, "West Points of the Confederacy: Southern Military Schools and the Confederate Army," *Civil War History* 43, no. 4 (1997): 310–31. For a review of the subject, see R. Don Higginbotham, "The Martial Spirit in the Antebellum South: Some Further Speculations in a National Context," *Journal of Southern History* 58, no. 1 (1992): 3–26; "Federal Writers' Project: Slave Narrative Project, Vol. 2, Arkansas, Part 1, Abbott-Byrd," online text, Library of Congress, Washington, DC, 20540, https://www.loc.gov/item/mesn021/.

3. The census records for James M. Holland are easy to confuse as there are two men with the same name, both married to women named Elizabeth. Tracking is possible through the names of the children.

4. The value of slave property increased dramatically in the 1850s, for somewhat unclear reasons. It may have been the sense that the institution was under threat from global and national abolitionism. It may have also been the more sophisticated use of slaves as capital, as the collateral for loans and the issue of financial paper.

5. Nansemond County neighborhoods were vaguely defined. "Lower Parish" is north of "Upper Parish." The families described in chapter 1 all lived in either

"Upper Parish" or "Holy Neck." The author would very much prefer to believe his ancestors were not slaveholders, but the evidence is clear.

6. *Richmond Dispatch*, August 4, 1862. Two Alexander W. Hollands served in the Confederate Army. One, described above, enlisted in 1861. The other enlisted in 1864 and was three years younger. The Alexander W. Holland held at Fort Monroe was released "to his home in NC," which suggests he might have been a different person. Historical Data Systems, comp., *US, Civil War Soldier Records and Profiles, 1861–65* (database online) (Provo, UT, USA: Ancestry.com Operations Inc., 2009).

7. Susan McKinnon, "Temperamental Differences: The Shifting Political Implications of Cousin Marriage in Nineteenth-Century America," *Social Analysis* 60, no. 2 (2016): 31–46; Martin Ottenheimer, *Forbidden Relatives: The American Myth of Cousin Marriage* (Urbana: University of Illinois Press, 1996).

8. Selena White married a man named David Holland, a descendent of the same Axy Holland who was Dempsey Hare's mother-in-law and the mother-in-law of Mary Holland, the murdered woman. Axy was David Holland's great-grandmother.

9. On the Prentis family, and Robert Prentis, see Kari J. Winter, *The American Dreams of John B. Prentis, Slave Trader* (Athens: University of Georgia Press, 2011). On the culture of Virginia college students, see Charese Coleman Wall, "Students and Student Life at the University of Virginia, 1825 to 1861" (PhD diss., University of Virginia, 1978), and A. J. Angulo, *William Barton Rogers and the Idea of MIT* (Baltimore, MD: Johns Hopkins University Press, 2009), chap. 2. Account of Peter's life from R. A. Brock, *Virginia and Virginians; Eminent Virginians* (Richmond, VA: H. H. Hardest, 1888), 662–63. Peter Prentis's grade reports at Webb-Prentis Family Papers, Accession #4136, Special Collections, University of Virginia Library, Charlottesville, Series 1B Boxes 6 and 7.

10. *Norfolk Virginian*, March 7, 1889, 4.

11. Brock, *Virginia and Virginians*, 663; *Norfolk Virginian*, March 7, 1889, 4.

12. Peter Bowdoin Prentis to Sister, Webb-Prentis Papers, Series 1B Box 7, Webb-Prentis Family Papers, Accession #4136, Special Collections, University of Virginia Library, Charlottesville.

13. *Norfolk Virginian*, May 12, 1875, 3.

14. *Richmond Enquirer*, June 10, 1863, 2.

15. *Richmond Enquirer*, April 24, 1863, 3; James Riley Bowen, *Regimental History of the First New York Dragoons* (Author, 1900), 22.

16. *Staunton Spectator*, February 10, 1863, 2; *Richmond Daily Dispatch*, August 4, 1862, 1.

17. Brock, *Virginia and Virginians*, 662–63. On the Bowdoin side, see "The Bowdoin Family," *Virginia Magazine of History and Biography* 38, no. 2 (1930): 191–94.

18. Nansemond County Will Books, Will Book, 4, 1885–92, microfilm reel 30, Library of Virginia, Richmond.

19. Samuel George Morton, *Crania Americana: Or a Comparatif View of the Skulls of Various Aboriginal Nations of . . . America* (Philadelphia, 1839), 16.

20. Ann Fabian, *The Skull Collectors: Race, Science, and America's Unburied Dead* (Chicago: University of Chicago Press, 2010), 15.

21. Morton quoted in Nott and Gliddon, *Types of Mankind* (Philadelphia, 1854), xli, 215.

22. Nott and Gliddon, 402.

23. *Hudgins v. Wright*, 11 Va. (1 Hen. & Mun.) 134 (1806); see also chapter 1.

24. Karl Jacoby, *The Strange Career of William Ellis: The Texas Slave Who Became a Mexican Millionaire* (New York: W. W. Norton & Company, 2017), 62.

25. Francesca Morgan used this marvelous sentence in her evaluation of the manuscript for this book, in which she waived anonymity and revealed her identity. I thank her for this sentence and for her acute and perceptive reading of the draft.

26. Records all found by searching "Virginia, Library of Virginia State Archive, Births, Marriages, and Deaths 1853–1900," database, FamilySearch.org.

27. Nansemond County Deed Books, Library of Virginia, Richmond. The deeds and indexes are on microfilm. Quote from Deed dated February 9, 1889, reel 44, 270. The first deed said "Bateman Station," which was at Elwood Road in Nansemond. Bateman was the manager of the Atlantic and Danville and got himself into legal and financial trouble. The station was renamed "Elwood Station." *Norfolk Virginian*, January 7, 1891, 2.

28. "Algorithmic Injustice? Racial Bias and Facial Recognition," May 6, 2021, https://www.pbs.org/wgbh/nova/video/algorithmic-injustice-racial-bias-facial-recognition/; Kade Crockford, "How Is Face Recognition Surveillance Technology Racist?," *American Civil Liberties Union*, June 16, 2020, https://www.aclu.org/news/privacy-technology/how-is-face-recognition-surveillance-technology-racist; "Racial Discrimination in Face Recognition Technology," *Science in the News*, October 24, 2020, https://sitn.hms.harvard.edu/flash/2020/racial-discrimination-in-face-recognition-technology/; Thaddeus L. Johnson, "Police Facial Recognition Technology Can't Tell Black People Apart," *Scientific American*, May 18, 2023, https://www.scientificamerican.com/article/police-facial-recognition-technology-cant-tell-black-people-apart/.

29. *Norfolk Virginian*, October 18, 1894, 5; *Weekly Virginian and Carolinian*, May 3, 1894, 8.

30. The handwritten record of Patrick's application for citizenship is in the possession of his great-grandson via his third wife, Rose Molloy. Photographic copy in author's possession.

31. On the racial classification cases, see Ian Haney-Lopez, *White by Law: The Legal Construction of Race*, and the website maintained by Haney-Lopez at

https://racism.org/articles/race/16-defining-racial-groups/372-the-racial
-classification-cases. The two Supreme Court cases are *Ozawa v. United States*,
260 U.S. 178 (1922), and *United States v. Bhagat Singh Thind*, 261 U.S. 204
(1923). Immigrants generally classified as white were certainly not exempt
from violence and discrimination. For a general overview, see Jacobson, *Whiteness of a Different Color*. For Italian Americans, see Thomas A. Guglielmo,
*White on Arrival: Italians, Race, Color, and Power in Chicago, 1890–1945* (New
York: Oxford University Press, 2003), and Jennifer Guglielmo and Salvatore
Salerno, *Are Italians White? How Race Is Made in America* (New York: Rout-
ledge, 2004). On the notorious anti-Italian riots in New Orleans, see Alan G.
Gauthreaux, "An Inhospitable Land: Anti-Italian Sentiment and Violence
in Louisiana, 1891–1924," *Louisiana History* 51, no. 1 (Winter 2010): 41–68.
Anti-Semitism has a long and frequently violent history: for an overview, see
Leonard Dinnerstein, *Uneasy at Home: Antisemitism and the American Jewish
Experience* (New York: Columbia University Press, 1987).

32. Ancestry.com, *Georgia, US, Property Tax Digests, 1793–1892* (database online)
(Provo, UT: Ancestry.com Operations, Inc., 2011). Personal correspondence
with Brian Brown, photographer, who documents vernacular architecture at
"Vanishing Georgia," https://vanishinggeorgia.com/.

33. Carl Lester, Grand Secretary, The Most Worshipful Grand Lodge of Georgia,
to Lawrence O'Malley, April 11 1977. Copy in author's possession.

34. *Mystic Star* (Chicago, 1870), 73.

35. On the lumber industry shifting to southern yellow pine, see William Cronon,
*Nature's Metropolis: Chicago and the Great West* (New York: W. W. Norton,
2009), 195–202. *Morning News*, December 7, 1896, 6; *Eastman (GA) Times-
Journal*, April 2, 1897, 1.

36. *Macon (GA) Telegraph*, November 6, 1898, 10; *Eastman (GA) Times-Journal*,
September 14, 1899, 4.

37. *Eastman (GA) Times-Journal*, September 14, 1899, 4; *Savannah Morning News*,
December 4, 1898, 6. The man accused of murder was named Will Williams.
He claimed to have been hired to kill the manager of the commissary at a turpentine mill by a white man named Strickland. Williams was convicted and
executed; Strickland faced no charges.

38. *Macon (GA) Telegraph*, December 4, 1898, 9; *Savannah Morning News*, December 4, 1898, 6.

39. A map of lynchings, state by state, has been compiled by the Equal Justice Ini-
tiative. See https://eji.org/reports/lynching-in-america/. On the formality of
lynchings, see Amy Louise Wood, *Lynching and Spectacle Witnessing Racial
Violence in America, 1890–1940* (Chapel Hill: University of North Carolina
Press, 2009).

40. Joel Williamson, *A Rage for Order: Black/White Relations in the American South
since Emancipation* (New York: Oxford University Press, 1986), 80.

41. C. Vann Woodward, *The Strange Career of Jim Crow* (New York: Oxford, 1955).
42. Leon Litwack, *Been in the Storm so Long: The Aftermath of Slavery* (New York: Knopf, 1979); Jane Dailey, *Before Jim Crow: The Politics of Race in Postemancipation Virginia*, Gender and American Culture (Chapel Hill: University of North Carolina Press, 2000); Glenda Gilmore, *Gender and Jim Crow: Women and the Politics of White Supremacy in North Carolina, 1896–1920* (Chapel Hill: University of North Carolina Press, 1996). At the Mount Sinai Baptist Church on Holy Neck Road, a historical marker commemorates Israel Cross and his advice. See also https://www.dhr.virginia.gov/wp-content/uploads/2018/04/133-5249_MtSinaiChurch_2006_NRfinal.pdf.
43. Copies of baptismal certificates in author's possession from the parish of what is now Saint Agatha/Saint James, 3728 Chestnut St., Philadelphia, all dated March 19, 1901.
44. *Philadelphia Inquirer*, December 10, 1902, 15.
45. A salary of $1,000 a year in 1920 is below average but not indicative of poverty. In 1905 the starting salary of a policeman in Chicago was $1,100. In 1922, auto workers in Detroit averaged about $1,500 a year before overtime. See O'Malley, *The Beat Cop*, and "Wages and Hours of Labor," *Monthly Labor Review* 28, no. 5 (1929): 179–97.

## Chapter Six

1. W. A. (Walter Ashby) Plecker to A. H. Crismond, August 21, 1940, Series IV: Eugenics and Racial Integrity, C. Correspondence concerning Eugenics: Plecker, Folder 41, Papers of John Powell, 1888–1978, n.d., Accession #7284, 7284-a, Special Collections, University of Virginia Library, Charlottesville. Hereafter "Powell Papers." On Italians and whiteness, see Guglielmo, *White on Arrival,* and the essays in Jennifer Guglielmo and Salvatore Salerno, *Are Italians White?*
2. Plecker to Cheatham, April 30, 1924, Powell Papers; June Purcell *Guild, Black Laws of Virginia: A Summary of the Legislative Acts of Virginia concerning Negroes from Earliest Times to the Present* (1936; reprint ed., Westminster, MD, 2011), 35.
3. Plecker to John Collier, April 6, 1943, Powell Papers. Searching Ancestry.com for Robert H. Cheatham makes it clear he was understood as white, and so was his wife, Buleah Childress, and the 1930 census lists the child Plecker found so awful, probably John Wesley Cheatham, as white. There is no record of Plecker's papers being destroyed, but more than thirty years' work would surely have left a more substantial paper trail. Helen C. Rountree, *Pocahontas's People: The Powhatan Indians of Virginia through Four Centuries* (Norman: University of Oklahoma Press, 1996), 237, describes an interview with an employee who later became director and who suggested the files had been destroyed.

4.  Plecker to Holsinger, June 11, 1940, Powell Papers.
5.  Plecker to Nancy Hundley, July 19, 1943, Powell Papers.
6.  Plecker to Hundley, July 27, 1943, Powell Papers.
7.  Plecker to Aileen Hartless, March 9, 1944, Powell Papers. The letter Ms. Hartless wrote to Plecker did not survive.
8.  Plecker to Rockingham Poultry Corp., April 16, 1945, Powell Papers. Census records for 1940 show Dorothy Lucille Floyd as race white, age eleven, which meant she was fifteen when she applied to work slaughtering chickens, and in 1952, age twenty-three she married; she and the groom were both listed as white. Her death certificate lists her as white.
9.  Plecker to Riverview Cemetery Superintendent, August 1, 1940, Powell Papers.
10. Plecker to Stokes, July 31, 1940, Powell Paper.
11. Plecker to Samuel Nixon, June 17, 1946, Powell Papers.
12. Plecker to Graham, August 9, 1940, Powell Papers.
13. Plecker to Quibel, March 10, 1934, Powell Papers.
14. Virginia Department of Health, Richmond, *Virginia, Births, 1864–2015*. The record is available at Ancestry.com, *Virginia, US, Birth Records, 1912–2015, Delayed Birth Records, 1721–1920*, including a scan of the certificate, front and back.
15. Plecker to Virginia County Clerks, "WARNING to Be Attached," Rockbridge County (VA) Clerk's Correspondence [Walter A. Plecker to A. T. Shields], 1912–43. Local government records collection, Rockbridge County Court Records, Library of Virginia, Richmond.
16. *Guild, Black Laws of Virginia.*
17. Plecker to Cunningham, September 11, 1940, Powell Papers.
18. Plecker to Cunningham, September 11, 1940, Powell Papers.
19. Edwin Black, *War against the Weak: Eugenics and America's Campaign to Create a Master Race* (New York, 2003); David E. Whisnant, *All That Is Native and Fine: The Politics of Culture in an American Region* (Chapel Hill: University of North Carolina Press, 1983); Arica L. Coleman, *That the Blood Stay Pure: African Americans, Native Americans, and the Predicament of Race and Identity in Virginia* (Bloomington: Indiana University Press, 2013); Katherine Ellinghaus, *Blood Will Tell: Native Americans and Assimilation Policy* (Lincoln: University Press of Nebraska, 2017); Helen C. Rountree, *Pocahontas's People: The Powhatan Indians of Virginia through Four Centuries* (Norman: University of Oklahoma Press, 1996); J. Douglas Smith, *Managing White Supremacy: Race, Politics, and Citizenship in Jim Crow Virginia* (Chapel Hill: University of North Carolina Press, 2002); Susan J. Pearson, *The Birth Certificate: An American History* (Chapel Hill: University of North Carolina Press, 2021); Laura J. Feller, *Being Indigenous in Jim Crow Virginia: Powhatan People and the Color Line* (Norman: University of Oklahoma Press, 2022); Gregory Michael Dorr,

*Segregation's Science: Eugenics and Society in Virginia* (Charlottesville: University of Virginia Press, 2008).

20. For a general biography, see *History of Virginia* (Washington, DC: American Historical Society, 1924), 397; Ancestry.com, US, Appointments of U.S. Postmasters, 1832–1971; Ancestry.com, US, Passport Applications, 1795–1925. On his death, see *Staunton Spectator*, December 3, 1890, 3.

21. Plecker's store advertised in the *Valley Virginian*, December 15, 1881, 3; *History of Virginia*, 397–98; *Alumni Bulletin of the University of Virginia* (Charlottesville, VA: Published Quarterly by the Faculty, 1894), 106; on the hotel, see *Staunton Spectator*, January 12, 1899, and July 12, 1907; *Richmond Virginian*, January 28, 1912, 7.

22. Commission of Lunacy, *Newport News Daily Press*, October 10, 1905, 6; sanitarium, June 17, 1905, 6; tuberculosis, May 4 1910, 5; typhoid, January 3, 1909, 7; drink, March 4, 1910, 2; chess, February 5, 1910, 5. Virginia Department of Education, *Virginia School Report: Biennial Report of the Superintendent of Public Instruction . . .* (Richmond, VA, 1910), 696.

23. Pearson, *The Birth Certificate*, 197–98.

24. Pearson, 3.

25. Pearson, 182.

26. American Bar Association quoted at https://www.americanbar.org/groups/public_education/publications/teaching-legal-docs/birth-certificates/.

27. Patrick Brantlinger, *Dark Vanishings: Discourse on the Extinction of Primitive Races, 1800–1930* (Ithaca, NY: Cornell University Press, 2003).

28. Kristin L. Hoganson, *Fighting for American Manhood: How Gender Politics Provoked the Spanish-American and Philippine-American Wars* (New Haven, CT: Yale University Press, 1998); Gail Bederman, *Manliness and Civilization: A Cultural History of Gender and Race in the United States, 1880–1917* (Chicago: University of Chicago Press, 2008); and Jacobson, *Barbarian Virtues*.

29. *Newport News Daily Press*, August 6, 1908, 6.

30. *Survey* 1 (April–September 1823): 119.

31. *Knoxville Journal and Tribune*, November 18, 1913, 2.

32. Lee Alexander Stone, *Eugenics and Marriage: A Treatise upon an Important Phase of Social Hygiene* (reprinted from *Journal of the Tennessee State Medical Association*, September 1915).

33. James Q. Whitman, *Hitler's American Model: The United States and the Making of Nazi Race Law* (Princeton, NJ: Princeton University Press, 2017).

34. Whisnant, *All That Is Native and Fine*, tells the story of the Whitetop Folk Festival in detail. On Powell, see Karen Adam, "'The Nonmusical Message Will Endure With It': The Changing Reputation and Legacy of John Powell (1882–1963)" (n.d.), 117; Ronald David Ward, "The Life and Works of John Powell, 1882–1963," Studies in Music, no. 55 (PhD thesis, Catholic University of America, 1973); J. Lester Feder, "Unequal Temperament: The Somatic

Acoustics of Racial Difference in the Symphonic Music of John Powell," *Black Music Research Journal* 28, no. 1 (2008): 17–56.

35.  Plecker, *Eugenics in Relation to the New Family and the Law on Racial Integrity* (Bureau of Vital Statistics, State Board of Health, Richmond, VA, 1925), reprinted the act.

36.  *Daily News Leader*, May 20, 1935, 14.

37.  Arthur H. Estabrook, *Mongrel Virginians: The Win Tribe* (Baltimore, MD: Williams and Wilkins, 1926); Plecker to Estabrook, August 29, 1924, Rockbridge County (VA) Clerk's Correspondence, Library of Virginia, Richmond.

38.  Coleman, *That the Blood Stay Pure*, 105–8; https://encyclopediavirginia.org /entries/atha-sorrells-v-a-t-shields-clerk-petition-for-mandamus-november -14–1924/.

39.  John Powell and Anglo-Saxon Clubs of America, *The Breach in the Dike: An Analysis of the Sorrels [sic] Case, Showing the Danger to Racial Integrity from Intermarriage of Whites with So-Called Indians* (Richmond, VA: Anglo-Saxon Clubs of America, 1920).

40.  Plecker to Smith, September 3, 1940. Luke M. Smith was then a grad student in sociology working with Professor Constantine Panunzio.

41.  Plecker, *Eugenics in Relation to the New Family*, 8.

42.  *Survey*, May 15, 1925, 535; "Virginia Marriages, 1785–1940," database, Family-Search (https://familysearch.org/ark:/61903/1:1:X518-SLC: January 29, 2020); Will of Frances B. Plecker, Circuit Court of Stanton, VA, December 16, 1909, executed February 15, 1912. On file at Staunton Courthouse, certified copy in author's possession. The 1860 census shows the Plecker household with Jacob, Frances, and two children: no Delia, although in 1860 she would have been thirteen and possibly enslaved and so not recorded.

43.  François Weil, *Family Trees: A History of Genealogy in America* (Cambridge, MA: Harvard University Press, 2013), 6; Daughters of the American Revolution Continental Congress, *Proceedings of the . . . Continental Congress of the National Society of the Daughters of the American Revolution* (Congress, 1911), 9. See also Francesca Morgan, *A Nation of Descendants: Politics and the Practice of Genealogy in U.S. History* (Chapel Hill: University of North Carolina Press, 2021), 11: "In the late nineteenth and early twentieth centuries . . . genealogists' methods and collections buttressed U.S. state and federal laws that served white supremacy—oftentimes, the even narrower category of white Anglo-American supremacy." See also Morgan, "Lineage as Capital: Genealogy in Antebellum New England," *New England Quarterly* 83, no. 2 (2010): 250–82.

44.  *Staunton Daily Leader*, December 17, 1914, 2.

45.  Plecker to John Collier, April 6, 1943, Powell Papers.

46.  "The Black-and-White World of Walter Ashby Plecker: How an Obscure Bureaucrat Tried to Eradicate Virginia's 'Third Race,'" *Virginian-Pilot*, May 18, 2004, accessed December 13, 2022, https://www.pilotonline.com/history

/article_654a811f-213f-5d97-a469–51cc43b1a77f.html. Kate Pecker's death record in "Virginia, Death Certificates, 1912–1987," database with images, FamilySearch (https://familysearch.org/ark:/61903/1:1:QVR4–9BRN: 16).

47. Plecker to Riggin, May 27, 1946, in Powell Papers. Eva Kelly continued to work for the state government, as a statistician, after Plecker's death. She and Plecker cowrote a short article in the *Eugenical News* in 1934, 26.

48. Plecker to John Powell, June 29, 1946, Powell Papers.

49. Walter Ashby Plecker, "Plecker to the Clerks of Virginia Courts," November 1935, Rockbridge County (VA) Clerk's Correspondence.

## Chapter Seven

1. Letter of Christine Rivers, Office of Vital Records, to Jeff O'Malley, November 16, 1998, copy in author's possession.

2. The paper copy made by John Powell is now stored off site by the Library of Virginia in Richmond.

3. Quotes from https://www.churchofjesuschrist.org/comeuntochrist/article/importance-of-family and https://www.churchofjesuschrist.org/study/general-conference/2008/04/salvation-and-exaltation?lang=eng.

4. The well-organized official website of the Church of Jesus Christ of Latter-day Saints explains the church's theology in detail. Quote from https://www.churchofjesuschrist.org/study/general-conference/2008/04/salvation-and-exaltation?lang=eng.

5. Doctrine and Covenants 127, https://www.churchofjesuschrist.org/study/scriptures/dc-testament/dc/127?lang=eng.

6. William Gladstone, "Mormons Quietly Baptizing Hitler, Oswald, Wilkes Booth," *Forward*, December 22, 1995. An overview of the controversy and of press coverage appears in Kris Boyle and Joel J. Campbell, "Baptism of Fire: A Comparative Analysis of Media Coverage of the LDS Church's Practice of Proxy Baptisms," *Journal of Media and Religion* 14, no. 2 (2015): 74–87.

7. Many of the "leaks" came from Helen Radkey, a convert to Mormonism who then became an ardent critic of the church. Radkey had access to the database of baptisms, which the church suspended. At the same time, the LDS issued a directive that proxy baptism was only for family members, not for strangers. *Salt Lake Tribune*, March 9, 2010, at https://archive.sltrib.com/article.php?id=53667482&itype=CMSID; Howard Berkes, "Mormon Church Limits Access to Controversial Baptism Records," March 9, 2012, at https://www.npr.org/sections/thetwo-way/2012/03/09/148318491/mormon-church-limits-access-to-controversial-baptism-records; Letter from the "First Presidency" to church members, February 29, 2012, archived at https://www.churchofjesuschrist.org/church/news/names-submitted-for-temple-ordinances?lang=eng.

8. "Pact Ends Mormon Baptism of Dead Jews," *Los Angeles Times*, May 6, 1995, sec. Metro.; "A Twist on Posthumous Baptisms Leaves Jews Miffed at Mormon Rite," *New York Times*, March 3, 2012, A12. On the Catholic response, see *Los Angeles Times*, April 20, 2001, A1; *New York Times*, April 24, 2001, A17; Catholic Review, "Vatican Letter Directs Bishops to Keep Parish Records from Mormons," *Archdiocese of Baltimore*, January 19, 2012, https://www.archbalt .org/vatican-letter-directs-bishops-to-keep-parish-records-from-mormons/; and Julia Creet *The Genealogical Sublime* (Amherst: University of Massachusetts Press, 2020), 64. As of this writing, "All Dead Mormons Are Now Gay" is still up: http://alldeadmormonsarenowgay.com/.

9. John G. Turner, "Mormons and Baptism by Proxy," *Wall Street Journal*, February 24, 2012, A11.

10. Thomasian and other Armenian historians quoted in Carissa Vanitzian, "Mormons Baptize Armenian Saints, Genocide Victims, Notable Figures in Growing Genealogy Scandal," *Armenian Weekly*, April 26, 2003, 7, archived at https:// tert.nla.am/archive/NLA%20TERT/Armenian%20weekly/2003/17.pdf.

11. Thomas Walter Laqueur, *The Work of the Dead: A Cultural History of Mortal Remains* (Princeton, NJ: Princeton University Press, 2015); Jerome De Groot, *Double Helix History: Genetics and the Past* (New York: Routledge, 2023); Alex Shoumatoff, *The Mountain of Names: A History of the Human Family* (New York: Kodansha USA, 1995).

12. There is a large literature on genealogy and the uses of the dead. Nadia Abu El-Haj, *The Genealogical Science: The Search for Jewish Origins and the Politics of Epistemology* (Chicago: University of Chicago Press, 2012); Laqueur, *The Work of the Dead*, chap. 7; Shoumatoff, *The Mountain of Names*; François Weil, *Family Trees: A History of Genealogy in America* (Cambridge, MA: Harvard University Press, 2013); Saidiya V. Hartman, *Lose Your Mother: A Journey along the Atlantic Slave Route* (New York: Farrar, Straus and Giroux, 2007); De Groot, *Double Helix History*; Alondra Nelson, *The Social Life of DNA: Race, Reparations, and Reconciliation after the Genome* (Boston: Beacon Press, 2016); Catherine Lee, Alondra Nelson, and Keith Wailoo, *Genetics and the Unsettled Past: The Collision of DNA, Race, and History* (New Brunswick, NJ: Rutgers University Press, 2012); Catherine Nash, *Genetic Geographies: The Trouble with Ancestry* (Minneapolis: University of Minnesota Press, 2015), and *Of Irish Descent: Origin Stories, Genealogy, and the Politics of Belonging* (Syracuse, NY: Syracuse University Press, 2008); Francesca Morgan, *A Nation of Descendants: Politics and the Practice of Genealogy in U.S. History* (Chapel Hill: University of North Carolina Press, 2021); Creet, *The Genealogical Sublime*; Jenny Reardon, *The Postgenomic Condition: Ethics, Justice, and Knowledge after the Genome* (Chicago: University of Chicago Press, 2017).

13. "Granite Mountain Record Vault," in *The Encyclopedia of Mormonism*, published in 1992 and now maintained online at Brigham Young University:

https://contentdm.lib.byu.edu/digital/collection/EoM/id/3739. William R. Lund, *Engineering Geology of the Salt Lake City Metropolitan Area, Utah* (Salt Lake City, UT: Utah Geological Survey, 1990).

14. https://www.npr.org/2011/03/26/134379296/the-secret-bunker-congress -never-used; Lund, *Engineering Geology*, 563.

15. Paul Foy, "Granite Storage Vault Has Rock-Solid Security," *Washington Post*, February 22, 2004, https://www.washingtonpost.com/archive/politics/2004 /02/22/granite-storage-vault-has-rock-solid-security/8732dca0–886d-4372 -ae15–30b1e54e56a5/.

16. The website changes frequently; https://www.FamilySearch.org/en/info /archive, accessed March 2, 2023. Cardinal Cardozo's video endorsement is at https://players.brightcove.net/1241706627001/default_default/index.html ?videoId=6286823408001 and https://www.FamilySearch.org/rootstech /session/interview-with-cardinal-baltazar-porras-of-venezuela?lang=eng.

17. The figure of roughly four hundred marriages comes from the fact that each marriage entry would typically include six names: the bride and groom and their four parents, thus 2,400 divided by six equals four hundred. For an excellent overview of how Ancestry and to a similar extent FamilySearch thwart historical investigation, see Katherina Hering, "The Representation of NARA's INS records in Ancestry's Database Portal," *Archival Science* 23 (March 2022), 29–44, https://doi.org/10.1007/s10502-022-09386-3.

18. John G. Turner, *Brigham Young, Pioneer Prophet* (Cambridge, MA: Harvard University Press, 2012), 223.

19. On Italians and racial identity, see Thomas A. Guglielmo, *White on Arrival: Italians, Race, Color, and Power in Chicago, 1890–1945* (New York: Oxford, 2003), and the essays in Jennifer Guglielmo and Salvatore Salerno, *Are Italians White? How Race Is Made in America* (New York: Routledge, 2004).

20. Katharina Hering, "The Representation of NARA's INS Records."

21. Recent books specifically about DNA and history include Abu El-Haj, *The Genealogical Science*; Nash, *Genetic Geographies*; Nelson, *The Social Life of DNA*; Lee et al., *Genetics and the Unsettled Past*; Morgan, *A Nation of Descendants*; De Groot, *Double Helix History*.

22. Morgan, *Nation of Descendants*, 225.

23. *Salt Lake Tribune*, September 6, 2013, at https://archive.sltrib.com/article .php?id=56830408&itype=CMSID.

24. http://www.ancestryinsider.org/2012/07/ancestrycom-laps-FamilySearch-in .html; Creet, *The Genealogical Sublime*, 87, 90. Munson also gives this quote in a documentary Creet directed and cowrote: *Data Mining the Deceased: Ancestry and the Business of Family* (2017).

25. Creet, *Genealogical Sublime*, 90.

26. Creet, 89; Hering, "The Representation of NARA's INS Records in Ancestry's Database Portal."

27. Quotations from the digitization partnership between NARA and Ancestry online at https://www.archives.gov/files/digitization/pdf/ancestry-2015 -agreement.pdf and via NARA's Digitization Partnerships Page (https://www .archives.gov/digitization/partnerships).

28. User comments taken from https://narations.blogs.archives.gov/2015/07/31 /ancestry-com-partnership-agreement-for-public-comment/.

29. James A. Jacobs, "Yet Another Digitization Contract Limits Free Access to Public Records," *Free Government Information (FGI)*, modified March 25, 2008, https://freegovinfo.info/node/1753/. Hering, "The Representation of NARA's INS Records," reviews and summarizes much of this criticism.

30. Copy of contract in author's possession. I obtained a copy of this contract with the help of Mary Dooley, legislative assistant in the office of my Virginia state delegate, Patrick Hope, who contacted Janet Rainey, the state registrar. "The Library of Virginia Newsletter, July 2015 Issue Stories," https://www.lva .virginia.gov/news/newsletter/stories/2015_07-july.asp. If you search for "Virginia Department of Health marriage records online free," you can possibly find this web page: https://www.vdh.virginia.gov/vital-records/genealogy/ which links to Ancestry.com.

31. McAuliffe quote in "Virginia Vital Records Are Here!," at https://www .Ancestry.com/corporate/blog/virginia-vital-records-are-here and at https:// web.archive.org/web/20161002104433/https://www.vdh.virginia.gov/news /PressReleases/2015/060215VitalRecords.htm. I spent a lot of time investigating this, looking at the contract and the record retention schedule agreed to between the Library of Virginia and the Department of Health and interviewing people at both places. It seems that physical records are retained by the Department of Health and then moved to the Library of Virginia, which may or may not store them in an off-site annex. Ancestry gets the digital information. One of our graduate students, who prefers to remain anonymous, worked in the Virginia County Courthouse and described how records were accessed in emails to the author, April 14, 2023.

32. Email to the author, October 3, 2023, from the state registrar and director of the Bureau of Vital Records. Ancestry terms and conditions at https://www .ancestry.com/c/legal/termsandconditions.

33. Pearson, *The Birth Certificate*, 159.

34. Levine quoted in "Virginia Vital Records Are Here!"

35. De Groot, *Double Helix History*, 178.

36. Greet, *Genealogical Sublime*, 126–32.

37. Nash, *Genetic Geographies*, Kindle ed. location 982. Ancestry does offer a summary history of the regions people come from: its history of Donegal starts, for example, in 1785, which is well after the successive invasions of Ireland and well into the era of global commerce and conquest. Alondra Nelson quoted in Creet, *The Genealogical Sublime*, 151.

38. National Academies of Sciences, *Using Population Descriptors in Genetics and Genomics Research: A New Framework for an Evolving Field*, 2023, https://nap.nationalacademies.org/catalog/26902/using-population-descriptors-in-genetics-and-genomics-research-a-new.

39. *Finding Your Roots*, season 7, episode 5, "Country Roots" (February 23, 2021), https://www.pbs.org/weta/finding-your-roots/watch/seasons/season-7.

40. Quotes from Bryan Sykes, *The Seven Daughters of Eve* (London: Bantam Press, 2001), 1.

41. Francis Galton, *Finger Prints* (New York: Macmillan and Company, 1892), 194; Simon A. Cole, *Suspect Identities: A History of Fingerprinting and Criminal Identification* (Cambridge, MA: Harvard University Press, 2001), 110, 117.

## Epilogue

1. John Eligon, "Quadroon? Moor? Virginia Sued for Making Those Who Wed Say What They Are," *New York Times*, September 8, 2019; Rachel Weiner, "'Aryan' and 'Octoroon': Couples Challenge Racial Labels to Get Married in Virginia," *Washington Post*, September 7, 2019. Dorothy Roberts recounts the story in chapter 2 of Nikole Hannah-Jones et al., *The 1619 Project: A New Origin Story* (New York: One World, 2021), 45–62.

2. The "race codes" appear in National Center for Health Statistics (US), *Vital Statistics: Instruction Manual, Data Preparation* (US Department of Health, Education, and Welfare, Public Health Service, Health Resources Administration, National Center for Health Statistics, 1991), and in *Instruction Manual: Demographic Classification and Coding Instructions for Death Records* (US Department of Health and Human Services, Public Health Service, National Center for Health Statistics, 1975); FARS coding manual, https://crashstats.nhtsa.dot.gov/Api/Public/ViewPublication/01CV; handbook for funeral directors, https://www.tn.gov/content/dam/tn/commerce/documents/regboards/funeral/posts/FuneralDirectorsHandbook-2012.pdf. The complaint, with descriptions of the plaintiffs, appears at the website of Glasberg's firm, https://www.robinhoodesq.com/docs/marriage/documents/va/Complaint.pdf.

3. *Spotlight on Heterogeneity: The Federal Standards for Racial and Ethnic Classification" at NAP.edu*, n.d., https://www.nap.edu/read/9060/chapter/1; "Initial Proposals for Updating OMB's Race and Ethnicity Statistical Standards," *Federal Register*, https://www.federalregister.gov/documents/2023/01/27/2023-01635/initial-proposals-for-updating-ombs-race-and-ethnicity-statistical-standards. See also "Revisions to the Standards for the Classification of Federal Data on Race and Ethnicity," *White House*, https://obamawhitehouse.archives.gov/node/15626.

4. *Richmond Times-Dispatch*, September 12, 2019, A3.

5. "Van Landingham Bill Striking Race from Marriage License," https://lis

.virginia.gov/cgi-bin/legp604.exe?031+sum+HB2106&031+sum+HB2106; "Blevins Bill to Reintroduce Race," https://lis.virginia.gov/cgi-bin/legp604 .exe?051+sum+SB1111; *Richmond Times-Dispatch*, September 10, 2019, A3.

6. Profile of Glasberg at https://www.robinhoodesq.com/victor-m-glasberg/. Information on Mildred Loving from Coleman, *That the Blood Stay Pure.*

7. https://casetext.com/case/rogers-v-va-state-registrar.

8. *Students for Fair Admission, Inc. v. President and Fellows of Harvard College* (June 29, 2023), 15, at https://www.supremecourt.gov/opinions/22pdf/20 -1199_hgdj.pdf.

9. See Nick Land, "The Dark Enlightenment," https://www.thedarkenlightenment .com/the-dark-enlightenment-by-nick-land/; Joshua Tait and Scott F. Aikin, "Deep Disagreement, the Dark Enlightenment, and the Rhetoric of the Red Pill," *Journal of Applied Philosophy* 36, no. 3 (2019): 420–35, https://doi.org/10 .1111/japp.12331; "Mencius Moldbug and Neoreaction," in *Key Thinkers of the Radical Right: Behind the New Threat to Liberal Democracy*, ed. Mark J. Sedg- wick (New York: Oxford University Press, 2019). On white nationalism, see Sara Kamali, *Homegrown Hate: Why White Nationalists and Militant Islamists Are Waging War against the United States* (Oakland: University of California Press, 2021); John Ehrenberg, *White Nationalism and the Republican Party: To- ward Minority Rule in America* (New York: Routledge 2022); Bradley B. Onishi, *Preparing for War: The Extremist History of White Christian Nationalism—and What Comes Next* (Minneapolis: Broadleaf Books, 2023); A. James McAdams and Alejandro Castrillón, *Contemporary Far-Right Thinkers and the Future of Liberal Democracy* (New York: Routledge, 2022); Wesley Lowery, *American Whitelash: A Changing Nation and the Cost of Progress* (New York: Mariner Books, 2023); Kathleen Belew, ed., *A Field Guide to White Supremacy* (Oak- land: University of California Press, 2021).

10. Rachel Weiner, "'Aryan' and 'Octoroon': Couples Challenge Racial Labels to Get Married in Virginia," *Washington Post*, September 7, 2019; John Eligon, "Quadroon? Moor? Virginia Sued for Making Those Who Wed Say What They Are," *New York Times*, September 8, 2019.

11. *Students for Fair Admissions v. Harvard*, 32, 40. Roberts quoted O'Connor's dissent in *Metro Broadcasting, Inc. v. FCC* (1990), at https://www.law.cornell .edu/supct/html/89–453.ZD1.html.

12. National Academies of Sciences, *Using Population Descriptors in Genetics and Genomics Research: A New Framework for an Evolving Field*, 2023, https://doi .org/10.17226/26902, xviii.

# INDEX

The letter *f* following a page number denotes a figure.

radical racism, 188–90

Radkey, Helen, 313n7

railroads, 134–36, 151–53, 152f, 180–81

Ramkishun, Ashley, 273–75

Ramon, Esther, 237

Reading Railroad, 136

Real ID regulations, 180

Reavey, Ed, 190

Reconstruction, 52–58; and Dempsey Hare, 58–60

records, 2–5; access to, 233–72; addendum to, 205–6, 207f; versus ancestry, 42–45; and detection, 143, 175–78; development of, 18–47, 194–95, 211, 249–51; digital genealogy and, 246–53; Freedmen's Bureau and, 52–55; free negro registers as, 32–34, 199; gaps in, 83–86, 143–44; Dempsey Hare and, 18, 45–47; and Mary Holland's murder, 55; and immigration, 119–23, 121f; in Ireland, 81–83, 88–89, 94; and lynchings, 17; Mormonism and, 237; Nansemond County Courthouse and, 61f; Walter Plecker and, 196–235; and race and marriage, 71–72; Racial Integrity Act and, 218–20; and Real ID regulations, 180; versus reality, 267; recommendations for, 263–64; storage of, 242–44; who qualifies for, 38, 83–84

Reeves, Peggy, 259

Regan, Michael and Ellen, 247

relationships: biological, genealogy and, 241; meaning of, 161–68, 277; racecraft and, 63–65; small communities and, 164; social versus biological, 7

religion: Dempsey Hare and, 16, 59; in Ireland, 99–101; Mormonism, and records, 233–72; and race, 115–

16. *See also* Catholicism; Protestantism

remittances, 132, 133f

resistance: to colonizer, 101–7, 112–17; to corporations, 136–40

respectability, 44

Richmond (Virginia), 196–232

Richmond and Danville Railroad, 151

Riggin, I. C., 229

Riverview Cemetery, 202

Roberts, John, 277–78, 280

Robinson, P. D., 216

Rockingham Poultry Marketing Company, 201–2

Rogers, Sophie, 273

Rogers, William Barton, 168

*Rogers v. State Registrar*, 275–77, 280

Rolfe, John, 160

Rooney, Michael, 86

Roosevelt, Theodore, 213

Rosenzweig, Roy, 285n3

runaway advertisements, 20–28, 30–32; changes in, 35–36; and detection, 36–38

Rundale system, 111–12, 114

sanity, Dempsey Hare and, 70–76

Sarfo, Samuel, 273

Saure, Philip N., 196

savage, Irish as, 94–96; religion and, 99–101

Schrack, Bonnie, 258

scientific research, and race, 266–69. *See also* race science

Scotch Irish, 116–17

Scott, James, 34

Scott, Julia, 227–28

Scott, Mary B., 68–69

seamen's protection papers, 33–34

segregation, 188, 214, 242

Seligman, Herbert, 226–27

servant, as term, 20